LONDON THROUGH RUSSIAN EYES 1896–1914

AN ANTHOLOGY OF FOREIGN CORRESPONDENCE

EDITED BY

ANNA VANINSKAYA

TRANSLATED BY

ANNA VANINSKAYA AND MARIA ARTAMONOVA

LONDON RECORD SOCIETY
THE BOYDELL PRESS
2022

Translation © Anna Vaninskaya and Maria Artamonova
Editorial matter © Anna Vaninskaya

First published 2022

A London Record Society publication
Published by The Boydell Press
an imprint of Boydell & Brewer Ltd
PO Box 9, Woodbridge, Suffolk IP12 3DF, UK
and of Boydell & Brewer Inc.
668 Mt Hope Avenue, Rochester, NY 14620–2731, USA
website: www.boydellandbrewer.com

ISBN 978-0-900952-02-9

A CIP catalogue record for this book is available
from the British Library

The publisher has no responsibility for the continued existence or
accuracy of URLs for external or third-party internet websites referred to
in this book, and does not guarantee that any content
on such websites is, or will remain, accurate or appropriate

This publication is printed on acid-free paper

Printed and bound in Great Britain by
TJ Books Limited, Padstow, Cornwall

MIX
Paper from
responsible sources
FSC® C013056

Dedicated to Ellen, who really wanted to read a book that had both sandwich men and Swiss Family Robinson *in it.*

CONTENTS

IV LONDON STREETS AND PUBLIC LIFE

ILLUSTRATIONS

The maps and plates can be found between pages 46 and 47.

MAPS

PLATES

FIGURES

The editor and publisher are grateful to all the institutions and persons listed for permission to reproduce the materials in which they hold copyright. Every effort has been made to trace the copyright holders; apologies are offered for any omission, and the publisher will be pleased to add any necessary acknowledgement in subsequent editions.

ACKNOWLEDGEMENTS

The London Record Society gratefully acknowledges a generous grant by the Jewish Historical Society of England that has helped considerably with the costs of this publication, as well as the funding provided by the Royal Society of Edinburgh that made this project possible.

Acknowledgements

The editor would like to thank her co-translator, Maria Artamonova, for providing a working text which made her job incalculably easier; her editor, Jerry White, for his interest in the project, his infinite patience and all his help; James Helling for the index; Simon Beattie for supplying physical copies of rare volumes and the Edinburgh University Centre for Research Collections for purchasing them; the organisers of the Anglo-Russian Research Network and numerous conferences for giving her opportunities to share her enthusiasm with others; and Aram Mikaelian for always helping out with the right word.

Portions of the Introduction appeared in Anna Vaninskaya, 'Under Russian Eyes', *Times Literary Supplement*, 28 November 2014, 17–19 and Anna Vaninskaya, 'Korney Chukovsky in Britain', *Translation and Literature* 20 (2011): 373–92.

Korney Chukovsky's articles translated and reprinted by permission of Dmitry Chukovsky.

ABBREVIATIONS

CW	Collected Works
KC	King's Counsel
KJV	King James Version
LCC	London County Council
LRC	Labour Representation Committee
LSE	London School of Economics
MP	Member of Parliament
OS	Ordnance Survey
SDF	Social Democratic Federation
TUC	Trades Union Congress

NOTE ON THE TEXT

Given the existence of numerous competing systems for the romanisation of Cyrillic, I have chosen to transliterate Russian words and names consistently but eclectically, combining conventions from several systems, such as British Standard and Library of Congress (except where a particular transliteration is universally accepted). Except in citations, titles of Russian books and articles are given in English translation for the benefit of English readers; titles of periodicals are transliterated.

In the main text, the authors' original formatting (of book and periodical titles, italicised words, etc.) has been retained. **Bold** is used for words printed in Latin script, as distinct from Cyrillic, in the original text. Where the original authors provide Russian translations of English phrases, these are only retained (i.e. back-translated) when they differ slightly from the literal meaning. Original punctuation has been amended to fit with English usage, with a few exceptions where it has been retained for stylistic purposes. Original typographical errors have been corrected silently. All footnotes are the editor's unless labelled otherwise. Major editorial interventions (e.g. in paragraphing) are indicated in the footnotes, but minor translation liberties (e.g. merging or breaking up of individual sentences) are passed over in silence. Where text is excerpted, long omitted sections are summarised by the editor in brackets to provide continuity. Short editorial omissions are marked by ellipses in brackets; ellipses which appear in the original text are reproduced without brackets.

NOTE ON MONETARY VALUES

Before decimalisation, the British pound sterling comprised twenty shillings (20s.) and a shilling comprised twelve pence (12d.). A shilling was equivalent to today's 5p; 1p is equivalent to about 2d. The Bank of England inflation calculator estimates that goods and services costing £10 in 1896 would cost £1,415 in 2021; and £10 in 1914 was equivalent to £1,227 in 2021. Values for intermediate years may be checked online.

The Russian rouble comprised 100 kopecks. In the period covered by the anthology, 1d. was worth 4 Russian kopecks; 1s. was worth 48 kopecks; and one pound was worth approximately 10 Russian roubles.

INTRODUCTION

FOREIGN CORRESPONDENTS IN LONDON

The reforming journalist George R. Sims's lavishly illustrated anthology *Living London*,[1] published in several volumes in 1902–03, provides a fascinating tour of the British capital at the turn of the twentieth century: from high to low and from East to West. Along the way, it takes its readers into the London inhabited by 'foreigners': 'Oriental London' ('Oriental' includes everything from Armenia to Japan), the 'cosmopolitan' 'Babel' of Soho and 'Russia in East London'. And it reminds its readers that the immigrant communities that formed such a distinctive part of the London cityscape retained strong links with the outside world, and with their countries of origin especially. There was a constant coming and going, a physical, intellectual and financial flow in both directions. For instance, according to Sims, every year 'nearly a million' roubles in remittances were sent 'by the Ghetto Bank of Whitechapel' to family and friends in Russia and Poland (1: 27). And winging their way back home were not just roubles, but personal letters and postcards, as well as articles written by resident foreign correspondents for newspapers and periodicals. Each personal letter found just a few isolated readers; the foreign correspondence reached audiences numbering in the hundreds of thousands. Sims does not ask what image of London was being produced by his fellow journalists for consumption beyond Britain's shores. But other countries had their own versions of *Living London*, and this anthology attempts to reconstruct one such version by shining a light on the city not as Sims's readers saw it, but as it existed in the minds of their contemporaries in Russia.[2]

---

[1] George R. Sims, ed. *Living London: Its Work and Its Play, Its Humour and Its Pathos, Its Sights and Its Scenes*, 3 vols (London: Cassell, 1902–1903). Sims's many London publications of the period provide an interesting counterpart to the Russian journalism reproduced here. See also his *Strand Magazine* series 'Off the Track in London' of 1904 and 'Trips About Town' of 1905, reprinted in *Off the Track in London* (London: Jarrold & Sons, 1911), especially 'Off the Track in London: I. In Alien-Land', *Strand Magazine* 27 (April 1904): 416–23 on the Jewish 'Ghetto'.

[2] Throughout this book, 'Russia' is used to refer to the entirety of the Russian Empire, which in the early twentieth century was subdivided into many administrative units, including several governorates in what were known as 'Little Russia' and the Southwestern Krai (or territory), i.e. Ukraine, in the Northwestern Krai (which included Lithuania and Belorussia) and in Congress Poland. The capital of the Empire was St Petersburg.

I

Newspaper correspondents have received relatively little attention from scholars of Anglo-Russian relations, who have tended to focus on prominent 'intermediaries' between the two cultures, such as translators, critics and travel writers. A list of notable Russians who visited or lived in London in the 1900s is indeed long and includes many individuals prolific with the pen.[3] One of them was the internationally

---

3 For accounts of Russian émigrés and visitors including writers and revolutionaries, as well as émigré press initiatives, see the work of John Slatter, Robert Henderson and Rebecca Beasley cited further down; see also Charlotte Alston, *Tolstoy and His Disciples: The History of a Radical International Movement* (London: Bloomsbury, 2014). Key Russian-language sources include: the biographical dictionary by Natalia Dissanayake, *Russkie Sud'bi v Londone [Russian Destinies in London]* (London: NED Publishing, 2016) (brief entry on 'Dioneo', a.k.a. Isaak Shklovsky, found on p. 193); Sergey Romanyuk, *Russkiy London [Russian London]* (Moscow: AST, 2009); the anthologies by O. A. Kaznina and A. N. Nikolyukin, eds. *'Ya Bereg Pokidal Tumanniy Al'biona...': Russkie Pisateli ob Anglii, 1646–1945 ['I Was Leaving Albion's Foggy Shore...': Russian Writers on England, 1646–1945]* (Moscow: ROSSPEN, 2001) (includes pieces by Shklovsky and Chukovsky) and Andrei Rogachevskii and Rose France, eds. *Russian Writers on Britain: An Annotated Reader* (Tallinn: Avenarius, 2001); Mikhail Parkhomovsky and Andrei Rogachevskii, eds. *Russkie Evrei v Velikobritanii: Statyi, Publikatsii, Memuari i Esse [Russian Jews in Great Britain: Articles, Publications, Memoirs and Essays]* (Jerusalem: Nauchno-Issledovatel'skiy Tsentr 'Russkoe Evreystvo v Zarubezhye', 2000), which includes pieces on Shklovsky and his wife; O. A. Kaznina, *Russkie v Anglii: Russkaya Emigratsiya v Kontekste Russko-Angliyskikh Literaturnikh Svyazey v Pervoy Polovine XX Veka [Russians in England: Russian Emigration in the Context of Russo-English Literary Connections in the First Half of the Twentieth Century]* (Moscow: Nasledie, 1997); the conference proceedings N. V. Makarova and O. A. Morgunova, eds. *Russkoe Prisutstvie v Britanii [Russian Presence in Britain]* (Moscow: Sovremennaya Ekonomika i Pravo, 2009) and the 'Russians in Britain' section of *Rossiya-Velikobritaniya: Pyat' Vekov Kul'turnikh Svyazey [Russia–Great Britain: Five Centuries of Cultural Connections]* (St Petersburg: Evropeyskiy Dom, 2015); Vyacheslav Shestakov, *Russkie v Britanskikh Universitetakh: Opit Intellektual'noy Istorii i Kul'turnogo Obmena [Russians in British Universities: A Record of Intellectual History and Cultural Exchange]* (St Petersburg: Nestor-Istoriya, 2009); Irina R. Chikalova, *Velikobritaniya: Osmislenie Istoricheskogo Opita v Rossiyskoy Imperii (XIX – Nachalo XX V.) [Great Britain: Interpretation of the Historical Record in the Russian Empire (19th – early 20th c.)]* (Minsk: Belaruskaya Navuka, 2018), which contains an excellent in-depth overview of Semyon Rapoport and an entry on Shklovsky, among many others. There are also numerous Russian-language dissertations dealing with Russian conceptions of England in the period; for London specifically, see L. V. Vorobyova, 'Londonskiy Tekst Russkoy Literaturi Pervoy Treti XX Veka' ['The London Text in Russian Literature of the First Third of the Twentieth Century'], thesis, Tomsk University, 2009; for Shklovsky specifically, see Z. S. Kanonistova, 'Mezhkul'turniy Dialog v Istoricheskom Kontekste: Vospriyatie Obraza Anglii i Anglichan v Russkom Obschestve vo Vtoroy Polovine XIX – Nachale XX Vv.' ['Intercultural Dialogue in Historical Context: The Reception of the Image of England and the English in Russian Society of the Nineteenth and Early Twentieth Centuries'], thesis, Saratov State University, 2006.

acclaimed writer Maxim Gorky, who visited the capital briefly in 1907 and published his impressions in a sketch entitled 'London'. Gorky's view of the city was a characteristic mix of romantic and critical clichés:

In the fog I see the face of London – it is the face of a giant from an old, wondrous fairy tale, wise and sad [...] The mighty, austere stone city is richly attired in a lush green cloak of gardens and parks; it is lavishly decorated with the precious works of an old, madly courageous art [...] You can grow to love the London fog, just like the paintings of Turner, for its soft, transparent colours.

And yet despite the city's 'strength' and its storied past, Gorky remarks, it is too preoccupied in the present day with 'narrow, crudely materialistic aims' – to the detriment of its 'spirit'. He mentions London poverty and the 'mechanical nature of life' there and is appalled by the extreme youth of the prostitutes he encounters in Piccadilly.[4] All of these descriptions, positive and negative, were commonplaces of the Russian view of London at the turn of the century. But even more typical was the fact that Gorky's sketch first appeared in a newspaper, *Kievskaya Misl'* *[Kievan Thought]*. The manner of publication is key. For it was not from the books of famous writers and critics that Russian readers picked up their ideas of contemporary London life, so much as from the pages of the mainstream periodical press, where both detailed in-depth surveys and superficial reinforcements of popular stereotypes could be found in abundance. In particular, readers could turn to the 'London Letters' and 'English Letters' of London-based foreign correspondents, whose articles were instrumental in forging the Russian public's conception of Britain's capital city, and in creating a particular discourse on the city's 'realities'.[5]

---

4   Maxim Gorky, 'London' in Kaznina and Nikolyukin, *'I Was Leaving Albion's Foggy Shore...'*, 323–26.

5   The role of the press, which disseminated both fictional and non-fictional images of London, was also much more important than that of guidebooks or entries on 'London' in popular encyclopaedias such as the *Brockhaus and Efron Encyclopaedic Dictionary*. For a contemporary assessment, see N. I. Kareev, 'How Far Russia Knows England' in Winifred Stephens, ed. *The Soul of Russia* (London: Macmillan, 1916), 96–101: 'articles on contemporary life published in monthly periodicals and newspapers [...] are read with very great interest, are subsequently collected and bound, and find yet other readers. Take, for example, Mr. Dioneo's (pseudonym) correspondence from London [...] Then the Russian periodical press carefully follows all that happens in England, thus sustaining the interest of the public. By the quantity of material distributed every month, the average Russian reader can follow the inner life of the English nation' (98–99). Shklovsky (Dioneo) himself contributed a chapter to Stephens's volume (132–41).

These correspondents were not always Russian themselves.[6] In the mid-1890s, the London correspondent for *Russkoe Bogatstvo [Russian Wealth]* – a prominent St Petersburg monthly of narodnik (i.e. populist non-Marxist socialist) tendencies – was none other than Eleanor Marx. In 1895, her reports covered

> 'political parties, social life and new trends in literature, arts and science [...] the Tories and the Liberal Unionists, the Factory Acts, unemployment, the May Day Demonstration, current data on alcoholism, London poverty, the Oscar Wilde trial, and Clementina Black's suffragette political novel *The Agitator* [...] the London County Council and the London School Boards and a mischievous piece on the lives and loves of her old sparring partner Annie Besant'.[7]

This catalogue sounds nearly identical to the list of topics – down to another piece on the lives of Annie Besant – covered by her Russian successor in the post, Isaak Vladimirovich Shklovsky (1864–1935),[8] uncle of the famous Formalist critic Viktor Shklovsky.

But though the topics they covered were similar, the Russian-born correspondents were writing from a fundamentally different perspective: they had to navigate a foreign culture while attempting to evaluate it and present information about it to readers back home. Some judged London from the standpoint of a member of the Russian *intelligentsia* appalled by British cultural backwardness; others from the contrary standpoint of the assimilated anglophile eager to contrast British respect for the rights of the individual with Russian contempt for personal autonomy. But whatever posture they chose to adopt, they were always keenly aware of the situatedness of the foreign observer's response. Shklovsky once compared the visits of two Russian friends of his to Whitechapel: one came in the summer and took away with him a wonderful impression of London as a great place unfairly maligned; the other came in the depths of winter and was so disgusted that he cut his trip short and returned to Russia horrified by what he had seen. Unlike these friends, the Russian correspondents lived in London year-round and had the chance to see it at its metaphorical best and worst. They could never write with the same kind of authority as their British counterparts, but they could, if they wished, occupy the position of outsider and insider simultaneously. Like Eleanor Marx – but unlike those Russian contributors who studied Britain from afar or paid fleeting visits there for research or tourism

---

6 For example, William Morfill, Oxford professor of Russian, was British correspondent of the Russian Symbolist journal *Vesi [Scales]*. Morfill's book, *A History of Russia* (London: Methuen, 1902), makes an appearance in one of Shklovsky's Letters: 'Chelovek s Prichudoy (Pis'mo iz Anglii)' ['The Crank (A Letter from England)'], *Russkoe Bogatstvo*, February 1903, 108–14. Korney Chukovsky mentions Morfill in his personal letters as well.

7 Rachel Holmes, *Eleanor Marx: A Life* (London: Bloomsbury, 2014), 386–87.

8 Many sources give 1865 as Shklovsky's date of birth.

4

– the London-based correspondents had the inestimable advantage of prolonged first-hand acquaintance. Their knowledge was practical as well as theoretical. The same could, of course, be said of other Russian immigrants who turned to journalism occasionally: such as the political exiles who made London their home before 1917, or writers such as Evgeny Zamyatin, who lived and worked in Britain for years at a time. But it was not their job to provide a detailed chronicle of and running commentary on all conceivable aspects of British life: from high politics, finance and the latest cultural developments to the everyday life of individuals right across the socio-economic spectrum. And this was precisely what the foreign correspondents were paid to do. Their Letters thus constitute a vast and almost wholly untapped resource, a unique window onto early twentieth-century London (and Britain) that has remained closed to English speakers until now.

Some of the correspondents that Russian periodicals sent abroad spent just one or two years in London; others lived out most of their lives in the city. While there, they wrote for a range of periodical formats: metropolitan monthly 'thick' journals such as *Russkoe Bogatstvo*, the liberal *Vestnik Evropi [The Herald of Europe]*, the liberal-tending-to-Marxist *Mir Bozhiy [Peace of God]* and the Constitutional Democrat *Russkaya Misl' [Russian Thought]*; popular illustrated weeklies for 'family reading' such as *Niva [Field]*, which had a circulation of between 200,000 and 300,000; and daily newspapers including the liberal Moscow and St Petersburg publications *Russkie Vedomosti [Russian News]* and *Birzhevie Vedomosti [Exchange News]*, the reactionary pro-government *Novoe Vremya [New Times]*, the Constitutional Democrat *Rech' [Speech]*, the popular provincial paper *Odesskie Novosti [Odessa News]*, and many, many others. Most also issued their articles in collected form. All these periodicals had clearly defined ideological positions and programmes, and no reader would have expected to see London portrayed in the same light in a socialist journal as in a mass-circulation illustrated weekly.[9] The correspondents also catered for all tastes, sending in feature human-interest stories and semi-fictional sketches,[10] book and

[9] It is worth noting that Russian correspondents wrote for the British press as well. While pieces by well-known Russian critics and writers such as Zinaida Vengerova and Valery Bryusov might occasionally appear in the *Fortnightly Review* or the *Athenaeum*, professional correspondents such as Rapoport and Shklovsky wrote for a much broader range of British newspapers and periodicals over the course of their lifetimes. Between them, Shklovsky and Rapoport contributed to the *Pall Mall Gazette*, the *Daily Mail*, the *Academy*, the *Daily Chronicle*, the *Daily News*, the *Echo*, the *Jewish Chronicle*, the *Progressive Review*, the *Novel Review*, the *Leisure Hour*, the *Christian Weekly*, *Sell's World Press*, the *Globe*, the *Independent Review*, the *Contemporary Review*, the *Polish Review*, the *Slavonic and East European Review*, and the *Socialist Review*. Shklovsky even contributed to the *Encyclopaedia Britannica*.

[10] The 'thick' journals, as well as various popular illustrated weeklies and monthlies, also published contemporary English fiction in translation, and Letters 'from our

5

press reviews, political and economic reports, social scientific analyses and accounts of public figures. Some articles were drawn predominantly from English-language printed sources, others from personal experience. Some dealt with specific locations from around the British Isles and the Empire, others with British life and national character in general. The correspondents had greatest scope in the 'thick' journals, which usually included sections devoted to literary criticism, politics and society, history and economics, in each of which one could regularly find extensive articles covering British topics.

To get a sense of the scale, consider the output of just one correspondent: Shklovsky. 'Thick' journal contributions were on average 10–15,000 words long. Shklovsky spent more than half of his life in Britain, and a 'Letter from England' – approximately thirty closely printed pages – appeared regularly in *Russkoe Bogatstvo* under his *nom de plume* Dioneo (a narrator of Boccaccio's *Decameron*) from the late 1890s onwards.[11] Some of these articles were later reworked and collected in well-reviewed and widely read volumes such as *Sketches of Contemporary England, English Silhouettes, On the Themes of Liberty, Reflections of Reality: Literary Portraits* and *Changing England*, each on average five hundred pages long.[12] Even leaving out of account Shklovsky's numerous post-revolutionary publications, not to mention his countless pre-revolutionary London Letters in other influential venues such as *Vestnik Evropi* and *Russkie Vedomosti*, where he published as *Sh.*, one is still left with something in the order of magnitude of a million words – and contained within them is what amounts to an encyclopaedic survey of turn-of-the-century London life. It is all there – the working-class pubs and funerals, the music hall acts and minstrel

---

London correspondent' appeared side by side with instalments from Ouida, Rudyard Kipling, H. G. Wells and Joseph Conrad, to list just the most famous of the English-language authors who were printed in *Russkoe Bogatstvo* from 1899 to 1902. There is a large Russian-language secondary literature on the reception of British writers in Russia in the late nineteenth and early twentieth centuries; for the press context specifically, see Maria Krivosheina's publications on Arthur Conan Doyle, R. L. Stevenson and Rudyard Kipling, as well as her 'Ob Odnom Anglofil'skom Proekte: Iz Istorii Petrogradskogo Zhurnala "Argus"' ['About One Anglophile Project: From the History of the Petrograd Journal *Argus*'], *Tekstologiya i Istoriko-Literaturniy Protsess: Sbornik Statey [Textual Criticism and the Historical-Literary Process: An Article Collection]* (Moscow: Buki Vedi, 2017), 134–45.

11   For instance, from 1897 to 1902, Shklovsky published in the vicinity of thirty English Letters in *Russkoe Bogatstvo*.

12   *Ocherki Sovremennoy Anglii [Sketches of Contemporary England]* (St Petersburg, 1903), *Angliyskie Silueti [English Silhouettes]* (St Petersburg, 1905), *Na Temi o Svobode: Sbornik Statey [On the Themes of Liberty: An Article Collection]*, 2 vols (St Petersburg, 1908), *Refleksi Deystvitel'nosti: Literaturnie Kharakteristiki [Reflections of Reality: Literary Portraits]* (Moscow, 1910) and *Menyayuschayasya Angliya [Changing England]*, 2 vols (Moscow, 1914–1915).

shows, the dance and fashion crazes, the cause célèbre trials, the raucous elections, the hymns of the Salvation Army bands, the magic lantern slides of Rational Dress Society lecturers, the Bovril adverts, the Derby, the gentlemen's clubs, the homeless on the Embankment, the retired Anglo-Indian colonels, the processions of the unemployed, the jingoists celebrating Boer War victories, and Londoners of all classes, factory girls and titled ladies, boating on the Thames. The selection of material never ceases to surprise. One day Shklovsky is writing about the practical jokes that stockbrokers play on each other at the Exchange, another day about the phenomenon of hooliganism, or the latest best-sellers of Marie Corelli, the poetry and novels of George Meredith, Southwark costermongers, the Reform Club, Satanists, etc. Nor is London his only topic. Shklovsky has as much to say about Chatham and Malvern and the Black Country, or about American tourists in Stratford-upon-Avon, as he does about Hammersmith or Hackney; he also writes at length about Ireland, Australia and South Africa. Taken together, the thousands of pages of his correspondence on British culture and society, published over several decades, constitute a kind of journalistic equivalent to *La Comédie Humaine* or *Les Rougon-Macquart*.

This anthology is meant to give a taste of the riches that lie hidden in dusty (though now mostly digitised) periodical archives, but it only scratches the surface. It presents translations from three Russian foreign correspondents: Shklovsky, Korney Ivanovich Chukovsky (1882–1969) and Samuil Yakovlevich Marshak (1887–1964), with a focus on the 'thick' journal contributions of Shklovsky. Other names could have been picked. Shklovsky's neglected contemporary, Semyon Isaakovich Rapoport (1858–1934), for instance, provides an equally interesting case study. He published numerous volumes of collected articles,[13] plus an

---

[13] The British Library catalogue lists, among others, *Narod-Bogatir': Ocherki Politicheskoy i Obschestvennoy Zhizni Anglii [A Warrior People: Sketches of the Political and Public Life of England]* (St Petersburg, 1900); *U Anglichan v Gorode i Derevne [With the English in City and Country]* (Moscow, 1900); *Delovaya Angliya [Business England]* (Moscow, 1903); *Stroiteli Angliyskoy Zhizni: Ocherki Reform i Sotsial'nikh Dvizheniy [The Builders of English Life: Sketches of Reforms and Social Movements] (Extracted from Mir Bozhiy)* [1905–1906]; *Statyi Ekonomicheskie i Politicheskie [Economic and Political Articles]* Extracts *from Periodicals* [1900–1916]; *Extracts from Periodicals Relating to English Life and Letters* [1895–1917]. For a much fuller bibliography of Rapoport's periodical and book-length publications and an in-depth analysis of his work as a foreign correspondent, see Irina R. Chikalova, 'England and Englishmen in Semen Isaakovich Rapoport's "Letters from London"', in M. P. Isenstadt and T. L. Labutina, eds. *Britanskiy Mir. Istoriya Britanii: Sovremennie Issledovaniya [The British World. The History of Britain: Contemporary Studies]* (Moscow: IVI RAN, 2015), 218–29 and the biographical account in Chikolova, *Great Britain*. For contemporary biographical sources on Rapoport, see his own account of himself in 'Rapoport, Semyon Isaakovich: Avtobiograficheskaya Spravka' ['Rapoport,

untold number of uncollected ones. Space considerations, however, have determined the anthology's emphasis on the more famous (in his time) Shklovsky.[14] Chukovsky and Marshak attained a very different kind of fame in subsequent decades as Soviet children's poets, as a result of which their early journalism was rescued from the archive and reprinted in their respective *Collected Works*.[15] No-one has edited or reprinted Shklovsky's prolific output, which is one reason, among others made clear below, to focus this volume around his Letters.

FACT OR FICTION? ISAAK SHKLOVSKY, SEMYON RAPOPORT AND THE ENGLISH LETTER

The Foreign Press Association, one of the oldest associations in the world for journalists from overseas media outlets, was founded in London in 1888 to serve the needs of foreign correspondents for Continental newspapers working in the United Kingdom. The FPA was instrumental in mediating the projection of Britain's image to the outside world: for instance, it had a direct influence on the foreign coverage of the Boer War. The first president of the FPA was a Russian nobleman, Gavriil Veselitsky-Bozhidarovich, and Shklovsky was one of the FPA's earliest members. Shklovsky – a Ukrainian Jew by origin – had started

---

Semyon Isaakovich: Autobiographical Notice'], in S. A. Vengerov, ed. *Kritiko-Biograficheskiy Slovar' Russkikh Pisateley i Uchyonikh [A Critical-Biographical Dictionary of Russian Writers and Scholars]*, vol. 6 (St Petersburg, 1897–1904), 201–03 and the brief 1912 entry for 'Rapoport, Semyon Isaakovich' in A. Harkavi and L. Katzenelson, eds. *Evreyskaya Entsiklopediya Brokgauza i Efrona [The Brockhaus and Efron Jewish Encyclopaedia]*, vol. 13 (St Petersburg, 1908–1913), 308–09.

14   Shklovsky's archive is held at the Russian State Archive of Literature and Art in Moscow. Contemporary biographical accounts of Shklovsky may be found under 'Shklovski, Isaac Vladimirovich' in Isidore Singer, ed. *The Jewish Encyclopedia*, vol. 11 (New York: Funk & Wagnalls, 1906), 299; *The Brockhaus and Efron Jewish Encyclopaedia*, 16: 44 and *Entsiklopedicheskiy Slovar' Brokgauza i Efrona [The Brockhaus and Efron Encyclopaedic Dictionary]*, vol. 39a (St Petersburg, 1890–1907), 622. Modern accounts may be found in O. A. Kaznina, 'I. V. Shklovsky (Dioneo) – Publitsist, Pisatel', Perevodchik' ['I. V. Shklovsky (Dioneo) – Journalist, Author, Translator'], in Parkhomovskiy and Rogachevskii, 260–72, in Kaznina's *Russians in England*, 89–91 and a few other brief articles, as well as in Chikalova, *Great Britain*.

15   See Korney Chukovsky, *Sobranie Sochineniy [Collected Works]*, 2nd ed., 15 vols (Moscow: Agentstvo FTM Ltd, 2012–2013) and Samuil Marshak, *Sobranie Sochineniy [Collected Works]*, 8 vols (Moscow: Khudozhestvennaya Literatura, 1968–1972), both abbreviated hereafter as *CW*. Unlike Shklovsky and Rapoport, who remained in London, Chukovsky and Marshak spent most of their lives in Russia. Chukovsky became a prominent literary critic and Marshak a famous translator of English poetry, and both achieved Soviet celebrity status for their children's poetry. Biographical accounts of both are legion.

his journalistic career as a teenager
and pursued it even after being
exiled to Siberia in the late 1880s
for association with the Narodnaya
Volya [People's Will] revolutionary
organisation as a student at Kharkov
University. He learned English on
his way to Siberia (the journey took
fifteen months) and while in exile he
developed ethnological interests,[16]
publishing both prize-winning
research and fictional sketches about
the local ethnic groups. In 1896,
he was sent to London as a correspondent for *Russkie Vedomosti* and
from 1897 he also started contributing to *Russkoe Bogatstvo*.

Fig. 1. Isaak Shklovsky.

Although there is no full-length
biography of Shklovsky, we can get
a fairly good sense of the kind of
Jewish background he came from
and of his time in Siberian exile from
his many autobiographical articles
and semi-fictional sketches dealing with Russia, as well as from the
flashbacks in his English Letters. His reminiscences about the 'Old
London Emigration', written in the 1920s, give a detailed picture of
the London revolutionary émigré circles he landed in in the 1890s.[17]
Shklovsky was well-regarded by London-based Russian exiles of
anarchist and socialist views, such as Prince Peter Kropotkin (whom he
translated),[18] Nikolay Chaikovsky and Feliks Volkhovsky (of the Russian

[16] For the journey to Siberia, see Shklovsky's letter, signed 'Dioneo, London, 26
February', printed in *Russkie Vedomosti, 1863–1913: Sbornik Statey [Russian News,
1863–1913: An Article Collection]* (Moscow, 1913), 275–76.

[17] See Dioneo, 'Staraya Londonskaya Emigratsiya (Chaikovsky, Kravchinsky i
Drugie) ['The Old London Emigration (Chaikovsky, Kravchinsky and Others)'],
Golos Minuvshego [Voice of the Past] 4 (1926), 41–62. For a description of
Shklovsky's parents, some of the wider family (he had thirteen siblings) and the city
he was from, Elisavetgrad, see the reminiscences of his nephew, Viktor Shklovsky,
Zhili-Bili [Once Upon a Time There Lived] (Moscow: Sovetskiy Pisatel', 1966).
As a child, Viktor did not know of the existence of his uncle.

[18] Shklovsky's Russian translation of Kropotkin's *Memoirs of a Revolutionist*
appeared in St Petersburg in 1906. In his foreword to the publication, Kropotkin
was much more complimentary about Shklovsky's competence as a translator
than he was in his reminiscences over a decade later. According to Chukovsky's
diary, this is what Kropotkin had to say about Shklovsky's translations in 1917: 'I
dictated "Memoirs of a Revolutionist" in English. Then Dioneo translated them.

Free Press Fund). But he was also close to Pavel Milyukov, historian and later leader of the Constitutional Democratic Party in the Russian Duma, who visited London in 1903–1904, and his wide circle of acquaintance included various prominent members of the Nabokov family. Many Russian émigrés left references to Shklovsky in their recollections and letters, and after the Revolution some of them, such as the Nobel prize-winning author Ivan Bunin and literary critic and University of London professor Prince Mirsky, applied to him for help and advice, for by the 1920s Shklovsky was well-connected in British public life and active in many Anglo-Russian organisations. He remained in London after the Revolution (being firmly opposed to the Bolsheviks) and continued writing about Britain – no longer for a mainstream Russian readership in the home country but for émigré publications across Europe.[19]

But although after 1917 he became a persona non grata, in pre-revolutionary Russia Shklovsky had been widely acknowledged as the foremost expert on Britain in the periodical press: 'none of his compatriots could compare with him either in the breadth of their coverage of various aspects of English life, or in the extent of their journalistic productivity'.[20] According to Milyukov's *Memoirs*, 'all of Russia followed the successes of progressive ideas in the old country of political liberty' in Shklovsky's columns in *Russkie Vedomosti*. In the 1900s, Shklovsky was 'the true mentor of the moderate current of Russian radicalism'; he 'did not idealise England [...] and was scepti-cally disposed. But all political currents respected him [...] and in this regard he could be considered one of the central figures of the Russian emigration in London', even though most of its leaders were 'to his left'.[21] Milyukov's assessment was confirmed by Harold Williams, special correspondent in Russia and later foreign editor of *The Times*, as well as a major player in Anglo-Russian relations during the War and Revolution, who described Shklovsky as 'well-known and highly esteemed throughout Russia as a skilful and enthusiastic interpreter of British democracy [...] It is safe to say that a large proportion of the

---

He would translate a page or a page-and-a-half and come to me in Bromley; I would spend the whole day correcting. He even got offended. I would completely redo it, write it anew. But it was not possible otherwise' (Chukovsky, *CW* II, 215).

[19] For an analysis of Shklovsky's anti-Bolshevik views and association with the Russian Liberation Committee, see Rebecca Beasley, *Russomania: Russian Culture and the Creation of British Modernism, 1881–1922* (Oxford: Oxford University Press, 2020), 388–89 and Kaznina, 'I. V. Shklovsky (Dioneo)', who devotes most of her biographical article to Shklovsky's post-revolutionary activities and publica-tions. Though Shklovsky was considered an 'enemy' by the Bolsheviks (in Maxim Gorky's words), his article collections continued to be brought to the notice of Bolshevik leaders like Trotsky in the early 1920s.

[20] Kaznina, 'I. V. Shklovsky (Dioneo)', 265.

[21] P. N. Milyukov, 'Zimovka v Anglii' ['Wintering in England'], *Vospominaniya [Memoirs]*, 1955 (Moscow: Izdatel'stvo Politicheskoy Literaturi, 1991), 152.

Introduction

younger generation of democratic Russians derive their knowledge of England almost solely from Dioneo's sympathetic articles.'[22]

Shklovsky's admiration for 'British democracy' was certainly evident in his English Letters. The Preface to his first collected *Russkoe Bogatstvo* volume did not mince words:

> My observations of the life of the Anglo-Saxon world have instilled in me a deep respect for the strong, persistent and talented race for whom broad civil liberty is not just an abstract principle. Whatever may happen to conditions in England itself under the influence of the inordinate development of financial capital [...] the mighty tree of Anglo-Saxon liberty [...] will continue to ramify gloriously in the colonies [...] The British Empire [...] is turning into a mighty federal union of independent democratic republics [...]. (*Sketches of Contemporary England*, v)

But all was not well with the Anglo-Saxon race in its native land, and Shklovsky framed the volume explicitly as a reaction to the dark and ugly elements in British life thrust into prominence by the Boer War. The scepticism and reluctance to idealise that Milyukov identified were all on show as Shklovsky chronicled the swift and disconcerting triumph of bloodthirsty militarism and attempted to come to terms with the blight rotting the tree of Anglo-Saxon liberty. In fact, the Boer War, imperialism and jingoism are in the background of most of the collected articles in this volume; the very first one, titled 'Imperialism', begins with a snapshot of the celebration of the fall of Pretoria. The documentary London street scenes, full of vivid colour and sound and close-ups of human flesh, are followed by a dissection of the phenomenon of the new imperialism from a cultural and economic point of view. Shklovsky traces the fortunes of British industrial output from far back in the nineteenth century, adduces tables of figures, cites Blue Books, Annual Statements of Trade and Joseph Chamberlain's speeches on tariff reform, and throws into the pot everyone from Kipling and the real-life 'Tommy Atkins' to J. A. Hobson, James Bryce, J. L. Hammond and Gilbert Murray, with asides on conscription debates and the use of colonial troops. Just a few pages in, the clichés of the Preface are all but forgotten, superseded by a desire to move and to inform the reader.

To move and to inform were the primary aims of most of Shklovsky's articles across his long career, and his method was calibrated accordingly as a mixture of four discrete modes: first-hand observation and accounts of personal experience; fictional slice-of-life scenes and composite characters; research summaries and statistics; and theoretical analysis.

---

[22] Harold Williams's Prefatory Note to Dioneo's pamphlet *Russia Under the Bolsheviks* (London: Wilkinson Bros. Ltd, 1919). This pamphlet is Shklovsky's best-known publication in English-language scholarship.

11

1) Here is what I saw and heard as I was walking down the street (with appropriate commentary from the standpoint of a foreign observer with his own cultural preconceptions – the juxtaposition of Russia and Britain).
2) Here are some biographical portraits, life narratives and snapshots of the thought and conversation of representative but not necessarily real individuals.
3) Here is some data on the cultural, political and economic aspects of the life of different classes of society.
4) Here is an analysis of the causes and effects and the broader significance of this or that social phenomenon.

The set-piece scenes and the vignettes full of memorably drawn characters that are such a distinguishing feature of Shklovsky's Letters are clearly intended to grip the reader's attention. Shklovsky's literary sensibility, his powers of description, his ear for vivid, fast-moving dialogue and his eye for detail all contribute to the powerful effect. But the facts and figures are never far away. One moment we might be laughing at a farcical breach-of-promise court case or marvelling at a gallery of British eccentrics worthy of *The Pickwick Papers*, complete with colloquial banter, and the next moment we are in the midst of a Hobsonian analysis of the economics of imperialism or an extensive reflection on the English national character, or ploughing through the minutes of government commissions and mammoth overviews of the periodical press, municipal politics, colonial literature or child labour. The cut-and-paste research is at times rather crudely shoe-horned in, inserted into the mouths of otherwise engaging characters, and in these sections one frequently catches the whiff of Shklovsky's New Grub Street hack-like drudgery in the British Museum. The selections in this anthology have been excerpted to prioritise the human-interest stories and to omit the numerous intervening pages listing statistics, quoting from official publications, referencing pamphlets and summarising press coverage of various burning issues of the day.[23] Shklovsky did not always reproduce his printed sources accurately or have time to properly research the public individuals he wrote about, and errors abound in the 'factual' interludes.[24] Any historian interested in this material would be better off going straight to the original documents, some of which have been identified in the footnotes or editorial summaries.

[23]   This kind of recycling of content was common journalistic practice across Europe in the period. It took various forms: from extended quotation to direct reprinting from other countries' newspapers, and Shklovsky, like many journalists of his time, was not above resorting to outright plagiarism or imaginative elaboration of the hints furnished by his British textual sources. See, for instance, his borrowings from Sims's *Living London* in the selections in this anthology.

[24]   However, it is worth noting that Shklovsky's misrepresentations often serve the purposes of a larger argument.

The only exception to this editorial approach is Shklovsky's first piece in this anthology, 'In the Russian Quarter', which has been reproduced in full to demonstrate his method. 'In the Russian Quarter' is what Shklovsky called elsewhere a 'half-belletristic' – i.e. fictionalised – account of the trials and tribulations of newly arrived immigrants trying to make ends meet in the East End of London in 1903–1904.[25] The characters are representative but also sensitively individualised working-class Ukrainians and Jews. We know their names; we hear their dialects (much of the dialogue in this piece is in Russian mixed with Ukrainian, Yiddish and bastardised English); we become acquainted with their personalities; and we follow them around from ship to sweatshop to soup kitchen to music hall. We witness their altercations, their reactions to the realities around them; we get insights into their different cultural and religious backgrounds. But then the perspective shifts: we are no longer in an imaginative sketch, viewing the world through the eyes of sympathetically presented individuals cast adrift in a poorly understood foreign city. We are now in a press overview summarising the spectrum of British public opinion on the social problem of immigration. We have gone from the personal insider to the abstract outsider perception of what 'immigration' is: from feet-on-the-ground to bird's-eye view, in which human beings with their own voices and feelings blur into one indistinguishable mass. And then we go back again. The individual foreigner's experience of Britain is offered as a studied counterbalance to Britain's perception of the faceless Other; the *public* discourse on 'alien immigration' embodied in the press overview is counteracted by the *personal* story of the alien immigrant him or herself. This is the ultimate significance of the fictionalised human-interest pieces in Shklovsky's oeuvre: they make the 'numbers live' (*Sketches of Contemporary England*, viii).

'The Working Quarter' is another good example of a fictionalised account, and it clearly shows that Shklovsky's literary technique was the formal counterpart of his ideological commitment to humanising political economy and putting some flesh on the bones of statistics. He is not just interested, he says, in the abstract laws, figures and formulas of the economists, but in the living and breathing individual. So he offers his readers a first-person narrative that combines novelistically described characters and impressionistic personal reflection with documentary reportage. The constant changes of perspective and abrupt transitions are hallmarks of Shklovsky's 'half-belletristic' writing. Eruptions of his own consciousness, extended scene-painting and fragmentary snapshots of people in the street (a six-year-old boy eating adulterated ice-cream;

---

[25] Robert Henderson uses the piece as a historiographical source in 'Liberty Hall: Apollinariia Iakubova and the East London Lecturing Society', *Revolutionary Russia* 28.2 (2015), 167–90.

an organ-grinder's wife harnessed like a horse) are spliced with political monologues and quotations from pamphlets and sociological surveys. To properly classify this portrait of working-class London, therefore, we should call to mind not just Charles Booth's *Life and Labour of the People in London* (1892/1902–1903) (which Shklovsky references extensively, along with the works of other contemporary doyens of slum sociology such as Seebohm Rowntree), or even the picturesque individual detail and outsider's perspective of a slumming memoir like Jack London's *The People of the Abyss* (1903), but also the stories and novels of so-called London slum fiction writers such as George Gissing and Arthur Morrison. Of course, in this particular sketch, Shklovsky is not describing a slum. The characters whose lives he shares for a few weeks are not the *lumpenproletariat* of Whitechapel, as he takes care to underline,[26] but the respectable, workhouse-fearing autodidact artisans, the aristocracy of labour. But there is no question that stylistically the account owes as much to the conventions of realist fiction as it does to the documentaries of the period.

Two other anthology selections offer clear examples of reportage straying into the formal territory of literature: the biographical narratives 'Frankie' and 'Richard Kelly', tracing the lives of a 'representative' suburban boy and a 'model' future Labour MP respectively. The degree of fictionalisation is difficult to ascertain, but Shklovsky is always present in some capacity within these stories as a friend or acquaintance of the main characters. Together with him, Russian readers can enter the homes of London's working- and middle-class families. In 'Frankie', for instance, they can follow Shklovsky to the house of a club acquaintance in a middle-class suburb near Kew Gardens, haunt of painters, novelists and well-off civil servants who guard their 'fashionable' street against the incursion of pubs and grocers. Shklovsky (and the reader) is given a tour of the house and garden by the owner's son, and the boy's public-school career, self-consciously paralleled with *Tom Brown's Schooldays*, then becomes the focus of the piece. The frame provided by this semi-imaginary portrait holds several essays' worth of factual information about everything from boys' reading habits to the loosening grip of the Classics in public-school education, as well as trenchant reflections on the inculcation of patriotic propaganda during the period of the Boer War. And, of course, no opportunity is lost – just as in the more straightforwardly documentary survey of pantomimes in Shklovsky's 'Father Christmas' article – to compare healthy British childhood with the sad fate of Russian schoolboys.

---

[26]   Shklovsky was perfectly aware of slumming as a social phenomenon, and in this piece he purposefully chooses not to focus on Whitechapel or Lambeth (as he did in other articles) because he knows that a whole literature already exists about those areas of London.

The method described here was by no means unique to Shklovsky. In her introduction to George Orwell's *The Road to Wigan Pier* (1937), Selina Todd assesses the practice of the documentary writer:

Orwell wanted to move his readers, and persuade them of his point of view. Statistics helped; so too did juxtaposing life in Wigan with life among the southern middle class. But he also wanted to hold his readers' attention. To this end, he followed Jack London in amalgamating situations (such as his several visits to mines) and creating characters who were composites of several people he had met, to make these more vivid and powerful. And [...] Orwell believed that his study would have greater credibility if he could claim to have first-hand experience of what he witnessed.[27]

Shklovsky blurs the line between fact and fiction for similar reasons. Aside from the outright invention of characters designed to embody particular social types (and to ventriloquise, in the form of political speeches or informal monologues, dry factual material), Shklovsky routinely composed life stories for individuals who only existed as names he had come across in surveys of the British press. He resorted to such devices time and again in order to personalise his material and to lend a narrative impetus to sociological analysis, but also to reinforce value judgments about British culture or institutions. If his own research and experience did not yield sufficiently compelling copy, Shklovsky was not afraid of resorting to fictional embellishments which he clearly considered 'true' in spirit, if not in fact.[28]

The same generic distinction that characterised Shklovsky's output – between informational reportage and fictionalised human-interest narrative – was also apparent in Semyon Rapoport's. Rapoport was another member of the Shklovsky generation of London foreign correspondents and like him a regular contributor of 'Letters from England' to top journals such as *Mir Bozhiy*, *Russkaya Misl'*, *Severniy Vestnik [Northern Herald]*, *Vestnik Evropi* and many others, not to mention a wide range of newspapers, including the financial press and the liberal daily *Rech'*.[29] Like Shklovsky, Rapoport was one of the earliest members of the London FPA, and like Shklovsky's, his road to foreign correspondence had been a long and winding one. Rapoport hailed from the

---

[27] George Orwell, *The Road to Wigan Pier* (1937; Oxford: Oxford University Press, 2021), xvii–xviii.

[28] For further discussion, see Anna Vaninskaya, 'Between Fact and Fiction: The Fabrication of Migrant Knowledge in Professional and Personal Correspondence', *Migrant Knowledge*, 16 December 2021, https://migrantknowledge.org/2021/12/16/between-fact-and-fiction/. In 'I. V. Shklovsky (Dioneo)', Kaznina examines at length Shklovsky's predilection for the hybrid autobiographical-fictional form in relation to his post-revolutionary publications.

[29] For a full list of the periodicals Rapoport contributed to, as well as the many pseudonyms under which he wrote, see Chikalova's publications.

Northwestern Krai and received a traditional Jewish education before moving to St Petersburg and eventually London in 1891. By then he had studied at an agricultural college, served as a soldier, and earned his living as a manual worker, a railway administration employee, and a writer for satirical and Jewish papers. There was little in all this to point to the future translator of Leo Tolstoy and G. B. Shaw, member of the Fabian Society and author of numerous article collections on British political, economic and business life.

For reasons of space, Rapoport's articles are only represented in this anthology by two editorial summaries. But it is important to give a brief overview of his output because – though it followed the same template as Shklovsky's and was addressed to similar readerships back in Russia – it has remained comparatively unknown. Like Shklovsky's, Rapoport's English Letters in the 'thick' journals and newspapers dealt with economic and political topics (Labour and Liberal party leaders, the aristocracy, etc.), social problems and social reform movements, notable books and individuals (W. T. Stead, Queen Victoria, J. S. Mill, Herbert Spencer), and the life of the country and the city. He contributed overviews of the London press, London music and theatre and the London police, as well as pieces on the book trade, education, suffragettes, socialism and religion. He published travel sketches of Ireland, Scotland and various English regions and cities. For the influential Jewish periodical *Voskhod [Ascent]* he also covered Jewish immigrant life in England, Jews on the English stage and similar topics.[30] One can get a good sense of Rapoport's range by looking at his English Letters in *Vestnik Evropi*, the 'thick' journal with which he had the longest-running association (and where he usually signed with his initials R---t, S.). In the decade from 1897, Rapoport wrote on topics such as: 'The English Village: Impressions and Notes', 'Impressions of the English Midlands', 'In South Wales: Some Travel Notes', 'My Trip to Scotland', 'Industrial "Republics": Observations of the Economic Corporations of England', 'Imports and Exports in Contemporary England', 'English Colonial Policy, Past and Present', and 'Church Schools in England'; while Letters dealing with London specifically included 'The Inhabitants of London and their Way of Life' (a review of the 1896 edition of Booth's *Life and Labour of the People in London*); 'A Failed Strike: Contemporary Life in London'; 'London Self-Government and Its Agencies'; 'Religious London: The Manners of London and Its Inhabitants'; and 'Sketches from the Life of London Youth'.

Brief summaries of two such London Letters: 'English Workmen at Leisure: A Sketch of Working-Class Amusements in London' and 'The

---

[30] He also contributed sections on Jews in English literature and Anglo-Jewish literature to the *Brockhaus and Efron Jewish Encyclopedia*, which also contained a very detailed article on Jewish London.

Story of One Street: The Domestic Life of the Poorest Stratum of the London Population' have been provided in lieu of translations in order to give the reader some sense of how Rapoport's articles would have complemented Shklovsky's. The first of these belongs unequivocally to the category of documentary reportage. The second is, simultaneously, an introduction to the workings of the London housing market and a Shklovskian 'belletristic' sketch – a first-person autobiographical narrative presenting a series of vignettes about the successive inhabitants (Rapoport himself included) of a house in a typical street undergoing the process of slummification. Rapoport's 'Garden Terrace' is very likely a composite portrait (several streets telescoped into one), which furnishes a suitable frame for a gallery of character sketches whose degree of fictionality is – as with Shklovsky's – difficult to ascertain. If the street existed, it was the closest Rapoport came to experiencing 'slumdom' himself,[31] and for both human interest and informational density his account matches anything produced in this line by Shklovsky.

THE NEXT GENERATION: KORNEY CHUKOVSKY AND SAMUIL MARSHAK

In 1903, another Russian foreign correspondent observed British life, as he later put it himself, from the 'slums': '[I was] destitute – from Russell Square I was kicked out to Titchfield Street – a street of the unemployed, of thieves and prostitutes: a real slum' (Chukovsky, *CW* 13: 329). This was Korney Chukovsky, the future literary critic and children's poet.[32] Chukovsky spent just over a year in London, writing

---

[31] Rapoport ended his life in a very different kind of London street: 6 Dagmar Road, Stroud Green. His obituary noted that he had 'lived in the district for 30 years' ('The Late Mr S. Rapoport', *The Hornsey Journal*, 23 February 1934, 22). He had apparently moved there from Sumatra Road, Hampstead, which is listed as the home of the Rapoport family in the 1901 census. Rapoport had two daughters, who married Englishmen, and a son, Julius West, who followed in his father's footsteps as a foreign correspondent – but in the other direction (i.e. to Russia). Though he came to London with his wife and son, in 'The Story of One Street' Rapoport is clearly unencumbered with a family, which supports the classification of this piece as semi-fictional.

[32] For an in-depth discussion of Chukovsky's visits to London, see Anna Vaninskaya, 'Korney Chukovsky in Britain', *Translation and Literature* 20 (2011), 373–92. The list of Chukovsky's lodgings in London is long and included Montagu Place; Store Street; 182 Great Titchfield Street and 39 Gloucester Street/Great Ormond Street (Gloucester Street ran into Great Ormond Street and was a short way from the British Museum; it is now Old Gloucester Street). He lived there in succession with his wife, and, after she left, moved to Upper Bedford Place. He photographed these streets for his diary (see the entry for 29 August 1904 in *CW* 11, 84–89), except Titchfield and Montagu (which had apparently been demolished). Some of these photographs, as well as his other photos of London street scenes (including a

short dispatches for the mass-circulation Odessa newspaper *Odesskie Novosti* rather than in-depth overviews for the metropolitan 'thick' journals.[33] In these newspaper columns, he was not aiming for the extensive research and analysis or the involved novelistic interludes that distinguished articles like Shklovsky's and Rapoport's. Where the latter routinely produced 10–15,000 words, Chukovsky's London Letters, broken into short paragraphs for the convenience of the newspaper reader, rarely came in over a thousand. He published eighty-nine Letters from June 1903 to August 1904, and taken together, they represent a mere fraction of the output of the 'thick' journal correspondents. The columns' topics, however – tariff reform, Hyde Park orators, Spiritualism, the Salvation Army, the British Museum, typical denizens of the streets like beggars and sandwich men, and public figures such as W. T. Stead, G. F. Watts and Herbert Spencer – match the topics of Shklovsky's and Rapoport's contemporaneous publications almost to a tee. And for Chukovsky, as for the others, the British popular press, from the *Daily News* and the *Daily Express* to *Reynolds's Newspaper* via the *Westminster Gazette*, served both as a major topic and an equally major source of information.[34]

Chukovsky, who was half-Jewish, half-Ukrainian, was also interested in the plight of immigrants, especially in the East End, and dedicated a number of dispatches to the parliamentary commissions that were laying the groundwork for the 1905 Aliens Act, which aimed to control the migration of poor Russian Jews into Britain. Chukovsky's writings on this subject, from reflections on the national immigration debates to descriptions of Whitechapel and its Jewish population, were effectively brief variations on the themes set by Shklovsky and Rapoport, who wrote at much greater length about the Jewish immigrant experience. Chukovsky's 'On Foreigners' from 1903 reads like a short and snappy starter to the massive main course of Shklovsky's 'The Law Against Aliens', an in-depth analysis published first in *Russkoe Bogatstvo* and then collected in the first volume of *On the Themes of Liberty* in 1908. Shklovsky's article takes thirty-four pages to recount the history of immigrant London going back centuries and to provide an account of the passage of the Aliens Act of 1905 full of excerpts from government

---

newsboy holding a 'Fall of Port Arthur' poster with whom Chukovsky got into an altercation while taking the picture), have been preserved. Chukovsky's descriptions of the various lodgings (with and without board), neighbourhoods, neighbours and landladies in this diary entry are a masterpiece of London portraiture in themselves.

33   Shklovsky had also written for *Odesskie Novosti* in the previous decade. Of course, newspaper circulations could be up to fifteen times larger than those of the top 'thick' journals (the most popular papers sold tens and sometimes hundreds of thousands of issues per day), so brevity was more than made up for by reach.

34   Chukovsky also devoted a whole article, 'English Clerks and *Tit-Bits*' to the lower-middle-class consumers of the New Journalism (*CW* II, 441–44).

commission documents and contemporary press coverage. Chukovsky contents himself with just a few quotes and tables.

Chukovsky had started freelancing for *Odesskie Novosti*, which had a largely Jewish editorial board and readership, in 1901 and when two years later the newspaper sent him to London (accompanied by his newly wed wife), he landed in a city whose contours had already been established in his own and his readers' minds by the older generation of correspondents.[35] But though his editor blamed him for spending too much time in the British Museum Reading

Fig. 2. Korney Chukovsky in London, 1904.

Room instead of seeking out newsworthy material (at one point, he lived just a few blocks away), Chukovsky did manage to get some first-hand experience of real London life – in no small part thanks to financial trouble at the newspaper. He spent long periods of time without money (not even enough for a shave), surviving on what he borrowed

[35] The surviving letters of Chukovsky's editor and friend Vladimir Zhabotinsky, reprinted in Evgeniya Ivanova, *Chukovsky i Zhabotinsky: Istoriya Otnosheniy v Tekstakh i Kommentariyakh [Chukovsky and Zhabotinsky: The History of a Relationship in Texts and Commentaries]* (Moscow-Jerusalem: Gesharim-Mosti Kul'turi, 2004), make for interesting reading – both for the explicit comparisons to Shklovsky and for the criticism of Chukovsky's memorable style (see www. uhlib.ru/istorija/chizh_chukovskii_i_zhabotinskii/index.php). Zhabotinsky cautions Chukovsky that another editor wants him to 'emphasise local life because, for instance, Dioneo wrote about some execution, but Chuk did not attend it. Let him henceforth attend all hangings' (28 July 1903). On 10 December, Zhabotinsky wrote: 'I am not pleased with your correspondence […] You are simply working too little for it […] [You] must devote more time to observations and less to the library […] Furthermore, *very important*: you should *never* include any witticisms or ironic remarks in your correspondence or allow yourself any humour at all […] Don't sit in the library, then everything will go well.' The last injunction could with equal fairness have been addressed to all the London correspondents: Chukovsky recounts meeting Rapoport in the British Museum in his letters (*CW* 14, 59) and Rapoport's obituary mentions how 'Day after day he journeyed to the reading-room of the British Museum to do his work'.

from his émigré friends, and the caustic irony that gave such a characteristic flavour to his dispatches doubtless stemmed in part from these experiences as a penniless foreigner. His descriptions of visits to see the Russian Jewish immigrants in Whitechapel (he knew a certain Katz family there) betray a degree of self-identification he shared neither with the better-off revolutionary exiles like Kropotkin (whom he saw from afar in the British Museum but did not actually meet until 1917 in Petrograd), nor with the other Russian expatriates and journalists with whom he associated. These included, aside from Shklovsky and Rapoport, Vl. F. Lazursky, a literature professor and former teacher of Leo Tolstoy's children who was in London doing research for his dissertation (and whom Kropotkin believed to be a Russian police spy); Milyukov, who also lived in a boarding house by the British Museum (in Russell Street); various correspondents for Odessa papers and the journalist and political activist A. F. Aladin, whom Chukovsky criticised mercilessly.

Chukovsky's relationship with Shklovsky was also rocky, not to say antagonistic.[36] Unlike the well-known Dioneo, Chukovsky was a nobody: a twenty-one-year-old working-class youth from Odessa who had only taught himself English five years previously after being expelled from school. His only relevant 'education' had been a typical autodidact reading course consisting of the English classics and contemporary English literature, and his acquaintance with the country was negligible by comparison with Shklovsky's. But this did not prevent him from mocking the older man's views and exposing his many factual inaccuracies and typographical errors.[37] In his diary, Chukovsky described Shklovsky's visit to him – with his 'gold-rimmed spectacles, bent back and quotations from all writers on all topics' (*CW* 11: 85) – as well as his own visit to Rapoport, in a way that left no doubt of his contempt for both of the older correspondents:

> Rapoport is not clever, a stutterer in speech and thought, envious and ambitious – but he always produces the impression of being loving and carefree. Just now I've read in 'Mir Bozhiy' a notice of his book 'Delovaya Angliya' which contrasts him with Dioneo, and it says that compared with Dioneo he is a complete fool and know-nothing. How the one must be raging and the other rejoicing. If I

---

[36] However, Chukovsky was on very familiar terms with Shklovsky's wife, Zinaida Davidovna, also a journalist. See Chukovsky's diary, as well as his letter to Shklovskaya in *CW* 14, 33–36 containing his trademark comic verses, and mentions of her in his letters to his own wife (43–44 and 389). When Chukovsky returned to London in 1916, he made sure to contact Shklovsky by phone and received a visit from his wife. Shklovskaya's obituary, by Gleb Struve, is reprinted in Parkhomovsky and Rogachevskii.

[37] See Chukovsky's articles written in the couple of years after he returned from London, in *CW* 6, 65–66, 428–29.

were the reviewer, I would console them both and say that they are both equally useless. The one tries to fit everything to his theories, and since theories are meat and drink to Russian readers, they don't notice that everything in Dioneo is pilfered from books, that if you were to take the quotations from his volume about England and return them to their authors, the only thing left of the whole volume would be the spine. Rapoport is also not without his 'theories'. But they don't quite conform with the leading articles in 'Russkie Vedomosti' – hence his lack of success. (II: 86)

And in a letter to his wife the same year, reflecting on his latest dispatches, he opined: 'I had almost lost heart and prepared to become another Rapoport or Dioneo [...] I [...] hold all these gentlemen in contempt, and that's a good sign' (*CW* 14: 44).

It was not just the Russian journalists that he held in contempt, but also the country that they were all meant to cover. In his London Letters Chukovsky often adopted the manners-and-customs-of-the-natives style of writing, confirming most of the entrenched stereotypes about the English national character in an inimitable tone of all-knowing world-weary disgust. He offered a few positive accounts of British philanthropy, respect for the law and safeguarding of individual rights, and some obligatory paeans to the Crystal Palace and the self-made man, but these were usually outweighed by criticisms: of the bizarre and punitive justice system, of the sway of tradition and the despotism of public opinion, of the cult of heritage, British conservatism, xenophobia, imperialism and jingoism. The English bourgeois, Chukovsky wrote, was primitive and had no spiritual life; the species was epitomised by the useless and ignorant 'middle-class woman', who occupied her mind with nothing nobler than her household, her purity, and her hymnbook (*CW* II: 452). Students were no better: they did not care for anything except 'the racing news' and 'who's who in football'. Mechanisation and narrow specialisation had killed off the national spirit which produced Chukovsky's beloved Romantic and Victorian poets. He ranted against the family hearth and the obsession with business, and 'Mrs Grundy' appeared in the dispatches with worrying frequency: the Englishman's censorship of plays, his prudery in sexual matters, his hypocrisy, were all castigated. He lambasted English anti-intellectualism at every turn – only foreigners, in Chukovsky's London, read for pleasure. Phenomena such as the breach-of-promise lawsuit, birth control, anti-vivisection campaigns, Spiritualism, the Salvation Army and Protestant theology all horrified him. Political topics such as tariff reform, women in Parliament or international trade competition immediately called forth harsh judgments on the status quo. He attended meetings in Essex Hall and in Hyde Park and was not impressed; he went to lectures and reading groups at the Working Men's College

and seasoned his awe with reservations;[38] he frequented the theatre
and criticised the hegemony of melodrama and the exclusive focus on
spectacle and special effects. He devoted a long article to the sad state
of English drama: censorship throttled everything of worth and avant-
garde foreign influences were non-existent.[39] He went to see Tolstoy's
Resurrection on stage but beheld instead 'the devil knows what. A
mockery of Tolstoy, syrupy sentimentalism, shrill melodrama' that even
the theatre-goers of a working-class suburb of Odessa would disdain
(*CW* II: 449). The only place in London where Russian literature was
properly appreciated was the Russian reading room in Whitechapel,
frequented exclusively by Russian Jews. British lack of interest in
Russia was a particular grievance. A 'silver shot glass', Chukovsky was
outraged to discover, was all that 'represented' his 'homeland' in the
British Museum (see 'The British Museum' piece in this anthology). If
a visitor wished to find out 'what goes on in that huge country which
has given him Tolstoy and Dostoevsky', what were its cultural achievements, there was nothing to point to but Russian 'drunkenness'. The fact
that Anton Chekhov's death in 1904 went completely unnoticed by the
British press stung him deeply. The British book market, Chukovsky
complained in another article, was flooded with pamphlets and sensa-
tionalist entertainment of the murders-and-ghosts variety. Literature
was produced not for serious purposes but for leisure and escapism.
Émile Zola and Guy de Maupassant, meanwhile, were sold in the same
shops as contraception.

Chukovsky's view of Britain was certainly a jaundiced one, but in his
condemnatory columns he still managed to pick up on most of the major
issues that were being explored at much greater length and, arguably,
with rather more balance, by the older generation of correspondents.
Although he was almost entirely cut off from the higher circles of
British life that were open to the likes of Shklovsky and Rapoport,
Chukovsky's acquaintance with the everyday realities of Edwardian
London – the working-class autodidacts, the alcoholic down-and-outs
and the lower-middle-class residents of the cheaper boarding houses –
gave his dispatches a flavour of authenticity that matched anything found

---

[38]   Chukovsky's wife was 'kicked out' of the Working Men's College, according to
        Chukovsky's letter of July 1904 (*CW* 14, 54).
[39]   'There are no foreign influences of any kind; just as Chekhov, Hauptmann, and
        Maeterlinck are wowing Europe with glimmering new aspects of life, the aims
        of the drama here are reduced to the recreation on stage of train crashes, floods,
        war, and so on' (*CW* II, 508). Elsewhere Chukovsky wrote: 'If you see a play
        at the theatre where the actors box rather more than act, and if you notice at
        the same time that every sock on the jaw elicits from the spectators an outburst
        of wild enthusiasm, know that you have found yourself in the company of [the
        English clerks] and that you are observing the highest expression of their aesthetic
        emotions' (*CW* II, 441).

in the older men's work. And the unflattering negative impressions of his first visit were eventually smoothed out by an idealising nostalgia. 'England is the dream of my life', he wrote in a letter in 1925. Despite his experience of poverty, he 'fell in love with that city [London] like a homeless dog', and he could never forget the London of his youth: 'In the most romantic way I still love the English, even their cant, even their snobbery' (*CW* 14: 621). Sixty years later, even his contempt for Shklovsky had evaporated. As he wrote in 1963 to Gleb Struve, who had found several of Chukovsky's comic verses addressed to Shklovsky's wife among Shklovsky's papers: 'I recall Isaak Vladimirovich and his wife [...] with a feeling of the liveliest gratitude. I was a deeply ignorant, destitute and awkward youth; only in their house, the only house in all of England, did I find shelter, food and affection.'[40]

A decade after Chukovsky, the Shklovskys welcomed another young correspondent to London. This was Samuil Marshak, a Russian-Jewish poet and journalist who arrived in 1912 after a stint as a foreign correspondent in the Near East the previous year. Although poetry was Marshak's real vocation,[41] he supported himself and his wife through their studies at the University of London by contributing sketches to a range of St Petersburg newspapers and journals (under the pseudonym Dr Frieken).[42] As he wrote in 1915, after his return to Russia:

The last few years I was forced to take up newspaper work in order to make a living (I contributed feuilletons, correspondence, articles and translations to the newspapers 'Birzhevie Vedomosti', 'Den' *[Day]*,

---

[40] This letter is not included in the *Collected Works*; it is reproduced in G. P. Struve, 'Pis'ma K. I. Chukovskogo k G. P. Struve' ['Letters of K. I. Chukovsky to G. P. Struve'], *Noviy Zhurnal [New Journal]* 101 (1970), www.chukfamily. ru/kornei/prosa/pisma/dva-pisma-ki-chukovskogo. Struve had sent the originals of Chukovsky's verses to Shklovsky's archive and also printed them in 1965. Chukovsky's other letters imply that the Shklovsky family lived in Shepherd's Bush in 1903 and in Richmond in 1904.

[41] For Marshak's activities as a specifically Jewish poet in this period, see Rita Genzeleva, 'Marshak, Samuil Iakovlevich', *The YIVO Encyclopedia of Jews in Eastern Europe*, https://yivoencyclopedia.org/article.aspx/Marshak_Samuil_Iakovlevich.

[42] Marshak was enrolled at East London College, now Queen Mary. He was in the Faculty of Arts and attended lectures on the history of English language and literature; his wife was in the Faculty of Science. It was here, especially in the College library, from whose windows he could look down on the busy Thames, that, as he later recalled, he first encountered and began translating the English poetry that would make him a household name in the Soviet Union. See 'O Sebe' ['About Myself'] in *CW* 1, 5–15 and I. S. Marshak, 'Ot Detstva k Detyam: Glavi iz Biograficheskoy Knigi' ['From Childhood to Children: Chapters from a Biographical Book'] in B. Galanov, I. Marshak and M. Petrovsky, eds. *Zhizn' i Tvorchestvo S. Marshaka [S. Marshak's Life and Work]* (Moscow: Detskaya Literatura, 1975), 426–28.

'Courier' *[Petersburg Courier]*, etc.).[43] But now I have, happily, quit regular newspaper work with its fuss and hurry and its hackwork and hope never again to return to it.[44] (*CW* 8: 81)

Until the outbreak of war in 1914 (he went back to Russia in July), Marshak was busy composing London Letters covering various aspects of English – and London – life: a Cornish fishing village, a Hampshire Simple Life school,[45] the Derby, an East End cinema, the Children's Welfare Exhibition, suffragettes, boxers, tourists, caravans, Parliament, as well as Captain Scott's death, various literary topics and the ballerina Anna Pavlova's tour. Some of the subjects had barely changed since the 1890s and 1900s; others reflected new political, technological and cultural developments, like the advent of the cinema as a mode of popular entertainment or the pre-war fad for Russian dance. Britain's greater openness to 'foreign influences', whose absence Chukovsky had bitterly lamented ten years earlier, was not just apparent in Marshak's correspondence, but in the list of his acquaintances: he met the poet Rabindranath Tagore, and was on familiar terms with Samuel Koteliansky, Virginia Woolf's future collaborator in the translation of Russian literature, who had come to London shortly before Marshak.[46]

---

43   From London, Marshak also contributed to other Petersburg publications such as *Nedelya 'Sovremennogo Slova' [The 'Contemporary Word' Weekly]* and the anglophile illustrated monthly journal *Argus*. Although the total number of his London Letters is smaller than even Chukovsky's (just over twenty), the listed periodicals represent just a fraction of his overall journalistic experience – he had been earning his living publishing under various pseudonyms and across a wide range of press outlets, 'thick' and thin, metropolitan and provincial, satirical and Zionist, since the late 1900s.

44   Compare the thoughts Chukovsky confided to his diary shortly before he left England: 'every day I hate newspapers more and more [...] I will bless the minute when I break free from the newspaper columns' (*CW* 11, 89).

45   Philip Oyler's Morshin School, where Marshak with his wife and sisters lived for long periods of time both before and after it relocated to Tintern in Wales in 1914, and which he invited the Shklovsky spouses to visit (see his letter to Shklovsky in *CW* 8, 57). Marshak was very interested in the 'simple life' and wrote about it in his newspaper sketches more than once. See also Yu. Ya. Marshak-Fainberg, 'Chastitsa Vremeni' ['A Piece of Time'], in B. E. Galanov, I. S. Marshak and Z. S. Paperny, eds. *'Ya Dumal, Chustvoval, Ya Zhil': Vospominaniya o Marshake ['I Thought, Felt and Lived': Reminiscences of S. Ya. Marshak]* (Moscow: Sovetskiy Pisatel', 1971), 13–42 for a detailed description of Oyler, the Simple Life School in both of its locations and the Marshaks' life there, as well as a description of their time in London and portions of his verse travel diary. Oyler's wife and sister, for their part, also left reminiscences of the Marshaks' time at the school (reproduced in *S. Marshak's Life and Work*, 432–34).

46   On Koteliansky, see Galya Diment, *A Russian Jew of Bloomsbury: The Life and Times of Samuel Koteliansky* (Montreal: McGill-Queen's University Press, 2011).

Fig. 3. Samuil Marshak (with Wife and Sister) at the Simple Life School, 1913.

Like Chukovsky, Marshak was straitened in means and forced to inhabit a succession of lodgings around London, near Canonbury, Mile End and St Pancras.[47] As he later recalled:

> Since my literary earnings were barely enough to make ends meet, my wife and I had occasion to live in the most democratic districts of London – first in its northern part, then in the poorest and most densely populated eastern one, and only by the very end did we make it out into one of the central districts near the British Museum where lived many other foreign students like ourselves. (*CW* 1:9)

The centrally located boarding house was also home to Swedes, Indians, Japanese and Chinese – an international assortment that would have seemed familiar to Chukovsky.[48] Unlike Chukovsky, however, Marshak also travelled extensively around the country by rail, boat and on foot. In 1912, he stayed in the environs of London, visiting various villages

---

[47] Specifically, 32 Beresford Road, 17 Campbell Road, and 56 Cartwright Gardens; one of Marshak's sisters, who briefly enrolled at the London County Council (LCC) Central School of Arts and Crafts in 1914, rented a room in 47 Great Percy Street.

[48] Chukovsky described the Australians, Germans and others he boarded with in Upper Bedford Place in his diary; see also Shklovsky's description of the inhabitants of a boarding house in 'Mr Muir'.

and towns in Essex, full of both London golfers down for the weekend and locals who had barely ever been to London at all. In 1913, he went on a walking trip with his wife to Cornwall and Devon, visiting Exeter, Plymouth, Tintagel, Fowey and Polperro; and in 1914 he travelled in Ireland along the banks of the River Shannon. The result of the second trip was a series of travel sketches, 'Across England', published in various periodicals in 1914 (the projected 'Across Ireland' remained incomplete due to the outbreak of war). He also kept a verse diary of his travels, took photographs and conducted a voluminous personal correspondence (some of it also in verse) that complemented his newspaper articles.[49]

Marshak's personal letters, mostly addressed to his wife, are full of detailed and frequently comical observations of London people and environments – the inevitable British Museum, the India Museum at South Kensington, the 'London Polytechnic' on Regent Street (where he studied before enrolling in East London College, and where he later unsuccessfully tried to place his sister), a Congregational church, landladies, and political and religious speakers in Hyde Park. He also describes the pubs and inns where he stayed and the farmers, tramps, riders, automobiles, cyclists and motorcyclists with whom he shared the road during his 1912 trip, reflecting in the process on the differences between London and country manners. During the 1914 trip, he similarly remarks on the contrasting attitudes of the Irish and the English (the topics in these letters range from Home Rule to fairies to vegetarianism). The greater friendliness and conversational openness of the people he encounters outside of London never fail to strike him, and Marshak keeps drawing his reader's attention to the distinctions between the capital's inhabitants and those of other parts of the United Kingdom. In Marshak's personal letters, London emerges as its own world with its own unique lifestyle.

NATIVES AND FOREIGNERS

But whatever they may have written in their personal letters, in their professional publications, all four correspondents strove, with varying degrees of success, to reconcile their awareness of London's diverse particularity with the stereotypical generalisations current in both Russian and British discourses of the city. Nowhere was this more evident than in their writing about their own compatriots, the economic and religious refugees from the Russian Empire. The first part of this anthology, 'Foreigners in London', is devoted to the East End immigrant

---

[49]   Some of Marshak's photographs are available on the main Marshak website: *Nedopisannaya Stranitsa: Samuil Marshak [An Incomplete Page: Samuil Marshak]*, http://s-marshak.ru/photo/molodost/molodost.htm.

community because, as we have already seen with Shklovsky's 'In the Russian Quarter', it was here that stereotype clashed most vividly with lived experience. It was also here that George Sims opened his Edwardian anthology *Living London*:

> We have been fortunate to-day, for we have seen the arrival of a ship laden with flesh and blood for the London slave market. The strange, white-faced, hollow-eyed men and women are Russian and Roumanian Jews. Not a word of English can they speak, but they have come to our crowded city to earn their daily bread. We shall see what happens to them from the time they land with a few shillings in their pockets to the Sunday morning when they stand in the streets to be hired by the sweaters at a wage which makes it a mystery how they can keep body and soul together. (Prologue 1: 5)

The mystery was no mystery to someone like Shklovsky. 'In the Russian Quarter' also begins on board a German steamer carrying a cargo of horses and Russian 'slaves' to the London docks. Among the 'slaves' are a Jewish tailor and a Christian joiner, who had left his wife and children at home in order to earn a living in far-off fabled London. The men, and two young Jewish seamstresses, are hired by a 'sweater' straight off the ship, but they do not stay with him for long and Shklovsky is able to document their attempts to 'keep body and soul together' in infinitely greater detail than Sims could ever envision. The joiner is soon dismissed from a factory job because the unionised British workers, incensed at his undercutting of their wages, get him sacked, and some months later he and his friend find themselves out in the street. Work is slack, the Tory newspapers are fuming rabidly about foreigners who are taking away British jobs, unemployment is rising and the immigrants, being outsiders who barely speak the language, cannot even join the workers' demonstrations. Besides, they are too afraid of the police. To keep warm one January evening, the tailor and joiner search out the Free Russian Library in Whitechapel – regularly packed full of unemployed, semi-starved men reading and discussing the news from back home – and pick up an out-of-work cobbler and tinker to go tramping the streets of London with them. They see women selling Russian food, the 'Jewish' Thomas Cook and the 'Odessa' restaurant in Whitechapel, a nursery sponsored by Anglo-Jewish philanthropists, a patent-medicine seller, and an outdoor meeting of the Social Democratic Federation.[50] They pass through the empty streets of the City, whose banks and shipping companies have shut their doors for the night, the homeless sleepers wrapped in newspapers, the fashionably dressed

---

[50] The Social Democratic Federation (SDF), the main Marxist group in Britain at the time, had an East End (Jewish) branch from the mid-1880s. The SDF's leader, H. M. Hyndman, was an acquaintance of Shklovsky's; he also pops up in Marshak's account of speakers seen in Hyde Park in his letters a decade later.

theatre and restaurant crowds, the prostitutes patrolling outside the big music halls, and a Salvation Army soup kitchen. As they leave the Salvation Army sermon in disgust, they get a bright idea – they will form a music hall singing and dancing troupe – The Samovaroffs – and make their living performing Ukrainian songs. Despite the objections of the Yiddish-speaking tinker, they land an engagement in an East End music hall and dress up for the part in a sorry imitation of Ukrainian national costume – with a little financial help from their former sweater. But no sooner are they thrust out on stage, than they are hooted off to the accompaniment of a hail of projectiles from the pit, and an enraged chanting of 'Kishenev', 'Kishenev'. For this is 1904, and the London (as well as the world) press is brimming with horror stories about the Kishinev Pogrom – the most significant of the pogroms that led to an upsurge in Zionism and a massive wave of Jewish emigration from Russia. 'You see,' explains the cobbler sarcastically as they escape from the stage, 'In Kishinev, they beat us for being Jews, and here they beat us to stick up for us.' The punchline, of course, is that the London working-class audience has mistaken the Jewish performers for Bessarabian anti-semites.

'In the Russian Quarter' provides a truly immersive experience for its readers, but its ironic portrayal of the encounter between native Londoner and Jewish immigrant only works because it comes from the pen of a journalist who felt as much at home among the London workers as he did among the 'alien' denizens of Whitechapel. For as parts II, III and IV of this anthology show, the Russian correspondents had many more strings to their bows than the obvious one of immigrant experience. In fact, the vast majority of their coverage had nothing to do with their compatriots in the capital at all; just as much, if not more of an emphasis was placed on the detail of 'native' working-class life. From Rapoport's Letters, as has been seen, Russian readers could learn about the leisure pastimes of London factory hands and the rent troubles of cabbies and carmen. In Shklovsky's articles, they could observe workmen returning home with their carpetbags full of tools or listen to the drunken voices issuing from a pub on a Saturday half-holiday. Shklovsky takes his readers to Battersea on a damp, cold autumn evening, when the factory whistles have stopped blowing and young working-class men are hurrying to the library or the Polytechnic. He follows some of them to an election meeting and witnesses the heckling and heated exchanges. On another occasion, he joins some maids, mechanics and clerks at a Hammersmith socialist club to sing hymns and listen to a lecture by a young autodidact carpenter – the kind who sits at his books after work until three in the morning and has nearly won a seat on the School Board. After the lecture, the entertainment: waltzes, polkas and barn-dances. There are some bicycles in the corner; on the walls hangs a print by Walter Crane, and newspapers scattered on the table include *Justice, The Labour Leader, The Clarion* and

Reynolds's Newspaper, as well as the club's own humorous magazine. It is as if the Russian reader has been transported bodily into the world of a late-Victorian working-class memoir. The public life of the London streets is also continuously on display: Shklovsky takes his readers to freak shows, penny gaffs and outdoor meetings; he shows little girls dancing the cakewalk and passing newsboys, quacks and hawkers; he squints at playbills, advertisements and political posters plastered all over the walls and in the pub windows of South London. Middle-class domestic life is not forgotten either, and readers are introduced to a Richmond schoolboy's routine, to Christmas dinners and pantomimes and the piano repertoires of patriotic villa-dwellers in as natural a fashion as they are regaled elsewhere with the sermons of a Jewish Orthodox tinker. Nor does Shklovsky shy away from the conventional journalistic fodder of sensationalism and celebrity. The anthology selections include pieces on Queen Victoria's funeral, the Old Bailey trial of serial killer George Chapman, and the scandalous behaviour of various religious sects, such as the Agapemonites in Clapton, whose leader proclaimed himself the Son of God.[51] In all of these accounts, even when they contain deliberate fictionalisations and inadvertent errors of fact, the sensitivity to detail and the grasp of cultural context leave no doubt as to their author's intimate acquaintance with 'native' London life. What is particularly noticeable about some of them is the degree of assumed knowledge on the part of the Russian observer – he is a participant too, confident in his ability to navigate his cultural surroundings. There are regular allusions to the 'typically English manner' of this or that – dancing, public speaking, fashion, pronunciation – and the reader is even led to believe that the Russian author's command of the English language is superior to that of the native Londoners he is describing. In articles such as 'The Working Quarter' and 'The Beck Case', the correspondent's ear is especially attuned to the accents around him.[52]

---

[51] Not included is Shklovsky's vivid account of American Mormon missionaries and Christian Scientist faith healers operating in London at the turn of the century, focusing on the 1898 inquest into the death of Harold Frederic, the American novelist and London correspondent of *The New York Times*. The death provoked an international scandal, and Shklovsky provided Russian readers with a transcription of the coroner's interrogation of the faith healer Mrs Mills, who, together with Frederic's mistress, was charged with manslaughter, but eventually acquitted.

[52] We do not know how good Shklovsky's English was in actuality: his renderings of English phrases in Latin script are full of typographical errors (silently corrected in this edition), but these may have been introduced by the compositors. We do know from his personal letters that Marshak's English was rudimentary when he arrived, although by the end of his stay he was being mistaken for an Irishman; and Chukovsky's accent was, according to Vladimir Nabokov, so thick that people could barely understand him.

But there was a limit to how 'native' correspondents were able or willing to go. Just as typical as the assimilated persona possessing insider knowledge, was the persona of the stranger in a strange land who sees all that he encounters through the spectacles of foreign habits and expectations. The natural comparative instinct of the immigrant was reinforced by the correspondents' professional duty of explaining British manners and customs in terms that were familiar to their readers back home. Shklovsky's and Rapoport's jarring use of words like 'vodka' (for whisky or gin), 'versts', 'desyatins' and 'arshins' (instead of English units of measurement), 'kopecks' and 'roubles' (instead of pounds and pence), or 'Duma' (for Council) in the midst of otherwise authentic-sounding descriptions is a literal case in point. British realities were to be understood by reference to Russian ones: 'Edinburgh is a kind of Scottish Moscow,' wrote Rapoport, 'whose historical kremlin is the Holyrood Palace [...] whereas Glasgow is a kind of Petersburg [...] livelier, more cosmopolitan than Edinburgh, and also more progressive and populous.'[53] There is no hint of judgemental intemperance in these kinds of comparisons, but occasionally, even a favourably disposed and knowledgeable correspondent like Shklovsky would give in to the temptation to interpret British culture from a position of bemused or exasperated incomprehension. Chukovsky, unsurprisingly, turned the damning comparison into a trademark of his colloquial style:

> Look at an Englishman when he has a newspaper in his hands. An English newspaper numbers on average sixteen large-format pages. The letters in it are tiny. You need a week to read all of it [...] One of us Russians would take it and give the whole thing a go right through. But an Englishman will pick out the headline he's looking for, read the twelve or so lines of interest to him, and lo! the newspaper is already on the ground. He couldn't care less about the rest. Serbia, Chamberlain, a car race, a cardinal's death – out of all this only one thing will interest him, *according to the nature of his business* – he has no notion of our Russkie's platonic interest *in it all*. (*CW* II: 439)

In Chukovsky's columns, the rhetoric of the explorer among the savages – 'enlightened savages in top hats' to be precise (II: 507) – was always threatening to break through: 'Their simple spiritual constitution demands events, story, action; "introspection" seems to them a trifling, useless thing. Of all human virtues these primitive people in top hats value strength, cunning, courage; and this is the primary proof of their cultural virginity' (II: 447).

Though extreme, Chukovsky's attitude was by no means exceptional. In the writing of all the Russian correspondents, the same

---

53 Semyon Rapoport, 'Moya Poezdka v Shotlandiyu' ['My Trip to Scotland'], *Vestnik Evropi*, July 1902, 82.

stereotypical British traits – 'spiritual mediocrity',[54] crass materialism, hidebound traditionalism and extreme religiosity – come in for criticism again and again. Detail is put in the service of cliché. Salvation Army bands appear regularly in both Shklovsky and Chukovsky as targets of light-hearted satire or heavy-handed condemnation. Even the generally even-handed Marshak cannot help remarking on the zealous evangelicalism of his Cornish hosts or on the shocking – 'especially for us Russians'– 'commercial nature' of the 1913 Children's Welfare Exhibition, whose organisers could not understand 'the selflessness and idealism' of the 'Russian lady' who volunteered her services for free (see 'At the Children's Exhibition' in this anthology).[55] In his personal letters Marshak referred to the English using the Finnish ethnic slur 'Chukhontsi' (*CW* 8: 53), while Chukovsky transformed the national insult into a veritable art form. Here he is on the female guardians of respectability whom he encountered in his boarding house:

> They will hold you in eternal contempt if instead of a fish knife you pick up one intended for the meat [...]
>
> A doctor's spouse [...] once asked me about my neighbour, a famous Russian professor:
>
> 'Tell me, has he received any kind of education?'
>
> 'Why, of course! His scientific works are known all over Russia. They have been translated into almost every language...'
>
> 'Then how can he not know yet that he must dress for dinner in the evening in tails and white tie, and not in the same jacket he wore for breakfast and tea?...'
>
> If I did not know that this was England, I would have thought it was the Chinese empire, so overwhelming is the despotism of public opinion here, whose mandarins are, of course, the women... (*CW* 11: 454)

Writing of the furniture 'symmetrically arranged' 'for show' in the 'home' of a London bourgeois family, he exclaims: 'It seems that if only you could overturn two or three chairs, strangle that canary in the cage, everything would breathe more easily, the sun would finally look in at the window' (11: 465). Russian openness and spontaneity, British formality and narrow-mindedness: they run like two intertwining threads through the cultural narrative of Chukovsky's dispatches. Of course, like Shklovsky, he was more than ready to sing the praises of British

---

54 Chukovsky, *CW* 11, 444.
55 This commercialism still rankled in Marshak's mind many years later when he told Maxim Gorky of the Exhibition. The latter proposed organising a non-commercial Soviet alternative, although nothing came of the idea (see *S. Marshak's Life and Work*, 434–35).

liberty, parliamentary democracy, individual autonomy and self-help, but his appraising foreigner's eye was always trained sceptically on the unsavoury peculiarities of native manners and customs. Most of Chukovsky's articles quoted above are not reproduced in this anthology, but the tone he adopts in them is just as apparent in the ones that are.

One may well ask why it is worthwhile to read today accounts so clearly marked by a former century's cultural prejudice? Why the Letters where dismissive stereotypes remain in unresolved tension with the rich particularities of London life, both native and foreign, are worth translating and reprinting at all? The answer becomes clear if we contrast Chukovsky's Letters with Russian journalists' coverage of London at war in the following decade. In 1916, a delegation representing both reactionary and liberal newspapers, as well as a popular illustrated weekly, was invited on what was essentially a public relations mission to Britain, shown military installations, and wined and dined by the King, the generals and the cultural establishment. The delegation consisted of Chukovsky, Aleksey Tolstoy, and Vladimir Nabokov (Sr), writing for *Niva, Russkie Vedomosti* and *Rech'* respectively, and several other journalists representing *Novoe Vremya, Russkoe Slovo [Russian Word]* and *Pravitel'stvenniy Vestnik [Government Herald]*.[56] The difference in tone between their articles and Chukovsky's Edwardian dispatches is profound, but hardly surprising – after all, the delegation had to fulfil its primary propagandistic purpose of presenting Britain in a positive light as a wartime ally. Much more telling is the fact that very little concrete or original information about wartime London can actually be gleaned from Tolstoy's and Nabokov's articles. As documents of observed London realities most of them are negligible: all they offer is a tourist's perspective, an elaboration of the delegation's itinerary and a formal account of the official aspects of the trip. Each correspondent had at least one, and sometimes more pieces devoted specifically to 'London Observations and Impressions' (as Nabokov called them), but only Chukovsky's managed to transcend the view from the car window and to give some feel for what life was really like in London in early 1916. Chukovsky produced a lively portrait of a city run almost entirely by women and children. In its anecdotal style, its attempts at catchy

[56]   A. N. Tolstoy published a series of articles in *Russkie Vedomosti* in March, April and May of 1916 which were reprinted in a collection called *V Anglii, Na Kavkaze, Po Volini i Galitsii [In England, In the Caucasus, Across Volhynia and Galicia]* (Moscow, 1916). Nabokov's articles appeared in *Rech'*, the Cadet newspaper, starting in February (as did at least one of Chukovsky's, in the issue of 26 February 1916: 'Iz Anglii: Letuchii Listki' ['From England: Flying Leaflets']). They were reprinted shortly thereafter as V. D. Nabokov, *Iz Voyuyuschey Anglii: Putevie Ocherki [From England at War: Travel Sketches]* (Petrograd, 1916). Chukovsky's articles for *Niva* appeared in book form as *Angliya Nakanune Pobedi [England on the Eve of Victory]* (Petrograd 1916).

dialogue and its magpie borrowings from the British press, if not in its framing (his brief being now to praise Britain), the approach was quite similar to that of his earlier columns – one could even call it Shklovsky-lite. The contrast with Nabokov's officialese is striking and though it could be explained partly by the popular middle-brow format within which Chukovsky was writing, the main reason was simply that Chukovsky was blessed with a naturally better eye for the detail of lived experience.

For at the end of the day, not all foreign correspondents are created equal. The pieces gathered in this anthology have been chosen because – for all their generalisations, biases and inaccuracies, their variations in perspective and degrees of knowledge – they can still cast a unique light on actual London life. In this regard, the anthology might well serve as a kind of counterpart to Sims's *Living London* – showing the city 'at work and at play', in all its 'humour and pathos', as seen through several pairs of particularly attentive Russian eyes.

I

FOREIGNERS IN LONDON

Fig. 4. Aliens Arriving at Irongate Stairs.

Korney Chukovsky, 'Ob Inostrantsakh' ['On Foreigners']
Odesskie Novosti, 5 August 1903[1]

London
(From our own correspondent)
12 August

A Commission whose remit concerns us closely presented its report yesterday evening.[2] The Commission's goals are officially formulated as follows: 'to enquire into the character and extent of the evils which are attributed to the unrestricted immigration of aliens to the Metropolis and to advise what remedial or precautionary measures it is desirable to adopt in this country, and to report whether it is desirable to impose any, and if so, what, restrictions on such immigration'. The Commission began its pleasant labours back in March 1902, and so far, it has met publicly forty-nine times and collected 175 most competent opinions. Moreover, it has sent Major E. Gordon to Russia and Romania in order to study in situ the causes of such an undesirable phenomenon.[3]

---

[1] Chukovsky published eighty-nine articles in *Odesskie Novosti* during his time in London from June 1903 to August 1904. The *Collected Works* reprints thirty-three, and thirteen of these have been chosen for translation. The translation follows the *Collected Works* text but corrects certain misprints. Titles for untitled articles are supplied in brackets. The publication dates of the issues are given in the 'old' pre-revolutionary style, as they appeared on the newspaper masthead (Russia changed from the Julian to the Gregorian calendar in 1918); the dates in the by-lines (not always supplied) are when Chukovsky actually wrote the articles in London according to the 'new'-style (Western) calendar. Chukovsky signed his articles 'K. Chukovsky'. Digitisations of the original issues from 1903–1904 are available from the Rare Books Library of the Odesa I. Mechnikov University: http://rarebook. onu.edu.ua:8081/.

[2] The 'us' in the opening sentence might refer to anyone from the Russian Empire generally, or to Jews in particular. Chukovsky's columns in *Odesskie Novosti* had a sizeable Jewish audience and the editorial board of the newspaper was also predominantly Jewish, so references here and in the following articles to Jewish immigrants in London would have been of particular interest to his readers and editors. See 'Odessa', *The YIVO Encyclopedia of Jews in Eastern Europe*, https://yivoencyclopedia.org/article.aspx/Odessa and Ivanova, *Chukovsky and Zhabotinsky*, who quotes a contemporary police report about the three main Odessa dailies, *Odesskie Novosti*, *Yuzhnoe Obozrenie* [*Southern Review*] and *Odesskiy Listok*, with all of which Chukovsky had some association: '"Odesskie Novosti" and "Yuzhnoe Obozrenie" are published and edited by Jews, and "Odesskiy Listok", though published by a Russian [...] is nevertheless also a Jewish organ in practice'. The newspapers are accused of being unpatriotic, too critical of Russia and too favourable to Western countries, especially Western socialism and social democracy, thereby predisposing the masses toward 'cosmopolitanism' and revolutionary ideas.

[3] Chukovsky is referring to and quoting verbatim from the Royal Commission on Alien Immigration (1902–1903), which laid the foundation for the 1905 Aliens Act. See Alison Bashford and Catie Gilchrist, 'The Colonial History of the 1905

37

What Mr Gordon said after he came back from his trip I shall not disclose: you know these causes every bit as well as he does. I shall move directly to the definition of the evils we are responsible for.

In financial terms, aliens are remarkably non-burdensome for the Metropolis. In 1901, there were 286,925 people here, of whom only 256 were receiving poverty relief.

Prison expenses on our fellow countrymen are, God knows, not particularly extensive either, although I am proud to say that some progress in this regard is nonetheless noticeable: in 1899, only 1,113 of us were put in English prisons, whereas in 1903, there were 1,864, and the following details are noteworthy:

	1889	1903
Habitual offenders	231	409
Imprisoned for 2 weeks or less	564	853
Imprisoned for 1 month	211	616

These are impressive numbers, but the English as enlightened mariners are mindful of the growth of their own crime rate and so are not especially inclined to claim this puny percentage for us.

In fact, aliens have even proved useful to England: the Commission has acknowledged that the best tailors and shoemakers are Russian and Polish Jews, and the best turners are Romanian. Hence the competition, which is all the more extensive because foreign labourers have substantially fewer wants than English ones. The English workman needs a daily bath, the English workman wants his paper, his roast beef, his ale – and the foreigner can easily go without all that.[4] This means he is prepared to accept working conditions so poor that an Englishman

---

Aliens Act', *The Journal of Imperial and Commonwealth History* 40.3 (September 2012), 409–37, which gives a good overview of the extensive historiography on this topic: the Commission's final report in August 1903 'recommended the establishment of an Immigration Department and the passing of legislation to prevent the landing, and to provide for the removal, of "undesirable" aliens' (418). See also Bernard Gainer, *The Alien Invasion: The Origins of the Aliens Act of 1905* (London: Heinemann Educational Books, 1972), which gives a very full account of the campaign for restriction and the Act's effect, as well as David Glover, *Literature, Immigration and Diaspora in Fin-de-Siècle England: A Cultural History of the 1905 Aliens Act* (Cambridge: Cambridge University Press, 2012) and Hannah Ewence, *The Alien Jew in the British Imagination, 1881–1905: Space, Mobility and Territoriality* (Basingstoke: Palgrave Macmillan, 2019). The anti-immigrant Conservative MP for Stepney, Major W. E. Evans Gordon (1857–1913), was the leader of the British Brothers' League and instrumental in the passage of the Aliens Act targeting 'foreign invaders'. The result of his research trip was the book *The Alien Immigrant* (London: Heinemann, 1903).

4   For an account of the actual English working-class diet, see contemporary works such as Maud Pember Reeves's famous *Round About a Pound a Week* (London: G. Bell and Sons Ltd, 1913).

would never agree to them. This is, of course, unpleasant for the worker, but it goes without saying that the employer has no problem with it at all. The main thing is the so-called 'overcrowding'. The issue is that nearly all the Russian Jews live in the eastern – and poorest – part of the city, the infamous Whitechapel.[5] Adjoining Whitechapel is a whole quarter of working-class neighbourhoods called Stepney. So when the foreigners became too numerous for Whitechapel, they began to settle in Stepney. As a result, the native population had to move out of their lodgings and hand them over to the aliens; the numbers show that the total number of Stepney inhabitants has remained nearly constant over twenty years, whereas the number of English people shrank with every year. See for yourselves:

	1881	1891	1901
Total population	282,676	285,116	298,600
Aliens	15,998	32,286	54,310

While the total population grows by 1, 1 ½%, the number of foreigners grows by nearly 50%. So around half of the population of Stepney would have had to surrender to the alien invasion. This is, of course, unfortunate and to be resisted. We aliens need to be cut down to size. To this end, the Commission has set up a certain organisation: the 'Immigration Department'. This Department will have many different functions: to ensure that no criminals or prostitutes (there is no registration here, so prostitutes have it easy) come to England, and no lunatics, idiots or other undesirables. But the Department's main task is to ensure that foreigners do not overwhelm the native population.

For this purpose, they are planning something like the Pale.[6] A list of places where foreigners are not welcome is being drawn up: the moment an alien sets foot on shore, Immigration Department officials will be quick to hand him a list of all the streets, alleys and squares he should steer clear of.

Simple, but hardly new or original.

---

[5]   The modern historiography and memoir literature of the Jewish East End is very extensive, ranging from Chaim Bermant and William Fishman's seminal studies *Point of Arrival: A Study of London's East End* (London: Eyre Methuen, 1975) and *East End Jewish Radicals: 1875–1914* (London: Duckworth, 1975) to Jerry White's *Rothschild Buildings: Life in an East End Tenement Block, 1887–1920* (1980; London: Pimlico, 2003) to popular 'guidebooks' to Jewish London. For a general history of migrant London, see Panikos Panayi, *Migrant City: A New History of London* (New Haven, CT: Yale University Press, 2020). For a contemporary map of 'Jewish East London', reproduced as Map 1 in this anthology, see Charles Russell, *The Jew in London: A Study of Racial Character and Present-Day Conditions* (London: T. Fisher Unwin, 1900).

[6]   Chukovsky is referring to the Pale of Settlement, the region of imperial Russia to which Jewish residency was legally restricted.

Korney Chukovsky, 'Britanskiy Muzey' ['The British Museum'] *Odesskie Novosti,* 25 October 1903

London
(From our own correspondent)
1 November

Fear not, my reader, I shall not speak of Assyrian antiquities. It is true that there are many of them here, but there is nothing special about them for a layman such as myself. They are antiquities like any other: dusty, cracked, labelled and numbered. You look at them, express your admiration for propriety's sake, but in your soul you say: 'I have already seen all this somewhere before'.

There are simply too many different kinds of rarities here. And it is well known that a rarity which can be found in abundance ceases to be a rarity.

There is, however, in the British Museum something more rare and valuable, which should elicit from you a shout of amazement and delight far exceeding all your previous exclamations!

This thing is small and inconspicuous. It is not even mentioned in the general catalogues. One needs to look long and diligently for it, but that is what makes it so much the rarer, so much the dearer.

Here is its little label. Read it:

'Tcharka'.[1]

I trust I do not need to translate this English word for you, especially as it is not English at all. The label is attached to a silver shot glass, and I can boldly declare that this shot glass is the only artefact in the British Museum that my homeland is represented by.

A museum which ought to offer a tangible demonstration of the heights of cultural creativity achieved by a given nation, of the degree of its spiritual flowering, of everything that this nation has attained thanks to its genius, at the price of its blood, tears and suffering, of all that it has, step by step, managed to win back from nature – this museum exhibits in its 'Russia' section a shot glass – and nothing more.

The Hottentots, the Papuans, the Negritos – every thread of theirs is under the glass, and there are so many of these threads that any European may form an accurate and detailed understanding of their lives. The whole Papuan, from cradle to grave, is in the palm of his hand. But if he asks what goes on in that huge country which has given him Tolstoy and Dostoevsky, is there really nothing more to point him to than our drunkenness?

'Well, and what are their manners and customs?' he will ask.

---

[1]   Small glass for alcoholic drinks; also a unit of measurement for liquids.

To that one would have to reply that there lived in Russia a renowned **writer Saltikov-Schedrin**, who, while carefully describing Poshekhonye,[2] wrote under the heading *manners and customs*:
'There are none. There used to be, but they are all gone.'
'Well, and what are the discoveries, the inventions of these strange people – what have they contributed to afflicted humankind?'
To this, the miserable foreigner, who is unfamiliar with the discovery of the Khadzhibey oil,[3] or with Mr Demchinsky's brilliant meteorology,[4] or with our wide-ranging researches in the field of deliberate self-mutilation, will shake his head no, point to the silver shot glass and say:
'Here are their manners, here are their customs, here are their discoveries – all of them.'
Perhaps alluding in this to the invention of the **toujours le même** Demchinsky,[5] who declared in 'Novoe Vremya' – remember? – that beer was a cure for all diseases.[6]
How is that for a recommendation!
Burning with envy of the Papuans, let us move on to the Reading Room.
I can never speak of it without enthusiasm. If the English had only created the Reading Room and nothing else, they would still deserve the name of a great nation.
Imagine the largest room you have ever seen, absolutely round in shape. The wall seems to have been built with a pair of compasses. Along the wall are books. Books three fathoms high.[7] The books can be lowered from the top by means of special hoisting machines, and that accounts for the amazing speed with which one receives them.
You can take as many books at once as you like – even a hundred. And what is more, you're not the one obliged to fetch the books – as is the custom in Odessa and Petersburg – instead, they are brought to your seat, thanks to which you can keep working without interruption or loss of time. Everyone has a separate desk; there is no noise because the floor is covered with a rubber mat; all the best books on medicine, poetry, current affairs, divinity, all dictionaries, reference books, directories are at your disposal. Go ahead, walk up to the shelves and take

[2]   The name of a town in Russia that had become a byword for provincialism – a godforsaken spot. Mikhail Saltykov-Shchedrin (1826–1889) was a famous nineteenth-century Russian writer and satirist.
[3]   Khadzhibey: a settlement and fortress – the site of present-day Odessa, where Chukovsky was from.
[4]   Chukovsky is being ironic in this sentence – N. A. Demchinsky (1851–1914/15?) was an engineer and journalist infamous for his controversial theories of weather prediction and widely considered a charlatan.
[5]   French: 'always the same'.
[6]   'Novoe Vremya': A major St Petersburg newspaper that by Chukovsky's time had acquired a reputation as a reactionary organ.
[7]   The original has '3 *sazhens*' or Russian fathoms, equivalent to 2.13 meters each.

them *yourself.* You are trusted to do so even though you have not given them *any guarantees*. The lack of oversight here is simply remarkable: the porters at the door won't even glance once to check what you are carrying out of the library, although sometimes you have to leave with a whole pile of your own books. How, one would think, could they know that these are *mine*? At the very least they could pass an eye over them – but no.

'Even we have failed to break the English of their habit of faith in human decency,' A. Herzen has said somewhere – and that is indeed extraordinary![8]

But how pleasant, how delightful, how calming it is to work in this atmosphere of trust, respect, considerateness! How human dignity revives here.

And this is more precious than any hoisting machine or rubber floor covering.[9]

---

[8]   Alexander Herzen (1812–1870) was a major nineteenth-century Russian writer and socialist political philosopher and publicist who spent many years in exile in London.

[9]   Chukovsky comes back to the subject of the British Museum Reading Room (where he spent much of his time while in London) in many other dispatches, considering, for instance, the proportion of female and foreign readers, the types of reading and research they engage in, the process of getting a reading pass, etc.

Korney Chukovsky, [Anti-Alien Sentiment]
Odesskie Novosti, 30 October 1903

London
(From our own correspondent)
7 November

I most humbly beg my compatriots, when they arrive in London, not
to pinch any handkerchiefs from English pockets.

Firstly, London is the most inappropriate place for this; and secondly,
it is beginning to pall a bit, upon my word.

Large-scale thieves are all of them natives, the indigenous population.
But whenever some penny pickpocket is caught, he will inevitably turn
out to be not just of Russian extraction but from Odessa to boot.

I went into **Guildhall** yesterday and what do I see: a creature infinitely
pitiful, infinitely ragged and infinitely hungry squirming in front of the
judge's grey wig and knitted brows.[1]

The name of the creature is Abram Guntvas; it has lived some sixteen
years in this world and only a week in London; it knows the English
language about as well as do many Russian translator-poets – and can't
do anything but weep and squirm.[2] It was vexing, and shameful, and
painful to witness this 'case'.

If only we were artful pickpockets; but we cannot boast even of that.
The accused had nicked four shillings (1 rouble 80 kopecks) – and at
once the long arm of the policeman stretched out and collared him.

To exacerbate the discomfiture, the powdered wig determined to give
the case a general, so to speak, complexion, and proclaimed:

'It is astonishing how all these aliens **abuse our hospitality**. The most
piffling request – and still they come. I bet they would not dare to show
their noses in America – there, before being allowed to disembark, they
are told: "Show sixty dollars. No money – back you go!". And here we
are still waiting for Parliament to approve a similar measure. And so it
turns out that over the last six months, 121 out of 486 sentences passed
are against foreigners. We need to take strong measures to tackle this
immediately...'[3]

---

[1]   Guildhall is located in the City of London and was the site of many famous trials
      throughout history.
[2]   'Translator-poets': almost certainly a tongue-in-cheek reference to Konstantin
      Bal'mont, the Symbolist poet, whose translations of Shelley Chukovsky criticised
      mercilessly.
[3]   Sir Alfred Newton made these comments when sentencing a 'young Russian Pole'
      at Guildhall in early November 1903; he had allegedly been in London two days and
      'was caught picking pockets in Holborn'. Chukovsky's figures are wrong: Newton
      said that 'no less than 121' 'cases of larceny' out of 365 considered 'at that court'
      were perpetrated by 'foreign subjects'. See 'A Straight Talk on the Alien Question',

43

How embarrassing! And all the more embarrassing because the Honourable Mr Newton is not speaking in his own voice but repeating the words that for three or four months past have hung like a nightmare over the freedom-loving British citizen.[4]

Strictly speaking, the English have always treated 'us' shabbily. They – to use a talented writer's astute expression – showed us hospitality not for our sakes, but for their own: to prove to themselves that they were the most freedom-loving people in the world... But what is currently happening in England has never been seen before.

You walk down the street and a huge poster looms in your face.[5] Some first-rate artist has depicted a hearth at which a red-bearded Russian, a slippery Frenchman, a goggle-eyed German and a long-legged American are all warming themselves. The hearth is called 'England'. And at the back behind them John Bull shivers with the cold. He asks ingratiatingly:

'Please, good people, allow me to warm myself too. After all, this is my hearth, in a manner of speaking.'

These posters are manufactured by the followers of Balfour in order to hammer into English heads the necessity of **retaliation** (reciprocal tariffs) – but it is unlikely that they produce *that* result.[6] At any rate,

---

Yorkshire Evening Post, 6 November 1903, 6 – one of the many provincial papers that syndicated this account. See also the much more detailed account of the case that appeared in the New Zealand paper *Evening Star* from their London special correspondent (writing on 20 November), who used it specifically to call for the passage of 'legislation based on the Alien Commission's report': 'Apart from alien street obstructors, the unchecked influx of undesirables from Russia and elsewhere is a serious menace to society [...] A sample of recent dumpings was before the Guildhall Court a couple of days ago, when Abraham Guntvas, seventeen, a Russian from Warsaw, was charged on remand with pocket-picking in Holborn. Guntvas, who could speak nothing but Yiddish, was caught in the act. He had landed in England only twenty-four hours previously.' See the full report in 'Topics of the Day: The Rubbish Heap', *Evening Star*, 29 December 1903, 4. Guntvas refused to be deported and was jailed. See also Severin Adam Hochberg, 'The Repatriation of Eastern European Jews from Great Britain: 1881–1914', *Jewish Social Studies* 50.1/2 (Winter 1988–Spring 1992), 49–62. For Newton, see Shklovsky's 'Imperialism'.

4   The words, and especially the comparison with America, do indeed sound like they were taken from the deliberations of the Royal Commission on Alien Immigration referred to in 'On Foreigners'.

5   A good selection of 'Political and Tariff Reform Posters' is available from the *LSE Digital Library*, https://digital.library.lse.ac.uk/collections/posters/politicalandtariffreform. See Plates 1 and 2 in this anthology.

6   Prime Minister Arthur Balfour (1902–1905) supported Joseph Chamberlain's project of Imperial Preference and Tariff Reform (imposing tariffs on imports from Germany and the United States) – one of the lightning-rod political-economic issues of the Edwardian period. Chamberlain (1836–1914) was a Unionist MP and leading imperialist. Both make very frequent appearances in Chukovsky's articles. See Oliver Betts, '"The People's Bread": A Social History of Joseph Chamberlain and the Tariff Reform Campaign,' in Ian Cawood and Chris Upton, eds. *Joseph*

Fig. 5. Advertising Sign.

the animosity that we have been experiencing lately has nothing to do with **retaliation**.

So who profits from this animosity? The very same people who are so quick to praise Chamberlain's absurd plans – the failing factory owners who have been beaten in the foreign markets. Their only hope is to at least secure the domestic market for themselves, and they'll stop at nothing to achieve this. Let the reader judge the degree of their success by the following minor example:

They have matches here of English make: the '**Swan**' brand.[7] Dreadful matches. They light up in your pocket of their own will, but when you need them to strike a flame, you can rub them all you like but you won't get anywhere. Besides which, they cost four times what the Swedish ones do.

And meanwhile, literally everyone uses these particular matches – working men for their pipes and gentlemen for their cigars. Why? Because on the box it says:

'If you are a true patriot, you won't use foreign products, you'll buy English "**Swan**" matches.'

Chamberlain: International Statesman, National Leader, Local Icon (Basingstoke: Palgrave Macmillan, 2016), 130–52.

7   The Swan brand had been around since the 1880s – it was acquired by Bryant & May in the early 1900s.

And this is enough. Positively, patriotism is a profitable thing... But the problem is not, of course, that Englishmen use dreadful matches – the problem is that in the wake of patriotism inevitably follows ethnic intolerance.

It is this latter that introduces such a mass of lies into English society that anyone would find it opportune.

For instance, take the recently published book by Colonel Gordon,[8] who was sent by Parliament to Russia, Romania and Austria to study the causes of emigration in situ.

And what do you know? This so-called investigator has delivered the following judgement. All emigrants live 'well, happily and prosperously' at home, much better than in Whitechapel. And if they must run for their lives wherever the road takes them, that must be because – one can only assume – they have too much of a good thing.

Alte, alte Geschichte![9]

---

8   See the footnote in 'On Foreigners' above.
9   German: 'The old, old story!'.

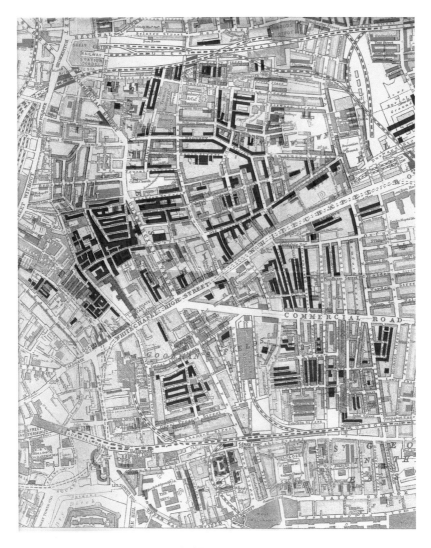

Map 1. Jewish East London.

JEWISH EAST LONDON

SCALE

This Map shows by Colour the proportion
of the Jewish population to other residents of East
London, street by street, in 1899.

EXPLANATION OF COLOURING.

Proportion of Jews indicated.

95% to 100%.

75% and less than 95%.

50% and less than 75%.

25% and less than 50%.

5% and less than 25%.

Less than 5% of Jews.

NOTE.—In all streets coloured blue the Jews form a majority of the
inhabitants; in those coloured red, the Gentiles predominate

Map 2. Dalling Road, Hammersmith.

The Streets are coloured according to social condition of inhabitants as under :—

Lowest Class

Very Poor

Moderate Poverty

Poverty & Comfort (mixed)

Fairly Comfortable

Well-to-do

Wealthy

Combined colouring (as Pink and Red) indicates a mixture of the Classes which the Colours represent.

Plate 1. Liberal Unionist Council Tariff Reform Poster.

Plate 2. Imperial Tariff Committee Poster.

Korney Chukovsky, 'Edinenie Narodov' ['The Union of Peoples']
Odesskie Novosti, 11 November 1903

London
(From our own correspondent)
19 November

Today, all the newspapers are overflowing with assurances that the English nation has offered a remarkably warm and ardent welcome to the Italian leader and that the bonds which had formerly existed between the two countries have now supposedly, due to this, been cemented exceedingly.[1]

But, first of all, what is the indicator of this warmth? The fact that a lot of people gathered to stare at the procession? But who doesn't know that the English are interested in this kind of thing exclusively as a spectator sport, and if it had been a motor race or a cock fight, the crowd would have been even larger? And secondly, where is the link between this spectating and the 'bonds'? Clearly, there is none.

It is in vain that the papers go on about the cementing of bonds.

Entirely in vain. Never before – a fact acknowledged by all truthful observers of English life – have the English evinced such hostility towards foreigners as now. Even during the last war,[2] which exacerbated jingoism and the nationalistic passions, nothing like it had been noted. Then, it was all based on the abstract grounds of 'patriotic feeling'. Now, it rests on economics. And for the English bourgeoisie, economic grounds lie much closer to home than any other.

And that's how it has turned out that we foreigners find life impossible in London. You try to hire lodgings but your accent betrays you as a foreigner and you get a refusal. A French family I knew hired an English maid. She spent two days with them and then turned obstinate. With tears in her eyes, she repeated: 'I don't want to serve foreigners, I'd rather throw myself off a bridge'.

And the French were offering her an easy job, much easier than the English would have done.

Jews, who until now had been living side by side with the English in remarkably friendly fashion, have started to complain. They, being the best tailors in London, had secured contracts to supply ready-made garments to nearly all the fashionable shops. Their work was famous. When buying yourself a cloak or a coat, you'd be told that they came from the East End, and this was the highest praise.

---

[1] Chukovsky is referring to King Victor Emmanuel's visit to England in November 1903, widely covered by the press.
[2] Chukovsky is presumably referring to the Second Boer War of 1899–1902.

47

Not so now. The Englishman, hypnotised by the Imperialists' shrieks about the demise of national manufacturing, demands from the seller, before all else, a guarantee that his goods have never been touched by 'the alien's impious hand'.[3]

And the Jews have started to lose their trade. Already, they are being looked at askance as competitors, which had never been the case before, when the false spectre of Chamberlain's prophecies did not hover over the English nation...

Chamberlain himself is always berating foreigners in his incendiary speeches. Only yesterday, he tried to discredit the Cobden Club by alleging that *its members were foreigners*.[4] In his opinion, that is the worst accusation conceivable. The Cobden Club *considered itself offended* – and invited the former Minister over to show him the members' list in order to restore the Club's honour by a parade of English names.

I have already written to you about the Immigration Commission, so you are already familiar with the plans to introduce a Pale of Settlement. All I have to add is that the English will retain this supposedly expedient distaste for their neighbours even when *the target itself is no longer there*. Faithful to tradition, they hold on for centuries to long-obsolete and pointless objects, institutions and relations.

After all, didn't one doctor here tell me when I asked him why he was a Conservative:

'My **daddy** was a Conservative – and I cannot very well betray my **daddy**!'

What a reason for a forty-year-old man!

It is just the same with misanthropic sentiments: they are inherited here – let England crush its rivals in the international markets thirty times over, the Whitechapel Jews will never get their clients back. **Daddy** will trump all other reasons.

Ergo: let kings visit London every day, let flags obscure the sky and thousands of noisy gawkers run after gilded coaches – but brotherhood, union, bonds will have nothing whatsoever to do with it...

---

3   The slogan 'Support Home Industries', with its corollary 'Employ British Labour', as exemplified in matchbox-making in particular, was already being satirised by Arthur Morrison nearly a decade earlier in *A Child of the Jago* (1896; Oxford: Oxford University Press, 2012).

4   London club named in honour of Richard Cobden (1804–1865), the famous Victorian Free Trade campaigner and Liberal MP. It furnished a natural target for the protectionist Chamberlain. The Cobden Club had no permanent premises of its own.

48

Korney Chukovsky, 'Whitechapel'
Odesskie Novosti, 8 August 1904

(From our London correspondent)

I once asked Mr Wide, my boarding-house neighbour:
'Let's go and see Whitechapel.'
He blinked his eyes in fright, refused, and advised me in a whisper to leave my wallet at home and take a stick with me instead. I was in no way surprised by his piece of advice, as I had only recently come across this strange pronouncement in Smith's **'Century Encyclopedia'**:[1]
'Whitechapel. A part of East London **inhabited by the poorer classes and by criminals.'**[2]
Finding my way through the crooked alleys of working districts – where, despite the heat, everything is shut up, locked and curtained, and only the garish pub windows disturb the overall sepulchral air – I reached the horse tram I was looking for, climbed to the top, and experienced the sensation of something peculiar, un-London-like and un-English. The horse tram was unusually dirty, stopped for long whiles at crossroads, and I was charged 1½ pence for the ticket, which is not in keeping with London customs since even the poorest Londoner regards a penny as such small coin that charging ha'pennies in the normal course of English life would come across as scrupulous unto beggary...
An hour later, I was in Whitechapel. It felt like whole millennia rather than a mere hour separated me from central London. The centre, too, has its share of poverty, but there it is covered up, silent, hiding out of sight. It lurks somewhere in the dark nooks and crannies, frightened lest its moan should break through the cheerful bustle of red-cheeked, self-assured, broad-shouldered people who are so good at working, loving themselves and laughing.
Here it is all in plain sight – in this rancid smell of spoiled fish which is fried and eaten right there in the street; these dirty, sickly children; these narrow, rotten back-alleys which seem to be forever forgotten by God and the sun and the sanitary inspector; in these clamorous, gaudy street-markets where faded, dyed, twice-turned rags are sold for pennies, where the curses, the hawkers' shouts, the exaggerated gestures all cry to you of squalor, lay it bare, thrust it in your face. One can hardly imagine a greater contrast with the calm and secretive life of London.[3]

---

[1] *The Century Dictionary and Cyclopedia* was a seminal American reference work issued in multiple volumes in many editions from 1889 onwards. New editions were published in 1903 and 1904, when Chukovsky was in London.
[2] Chukovsky gives the English in parentheses after a Russian translation.
[3] Compare this description not just with Shklovsky's accounts later in this anthology but also with Jack London's *The People of the Abyss* (New York: Macmillan, 1903).

49

Fig. 6. An Old Clothes Shop in the East End.

And this is not the only contrast. For instance, I need to find out where the Russian library is, so I approach a man and ask him.

He stops, takes a long while to explain the route, leaves, then returns and says:

'You know what: though I'm busy now, no matter, I'll go with you and lead you right up there.'

That is so unlike London. An Englishman would just nod his head towards the nearest policeman, and that would be the last you'd see of him.

You walk down the street – the longest, dirtiest and most garish **Commercial Road** in the world – and stop in your tracks, amazed. A sign says in Russian letters: '*Odesskiy restoran*'.[4] But that is, of course, an exception. The language of Whitechapel is a Jewish jargon mixed up with corrupted English words.[5] Many houses display black-bordered

---

4   Russian: 'Odessa Restaurant'.

5   'Jewish jargon' means Yiddish: a common usage in Russia – or, at any rate, in Ukraine – at the time; but also in Britain. 'Yiddish jargon' appears in S. Gelberg's chapter 'Jewish London' in Sims, *Living London* 2, 29–35; and in Sims, 'Off the Track in London: I. In Alien-Land': 'the German Hebrew jargon known as "Yiddish"' (416).

Fig. 7. In an East-End Russian Restaurant.

mourning portraits of the late Herzl in their windows.[6] There are many Jewish-language newspapers, and it is so strange to see their contents bills about the expedition to Tibet, about Port Arthur,[7] and so on.

With the adaptability typical of Whitechapel denizens, they learn English very quickly, but they are even quicker to forget their Russian. I once met a thirty-year-old Jew here who had completed four standards of a gymnasium in Russia, but now all he could do when addressed in Russian was smile politely. And he had only lived here just over two years.

Although English newspapers are forever berating immigrants for being ignorant, uncultured, and so on, it is clear to any objective observer that the spiritual and intellectual interests of Whitechapel are much higher and fresher than in London itself.

Can you find me an Englishman, not a professional or a rich man, who would spend his time reading books in the British Museum? You cannot... The British Museum is frequented either by so-called **literary**

---

6   Theodor Herzl (1860–1904) was the father of political Zionism who advocated the foundation of an independent Jewish state. He died on 3 July.

7   Probably a reference to the siege of Port Arthur in the Russo-Japanese War (1904–1905).

hacks,[8] or by people who do not know what to do with their spare time, or by foreigners. And now take a look inside the Russian reading room in Whitechapel. I once visited it in winter. The windows were shut. A room the size of a thimble. And people on the windowsills, in the hallway, on the stairs. There is a bench and chairs, but no-one is sitting down, because you can pack more people into the room standing up. The purpose of the library is to help newcomers not to forget the Russian language, the Russian culture, so that they, lost as they are in a great indifferent city, can have a hospitable and homely nook to turn to. There are a lot of Russian newspapers in the library; there is Pushkin, Dostoevsky, Tolstoy, Pavlenkov's 'Lives of Remarkable People', and so on. There are even 'Plato's Dialogues' translated by Vladimir Solovyov.[9]

But as I came up now to the place where the library used to be, I found only an 'Emigration Bureau'. In its window was a notice stating that *two pounds* (twenty roubles) would buy you a ticket from London to New York. Right by the Bureau, pale and dirty people stand around offering to sell a watch, a bicycle or a sewing machine, because they have no money for the passage to America. And they immediately exhibit these objects to you, in their far-from-ideal state.

It was with some difficulty that I found the new library premises.[10] They are roomier and cleaner; there are even two gas fixtures. Downstairs is a tearoom which could be transformed, if one wished, into a lecture hall, a ballroom, and even a theatre. At one end of the room hangs a curtain depicting – according to some – the sea, or – according to others – a battle between the Russians and the Kabardians. The tearoom is open to everyone, and you can visit it any time you like, so there are at most two or three people there actually drinking tea, and the other thirty or forty are debating, reading, listening. The debate is conducted

---

8   For the Reading Room's 'literary hacks', see George Gissing's well-known novel *New Grub Street* (London: Smith, Elder & Co., 1891).

9   Vladimir Solovyov (1853–1900) was a major nineteenth-century Russian philosopher and poet. Florenty Pavlenkov (1839–1900) was a nineteenth-century Russian publisher and librarian who in 1890 founded the influential biographical series 'Lives of Remarkable People', aimed at the mass autodidact market.

10 For an excellent in-depth account of the Library's history, including the move from Church Lane to Princelet Street, just off Brick Lane (to premises owned by the East London Jewish Branch of the Social Democratic Federation), in summer 1904, see Robert Henderson, '"For the Cause of Education": A History of the Free Russian Library in Whitechapel, 1898–1917' in Rebecca Beasley and Philip Ross Bullock, eds. *Russia in Britain, 1880–1940: From Melodrama to Modernism* (Oxford: Oxford University Press, 2013), 71–86. The library was, in fact, a much more impressive cultural institution than Chukovsky's account lets on. Isaak Shklovsky lectured there.

Fig. 8. The Free Russian Library.

in Yiddish. I do not understand the language and instead strike up a conversation with a youth who joins me at my table.[II]

'When I lived in Russia, all I could hear was England this and England that, and there is no country better than England. But let me tell you, nowhere do they suck the poor man dry like they do here. I arrived here two months ago – went out into the street – no idea where to go. And look, there are three hundred others just like myself. So we huddle up and stand there. A man comes up – a rich one, in a top hat, and says: "If I could find a good tailor, I would hire him on the cheap". And all three hundred of us just swarm around him. He seemed to consider me, but seeing my boots, "No", he says, "I don't need you, you are a **greener** (a derogatory term for newcomers)". And wherever I went, everyone looked at my boots. The English won't hire me – they have some kind of trade unions, and the Jew won't pay me more than three shillings a day.'

'But three shillings is a very good fee', I said.

'Yes, it is, if you have work every day… But they mostly hire you for half a day, or a quarter of a day, and then you walk around jobless for two weeks. And besides, it's shameful to have to compete with your own people. Recently an employer in Brick Lane chose me, but then

---

[II] The original has 'Jewish' rather than 'Yiddish'. Chukovsky did not know it because he was raised by his Ukrainian single mother, who had been a servant in his Jewish father's household.

53

all the others rushed towards him begging for work, and as soon as I looked at them, I had to step aside… And even if you find permanent employment, like I have now, it's still bad. You work from six in the morning till ten at night, with one hour for lunch. And the journeymen are like beasts. You don't dare straighten your back. Why does no-one print it in the papers, why don't they tell the poor people that life here in London is worse than anywhere else, that they should not come here. Here they are tossed about like cucumbers in Lithuania, but they still come, still run here, and what will happen to them here in the end doesn't bear thinking about.'

I left my melancholic companion after about ten in the evening. The whole of London was already deserted, but in Whitechapel, human misery was still pouring through the streets, clamorous, lurid and unashamed.

There are not many English people in this 'quarter inhabited by criminals'. You notice it at once, for there are few pubs in Whitechapel.

Isaak Shklovsky [Dioneo], 'V Russkom Kvartale' ['In the Russian Quarter'] English Silhouettes (St Petersburg, 1905): 469–501[1]

I.

In late May of 1903, a huge cargo steamer named the *Blücher* set out from Hamburg to London.[2] There were horses and people on the ship. Horses are an extremely valuable cargo and quite susceptible to seasickness, from which they suffer greatly, and for this reason they were allocated the best spot on the *Blücher*. People also suffer from seasickness, but the *Blücher* passengers belonged to a class one does not make a fuss over. They were mostly the natives of Northwestern shtetls,[3] cowed, small, plain, very poorly clad, marked with the seal of centuries-long chronic malnutrition. The burly sailors shouted at them as they drove them into the black depths of the hold. Men, women and children crawled in obediently, dragging behind them huge bundles and dirty flock-mattresses. Of course, none of them could have said why they had brought along these dirty and worthless rags to their new homeland. Among the scrawny, curly-haired, hook-nosed natives of the

---

[1] Originally published as a Letter 'From England' under the pseudonym Dioneo in the monthly journal *Russkoe Bogatstvo*, August 1904. Digitisations of *Russkoe Bogatstvo* issues are available online in various repositories and may be accessed via *Wikisource*: https://ru.wikisource.org/wiki/Русское_богатство. Shklovsky's Letters were regularly collected and published in volume form by the journal's publishing house. I have used the collected volumes rather than the original periodical publications as translation sources for all of Shklovsky's Letters because while changes between the two formats were generally minimal (in many cases the same plates appear to have been used and the same typographical errors preserved), Shklovsky did occasionally introduce significant amendments when reprinting (and included explanatory prefaces). Such amendments and important prefatory material are noted throughout. The collected volumes thus represent the author's 'final' version. Aside from the Letters translated here, the *English Silhouettes* volume also included articles dealing with political-economic topics like protectionism and female and child labour, public figures such as Arthur Pinero and Shaw, Meredith and Spencer, and cultural and social topics such as 'The English Character', 'The Crank', English police and the Derby, among many others.

[2] According to the collections of the Museum of America and the Sea, the *Blücher* was an immigrant steamer built by Blohm & Voss in Hamburg, Germany in 1901 which operated on the Hamburg–America (New York) Line. It could accommodate 550 third-class passengers. A chromolithograph postcard, 'Steamer BLUCHER, built 1901', may be seen in 'Immigration and Steamships', *Mystic Seaport Museum*, http://mobius.mysticseaport.org/detail.php?kv=109051&module=objects.

[3] 'Northwestern' refers to the Lithuanian and Belorussian portions of the Russian Empire. A shtetl is a small Jewish town or village in Eastern Europe: this Yiddish word, assimilated into English, is the closest equivalent to the Russian 'mestechko' (which has the same meaning) that Shklovsky uses.

Northwestern Krai one could discern emigrants from a different region of Russia, mostly fair-haired ones, and veritable giants by comparison with the Lithuanian starvelings. Jews predominated here, but there were also quite a few Estonians and Poles. Some had already parted with their national caftans and 'suknyas' at the border or in Hamburg,[4] but a few proved obstinate conservatives. Among their number was a tall, broad-shouldered Ukrainian in an astrakhan hat, a black peasant overcoat girt with a colourful belt and a pair of enormous boots.[5] This passenger seemed especially bewildered when the emigrants were being driven into the hold in Hamburg.

'Tell me, are we going?!' he questioned the sailor desperately.[6]

'**Vorwärts! Schneller!**' the sailor shouted.[7]

'But I need to know if we'll go soon?' the passenger kept repeating.

Instead of replying, the sailor gave the Ukrainian a shove in the neck. The latter grew furious, threw down the sack he was holding, ground his teeth, quickly turned around and took a swing with his huge heavy fist. But at that moment, somebody grabbed the Ukrainian by the hand and spoke quickly.

'Let them be! don't raise a ruckus! He didn't understand you. I'll ask for you. Upon my soul, it's better if you calm down! come! we'll lie down together,' said a puny, very nervous and fidgety young man. The Ukrainian sighed, picked up his sack and descended into the hold.

'**Um wie viel Uhr fährt das Dampfschiff?**' the little man asked in a Jewish accent of another sailor in the depths of the hold. The sailor replied.[8]

---

4   'Suknya': Ukrainian dress-like garment.
5   'Ukrainian': the original text has 'Maloross', meaning 'Little Russian' – a term widely used in the nineteenth century to refer to ethnic Ukrainians. 'Little Russia' was a historical designation of the part of the Russian Empire coinciding with certain parts of present-day Ukraine. 'Ukrainian' has been substituted for 'Little Russian' throughout the translation. The man's attire is stereotypical, see George R. Sims's descriptions and illustrations of Eastern European immigrants (including Jewish ones) fresh off the boat in 'Trips About Town: IV. Round St. George in the East', *Strand Magazine* 29 (June 1905), 685–91: 'The high boots and the astrachan [*sic*] caps give them a picturesque appearance to the English eye' (686); see also images of immigrants dressed like Shklovsky's characters disembarking from steamships in Sims's *Living London*.
6   This character, Onisko Blagovistnik, speaks Ukrainian, not Russian, throughout the sketch. However, his speech has been translated into standard English, so the linguistic contrast that would have played a large role in the apprehension of the original Russian readership has, unfortunately, been lost. The effect could have been more closely approximated by translating his speech into Scots. —
7   German: 'Forward! More quickly!'
8   German: 'What time does the steamer leave?'

'You see, it was all a misunderstanding. You are Russian, you are not used to being pushed around, so you get angry. But we little Jews,[9] we say "Thank you, God be praised" when we're not being disembowelled or having our teeth knocked out with a log. What is your name?'
'Onisko Blagovistnik, a joiner from Shirokaya Greblya.'[10]
'And I am Hatskel Baltyansky, a tailor from Kishinev. Pleased to meet you.'[11]

Many have sung of the stormy sea. Usually, the poet stands at the mast, and fixing his prophetic gaze upon the foaming billows, exclaims: 'You are mighty, ocean, but I, too, contain the whole universe in my breast. Let's see who shall win!' No poet apart from Byron seems to have dared to break the mould and sing of seasickness.[12] Don Juan was aboard ship lamenting his separation from Donna Julia when, owing to the tossing of the keel –

He felt that chilling heaviness of heart,
Or rather stomach, which, alas! attends,
Beyond the best apothecary's art,
The loss of love, the treachery of friends.[13]

Now we need to imagine what the emigrants driven into the *Blücher*'s hold must have experienced in the stormy German Sea. None of them had ever seen the sea before, and many felt sick as soon as they came aboard from the mixed smell of oil, steam and tar. By the time the *Blücher* went out to sea and started lurching from wave to wave, all in the hold were sick. The ship swayed from port to starboard. The waves, as if made of cast-iron, beat its sides. Their buffets caused the *Blücher* to bob up and down, groan and creak. In the hold, children cried, women screamed, and men moaned. Some who would not perhaps have turned

---

9   The original is not just diminutive but derogatory, the closest equivalent in English would be something like 'little yid'.
10   A village in Ukraine – Shyroka Hreblya in Ukrainian.
11   Kishinev was in the Bessarabian part of the Russian Empire (present-day Moldova, which borders Ukraine). However, the man's name is typical for a Lithuanian Jew: a search of Lithuanian Jewish records and records of 'Russians' immigrating to the US in the period (see the 'Lithuanian-Jewish Records from LitvakSIG, 1795–1949' and the records of 'Russians Immigrating to the United States' at *MyHeritage*, www.myheritage.com/research/collection-10951/lithuanian-jewish-records-from-litvaksig-1795-1940 and www.myheritage.com/research/collection-10029/russians-immigrating-to-the-united-states) reveals many Hatskels/Hatzkels and Boltianskis/Baltunskys (and other variations).
12   Rupert Brooke would shortly describe seasickness naturalistically in his sonnet 'A Channel Passage' (1909), see *The Complete Poems* (London: Sidgwick & Jackson, 1950), 85. Aside from poets, seasickness had been memorably depicted by Jerome K. Jerome in *Three Men in a Boat* (London: J. W. Arrowsmith, 1889).
13   Shklovsky provides a Russian translation in parentheses here and for most English words and phrases that appear in the text.

nauseous from the tossing and rolling, grew sick at the sight of the others' vomit. The already heavy air in the hold grew even worse from the stench caused by the aftereffects of seasickness. It seemed to the little tailor Hatskel that he was tied to a huge wheel and spun upside down. First, he felt a cold in his stomach, then along his entire back, as if the wheel to which he was tied were hewn out of a huge slab of ice. When feeling better for a few seconds, he would say with a moan: 'I wish they had killed me with that log back then! I wouldn't be in so much torment now!'. Onisko Blagovistnik was also suffering, but he held out and kept silent.[14]

Stormy as the German Sea might be, in May even it grows calm occasionally. By the morning, the wind had fallen completely, and by lunchtime, the sea was as smooth as if someone had levelled it with a gigantic plane. Everyone crawled out of the stifling, fetid hold. The emigrants' faces were green, their cheeks hollow, their noses peaked; all bore the same sourly doleful expression that one usually sees after a good roll on the waves. After another hour, the people cheered up and began to observe with interest the fishing schooners that slowly glided by the *Blücher* under their faintly billowing tar-painted sails. From the clear pale-blue sky, which was only beginning to assume its summertime depth of hue, dazzling rays of light fell, like a quicksilver rain, onto the slightly wrinkling surface of the sea. A fresh, salt breeze blew gently in the emigrants' faces and quietly whispered something to them. These whispers cheered the soul and caused the blood to flow more strongly to the cheeks. Hope was born that all sorrow and darkness had been left behind, while ahead lay a new life, as dazzling as that quicksilver rain which so hurt the eyes. As if wishing to reinforce the hope that had awakened in the emigrants' hearts, terns cried fiercely, now rising, now falling to the sparkling sea. Hatskel was getting acquainted with everyone and striking up conversations with one emigrant after another. He made the acquaintance of two comely young women who were sitting, wrapped up in a single shawl, on a coiled length of cable in the very bow of the ship. He found out that they hailed from a small shtetl in the Podol'skaya Governorate and were 'seeking their fortune'.[15]

'There is nothing to eat in our shtetl', said one of the young women. 'There are ten seamstresses for each blouse that the priest's wife,[16] the bailiff's wife or the superintendent's daughter might want sewn. And other than waiting for that blouse order to come, there is nothing, nothing at all ahead until you grow old, if death doesn't come sooner.

---

[14] Editor's paragraph break.
[15] Also known as Podolia, a region spanning parts of present-day Ukraine and Moldova. There were many Jewish settlements there, see the *JewishGen Communities Database*, www.jewishgen.org/Communities/jgcd.php?get=y&prov1900=Podolia.
[16] The original text refers to a Russian Orthodox local priest's wife and is slightly derogatory in tone.

And the hardest thing of all is that they look at us as if we were mangy dogs. Why? How have we offended them? All we wanted was some work. If only we could make it to America! There are some people from our shtetl there already. They write that if you work hard, you'll quickly become a real somebody there. The only trouble is, where could we get the money for the journey? We've worked, raised money, wheedled it out of our families, and all of that has only proved enough to get us as far as London.'

'Oh, girls, you'll have your fill of crying in the new place', broke in an old Jewish woman who was pressing her sick granddaughter to her breast, 'You'll famish there'.

'And have we not gone hungry before? Could anything be worse than what we've had? At least we'll be treated like people! Is a log to the head better?'

Hatskel nodded his head approvingly.

'Nice to meet you. What are your names?'

The young women turned out to be friends rather than sisters. One of them was called Golda and the other Pearl.

'From now on you will be Miss Golda and you Miss Pearl', Hatskel said gallantly. He also sneaked up to Blagovistnik, who was standing by the side of the ship alone, away from the others. Hatskel was intrigued to know how this big strapping joiner from a remote woodland village had ended up on the emigrant steamer. The explanation turned out to be rather simple.

There was nothing to eat in Shirokaya Greblya, especially for him, Onisko Blagovistnik, who had learned his joiner's trade from a German whom an unfortunate fate had cast away in Vinnitsa.[17] Once, when Onisko had come to town from Shirokaya Greblya, he found out from a friend at market that Makar Gnibeda, who had also studied with the German and had joined a party of emigrants some five years ago, had turned up. He had sent his wife some money and a letter, in which he recounted that he never made it to America, but had remained in the city of London, where there were many Russians. There he was employed in a workshop and earned up to twenty shillings a week, 'which in our money would be forty roubles a month'. This news astounded Onisko. Makar was a worse craftsman than he, and here he was earning forty roubles a month, when a superintendent acquaintance of Onisko's from Burmachina was only making twenty-five. And the position of superintendent had seemed to Onisko to be the highest happiness a man could aspire to.

'If Makar can get it, why not me?', the thought passed through Onisko's mind.

[17] At the turn of the century, Vinnitsa was one of the largest historic cities in the Podol'skaya Governorate.

He visited Makar's wife, who told him that she was going to London. Onisko spared a five-kopeck coin and asked a literate man to copy down Makar's address for him onto a piece of paper. He hid the paper, written over in pencil, in a tobacco pouch. Since then, the thought of seeking his fortune was lodged like a nail in the joiner's head. At last, he made good on it; but he must have set out in an unlucky hour. At the border, he had become separated from his own emigrant party, attached himself to another, and together with them ended up on the steamer *Blücher*.

'Good thing at least that the piece of paper isn't ruined', Blagovistnik finished. 'Here it is, read it if you please.'

Hatskel turned over the tobacco-yellowed scrap of paper the joiner had taken out of the pouch and whistled. The pencilled scribbles had almost completely faded from the effects of time and tobacco.

'Well, we'll be in for a lot of bother trying to decipher this address! But never mind, we'll stick together! Just let me give you some advice: take off your overcoat, your boots and hat. It's important to fit in with everyone else…'

Onisko agreed. Right there on board the ship, with Hatskel's help, Blagovistnik exchanged his attire for a little old suit coat, a bowler and a pair of trousers worn outside the shoes.[18]

Night came, calm and clear. The emigrants descended into the hold. Only a couple of people remained on deck and watched the coloured signal lights demarcating a huge shoal.

Onisko grew melancholy. He thought of his wife and children, Shirokaya Greblya, the vast forest stretching all the way to the Austro-Hungarian border, and started singing softly, then more loudly.

'You sing so well, Blagovistnik', said Hatskel, deeply moved, 'it makes me want to cry…'.

II.

When the emigrants spilled out onto the deck in the morning, the *Blücher* had long entered the Thames and was already drawing near London. Along both banks of the river the masts of numerous ships towered like reeds. Then came into view huge soot-covered buildings with darkened gold inscriptions. The river resounded with the din of steamship whistles, the rattling of machinery, the clangour of steam hoists, the howling of sirens, and the shouts of men. The emigrants stood as if turned to stone. They were dumbfounded by this feverish

[18] Many elements of the opening of Shklovsky's sketch were inadvertently recreated by Charlie Chaplin in his famous silent film *The Immigrant* (1917), down to the crowding on board ship, the seasickness, the ironies of arrival, and characters like Onisko, Golda/Pearl and the old woman. One still from the film features a bearded immigrant wearing an overcoat, high boots with trousers tucked inside and an astrakhan hat seated side by side with the little tramp in an old suit and bowler.

energy, this incredible activity. They had a dim feeling that in this hectic hubbub they, too, had to be as energetic and as strong as all the others, or else life would sweep them mercilessly aside. And in each emigrant's mind burgeoned the same more or less defined thought: 'shall I, too, be given an opportunity to chase my daily bread, or will I be pushed at once to the side?'. And now the silhouette of a huge drawbridge with tall towers appeared against the pale sky.[19] In the depths of the steamer a signal bell jangled, and the *Blücher* shuddered to a halt.

When the gangway was lowered, some people ran onto the deck and started explaining something quickly to the emigrants.[20]

The grating sounds of the unfamiliar language completely bewildered the newcomers. A few were approached by relatives. Hatskel, Blagovistnik, Pearl and Golda kept together, not knowing where to go. But then a well-fed, rosy-cheeked and nicely dressed man with a gold pince-nez and top hat came up to them. He looked our acquaintances over and spoke condescendingly in Russian with a characteristic accent.

'From Russia?'

Hatskel and the others brightened up immediately.

'You know how to work?' continued the gentleman in the top hat. Hatskel replied for everyone that he was a skilled tailor, that the young women knew how to sew, and that 'he over there was an excellent joiner'.

'And have you any friends?' continued the gentleman in the top hat.

'No.'

'Have you brought much money?'

This question received no answer. Hatskel had seventy Russian kopecks in his pocket, the girls had even less, and Blagovistnik had a silver rouble.

'Well, what can one do', the gentleman continued condescendingly, adjusting his gold pince-nez, 'one must help one's countrymen. I have work for everyone. You, young man, will sew cut-out trousers; you, ladies, will get to stitch buttonholes; and you, if you wish, can nail together crates for packaging. I will give you room and board, and as for wages (here the gentleman cast a sidelong glance) three shillings

---

[19]   There are many contemporary photographs of the Port of London with Tower Bridge in the middle distance.

[20]   Probably representatives of the Jews' Temporary Shelter. According to Prue Baker in 'House of a Thousand Destinies – The Jews' Temporary Shelter', *Jewish East End of London*, www.jewisheastend.com/shelter.html, in 1903–1904 five thousand people came through the shelter, which was in direct communication with 'ships entering the Thames from Hamburg' so that its superintendent could meet 'every incoming ship in the Port of London' in order to prevent immigrants 'being robbed or taken in sweat shops as slave labour' – precisely the fate that befalls Shklovsky's characters.

per week. If you accept, here is my address. This is my man. He'll bring your belongings'.

The whole party was delighted to accept the conditions offered by Mr Kaun,[21] as the gentleman called himself. The newcomers were led through a maze of dirty and noisy streets to a huge, gloomy house. The men were shown to a corner of the floor in one room, and the young women in another. They were given some lunch: a herring and a slice of white bread apiece, and tea. The following day, work started at six in the morning and continued until eight in the evening. English people would have been horrified by the long working day, the paltry wages, the accommodation and the food. But not only did all this not seem horrible to our countrymen, on the contrary, they found the conditions quite passable 'for a start'. They were used to sleeping on the floor, the fare in the shtetls had been much worse, and the wage of six roubles a month seemed to the girls positively magnificent.[22]

I met Hatskel and Blagovistnik at the end of the summer of 1903 at a Russian stage production in Whitechapel. The performance itself was most interesting and accompanied by a whole range of small incidents.

[21] The surname can be transliterated in a number of different ways (Kaun is a south Russian name, but it could equally be Cohen), so the exact ethnicity of the man remains a mystery, which is significant given the stereotypical depiction of East End sweaters as Jews.

[22] Compare the depiction of the capture of newly arrived immigrants by sweaters (a much-investigated topic in the period) in the 'Sweated London' chapter of Sims, *Living London* I, 50, 54: 'the immigrant is not even safe when he has reached London. Men, frequently of his own faith and country, wait for him outside the docks, and because he is ignorant and friendless in a strange land, and speaks only his own language, seize upon him and convey him to a shark's boarding house [...] The Jewish community, fully aware of these evils, does its best to guard against them. They have agents who meet every boat, and, addressing the poor aliens in their own language, help them [...] Let us meet a ship from Hamburg, laden with men and women who will presently be working in the dens of sweaters [...] Fortunately [...] the Superintendent of the Poor Jews' Temporary Shelter, is here also. As the scared and shivering foreigners step ashore he speaks to them either in Yiddish or Lettish [Latvian], and finds out if they have an address to go to. Most of them have something written on a piece of paper which they produce creased and soiled from a pocket. It is the address of a friend or relative [...] it may be only a fellow townsman or fellow villager, who came to London years ago'; 'Others have no idea where they are going. Many, asked what money they have, confess to twenty or thirty shillings as their entire fortune. [...] Let us enter a "dwelling" workshop. It is a room nine feet square. In it fourteen people are at work. [...] The poor wretches have been at work since six o'clock in the morning. They will go on probably till midnight [...] The wages these poor foreigners can earn by their ceaseless toil will perhaps be eighteen shillings at the week's end. [...] The Russian "greener" lives on next to nothing. A cup of tea and a herring are frequently all the food he will have in the twenty-four hours. [...] Not long ago a Russian who appeared before the Sweating Committee said [...] He worked harder in London than in Warsaw and made less.'

Fig. 9. An East-End Den.

For instance, Natalia Stepanovna Chubukova (in the drama piece 'The Proposal') forgot her lines in the most interesting place and ran offstage to consult her notebook, leaving her fiancé to his fate.[23] Lomov had to sit around for at least twenty minutes because the notebook somehow got mislaid. The stage manager started arguing with the director about a programme matter and got so carried away that he forgot to draw the curtain, although Chubukov, having called several times for 'champagne!', was signalling desperately. Finally, a member of the audience took pity and drew the calico curtain. The stage manager got a dressing-down backstage and was told that there is a proper time for everything. The result was that during the next piece, 'The Bear',[24] he

---

[23] Shklovsky is describing characters from a one-act farce by Anton Chekhov, *Predlozhenie: Shutka v Odnom Deystvii [A Marriage Proposal: A Joke in One Act]* (in *Novoe Vremya [New Times]*, 3 May 1889). Note that Chekhov's plays are being performed in Russian in East End theatres several years before the first English-language production of a Chekhov play: *The Seagull* in Glasgow in 1909.

[24] Another Chekhov farce: *Medved': Shutka v Odnom Deystvii [The Bear: A Joke in One Act]* (Moscow, 1888). This was, incidentally, the second Chekhov play performed in English in the UK: at the Kingsway in 1911, and in 1914 it was 'put on as a curtain-raiser to a cinematograph entertainment at a London theatre [...] and had quite a pleasant reception from a thoroughly Philistine audience. The humour

displayed more zeal than necessary and lowered the curtain long before the end, as soon as Luka started imploring Smirnov. But none of these trifles prevented the Whitechapel audience from enjoying the show.

Blagovistnik and Hatskel (especially the latter) were by now in some measure accustomed to London and their new life. Hatskel could already stick together several English phrases. Both knew now that 'Mr Kaun' was not a benefactor but a ruthless 'sweater', who exploited newcomers or 'greeners'.[25] They had long ago left Kaun's den, and he had found new 'greeners' to replace them. Now Hatskel and Blagovistnik were earning eight shillings a week and knew that the English took in three or four times as much, but they had not yet attained any consciousness of the necessity of acting in concert, all together. Until now it seemed to them perfectly normal to hire themselves out bit by bit for a smaller wage than the English. Hatskel was only just beginning to understand why the English joiners berated Blagovistnik so bitterly when he once took a job at a factory for eighteen shillings a week. Blagovistnik thought the terms magnificent, although his fellows were earning thirty-eight shillings. He was very distressed when the other joiners, having learned how much Onisko got engaged for, demanded that the manager dismiss the foreigner.[26] Our friends were still trying to measure the new life by the old measure and found themselves at a loss every time they realised that the measure did not fit at all.

III.

Now I would like to tell the story of the creation of 'The Samovaroff Troupe of Russian Singers and Dancers', which is at present enjoying great success at one of London's most fashionable music halls.[27]

---

is very nearly of the variety most popular over here, the psychology is a shade subtler.' This was the view of Julius West, Semyon Rapoport's son, in his introduction to the translation of *Plays by Anton Tchekoff: Second Series* (New York: Charles Scribner's Sons, 1916). See also Jan McDonald, 'Chekhov, Naturalism and the Drama of Dissent: Productions of Chekhov's Plays in Britain before 1914' in Patrick Miles, ed. *Chekhov on the British Stage* (Cambridge: Cambridge University Press, 1993): 29. Shklovsky's assumption in this whole paragraph is that readers will be familiar with the characters from both plays – a safe bet given the popularity of Chekhov's farces in Russia.

[25] The words in quotations marks are all English directly transliterated into Russian.

[26] The anti-immigrant sentiments of unionised British workers were frequently explained by reference to alien undercutting. Shklovsky, however, is not criticising the British but the immigrants themselves for their lack of class consciousness.

[27] There was a Peschkoff Troupe of Russian Dancers performing with George Robey on the bill at the London Pavilion Music Hall in November 1903. In fact, there were many similar Russian troupes performing in London and elsewhere since the turn of the century, if not before, though 'Samovaroff' appears to be a pseudonym.

64

Great ideas always strike one unexpectedly. This is an old saying; but our heroes, Hatskel Baltyansky and Onisko Blagovistnik, learned it from their own experience. It happened last winter, after Christmas. All the London papers were full of stories about unemployment. Dozens and hundreds of workshops had either closed down altogether or considerably cut the number of 'hands'. People seemed to have conspired not to order new coats or buy new furniture so that our compatriots would have to remain jobless. In addition, the gutter press was shouting in every issue: 'No wonder our workers are starving when foreigners are stealing their bread!'.

Fig. 10. Conservative and Unionist Party Poster.

'The alien has taken the jobs of British workers', asserted an economist in the '**Daily Express**'. 'He can live in conditions which any self-respecting Briton would find impossible. The alien is used to sleeping in one room with his whole family. He can do without beds, without mattresses and without linen. In his homeland the alien is used to eating the kind of food that our pigs would not touch. The people who have robbed our workers of their wages are able to live on black bread, thin tea and herrings alone. They agree to work twelve and fourteen hours a day and are content with six or eight shillings a week.'[28]

---

[28] Shklovsky's note: All of these arguments are repeated in the book '**Alien Immigration**' by Frederick Bradshaw, London, 1901, p. 74–82.
Editor's note: There is no record of such a book from 1901. Shklovsky might have in mind Frederick Bradshaw and Charles Emanuel, *Alien Immigration: Should Restrictions be Imposed?* (London: Isbister and Co, 1904), which contained 'pro' and 'con' cases for immigration restrictions. For a very detailed account of the book's contents and the context of publication in relation to the alien immigration debate at the turn of the century, see Jim Thomas, *Alien Immigration and the London School of Economics: Some Early Connections*, Technical Report, February 2016, *ResearchGate*: DOI: 10.13140/RG.2.2.19986.25286. The arguments Shklovsky

The author further asserted that only one thing could save England: a ban on foreign workers settling in the country. Heated debates raged in the press.

The official papers were writing that the government had promised workers an old-age pension.[29] 'It would, of course, be happy to fulfil those promises; but is it possible at the present time, when England has become a Mecca for immigrant ships to flock to unhindered from all directions? If the government provides a pension for elderly workers, even more foreigners will swarm in and get their hands on those pensions. That is why first we must have Parliament pass a law restricting immigration to England. Then the material conditions of British workers will immediately improve. There will be enough jobs for everyone. Wages will rise. Working hours will decrease. The government will build good houses for the workers and provide for the elderly.'

The Liberal and Radical papers asserted that all this was just empty talk. Until the eighties, there had been virtually no immigration to England,[30] and yet the condition of British workers was even worse than now. At the present time, the absolute number of foreigners in England in comparison to Germany or France, not to mention America, is negligible. Communities of foreign labourers are found only in two London boroughs and a single district of Leeds. Only there can complaints about competition be heard. In the rest of England, the alien question is completely non-existent. A law that would give government authorities the right to stop incoming migrants would only cause immeasurable harm. The executive branch would then receive much more power than is desirable. The government would cease to be subject to strict public control, which would have disastrous consequences. The necessary result of an immigration control law would be a passport system, the mere thought of which strikes terror into the hearts of Radicals and Tories alike. The opposition papers also asked sarcastically: since when had the Tories become interested in the reduction of the working day? Had not the '**Times**' just recently come out with thunderous leading articles against trade unions and had it not held them responsible for ruining English industry by their defence of the short working day?

Newspaper battles raged all along the frontline. Every day, in the weather-beaten and smoke-blackened offices of Fleet Street, dozens of 'leader writers' picked the labour question to pieces. They elucidated

---

recounts in this and subsequent paragraphs summarise the 'pro' and 'con' cases in the public debate (the Commission testimonies and divergent opinions, etc.) point for point.

29 'Official papers': the original has 'Ministry', i.e. Government papers ('Ministry' has been translated as 'Government' throughout this volume). In light of the preceding and following paragraphs (on the tabloid and Liberal/Radical press respectively), one can assume the reference here is to national papers like *The Times*.

30 Evidently, Irish immigration does not count.

wage laws, analysed the outcomes of free trade and protectionism, sifted through bulky Blue Books, cited Adam Smith, Mill and Ricardo,[31] made scientific forecasts; but unemployment still continued to grow with every passing day. More and more often processions of the unemployed appeared in the streets of London. Old men marched, and so did young men. Since no demonstration in England can do without three things: music, banners and songs, the unemployed marched to the sound of drums and pipes, following a banner which read 'Buy the strength of our muscles or give us bread', and chanted 'No work!'. This dreadful song was composed by the grandfathers and fathers of the current generation, in Lancashire during the cotton famine, when millions of spindles fell silent and hundreds of thousands of workers begged for alms along the high roads.[32] The Smiths, the Joneses, the Palmers and the Taylors were having a rough time; but being British, they could at least protest and threaten. Hatskel Baltyansky, Onisko Blagovistnik and many more Hatskels and Oniskos had it much worse. They were left jobless, breadless, homeless, and all they could do was groan. What could they have said to this rich city if they too came out with drums and banners?[33] How could they say it if they didn't speak the language? Would they not hear in reply: 'Why have you come? Who invited you?'.

It may be that no-one would have said this, but the Hatskels and the Oniskos brought with them an ingrained fear of the police.[34] When

---

[31]   Founding fathers of classical political economy.

[32]   Shklovsky is referring to the Lancashire 'Cotton Famine' or depression in the cotton industry of 1861–1865, which was caused in part by the interruption of raw cotton supplies due to the American Civil War. It led to mass unemployment and emigration.

[33]   In fact, immigrant Jewish sweated workers in the East End had a long tradition of unionising, striking and demonstrating, going back to the tailors' strike of 1889 and continuing into the 1900s and 1910s, and there were separate Jewish tailors' unions. More generally, in London in the early 1900s, there was a range of formal labour, socialist and anarchist organisations that welcomed immigrants and that Hatskel and Onisko could have joined. Shklovsky, who had close connections with the London socialist scene, must have been aware of immigrant labour militancy, but in this sketch he is depicting the depoliticised majority. See David Rosenberg, *Rebel Footprints: A Guide to Uncovering London's Radical History* (London: Pluto Press, 2015), chapter 4 and the Yiddish banner of the Trousermakers' Union at www. jewishgen.org/jcr-uk/london/East_End_London.htm. See also works ranging from William Fishman's seminal *East End Jewish Radicals* via Geoffrey Alderman's *London Jewry and London Politics, 1889–1986* (London: Routledge, 1989), to Karin Hofmeester's *Jewish Workers and the Labour Movement: A Comparative Study of Amsterdam, London and Paris, 1870–1914*, trans. Lee Mitzman (Aldershot: Ashgate, 2004).

[34]   According to the testimony of observers like Sims and one of the heads of the Jews' Temporary Shelter, new arrivals 'feared to call for the assistance of the police because they thought the English police were much the same as the dreaded *objescik* whom they had left behind' (qtd in Baker, 'House of a Thousand Destinies

Fig. 11. Unemployed Workers Processing Along the Strand, London, 1903.

they came across a street procession with drums and banners, they hastened to turn aside into an alley to keep out of harm's way. Our friends only wondered that everything was so calm, that one heard no alarm whistles followed by screaming, crying, swearing and the tramp of people scattering in all directions.

It was January. Thick fog covered Whitechapel like a hat. It was hard to tell the time of day. Streetlamps burned everywhere, their light fading into the gloom, but the factory whistles were just proclaiming the midday break. Hundreds of dejected, hungry and cold people wandered along the sticky pavements, their hands thrust deep in their pockets. Among them were Onisko and Hatskel.

'It's rotten luck, mate!' said Blagovistnik gloomily. 'What do we do now? There's no hope. We might as well croak!'

'People have told me that it's *slack* now, but it will be over shortly because spring is coming', answered Hatskel, mixing English words, like all immigrants, into his broken Russian. 'There is "hope".'[35]

– The Jews' Temporary Shelter'). However, their fears were not entirely unfounded – one need only recall police behaviour during the Bloody Sunday demonstration of 1887 in Trafalgar Square.

[35] The linguistic contrasts in the following dialogue are extremely difficult to get across in translation. The italicised words are English transliterated into Cyrillic; Onisko is speaking throughout in Ukrainian with untranslatable idioms; Hatskel's

'What hope? To drop dead or what!' remarked Onisko in the same funereal tone.

'And what "hope" did you have back in Shirokaya Greblya? Once work picks up here, will you be earning the same as there? Have you spoken to Makar? How much is he making in his *furniture shop*?'[36]

'Twenty shillings a week', said Onisko, cheering up.

'That's ten silver roubles.[37] And people say that's too little. A *joiner* here earns thirty-five or forty shillings a week. What will you say, Onisko, when you have eighty silver roubles a month? Eh? We've just got to wait out the *slack*! Let's go warm ourselves in the meantime. I can't stand it. There's no frost, but I'm absolutely freezing. Come, Onisko.'

Blagovistnik had become used to obeying Hatskel since he had first met him, being entirely convinced that the latter was 'a very crafty schemer' and would always find a way to wriggle out of any difficulty. By force of old habit, he adjusted his bowler instead of his astrakhan hat and wandered off after Hatskel.

'Isn't it strange, Onisko', said Hatskel, who was physically unable to endure silence, 'In Kishinev I would have been afraid of you as a pogromist. You are a very good man, Onisko, but you wouldn't have been able to restrain yourself and would have followed the others. Isn't that so? Because over there I wasn't a human being in your eyes but a dog that wants beating. You are a just man, Onisko, but you would have smashed up all my furniture and all my tools, even though I'm a poor worker just like you. But here we've met, I've got to know you and you me. And there's no problem, we're good comrades. We help each other out. Isn't it a wonder, Onisko?'.[38]

Blagovistnik nodded his big head, from which the bowler was always slipping, in affirmation, but did not say a word.

IV.

From the main thoroughfare the friends turned into a side-street, even dirtier and gloomier in appearance, built up with crooked black houses

---

Russian grammar is indeed broken (his native language almost certainly being Yiddish), but here he echoes Onisko and says 'hope' in Ukrainian.

[36] Shklovsky gives the English word transliterated into Cyrillic, then in parentheses in Latin script with Russian translation; 'joiner' in the paragraph below is also transliterated and then translated into Russian in parentheses for the benefit of readers unfamiliar with English.

[37] Hatskel actually says 'karbovanets' here and below, which was the name of the Ukrainian unit of currency in the post-revolutionary period, but also the Ukrainian name for the silver rouble in the imperial period, which is its likeliest meaning here.

[38] Britain is being presented by Shklovsky as a place where former ethnic and religious antagonisms can be overcome in class camaraderie.

whose windowpanes had become iridescent with age. In places, there were no panes of any kind, and in their stead one saw pillows in chintz cases. These houses were living out their last days. Enterprising people had rented them and were now letting them out room by room and even corner by corner to destitute foreign riffraff. No Englishman would have agreed to live in a slum like this. Every corner here was to let for three shillings a week. Sometimes, a single bed had three 'tenants' in it. Each of them took his turn to sleep in it for eight hours. When one lodger came back from work, another left. In this way, the bed never grew cold. On the whole, these half-ruined hovels rented out piece by piece to the undemanding and uncomplaining foreign paupers brought the entrepreneur six or seven times more in earnings than good new comfortable houses let to well-to-do people in respectable areas.[39] From open doors came the ringing of hammers, the screeching of rasp files and the hissing of irons. The foreigners worked in the very same rooms in which they slept. In their home countries, they had been accustomed to regard this as a normal occurrence, but the English were horrified by such low standards. The walls were gaudy with Jewish-language and, in places, Russian-language bills, like white, red and yellow patches on a coal sack.[40] They announced meetings, play productions in Yiddish, the newly formed bakers' cooperative union.[41] On the pavement, in the dirt, little children were bustling about among the cabbage stalks, old newspapers and other rubbish. The whole of eastern Europe had its representatives here. An old Italian woman with a dried, chapped face, wrapped up in a shawl whose corners formed a huge knot on her bent back, was cranking a battered barrel organ like an automaton. A dozen girls, dirty, with tangled hair falling from under their straw hats or greasy

---

[39] The observations about East End slums in this paragraph were the stock-in-trade of late-Victorian and Edwardian social reportage, as well as literature. See, for instance, G. B. Shaw's play *Widowers' Houses* (London: Henry & Co., 1893) about slum landlordism. The practice of lodgers sleeping in a single bed by turns was certainly not limited to foreigners – Jack London in *The People of the Abyss* shows doss house lodgers on the 'two relay system', whereby day and night-shift workers shared the same bed.

[40] 'Jewish language' refers to Yiddish most likely written in Hebrew characters, as was common in East End posters and advertisements, restaurant bills of fare, etc.

[41] For the bakers' cooperative, see Rosenberg, 88–89; a banner of the 'London Jewish Bakers' Union' may be seen in the collections of the Jewish Museum London: https://jewishmuseum.org.uk/50-objects/1984-126_0001/. London had a thriving Yiddish theatre scene at the turn of the century, see https://jewishmuseum.org.uk/50-objects/2000-60-1/, as well as David Mazower, 'London-New York, or The Great British Yiddish Theatre Brain Drain', *Digital Yiddish Theatre Project*, https://web.uwm.edu/yiddish-stage/london-new-york-or-the-great-british-yiddish-theatre-brain-drain and Bernard Mendelovitch, *Memories of London Yiddish Theatre* (Oxford: Oxford Centre for Postgraduate Hebrew Studies, 1990), www.ochjs.ac.uk/wp-content/uploads/2011/09/7th-Stencl-Lecture-Memories-of-London-Yiddish-Theatre.pdf.

sports caps, were dancing on the pavement to the music – dancing the *cake-walk*, imported from the Negro plantations to the aristocratic drawing-rooms of the West End, and from there to Whitechapel.[42]

'Look, Onisko', said Hatskel suddenly, stopping before a little shop, 'our little Jews have brought the whole of Kishinev with them to London'.

In the little shop, a stout Jewish woman in a tucked-up red flannel skirt was selling buckwheat groats, black rye bread, pickled cucumbers, poppy-seed honey cakes with nuts, herrings – in a word, all those foodstuffs that so horrify the English. Migrants from the Northwestern Krai can adapt themselves quite quickly to new surroundings, to a foreign language, to an unfamiliar way of life; but their stomach remains conservative and faced with 'fleshpots' still pines for porridge, herring, and pickled cucumbers.[43]

'And here is the Jewish Cook',[44] pointed Hatskel to a shabby booking office in whose window hung a poster depicting an ocean liner, with an inscription below in the Jewish language. 'If you want, he'll give you a *Schiffkarte* (ticket) to New York, Argentina or South Africa![45] Maybe

---

42 Cf. the long description of street dancing in George R. Sims, 'Off the Track in London: V. In the Shadow of St. Stephen's', *Strand Magazine* 28 (August 1904), 152–58, especially: 'An organ is playing, and the music has brought a mob of children into the street to trip a *pas de quatre*, or indulge in a marvellous infantile imitation of the American Cake Walk, which is now the favourite dance of the by-way ball' (157). See also the illustration of 'Little Jewish Children' dancing in Sims, 'Off the Track in London: I. In Alien-Land', 423 and Jack London's description (and photograph) of East End children dancing in 'The Children' chapter of *The People of the Abyss* beginning: 'There is one beautiful sight in the East End, and only one, and it is the children dancing in the street when the organ-grinder goes his round' (274); and Mathilde Blind's poem 'The Street-Children's Dance'. Children's street life was a common motif of East End social investigations, and Shklovsky included similar scenes in many of his articles.

43 'Fleshpots': the original text has literally 'cauldrons of meat', which, being placed in quotation marks, is almost certainly a reference to the Russian for 'fleshpots of Egypt' from Exodus 16:3, and a play on the stereotypical English predilection for meat dishes. One wonders what Shklovsky would have made of Harry Champion's 'Boiled Beef and Carrots' and 'A Little Bit of Cucumber' music hall songs about East End cockney tastes in food. The description of immigrant shops, etc. is a staple of East End writing of the period such as Sims's. Shklovsky is giving Russian readers a guided tour of the Jewish East End.

44 This is a play on Thomas Cook, the famous travel agency. Hatskel is describing an emigration agency – for a very negative assessment of the operation of emigration agents, see Sims, 'Sweated London'.

45 All major destinations of mass Jewish emigration, and specifically 'transmigration' (migrants who passed through London on their way elsewhere). Rosenberg recounts how 'unscrupulous travel agents in Hamburg' sold 'tickets to New York, which were actually marked "London"' (83). On transmigration, see Tobias Brinkmann, ed. *Points of Passage: Jewish Migrants from Eastern Europe in Scandinavia, Germany, and Britain 1880–1914* (Oxford: Berghahn, 2013). See also Sims, 'Trips

---

you wish to send for your wife and children from Shirokaya Greblya? Just go in and say: "Here is the money, bring me Madame Khima Blagovistnik with her children Panasik, Grits, Ganusya, Motrya and Khivrya".⁴⁶ And all will be done in a trice. The Jewish Cook will write to their agent in Vinnitsa or Proskurov,⁴⁷ whichever town is nearer to Shirokaya Greblya. The agent will go there, get the children ready, pack the household odds and ends, and sort out the passport. Or you could forget the passport, if you pay three extra roubles. Then Madame Khima will be allocated to a consignment, sent by special train to Hamburg, and from there to London, straight to Mister Onisko. Here are the goods, all in order if you please!' Chattering in this manner, Hatskel, together with his friend, approached a lopsided house, whose wall had bulged out. Above the doors was a conspicuous blue sign with the words: 'Russian Odessa Restaurant'. Under the Russian inscription, one in the Jewish language communicated that dishes here were prepared using

---

About Town: IV. Round St. George in the East': 'Look at this group of immigrants making their way from the docks to the Jewish shelter in Leman Street. They have just come from one of the Pales of Settlement in the land of persecution. It has been a desperate effort to raise the passage-money, and they have probably been robbed and cheated by the way. But, poor as they are, miserable as they are [...] they will make a bold fight with fortune, and presently they will be prospering and saving money [...] To-day they are nervous, anxious. Some have a journey of thousands of miles yet before them. They are making their way to America, or to some far-off Jewish colony. But some will remain' (686). See also his 'Off the Track in London: I. In Alien-Land', for a long description of the Jewish shops, the 'Russian post-office' in Brick Lane, and 'the shipping agents and bankers [...] taking money for remittance to relatives abroad who are to leave the Russian Pale and come to the city paved with gold, or booking passages to America and the Colonies for the immigrants who are "moving on"' (419).

⁴⁶ The appellation Madame is of course ironic and is meant to look incongruous in conjunction with the typical Ukrainian names, of the kind that may be found in a work by Nikolay Gogol, one of Shklovsky's favourite writers, to judge by the frequency with which allusions to him crop up in his articles.

⁴⁷ Towns in western Ukraine in neighbouring governorates, both sites of anti-Jewish pogroms. See the entries for Vinnitsa and Proskurov in *The Untold Stories*, Yad Vashem: The World Holocaust Remembrance Center, www.yadvashem.org/untoldstories/database/index.asp?cid=686 and www.yadvashem.org/untoldstories/database/index.asp?cid=748.

kosher meat.[48] Beneath this sign was another, which read: 'The Free Russian Library'.[49]

'Here's where we'll get warm!' Hatskel said, pointing to the second sign. 'Have you got anything like it in Shirokaya Greblya?' he asked boastfully. It has to be admitted, however, that the entrance to the library was not at all presentable. The friends had to grope their way along a dark corridor, through which spread, evidently from the 'Odessa Restaurant', an insupportable stench of cabbage and fish fried in vegetable oil.

'Take care going up!' someone shouted to the friends from above, 'or you'll break a leg'. This was no idle warning. Someone had spilled water or slops on the staircase. Many banisters were missing. They had been taken out by the poor tenants in the cold nights to kindle fires in their grates.[50] Doors leading to dirty rooms, in which cobblers and tailors were working, opened out onto each landing.

'Have you seen anything like it in Shirokaya Greblya?' Hatskel continued to rhapsodise. 'Look: the walls are covered in wa-a-allpaper. Have any of these people ever lived in wallpapered rooms back in Shepetilovka or Smela?'[51]

Onisko agreed with this silently. A scrap of paper pasted to the doors declared that it was indeed here that the free library was located. Five or so very poorly clad Russian Jews stood on the landing. Some of them smoked in silence. Others were heatedly discussing some question.

'So, Benzion,[52] same old thing?' Hatskel called out to a scrawny young man with a gloomy cadaverous face and sunken cheeks.

[48] As Chukovsky mentions, there was an Odessa Restaurant in Commercial Road, so it must have been a common name. See Sims, 'Off the Track in London: I. In Alien-Land': 'Here is a little restaurant with its bill of fare in Hebrew characters. We push the door ajar and enter, for we know that it was once the haunt of the Bessarabians, the formidable gang who had a standing vendetta with the Odessians, and who fought them not long ago outside the Yiddish theatre, the fray ending in a man being stabbed to death' (423).

[49] Cf. the description in Chukovsky's 'Whitechapel'. Shklovsky had more extensive first-hand experience of the Library than Chukovsky, being not just a visitor but a lecturer there.

[50] These are all typical details – compare Arthur Morrison's description of an East End slum in *A Child of the Jago*: 'Front doors were used merely as firewood in the Old Jago, and most had been burnt there many years ago'; the main character climbs 'up the first stair-flight with the necessary regard for the treads that one might step through and the rails that had gone from the side' (14).

[51] 'Smila' in Ukrainian – town in central Ukraine. 'Shepetilovka' might be a misprint for Shepetovka (Shepetivka in Ukrainian), a town in western Ukraine, although a village named Shepetilovka is mentioned in nineteenth-century Russian periodicals. The reader must surely take Hatskel's continued insistence on the superiority of London life with a pinch of salt.

[52] Benzion or Ben-Zion is a Hebrew name which means literally 'son of Zion'. It was the middle name of Morris Winchevsky, a prominent Jewish socialist leader who lived in London in the 1880s.

'The same', he replied laconically.
'No work?'
'None'.
'*Strike*'.
'No, *slack*'.
'How long for?'
'Till *Easter*'.
'Bad *job*'.[53]

'Tell me about it, Hatskel, we might as well die! At least I can keep warm here, otherwise I'd be lying right in the street.'[54]

'And why wouldn't you rather go back home?' Onisko interjected suddenly.

'Why? Here at least I have hope. By *Easter*, the *slack* will be over, and then everything will be great; but *over there* I have nothing to look forward to. Here, I am my own master. I have no-one to fear. But there, I've got to be quaking before everybody. They don't even take me for a human being there.' Hatskel shot a triumphant glance at Onisko.

'Benzion the cobbler will find work!' Hatskel began boastfully, as if speaking of himself. 'He's only been here a year and look at him blazing away in English like a proper *Englishman*. He can say anything, and he understands everything!'

Only an extreme infatuation with England can explain Hatskel's exultant enquiry: 'Have you got anything comparable?'. For in reality, the free Russian library, supported as it is by voluntary donations from very impecunious people, produced a dispiriting impression. The seal of desperate, cruel poverty, or more precisely destitution, was stamped on everything: on the peeling room, the wretched tables and the rough benches, and especially on the numerous patrons buried in their newspapers and books. These patrons, for the most part unemployed, poorly dressed, pale, very likely hungry, were softly rustling the pages of Russian and Jewish newspapers. Rows of books stretched along the walls on roughly jerry-built handmade shelves. In this faraway alien land, they offered the library visitors a treasured fragment of home.

---

[53] Shklovsky includes the English words in Latin script and provides Russian translations of the English words in parentheses, for instance, 'slack' is defined as 'the dead season' or 'interruption'. He is also illustrating here the practice of mixing in words from the host language in immigrants' speech, known as code-switching in linguistics.

[54] The practice of unemployed men keeping warm in public libraries is frequently described in social documentary writings, as late as the 1930s by Orwell. Benzion could perhaps have gone to the Jews' Temporary Shelter in Leman Street, which had been operating since the 1880s, although this was aimed primarily at newly arrived homeless migrants and transmigrants. See Aubrey Newman, 'The Poor Jews' Temporary Shelter: An Episode in Migration Studies', *Jewish Historical Studies* 40 (2005), 141–55.

These paupers, driven from the ghettos of the Pale by extreme destitution and sometimes by horrific, bloody catastrophes, lived and breathed the interests of the old country, preserved the Russian language, even though most of them did not know it well. In particular, there was great demand in the reading room for provincial newspapers, the various 'Heralds' and 'Leaflets' issued in the large centres of the South and the Northwestern Krai.[55] Such 'Leaflets' were read from beginning to end. From the large room, a door led to a small one, even more dirty and airless, piled up to the ceiling with books and dust-covered corded bundles of old newspapers. Here, huddled behind a simple desk, a ginger-haired youth with a very kindly and very sickly face was diligently binding. The librarian, a tall, broad-shouldered man with a large black beard, was, to all appearances, the highest authority in both rooms.

Among all these undersized and sickly natives of the ghetto, the librarian seemed a giant. He could even stand as tall as Blagovistnik.[56]

The group could barely find a place to sit. Hatskel, ever curious, reached immediately for '*Odesskiy Listok*'. He carefully read the correspondence from Kishinev, then put the paper aside, being physically unable to abide silence. Next to Hatskel sat a long-bearded man, no longer young, who held before him in his strong calloused hands an issue of a newspaper in Hebrew.[57] It appeared that he was highly agitated by his reading, for he would shake his head, sigh, set the newspaper aside, then pick it up again. In one of the moments when the issue was set aside, Hatskel spoke to his neighbour in a whisper:

'Bad news?'

Instead of replying, Hatskel's neighbour, lifting his eyes and swaying his body slightly, began to quote from memory Hebrew verses from the Bible:

'And the Lord said, I have surely seen the affliction of my people which are in Egypt, and have heard their cry by reason of their taskmasters; for I know their sorrows... I have also seen the oppression wherewith [they] oppress them.'[58]

Hatskel understood only that this was from the Bible; but he sighed sympathetically just in case and, after a moment's silence, changed the subject.[59]

---

[55] One famous example is *Odesskiy Listok [Odessa Leaflet]*, a popular liberal newspaper of the period to which Chukovsky, among others, contributed.

[56] On the Chief Librarian Aleksey Teplov, see Robert Henderson, 'For the Cause of Education' and 'Aleksei Teplov and the Free Russian Library in Whitechapel', *Solanus* 22 (2011), 5–26.

[57] Here and below the original text has, literally, 'the ancient-Jewish tongue' – as opposed to 'the Jewish language' or 'jargon', which designates Yiddish. The likelihood is that this is a Yiddish-language newspaper printed in Hebrew characters (see Sims, 'Off the Track in London: I. In Alien-Land', 419).

[58] KJV Exodus 3:7 and 3:9 (the word 'Egyptians' is omitted).

[59] The contrast between religiously orthodox and secular Jews is well evoked here.

'Where are you from?'

'From Veprik,[60] Poltava Governorate.'

'Ts-s-s! That's not too near London! Have you got a trade in hand?'

'I'm Zelman Soloveychik,[61] a whitesmith and tinker, except in our shtetl there are more tinkers than samovars. You can't get work there at any price! On Saturdays, I used to be a cantor in our little synagogue. Oh, woe to the Jews: there is nothing to eat.'

'Have you been here long?'

'Over three months. I have towed steamships in the docks, I have cranked engines, I have sewn peaks to caps. I've tried everything. And now it's *slack*... I've got hands. I've got a trade. I have a will to work too, and here I am going hungry. At least I can warm myself here in the library... Oh woe, woe! I have children in Veprik, a daughter with a child of her own. Her husband has been conscripted into the army. Everyone is expecting help from me, but no-one is buying my hands!', the tinker shook his head.

The other readers had begun to look askance at the talkers, so Hatskel, the tinker, and Benzion went out onto the landing. They also called out Blagovistnik, much to his pleasure.

'Listen, let's go call on this one young lady', Benzion suggested. 'She's very kind and helps out a lot with work. She has many acquaintances among the rich Englishwomen.' Since neither Hatskel nor the tinker nor Blagovistnik had anything better to do, they accepted the suggestion without objections. Along the way, Hatskel began to enquire who this tender-hearted young lady was. He found out that the English Jews had organised a nursery for children whose mothers, newly arrived from Russia, were busy all day with work.[62] The children were brought in the morning and remained in the nursery for the entire day. There, they were immediately bathed, changed into clean clothes, fed and played with until evening. And the young lady was in charge of the nursery.

---

[60]   A village in eastern Ukraine.

[61]   Zelman is a typical Ashkenazi name, a variant of Solomon. Soloveychik is a popular Jewish surname, including that of a Belorussian rabbinical dynasty.

[62]   Shklovsky is almost certainly referring to the Jewish Day Nursery for children of working parents established in 1897 by Alice Model, an important Anglo-Jewish philanthropist active in mother- and child-care. It relocated to New Road, near the Royal London Hospital, in 1901. According to Susan L. Tananbaum, 'Britain: Nineteenth and Twentieth Centuries' in *Shalvi/Huyman Encyclopedia of Jewish Women*, 31 December 1999, *Jewish Women's Archive*, https://jwa.org/encyclopedia/article/britain-nineteenth-and-twentieth-centuries, the Nursery was 'committed to using the latest methods and to encouraging mothers to adopt English child-rearing styles'; and according to Rachel Kolsky and Roslyn Rawson, *Jewish London: A Comprehensive Guidebook for Visitors and Londoners* (London: New Holland, 2012), 'facilities for the 50 children included daily medical checks, defumigating the children's clothes to prevent the spread of disease [and] subsidized meals'.

The nursery was located in perhaps the dirtiest and poorest passage in poor and dirty Whitechapel. The wonderful cleanliness of every nook and cranny inside furnished a striking contrast with the general look of the street.

As our little group came up, several young children ran out towards them. From the entrance hall, Hatskel saw a huge room with about forty children bustling about. Some of them were still mastering the art of walking on two legs instead of on all fours. Others were riding rocking horses. Still others were sitting decorously in a row on little chairs, their faces uncommonly serious, engaged in their private business. Several nurses in blue dress uniforms were promptly and skilfully tending to the children. 'The young lady', also in a dress uniform, greeted the group affectionately; but here a little incident occurred. One of the boys, the enterprising three-year-old Sammy, tempted by the open door, ran out into the street and disappeared. A fearful commotion ensued. The young lady wrung her hands in despair and kept repeating that Sammy was sure to be run over.

The imperturbable English nurses suggested going to the police. And indeed, to the young lady's great delight, Sammy was soon delivered from the nearest police station, where a 'bobby' had brought the little vagabond in his arms. Sammy turned up with a huge slice of bread and butter that the policeman had provided him with.

'No work!' the young lady declared with disappointment having heard the companions out. 'If I learn of something, I shall let you know, but there is nothing at present.'

'Would you like to have some soup today?' asked Benzion when they all came out into the street. 'Then let's go to the Strand tonight. The Salvation Army is distributing soup to the unemployed there. Except it's too early now. Let's keep warm in the library in the meantime.'

V.

The library closed, and the company of friends, with Benzion at its head, set off in search of free soup.[63] Whitechapel's main street was still busy. People, though in thinner groups than before, crowded around stalls lit by smoky kerosene torches quivering in the fog, and harkened to the costers' howling cries.

'I bet they don't know where to spend the night either!' said Hatskel, pointing to a group of cheerless people who – the collars of their

---

[63]   As Jewish immigrants, the group could have gone to the Soup Kitchen for the Jewish Poor, dating from 1854, which relocated to Butler (later Brune) Street, Spitalfields, in 1902. But instead, readers get a typical satirical portrayal of Salvation Army charitable relief, preceded by a long tour of central London. See 1930s footage of the Soup Kitchen for the Jewish Poor at the British Film Institute: https://player.bfi.org.uk/free/film/watch-soup-kitchen-1934-online.

coats raised for warmth – were listening attentively to the shouts of a gentleman in a top hat, spectacles and black frock coat, mounted on a cart. The gentleman was gesticulating desperately and shouting himself hoarse, all while demonstrating some small box.

'Do you know what he wants?' asked the tinker.

'He is selling pills to cure all diseases', Benzion answered with a smirk. 'Many are sick here, and you need money to call a doctor. So they buy the stuff.'

'He wants to eat too!' Hatskel ventured a reply.

'The poor man is working, and if he ruptures himself, there's nobody to save him!' sighed Onisko.[64]

A little further on, on a little lawn, the group ran up against several hundred people who had tightly encircled a speaker mounted on a railing. Next to the speaker on one side stood a person with a red flag, and on the other, two old men were holding the rods of a huge painted banner. It depicted Adam and Eve in aprons of fig leaves, then two men without frock coats, holding hands. A long inscription sparkled in gold over it all.

'What is that?' asked the tinker.

'The *mantlemakers union*', Benzion answered. *Middlemen* are offering them new *conditions* now, so that *branch* of the *S. D. F.* is telling them not to listen to the *bamboozlers* but to go on *strike*.[65]

The only thing Onisko understood from this whole explanation was the word *strike*. He looked around apprehensively and pulled at the tinker's coattails.

'Let's get a move on: they're talking about a *shtraik* here! And here's a *desyatsky*!'

---

[64] The scholarship on the patent medicine industry, especially in relation to the medical profession and as a business practice, is extensive. See, to begin with, Roy Porter, *Quacks: Fakers and Charlatans in English Medicine* (Stroud: Tempus, 2000); Louise Hill Curth, ed. *From Physick to Pharmacology: Five Hundred Years of British Drug Retailing* (Aldershot: Ashgate, 2006); Takahiro Ueyama, *Health in the Marketplace: Professionalism, Therapeutic Desires, and Medical Commodification in Late-Victorian London* (Palo Alto, CA: Society for the Promotion of Science and Scholarship, 2010) and J. Worth Estes, 'The Pharmacology of Nineteenth-Century Patent Medicines', *Pharmacy in History* 30.1 (1988), 3–18. For some illustrations of quack cures, see Liza Picard, 'Health and Hygiene in the 19th Century', *British Library*, www.bl.uk/victorian-britain/articles/health-and-hygiene-in-the-19th-century.

[65] This is another great example of immigrant code-switching – Shklovsky provides Russian translations of the English words in parentheses. The iconography of the banner is typical of nineteenth-century union and socialist visual culture: clasped male hands were a common symbol of unity in nineteenth-century banners (see also Walter Crane's frontispiece to William Morris's *A Dream of John Ball* (London: Reeves & Turner, 1888): 'When Adam delved and Eve span / Who was then the Gentleman?'). SDF activists were a common presence in the streets of London.

To Blagovistnik's great surprise, the 'desyatsky', i.e. 'bobby', came up to the crowd, stood impassively for a couple of minutes, and then went on.[66] Onisko would have remained gawping, had he not received a dig in the ribs and a reminder that it was time to go. The bustling street came to an end at the brightly lit Three Nuns tavern.[67] Ahead stretched the streets of the City, completely deserted at this time of night. Banks and trading offices, brimming with life during the day, where responses were drafted to letters received from far-off Australian and South American cities, now stood dark and dead. It was hard to believe that here business boiled over in the daytime, that in these banks the destinies of entire nations were decided and the politics of the greatest state in the world were determined. Brass plates with black inscriptions stood out indistinctly in the damp gloom: 'The Bank of Australia', 'The Russian Foreign Trade Bank',[68] 'The Bank of China', etc. There were so many banks that all the windows of the huge six-storey buildings were dotted with signs. In one of them, Hatskel counted no fewer than fifteen banks. The banks alternated with offices of giant steamship companies which regularly sent mail boats to Australia, South America, and the Far East. Their steps echoed hollowly in the deserted and winding ancient streets. This city of business, in the grip of a deathlike sleep after a frenetic working day, produced a dim sense of dread. At last, the group came up to a huge building with columns. Before its portal, on a granite pedestal, a colossal bronze figure of a horseman loomed in the fog.

'The Exchange,' Benzion explained laconically. 'And this is a famous English general. He beat everyone, even Napoleon. Look what practical people the English are: they really revere the general, but meanwhile, see what's under the monument!'

From the pavement under the pedestal, a staircase led underground. On the doors was nailed a plate with the image of a hand and the inscription '**Gentlemen**'.[69]

---

[66] 'Desyatsky': in Tsarist Russia, a local rural policeman elected from among the peasants of a village. As George R. Sims wrote in *Living London*, 3, 220, with reference to political public meetings and demonstrations: 'Good order' prevails even when 'the capitalists, or the Government' are 'denounced' because 'our London police are taught and trained to avoid any interference likely to provoke hostilities.'

[67] The Three Nuns was at 11 Aldgate High Street. The group travels from Whitechapel to Aldgate High Street to the City.

[68] A large private commercial bank established in 1871 and headquartered in St Petersburg, with branches abroad. In 1899 its London branch address was listed as 61–62 Gracechurch Street (City of London). The Ordnance Survey map of London for 1893–1895 does indeed depict this entire area as dotted with banks.

[69] The statue (general) in front of the Stock Exchange in Threadneedle Street is the Duke of Wellington. The Ordnance Survey map of London for 1893–1895 does appear to show the steps (OS London, 1:1,056, 1893–1895).

The companions exchanged glances. Hatskel snorted. The tinker formulated his impressions at somewhat greater length.

'When a man is born, the Talmud says, his arms are folded. When he dies, his arms are outstretched. When a man enters this life, he wishes to grasp and seize everything. When he leaves the world, he casts away all his earthly riches. He comes into the world poor and naked. He leaves life poor and naked. You say this man here conquered everyone? The Talmud tells of another warrior, Alexander Ga-Mogden (of Macedon), who passed over the whole world and finally came to the gates of paradise and knocked on them with his sword.

"Who knocks?" asked the angel who guarded the entrance.

"Alexander."

"Who is Alexander?"

"Alexander, Alexander the Great, conqueror of the entire world."

"We do not know him here. Only the righteous dwell here. Go!"

Alexander asked for a memento of some kind. Ga-Mogden wanted to have something to remind him that he had reached the gates of paradise. And the angel gave him a piece of a human skull. Alexander showed the piece to his wise men, who put it in the bowl of a scale. And the king placed in the other bowl all his gold and silver, but the skull piece outweighed it. Then Alexander added his crown and all the precious stones he had acquired in his campaigns; but the skull piece still outweighed them. And one of the wise men approached, took a pinch of dust and sprinkled it over the skull piece. And the bowl of the scale containing it rose at once on-high. The piece was the eye socket of a conqueror. Nothing can sate the eye but the dust that will cover it in the grave… Just so this chap on the horse. You say he defeated the great Napoleon himself! And now there's a privy under him.'

The clock struck twelve.

'It's still too early. They distribute the soup at 2 a.m.', Benzion said. 'Let's come out onto the Embankment in the meantime, there are people there.'

There were indeed people there. Along the granite embankment stretching for three or so versts,[70] men, women and children were roaming silently, like nocturnal animals. People were sitting on all the benches under the bare trees dripping with water. A whole family, by the looks of it, were asleep on one bench: the husband with his bowler hat pulled over his eyes, the wife and two children wrapped in a shawl. The heavy tread of a policeman resounded nearby; but the 'bobby', as he passed by the sleepers, turned the other way as if he were scrutinising something in the fog streaming over the great river.

---

[70]   Old Russian unit of distance, equalling approximately one kilometre.

Fig. 12. The Houseless Poor of London: A Midnight Scene on the Thames Embankment.

'The policeman pretends he doesn't see the sleepers', Benzion explained, 'or he'd have to wake them and move them on'.[71]

'My God! My God! So many homeless!' the tinker sighed.

Instead, the policeman was carefully watching those who stood, as if petrified, at the stone parapet. There, where the gas lamps, cutting through the fog, lighted the river, the water sparkled like someone's glazed, baleful eyes. And this light, it appears, held some irresistible fascination for those who gazed over the parapet. The tide was high. Down below the water hissed and splashed against the cut stones. It seemed that someone there was beckoning to the hungry and frozen people, promising them, at the very least, peace...[72]

'Look here', Hatskel suddenly whispered and pointed to some man who lay on one of the benches. To keep warm, he had wrapped himself in several issues of a newspaper as in a blanket.

---

[71] There were many accounts (and images) of the homeless on the Embankment benches and the police moving them on in the press and social documentaries of the period, as well as in later fiction (see the similar Trafalgar Square scene in George Orwell's *A Clergyman's Daughter* (1935; Oxford: Oxford University Press, 2021): '*The Policeman* (shaking the sleepers on the next bench): "Now then, wake up, wake up, you! Rouse up, you! Got to go home if you want to sleep. This isn't a common lodging house. Get up, there!"' (127).

[72] The Thames suicide was another common cultural trope inherited from the nineteenth century. Cf. Chukovsky's 'Beggars in London' piece.

The Embankment ended in a colossal, magnificent building; on its tall tower, which seemed to be woven of stone lace, a huge electric lamp blazed brightly. This light demonstrated to the English that their representatives were awake and discussing matters of state in Parliament. Here was the beginning of a brightly lit central London street.[73] The theatres and fashionable music halls, of which there are many in this quarter, had already closed; but the expensive night restaurants were still open. At their doors, enormous attendants in embroidered liveries were helping in and out of carriages ladies in ballgowns and white wraps trimmed with swansdown and men in tailcoats and white ties. Gentlemen in top hats and tails visible from under their unbuttoned coats staggered and swayed along the wide pavement. There were youths here as well, but one came across fewer of them than grey, glossy, stout old men. Both the young men and the old were alternately singing and swearing. The swearing of the old men grew particularly ugly when they met the gaily dressed painted women who were strolling in pairs up and down the pavement. The women looked at the old men ingratiatingly and – probably seeking to appeal to them – also replied with lewd obscenities in English, French and German. Among these women one came across a few who were very young, sometimes almost children no older than thirteen years of age. It was at them that the old men stared most lustfully.

The tinker sighed heavily and started chanting verses from Ecclesiastes: 'So I returned, and considered all the oppressions that are done under the sun: and behold the tears of such as were oppressed, and they had no comforter; and on the side of their oppressors there was power; but they had no comforter... Yea, better is he than both they, which hath not yet been, who hath not seen the evil work that is done under the sun!'[74]

Hatskel, meanwhile, was busy with something else. For some time past, he had been gazing at the huge, wall-sized colourful posters that one came across here and there. Their bold, elegant and mysterious drawings intrigued Hatskel. One of the posters, for instance, depicted a gigantic bull crying over a little bottle labelled '**Bovril**'. Some words were printed underneath.

---

[73] The group, having walked from Whitechapel through the City and via the Victoria Embankment, have arrived at (Westminster) Bridge Street in front of Big Ben, which turned into Great George Street, leading to St James's Park: see OS London, 1:1,056, 1893–1895. The contrast between the homeless on the Embankment and the rich of the West End, as well as the prostitution for which the entertainment district had been famous since the nineteenth century, were the stock-in-trade of London commentators, from reformers and sociologists to writers and campaigning journalists like W. T. Stead.

[74] KJV Ecclesiastes 4:1 and 4:3. Shklovsky again takes up the contrast between the traditional-religious and the secular worldviews here: as the tinker quotes the Old Testament to bemoan the iniquities of modern life, Hatskel is busy trying to understand it and find ways to adapt to and succeed in it.

'What's that, Benzion?' Hatskel could no longer contain himself. 'An advertisement for a meat extract. The bull is crying and saying: "My poor brother, how did they manage to thrust you into such a small bottle!". They're doing good business! The man who came up with the word "**Bovril**" received a considerable sum from the firm. You see, there isn't even any such word in the English language, but it signifies an awful lot. There's this novel. It describes the people of the future who can do anything because they've discovered the life force of everything – *vril*. So *bovril* means *vril*, i.e. the very essence of a bull, or *bovis*.'[75] 'And what's the meaning of this one?' Hatskel pointed to a picture depicting a cheerful little old man with a braid jumping over a fence. 'Simply an advert for oatmeal. The manufacturer is saying: it gives so much strength – look how nimble even an old man becomes.'

Hatskel now kept asking for explanations of every striking picture, until the company approached a demolished quarter. Here used to spread the labyrinth of dark, gloomy, poverty-stricken streets and alleys immortalised by Dickens. In this quarter once stood the 'Old Curiosity Shop' owned by Little Nell. The Council had bought up all the hovels, evicted the riffraff to new lodgings, pulled down the old houses and decided to construct a magnificent new avenue.[76] Heaps of rubble, pits left by old

---

75 According to the object record for the poster 'Alas! My Poor Brother', 1905, Victoria and Albert Museum, London, *Victoria and Albert Museum Collections*, https://collections.vam.ac.uk/item/O74315/bovril-alas-my-poor-brother-poster-benson-s-h/, 'The advertising agent S. H. Benson, whose first account was that of Bovril, successfully established it as a household name. First conceived in 1896, "Alas! My Poor Brother" had enduring popularity. It won second prize in a Bovril competition for the most popular poster in 1923 [...] The image was then used in posters, colour throwaways, press advertisements and plaster models for shop window display.' Benzion, who appears to be giving a guided tour of central London for the benefit of Shklovsky's readers, as much as his companions, explains the derivation of the name from Edward Bulwer Lytton's novel *The Coming Race* (Edinburgh, 1871).

76 Shklovsky is referring to the location of the 'Old Curiosity Shop' building in Portsmouth Street, Lincoln's Inn Fields, not the location that Dickens had in mind when writing the novel in Green Street (now Irving Street) behind the National Portrait Gallery. See Richard Jones, 'Immortalised by Charles Dickens?', The Old Curiosity Shop: A Detailed History, *London Walking Tours*, www.london-walking-tours.co.uk/dickens-london/old-curiosity-shop.htm. The 'labyrinth' of streets, still visible on maps of the 1890s (see OS London, 1:1,056, 1893–1895) was indeed being demolished in 1903. See *Kingsway Conservation Area Statement*, Conservation & Urban Design Team, *London Borough of Camden*, www.camden.gov.uk/documents/20142/7871262/Kingsway.pdf/: 'In 1898 the LCC agreed a scheme for the development of a road linking Vernon Place in the north to the Aldwych in the south. This scheme completely altered the character and appearance of the area. The new road resulted in the demolition of the medieval street layout around the Aldwych as well as a complex 17th century street layout to the east of Drury Lane to create a north/south access route. The scheme meant the demolition of a very densely populated area, 3,700 residents were displaced from their homes. [...] The LCC created a broad avenue 30 metres wide [...] and described it as "the largest

cellars, half-ruined walls with smashed windows and torn wallpaper, stood out everywhere. The future streets were marked out by wooden hoardings plastered with colourful posters. Now, despite the late hour, the ruins were teeming with life. Black-dressed groups of men, women and children flowed in from all directions. From afar came the sharp beat of a drum and the blaring of brass instruments.

Several huge braziers filled with blazing coal that emitted heat on all sides stood in the square. Frozen people huddled around the braziers. Nearby, a cauldron was suspended from three rails, with something hissing and bubbling inside. Beside the cauldron stood men and women in uniforms. Some held brass instruments and drums, others faded banners of blue and red cloth with a yellow inscription: 'Fire or blood! What will you choose: hellfire or eternal salvation!'.[77]

In this time of unemployment, the Salvation Army had collected a lot of money from generous and tender-hearted people in order to distribute nightly bowls of oatmeal to the hungry. But while attending to the salvation of those who had lost their jobs, the Army treated them to very long sermons and very small cups of soup.

'Rejoice and sing!' shouted the precentor, a fat old man with a fleshy nose, dressed in a blue jacket over a red shirt. The brass instruments blared out. The soldiers began to beat their drums with all their might. The more they played, the livelier the tempo became. The young women struck up a religious hymn to a dance tune. In the language of the Salvation Army, this was called 'simplifying the Gospels'. The purpose of the dance tune was to raise the sinner's spirits and inspire him with hope.

'Livelier, livelier!', urged on the big-nosed precentor in the meantime. He shook his head, waved his arms about, then began to stamp his feet, wriggling his fat haunches.[78]

---

and most important improvement which has been carried out in London since the construction of Regent Street in 1820". It was opened in 1905 by Edward VII. [...] Most buildings were completed before 1914.'

[77] Compare the following description of the Salvation Army with Chukovsky's in 'Barrack-Room Philanthropy'. But compare it also with George Orwell's depiction of very similar scenes criticising charity that comes with religious strings attached in chapters 26 and 33 of *Down and Out in Paris and London* (1933; Oxford: Oxford University Press, 2021), as well as his unflattering comments about Salvation Army shelters in the same book.

[78] This is one of numerous such scenes in Shklovsky's (and Chukovsky's) Letters. See the Salvation Army's own collections in the 'Virtual Heritage Centre' for photographs of many of the elements described in such scenes: www.salvationarmy.org. uk/about-us/international-heritage-centre/virtual-heritage-centre and the extensive secondary literature on the Army. The Salvation Army was a favourite butt of satire and criticism not just for Russian journalists, of course, but for British humourists and social observers as well – see above all G. B. Shaw's play *Major Barbara* (London: A. Constable & Co., 1907).

The unemployed stood quietly and respectfully. They were waiting for the soup, afraid to stir lest they should be left with only the prayer and the dance, and no oatmeal. The orchestra fell silent. The crowd heaved a sigh of relief and moved a step closer to the cauldron; but it had been too hasty: there was the sermon to hear out first.

The precentor began to speak, like all English clergymen, with moans, with exclamations of the word *Lord*, with wearisome repetitions of the same sentence in divers tones. The sermon consisted of a commentary on the story of Samson. First, the precentor told of the life of the biblical hero and enumerated all of his exploits.

'And now let us see what lesson we can draw from Samson's life. Consider him first as a warrior of the Lord, for he was doubtless both a soldier and a captain. True, there are a few big, ugly stains on Samson's character; but as thousands of years have passed since that time, we should not be too exacting... And now that we have thoroughly scrutinised Samson's sins, I shall put the question to you: what feat have you performed? Have you done some great deed that you could only accomplish with the help of the Holy Spirit? Eh?' The preacher paused. The huge, dejected crowd remained silent, as if it were afraid that an incorrect answer would dash the hope of soup.

'Do your neighbours', the speaker continued, 'know anything favourable about you? Have you done some good worth mentioning? Have you killed a Philistine? Have you vanquished the enemies of the Lord? Have you won any victory over the Philistines that dwell in your soul? What have you done with them? If you have not yet killed these enemies, they are still living within you. You are permitting them, like Goliath, to walk free and to mock the hosts of the Lord. You must choose one or the other: either fire or blood, to wit, either the fires of hell or eternal salvation'.

The dejected crowd heaved a deep sigh. They were waiting for the soup to come at last.

'Sing hymn no. 42', shouted the big-nosed preacher. The drums rattled, the brass trumpets roared. The male and female soldiers of the Salvation Army started singing sullenly and discordantly from their hymnbooks:

> **There is a fountain filled with blood,**
> **Drawn from my Saviour's veins;**
> **And sinners plunged beneath that flood,**
> **Lose all their guilty stains.**[79]

---

[79] Shklovsky gives a Russian translation in parentheses. This is the first stanza of William Cowper's popular hymn 'There is a fountain filled with blood' (1772), which has many musical settings. However, either Shklovsky or the Salvation Army have substituted 'Saviour' for the original 'Immanuel' in the second line.

85

The singers were trying hard. The musicians strained to blow till they were blue in the face. The preacher now clicked his fingers, now smacked his lips, now shrugged his shoulders, and finally, to Onisko's great indignation, began to skip and hop.

'You're gaga, you loon!' Onisko shouted. Hatskel pulled sharply at his friend's jacket. At his companions' request, the little cobbler translated the sermon.

'No, I don't need any soup,' the tinker grew agitated. 'I'll leave. I cannot stand here.'

'Why not?' Benzion asked in amazement in Yiddish.[80]

'Your name means *son of Zion*', the old man said reproachfully, 'and you should know what the Talmud says about the daughter of Zion. There was once a man', he continued in chanting tones, 'who vowed to love a fair and loyal maid. For some time, the maid lived happily, and there was perfect accord between the bride and groom. But there came a time when the groom had to leave his bride and go away. And she waited for a long time; but the groom did not return. Her friends pitied her, and her rivals laughed at her. In mockery they would point at her and say: "He has left you and will never come back". And so the maid removed herself from them and in secret reread the letters the groom had written to her, those letters in which he pledged loyalty and devotion. And weeping she reread these letters, and she found solace in them, and then she would wipe away her tears and be consoled.

'And a joyful day dawned for her. Her beloved came back. And he learned how others had doubted his return and he asked the maid how she had retained her faith in him. And she showed him the letters in which the groom had vowed his loyalty.' The tinker's lips trembled; a tear rolled down his hollowed cheek and, like a lamb in the wood, disappeared in his grey beard.

'Israel!' he continued. 'In poverty, in captivity all the nations mocked you. They laughed at your hopes of rebirth. They scorned your wise men, and they spat at your righteous men. The daughter of Zion retreated into her schools and synagogues. She read the scriptures that the Lord had given her and had faith in His holy covenants. A day will come when the Lord will free you, daughter of Zion. And when He asks: "How could you have remained loyal, when all the nations mocked you?", she shall point to the Bible. "Was not Your Testament mine only joy?" the maid shall say. "Would not I have perished long ago from grief without it?".' The tinker began to cry and concluded in a quavering voice: 'Can I listen to these fools blaspheme the Testament – for a bowl of food? I am leaving'.

Hatskel, who had found the incomprehensible sermon boring, became interested, meanwhile, in a huge colourful poster that took up

[80]   Original has just 'jargon'.

an entire wooden hoarding.[81] The poster portrayed a gigantic Chinaman surrounded by a ring of squatting Chinese children.[82]

'Tell me, please, what is this?' he asked Benzion.

'A music hall, that is to say, a café chantant advert. A troupe of Chinese singers and dancers is performing there.'[83]

'Go on?' asked Hatskel with breathless curiosity.

'These Chinese are making big money. I read it in the paper. Good *job*!'[84]

Hatskel looked at the Chinaman and then a sudden thought struck the tailor – a pleasant one, it seems, because he started, burst out laughing and slapped himself on the knee!

'Oh, what an idea I've had!' he shouted. 'Gentlemen, let's go at once! To hell with all these charlatans and their soup!'

The company followed Hatskel obediently as he rubbed his hands together in glee.

'Oh, what an idea I've had!' he repeated. 'I read in a book that some Greek or Turk, or maybe an Armenian, can't remember now, came up with a clever notion when he got into a bath. In order not to forget, he jumped out immediately and ran straight home from the bathhouse stark naked, shouting in the street: "I've found it! I've found it!". Well, and I've found it too!'[85]

'So tell us already!' Onisko demanded.

'If there can be Chinese dancers, why not Russian ones? If the Chinese are making money in the music hall, why can't we make it too?' Hatskel answered with a question. 'I can sing. I know how to dance too. Benzion can sing. Blagovistnik can sing very well indeed. At night on the *Blücher* we listened to him spellbound. And I know rabbi Zelman was a cantor, so he must have a singing voice too. Let's put together a Russian troupe of singers and dancers. They flock to see some mangy Chinese. And how are we worse?'

Hatskel's project amazed everyone by its unexpectedness and eccentricity.

'We will sing Ukrainian songs.[86] And we have a teacher right here', Hatskel pointed to Blagovistnik, who gaped with astonishment.

[81] The secular and enterprising Hatskel is no more interested in his companion's Jewish sermon than in the Salvation Army's Christian one.

[82] Although 'Chinaman' is an ethnic slur, it is appropriate in context, especially given Hatskel's bright idea of capitalising on ethnic stereotypes.

[83] There were indeed such Chinese troupes of dancers performing in the London music hall in this period.

[84] As above, italicised words are Shklovsky's transliterations of English words into Russian, with a Russian translation provided in parentheses.

[85] Hatskel is embroidering the story of Archimedes, who is held to have shouted 'Eureka!' ('I have found it') after stepping into a bath.

[86] The original text here and in Hatskel's lines below has 'Little Russian' – see the explanation in note 5 above. It is a mystery why the majority-Jewish group decide

'How can I, an old man, play the buffoon?' the tinker asked at last. 'If you want to eat, you'll start singing in goose language, let alone Ukrainian!' Hatskel replied sententiously. 'And besides, why would we need to stay on the stage permanently? The winter will pass, the *slack* will be over, there'll be work; then you, rabbi Zelman, will go into a workshop, and you, Onisko, into a *furniture shop*. Then we'll quit the theatre. We just have to make shift to get through the winter. Is wandering the streets better than dancing on the stage? We won't be doing anything wicked if we sing.'

Hatskel's logic seemed convincing. In spite of all the eccentricity of the project, even the obstinate Onisko was swayed by the argument: 'If the Chinese can do it, why can't we?'.

'Listen, Hatskel,' the tinker remarked indecisively, half admitting defeat, 'But I speak Russian very badly'.

'Oh, nonsense! Who's going to care? Who can understand you here? Just sing well and say "la-la-la" instead of the words.'

The practical Onisko pointed out that they would need some 'money' to 'make good clothes';[87] but Hatskel had an answer ready for everything. Indeed, they would need costumes; but they could get the money from Kaun, the *middleman* with whom they had fallen in straight from the ship. Kaun, to put it bluntly, was a scoundrel, but he had a shrewd eye when it came to **business**. If he was promised a good share of the proceeds, and if he saw the business as profitable, then he would give the money for costumes.

'And we don't need much money', Hatskel expounded his plan, 'only for the cloth. It's cheap here. I am a tailor, after all, so I can sew any costumes you like myself. Benzion will cobble together some boots. Hooray! I wish it were morning already! We'll find Kaun. You'll see, we'll even manage to squeeze a shilling or three out of him for food. What do you think, Onisko, won't it be nice to drink some hot tea in a *coffee shop* of a cold morning? Eh? With a bun!'.

---

to try their luck pretending to be Russians/Ukrainians, when they could have made a living performing in the East End's thriving Yiddish theatre scene, such as the Pavilion Theatre and the Wonderland Music Hall in Whitechapel Road. Though it is less of a mystery if Hatskel is already planning to make his way outside the Jewish East End in the prosperous West End and other London music halls, where Slavic culture might have been more marketable than Jewish. See the article on 'The Pavilion Theatre and Wonderland, Whitechapel Road, Stepney' in *ArthurLloyd. co.uk*, www.arthurlloyd.co.uk/PavilionTheatreAndWonderlandWhitechapelRoad. htm and 'Music-Hall London' in Sims, *Living London 2*, 222–28 for a description of the Wonderland music hall where 'plays, songs, and sketches, [are] given first in Yiddish dialect and afterwards translated into more or less choice English' to an audience composed of 'greeners' and 'East-End "sweated" Jew toilers' (225). An example of a London Yiddish music hall song-sheet from c. 1903 may be seen in Mazower, 'London-New York, or The Great British Yiddish Theatre Brain Drain'.

87 The quoted words are in Ukrainian.

I won't recount in great detail the negotiations with Mr Kaun, who did indeed turn out to have a shrewd eye for *business*. First, he put them through an examination: Hatskel hastily knocked off a Cossack dance, while Onisko sang in a deep bass

> Oh, why haven't you come
> As I asked you,
> The candle was burning all evening
> By the bed.[88]

The tinker also sang very well, albeit in an oriental manner, with plaintive modulations, but in tune and pleasantly. The gloomy Benzion gave every hope of becoming as lively a dancer as Hatskel. After the examination, Mr Kaun knitted his brows imposingly and thrust out his lips.

'Yes!' he said finally, adjusting his pince-nez. 'Not bad, but you need some lady singers. At least two. The manager will not accept a troupe without them. Find the ladies and show them to me. If they're acceptable, I'll give you three pounds for the costumes and have a chat with the manager.'

The troupe very nearly despaired, but then Hatskel remembered Miss Golda and Miss Pearl, who had arrived in London together with him.

The young women were just then running out of work: they had completed a large consignment of waistcoats and *slack*, with all the horrors of hunger, was looming ahead. They agreed to join the troupe at once. Hatskel brought them to Mr Kaun, who was quite pleased with their singing and dancing (the young women took a turn together with Hatskel), but here everything nearly fell apart.

'Misses, for the stage, you'll need to sew yourselves some costumes that are different from the kind the Russians wear: you need knee-length skirts, and the blouses should be open at the top up to here.'

Miss Golda and Miss Pearl stated categorically that they were 'honest girls' and would rather starve than show themselves in public with bare shoulders and in short skirts. Some protracted bargaining over bodices and skirts followed, and finally a compromise was achieved: the young women stood out for blouses buttoned up to the throat but accepted the short skirts. Everything was settled.

'Well, and what will you call your troupe?' asked Kaun after having negotiated thirty per cent from each performance for himself.

'You are the oldest one among us, rabbi Zelman,' answered Hatskel. 'You tinplated samovars, so let it be "Samovaroff's Russian Troupe".' Everyone agreed to this.

---

[88] Most likely a Ukrainian folk song (original not found). Shklovsky's original text is in Ukrainian.

Rehearsals started the following day. And two weeks later, Mr Kaun talked it over with the manager, and 'Samovaroff's Troupe' secured an engagement at a music hall in Cambridge Road, Whitechapel.[89]

VI.

'If you want to eat, you'll start singing in goose language, let alone Ukrainian!' This aphorism of Hatskel's was on the minds of all the members of 'The Samovaroff Troupe of Russian Singers and Dancers' – **'The Samovaroffs'**, as the bill proclaimed – when with beating hearts and clutching the bundles containing their costumes to their breasts, they approached the actors' entrance of the music hall in Cambridge Road.

'Dance, you poor devil, as the master commands!' Onisko shrugged hopelessly and clicked his tongue.[90]

'Well, what do you expect?' the tinker immediately guessed his meaning. 'What choice have I but to dance when no-one needs my hands! I understand you very well, Mr Blagovistnik! Do you think it's easy for me, at forty-five years of age, an honest craftsman and not the least of Talmud scholars, to dance and be a jester? I already have a granddaughter, sir!' the tinker shook his head dolefully.

Miss Golda and Miss Pearl shivered as in a fever and walked with downcast eyes, clinging to each other timidly. Benzion was grim, frowning bitterly, and his lower lip quivered repeatedly. Only Hatskel comported himself with an unusual, not entirely natural swagger.

The actors' entrance was not easy to reach. Nearby, around the corner, were the doors leading to the '*pit*', i.e. down into the stalls, where the

89 This is most likely the Forester's Music Hall in Cambridge (now Cambridge Heath) Road, Bethnal Green, famous at the beginning of the century for its 'trial turns', as recalled in numerous music hall histories and memoirs, e.g. Leon M. Lion's *The Surprise of My Life: The Lesser Half of an Autobiography* (London: Hutchinson & Co., 1948), 71: 'No "turn" could get a showing save through some agent [...] my most thrilling adventure was the "try-out" at the "Foresters" in the far remote East End. I was to supply the playlet, the scene, the rest of the cast, and myself, at an all-in emolument of twenty-five pounds, subject to 10 per cent.' See also Walter Macqueen-Pope's *The Melodies Linger On: The Story of the Music Hall* (London: W. H. Allen, 1950) and Clarkson Rose's *With a Twinkle in My Eye* (London: Museum Press, 1951). According to an article by Ronald Mayes printed in a programme for 'Dirty Work' at the Aldwych Theatre in 1932 (quoted at 'Foresters Music Hall, 93 Cambridge Heath Road, Bethnal Green, London', *ArthurLloyd. co.uk*, www.arthurlloyd.co.uk/Foresters.htm), the 'trial turns' were instituted for one matinee each week by the MacNaghten Vaudeville Circuit, which took over the Hall in the early 1900s. Here aspiring performers had their 'auditions' with critical audiences, 'and if they were not pleased, the curtain was very quickly rung down upon the unfortunate artiste. In this way the circuit was able to acquire talent for their theatres.' An illustration of the auditorium and stage of Forester's Music Hall may be seen at www.arthurlloyd.co.uk/FrankMacNaghten.htm.

90 An old Ukrainian proverb. Shklovsky's original text is in Ukrainian.

cheapest seats are to be found in English popular theatres. Here stood the audience, already lined up in pairs in an endless queue. For the most part, these were young people in tweed caps, with bright silk cravats which served them for both collar and tie. Here also stood sailors, soldiers in bright red coats, and lads who came, it seemed, from the docks. The men had come with their **sweethearts**,[91] young women in enormous hats with bright feathers of incredible colours. They shrieked often in response to their young men's witticisms or in sheer delight.

Rain started to pour, as heavily as from a watering pot. The crowd opened their umbrellas, but their buoyant mood was not dampened in the least. Then appeared those who wanted to wrangle something out of this good-humoured throng that had assembled to amuse itself.

Four 'minstrels' dressed up as negroes came up and – butchering the language – began to sing comic verses.[92] Some cleanly dressed, sleek, well-fed man with the face of an actor started doing impressions of Napoleon, Chamberlain, Lord Beaconsfield, Gladstone,[93] and then of an old lady who fell asleep in church and swallowed a fly. The man pulled all his props, viz. an old hat, a bonnet, and several fake beards and moustaches, from his side pocket.

'Why so glum?' Hatskel fidgeted nervously. 'You should look at this man! This, people say, is a real actor. He was earning good money on the stage. And now he's unemployed. He has no home. So there he is, playing the buffoon in the street. Hell! What a machine London is! If you're brave and know how to wait for your moment and jump well, you'll rise to the very top. But miss out on your luck just a bit, and the wheel will cut you to pieces, spew you out like a rag, and no-one will even notice that a human being has disappeared!' But here the sententious speech was cut short.

91 See the 'London Sweethearts' chapter, including illustrations of behatted girls strolling with a soldier and a lad, in Sims, *Living London* 2, 15–21.
92 For the minstrelsy context in these years, see Jeffrey Green, '*In Dahomey* in London in 1903', *The Black Perspective in Music* 11.1 (Spring 1983), 22–24 and his 'Minstrelsy' in *The Oxford Companion to Black British History* (Oxford: Oxford University Press, 2007), www.oxfordreference.com/view/10.1093/acref/9780192804396.001.0001/acref-9780192804396-e-271. See also Michael Pickering, *Blackface Minstrelsy in Britain* (Aldershot: Ashgate, 2008), George F. Rehin, 'Blackface Street Minstrels in Victorian London and Its Resorts: Popular Culture and Its Racial Connotations as Revealed in Polite Opinion', *The Journal of Popular Culture* 15.1 (Summer 1981), 19–38, and Simon Featherstone, 'The Blackface Atlantic: Interpreting British Minstrelsy', *Journal of Victorian Culture* 3.2 (1998), 234–51.
93 All political figures, including Disraeli and Gladstone, the two famous Victorian prime ministers, and Joseph Chamberlain, Secretary of State for the Colonies until 1903 and leading proponent of tariff reform (see Chukovsky's articles and Shklovsky's later in the anthology).

The doors into the *'pit'* were opened, and the queue began to crawl inside. Here finally was an opportunity to reach the actors' entrance. In two minutes, the Samovaroff troupe was already in the dressing room, and in a few minutes more they were fully made-up and changed. And now they huddled together in the wings, waiting for the director's signal.[94] The would-be singers quailed fearfully listening to the laughter, the female shrieks and the whistles coming from the half-lit auditorium beyond the curtain. Even Hatskel, who had constantly put on a brave face, was now stroking with a trembling hand the long Cossack moustache that had just been pasted there. Blagovistnik spread his legs and hung his head so his whole figure expressed complete helplessness. The tinker, whose cheeks had been heavily rouged and beard blackened, and who had been provided with a shaggy wig, swayed to and fro as if in prayer and whispered something. Miss Golda and Miss Pearl were shaking with fear and, at the same time, burning up with shame: they kept squatting to make their skirts, which barely covered their knees, seem longer. Benzion was still as gloomy as a storm cloud. It is worth saying a few words about the troupe's costumes. The tinker was kitted out in a coachman's plush sleeveless jacket edged with braid, baggy velvet Cossack trousers with golden braiding, and tall lacquered boots. The rest of the men wore fantastical Ukrainian costumes that had been decorated, for added brilliancy, with lots of sparkling braid. The young women were given Hussar boots with spurs, short skirts, Spanish bolero jackets trimmed with galloons and small bells, and for their heads something resembling a huge traditional Russian headdress, about a foot and a half high.[95]

Past them walked acrobats ready for the stage, with large shawls thrown over their leotards for warmth; red-nosed clowns in long baggy trousers and frockcoats, with tiny top hats perched on their ginger wigs; some people decked out as either Turks or Moors, in white robes, green satin bloomers and red jackets. The fat snub-nosed director in tails and white tie, with an enormous fake diamond on his shirtfront collar stud,[96] who was bustling about on stage, noticed the despondent 'Samovaroff Troupe' and threw them a few words in passing, of which Hatskel understood only '**Cheer up!**'.

'What is he saying?' asked Blagovistnik.

---

[94] For a visual depiction of a similar scene, see the photograph 'Waiting to Go On (Royal Music-Hall)' in Sims, *Living London* 2, 223.

[95] Shklovsky uses Russian measures ('vershok') and dress terms ('kokoshnik') that have no direct equivalents in English. The costumes underline the absurdity of the act, with Jews donning the national costumes of their traditional oppressors.

[96] Compare Oscar Wilde's description of a theatre entrepreneur in a poor district of London in *The Picture of Dorian Gray* (1891; London: Penguin, 2003), who also has 'an enormous diamond blaz[ing] in the centre of a soiled shirt' (49).

'He says we shouldn't lose our nerve. We should be braver because we are certain to be a success', Benzion translated. 'The director also says that Miss Golda's and Miss Pearl's singing will be especially well received.'

'My God!' sighed Blagovistnik. 'I'd rather there were Turks or Tatars sitting there with their guns than Englishmen! Fighting in a war is probably not as hard as dancing and singing!'

Presently it became a lot lighter backstage. The curtain was raised, and all the chandeliers in the auditorium sparkled. Samovaroff's troupe felt their legs buckle under them with fright, as if they were made of cotton wool. Peering from the wings, the dancers could see the huge auditorium directly in front of them, and the thousands of attentive eyes and sweaty faces whose expression seemed to Hatskel incredibly malicious and expectant. The thought, 'They're lying in wait for us', struck Hatskel inexplicably. The audience was indeed somewhat out of temper. Firstly, many had been unable to find seats in the *'pit'*; secondly, a slight misunderstanding had arisen between the sailors and the soldiers. The kind of atmosphere was brewing that on the Continent, where the police patrol theatres, blows up into an outright confrontation accompanied by police reports, and in England, where 'bobbies' have no right to enter theatres, usually concludes with a few extra police whistles.

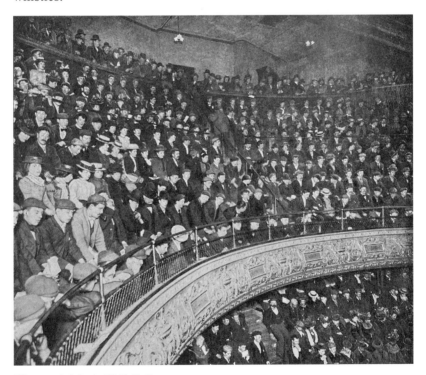

Fig. 13. A Music Hall Gallery.

93

Several disgruntled spectators began to catcall an oriental magician for no good reason when one plate he let roll over an open umbrella wobbled slightly.[97] But the rest of the audience shouted to the catcallers: **'It is not fair play. Give him a chance!'**. And the magician really did take his chance! Several more plates went rolling over the open umbrella, with water pouring and fire blazing from them in turn. The candles in the candelabra now flared up, now went out, now turned into plants, now into live doves. Those who had been shouting '**give him a chance!**' were now applauding, especially when the magician's assistant, a red-nosed clown in an excessively long coat, took all the candles and ate them. The discontented ones were silent. They were no longer catcalling, but neither did they applaud. The irritation had not dissipated; it had only been internalised. The next turn gave the discontented ones even fewer grounds for catcalling. The programme listed the number as 'The Laziest Juggler in the World'. Indeed, when the curtain rose, the juggler was lying in bed, wrapped head to toe in a blanket. An alarm clock on the bedside table rang shrilly. 'The laziest juggler in the world' woke up, stuck his head out from under the blanket, grabbed a slipper, smacked the alarm clock so that it shattered to pieces, and again crawled under his blanket. Applause rang out in the auditorium. Some women even squealed with excitement. The juggler then left his bed and, still in his night clothes, began to search for something under the bedstead and in the drawer of the bedside table. There were more squeals. The sluggard finally found what he was looking for – the slipper, and then began to toss up first a washbasin, then a jug and plates. It did not go well. The juggler was still sleepy, and he took every chance to climb under the blanket – to the spectators' great delight. The washbasin and jug would fall to the floor, and the juggler would jump out of bed and smash them with a hammer. And the more fragments were scattered on the stage, the wilder grew the public's enthusiasm. The lazy juggler then put on a moustache and beard of twisted wire, tossed up several turnips and caught them on his moustache. Then he asked someone from the audience to throw him a turnip, so he could catch it on his moustache too. But the turnip struck the juggler on the forehead instead of the moustache, and he collapsed. All his undergarments came apart, and the juggler was left in his leotard. The orchestra drums rolled. The juggler, holding up his drooping underwear, clambered back under the blanket. Prolonged applause followed.

Meanwhile, the misunderstanding in the '*pit*' between the soldiers and sailors continued to grow. Some shaven sailor, in the widest of trousers dangling over his boots like the hems of a skirt, was trying to convince a soldier, laced as tightly as if he were wearing a corset, that stealing

---

97   For a vivid description of pre-war music hall oriental magic acts, see J. B. Priestley's *Lost Empires* (London: Heinemann, 1965).

other people's 'sweethearts' was a dirty trick. The sailor had just returned from Valparaiso and met his sweetheart in the music hall on the arm of the soldier. There were those who took the side of the sailor. There were also those who defended the soldier. In the street or in a square, the misunderstanding would have been quickly resolved by a good boxing match; but in the '*pit*', professional honour and the presence of 'sweethearts' did not permit of any fighting. The discontent accumulated and looked for release. Both the sailors and the soldiers would have welcomed it now if someone on stage embarrassed himself, flopped shamefully, so that he could be jeered, deafened with catcalls, pelted with apples, potatoes, rotten eggs and tomatoes. The third turn, meanwhile, also failed to act as a lightning-rod. Two wrestlers in leotards and shorts akin to swimming trunks stepped

Fig. 14. Ahmed Madrali.

out on stage. The shorts of one wrestler were sewn from an American flag, and of the other from red cloth with crescent moons. These were the heroes of London's popular music halls: the American strongman Billy Pipkin and the 'Terrible Turk' Ahmed Madrali, 'champion of His Majesty the Sultan Abdul Hamid'.[98] The wrestlers shook each other's hands and then entwined and began to squeeze one another. An English crowd can spend hours admiring a match. The soldiers and sailors forgot their quarrel for the time being and watched the wrestling with baited breath. Only broken exclamations could be heard.

---

[98]   Ahmed Madrali was a well-known Turkish wrestler of the period (and not the first to be promoted as 'The Terrible Turk'), but no Billy Pipkin appears in the list of Madrali's opponents on the Wrestling Data website, so he is probably one of Shklovsky's fictional characters. See 'Ahmed Madrali', *WrestlingData. com*, www.wrestlingdata.com/index.php?befehl=bios&wrestler=5933&bild=0&de tails=10. In 1904, Madrali lost the world wrestling championship match at Olympia to a Russian. He appeared on the front cover of *The Tatler* on 3 February 1904.

'Go on Billy.'

'Push, Ahmed! Don't be shy.'

But now Billy squeezed the Turk as if in an iron band and lifted him up. The American's face went blue with the dreadful exertion, his biceps tensed like balls, and he threw his opponent to the floor.

'Knock out!' someone shouted in the auditorium.

'Not yet! Hardly! Only one shoulder is touching the floor.'

Billy fell upon the Turk with all his immense weight, trying to press both of his shoulders, as per the rules, to the ground. Ahmed struggled. His black eyes flashed angrily, his teeth were bared. It seemed that two troglodytes were engaged in mortal combat. But now something completely unexpected happened. The Turk made an inhuman effort, tossed the American up, flung himself on top and pressed him to the floor. Billy was carried offstage in a faint, and water was poured over him.

The audience in the auditorium applauded, shouted *hurray* in honour of the Turk, and women shrieked with delight...

'Samovaroff's Troupe, get ready!' shouted the director. Both the men and the women felt their hearts sink suddenly. Meanwhile, the curtain was raised again, and the orchestra played a ritournelle. To these sounds the whole Samovaroff troupe was supposed to jump out whistling and whooping (the director believed that war cries behoved Russian singers as much as Red Indians). Hatskel was to dance squatting from the wings to the footlights, followed by Benzion, Blagovistnik and then the tinker with a large tambourine in his hands. The men were instructed to line up before the footlights and await Miss Golda and Miss Pearl, who were supposed to run up to them, shaking their heads playfully, with arms akimbo.[99] Then they were meant to sing. All of this had been rehearsed many times, and notwithstanding their fierce terror, was not gone from the troupe's memory. When the ritournelle finished and the conductor gave a tap with his baton, Hatskel, with the desperate resolve of a rabbit who knows he has no choice but to fire a pistol, shut his eyes tightly, whooped and leapt out on stage, arms akimbo. He did not hear either Benzion's whoop or the tinker's tambourine. All these sounds were drowned out, like the clatter of horses' hooves is drowned out by rolls of thunder. Something terrible had happened. The disgruntled sailors and soldiers had found an object of hate. The pent-up irritation which had been accumulating all evening poured out. It had already been condensed by the sight of the fighting men. So when the Samovaroff troupe appeared on stage, a violent, vicious cry of 'Off with them! Don't want 'em!' resounded in the auditorium. Those shouting dimly understood that they needed some reason in order to hurl hateful insults at these strangely apparelled people who had only just emerged from

---

[99] Shklovsky is describing the moves of traditional Russian folk dances.

96

the wings. And the pretext was found as swiftly as the torrent of hate had burst forth. 'Kishinev! Kishinev!' shouted the mob.

Hatskel shifted his feet in one spot. Blagovistnik spread his arms widely, as if asking the audience: 'why?'. The tinker stood as if struck by lightning and quietly murmured the words of the prayer: 'Hearken, Israel, our Lord is the One God!'. And the audience was beginning to enjoy the row more and more. A thousand throats were intoning: 'Off the stage with them!'. Apples, oranges and baked potatoes flew like hailstones.

Someone hurled a stick onto the stage. Someone flung an open jack-knife of the kind that English sailors usually carry. Things could have taken a serious turn, so the curtain was lowered. The panting director ordered the orchestra to play '**Rule Britannia**'. At first, nothing could be made out; but then the sounds of the patriotic song had their calming effect. When the crowd had quietened down, the director announced that 'The Samovaroff Troupe' would not perform, in accordance with the audience's wishes. This announcement was met with loud applause.[100]

In the wings, the Samovaroff troupe stood stupefied. Then Miss Golda and Miss Pearl burst into bitter tears.

'But why? How did we offend them?' Onisko began at last.[101]

'You, Blagovistnik, are a Christian, and that's why when you get a beating you try to find out what exactly for', Hatskel answered bitterly. 'But we've been used to this for the last two thousand years.'

'What were they shouting?' the tinker asked.

'You see,' Benzion explained sarcastically, 'In Kishinev, they beat us for being Jews, and here they beat us to stick up for us.'[102]

---

[100]   See the account in Stephen Weissman's *Chaplin: A Life* (New York: Arcade Publishing, 2008), ch. 11 of Chaplin's equally violent reception in the same place two years later: 'After the first couple of jokes, the audience started throwing coins and orange peels and stamping their feet and booing.' Chaplin tried a 'comic Jew' act at Forester's Music Hall in 1906 (he recalled later that 'Jewish comedians were all the rage') and was also booed off the stage. According to Weissman, 'New acts were usually required to perform at "trial turn" matinees before they were given a regular booking', but as Chaplin had already done a successful Irish act at Forester's, the management gave him an 'unpaid tryout on their regular bill'. Weissman characterises the audience at Forester's as largely working-class religious Jews (and Irish) rather than 'rowdy Aldershot soldiers who had reeked of beer and delighted in baiting [Chaplin's] mother for the sport of it'.

[101]   Cf. Pearl's and Golda's words in the first section of the Letter.

[102]   Benzion is referring to the Kishinev pogrom of April 1903, which received massive sensational press coverage in Europe and America and elicited much sympathy for the Jewish plight from the Western public. See Steven J. Zipperstein's *Pogrom: Kishinev and the Tilt of History* (New York: Liveright Publishing Corporation, 2018) and Rosenberg 92, quoting Rudolf Rocker, on the '25,000 immigrant Jews [who] marched from the East End to a protest rally in Hyde Park after a pogrom in Kishinev in 1903 left 49 Jews dead, approximately 500 wounded and 2,000

The girls were crying more and more bitterly. Clowns, gymnasts and magicians surrounded the Russian troupe. They all sympathised with the predicament of colleagues who were driven from the stage without even being given a chance to prove themselves.

'**Cheer up!**' shouted the fat director, rolling up to them. 'Things can still be mended. The entrepreneur says that if the audience hadn't gone as mad as March hares, you'd have been a great success. **Cheer up, misses! Cheer up, old chap!**', he slapped the tinker, who had still not dared to let go of the tambourine, on the shoulder. 'I have some good news for you. Tomorrow you'll perform at a different [illegible] music hall in North London. There you'll most likely prove a success. And now the entrepreneur wants you to go to the cashier and get your ten shillings each. **Cheer up!**'

And the Samovaroff troupe did indeed cheer up. Ten shillings, in any case, was already something that, even with a poor knowledge of English, one could easily turn into a dinner and a night's lodging. And ahead of them more guaranteed dinners and lodgings beckoned...

The experienced entrepreneur was not mistaken. The Samovaroff Troupe was indeed a great success. At present, however, only Hatskel, Miss Golda and Miss Pearl remain of the original members. Hatskel now dresses like a dandy, is partial to red waistcoats with black spots and inserts 'we artistes' before every other word. Onisko Blagovistnik works at a furniture workshop, earns thirty-five shillings a week, is quite content, has opened an account at a savings bank and is conducting negotiations with the 'Jewish Cook' to send for his wife and children from Shirokaya Greblya. The tinker has found a job at a factory that makes tins for preserves. On Saturdays, you can see him in a top hat and a black frockcoat with a red handkerchief peeking out of the back pocket. The tinker is great friends with Blagovistnik. Benzion used his very first savings to buy a ticket and leave for Canada. He has his own wide-ranging plans, which I may tell you about one day.

---

homeless [...] "the onlookers [...] took off their hats to the marchers"'. It should be recalled that Hatskel is from Kishinev.

II

LONDON LABOUR AND THE
LONDON POOR

Fig. 15. Postcard, Early Twentieth Century: 'London Life. Coster in His Donkey Cart at Covent Garden Market'.

Korney Chukovsky, 'Nischie v Londone' ['Beggars in London'] *Odesskie Novosti*, 17 December 1903

London
(From our own correspondent)
24 December

A long building. A dim lantern swings in the wind above the gates, and the yellow spot of its light dances on the board nailed to them.

A man exhausted by hunger, damp and enforced idleness, dirty and bedraggled, comes up to that board in the night and reads:

'Anyone who is shelterless, hungry or in need of medical assistance, come right in. The doors are open day and night.'

The man reads this and walks on. He walks past libraries, art galleries, charitable institutions, museums – past everything that has been gained by centuries of suffering for his happiness, and makes his way to the Thames, above which tower majestically the patterned Houses of Parliament.

There he stands, his teeth rattling, looking long into the distance, to the other bank of the river, where a thousand factory chimneys noisily spew forth red masses of fire into the empty sky – also in the name of his human happiness.

And as if in mockery of all these caring institutions, the following morning his cold blue corpse is dragged from the Thames, no longer in need of any acts of Parliament, any workhouse charity, or any thundering of factory wheels.

What does this mean?

A liberal-minded man would find it easy to explain all this in approximately the following way:

The pauper did not go to the workhouse because anyone who makes use of the hospitality of such a house loses his right to vote. And a Briton values his right to vote so highly that he would rather part with his life than with that.

As for Parliament, it proved unable to keep the suicidal man from taking his life because it failed to pass this or that law. (The liberal man even knows which ones.)

And so on. It turns out that you only need to change one or two screws in the huge machinery of state, and all will be well in this green isle. That is why the people here only ever trouble themselves about these screws, and it never occurs to them to think of destroying the machinery and replacing it with a new one. An Englishman – in the words of the poet –

... has determined, calculated and measured everything;
All that is needful is about him, and so cleverly arranged,
That he shall be laughed to scorn who is impudent enough to disbelieve

That this is the life that everyone must lead.[1]

It is about one of these 'screws' – the fight against mendicancy – that I wish to tell you today. This subject is the most topical in the run-up to Christmas.

It is common knowledge that mendicancy is strictly forbidden in England. Only cripples have the right to lay a verbal claim to your pocket. But prohibition does not mean eradication, which is why you will nowhere see so many beggars as in the streets of London. And because of the parliamentary ban, begging has to be camouflaged by various pretexts, so that lying has become nearly synonymous with it. So how can one combat this lying?

It would seem logical to destroy the cause of the evil – namely, the parliamentary ban. But no. A new and additional screw is inserted into the machine, while the old one is left fully intact. I mean a secret police agency charged with eradicating deceit and feigned illness amongst the beggars.

This, of course, only makes the denizens of the London slums even more skilled at their art, and soon a whole school of sham self-mutilation emerges, which produces its own geniuses, its own heroes, its own charter, and so on.

The head of the Society for the suppression of '**Mendacity in Mendicity**' has been, until lately, Mr Joseph Bosley,[2] and I shall now quote from a conversation with him:

'Are there any cases of deliberate bodily harm for the purposes of mendicity?'

'Oh, they are very frequent. All Londoners remember the man who had sat for twenty years on **Blackfriars Bridge**, showing his leg covered in ulcers. He produced these ulcers by applying an ordinary brass penny

---

[1]   Quotation from the poem 'On the Island' (1861) by Nikolay Scherbina (1821–1869), a nineteenth-century Russian poet who lived in Ventnor on the Isle of Wight in 1861.

[2]   Joseph Bosley, referred to as the 'Beggars' Terror' or 'Champion Beggar Hunter' by the *Daily Mail*, was an officer of the Mendicity Society, founded in 1818 for the suppression of begging via the carrot and stick of charity and prosecution. He appears from the 1880s onwards in numerous local and national newspaper reports of beggar convictions for various ingenious forms of fraud and trickery, including cross-dressing; he retired in 1904 and died in 1908. His obituary in the *Daily Mail* ('Tramps' Terror', 22 May 1908, 3) refers to several of the examples Chukovsky gives here, including 'a sheep's tongue in pickle', the £300, and the 'Soapsuds King'. The 'Soapy Fits King' was the subject of articles himself circa 1900; so were pavement artists, etc. The conjunction of the words 'mendacity' and 'mendicity' appears quite frequently in articles about begging fraud from the mid-nineteenth century to the 1910s and the phenomenon provided excellent material for fiction. Arthur Conan Doyle's Sherlock Holmes story 'The Man with the Twisted Lip', *Strand Magazine*, December 1891, for instance, turns on the prosperous living to be made from sham begging in London.

to his scratches. He died of it not long ago.'

'But most of the time, their ailments are completely simulated, aren't they?'

'Yes. There are masses of fake blind beggars, fake dumb ones, lame ones... Do you remember the case of **Hurley**, the beggar who shammed a fit by using Pears soap to generate foam at the mouth?[3] He is in a workhouse now. But I am keeping an eye on a couple of chaps like him, who are still at large', **Mr** Bosley added portentously...

Fig. 16. The 'Soap Fit' Dodge.

'...There was another man who simulated epilepsy. He had sewn a horseshoe into the lining of his hat, and when he banged his head against the pavement, people thought that his head was about to split open. We put him away in an appropriate facility, too.'

'And what about those mendicants who exhibit in the street the pictures they have drawn depicting their sufferings – could it be that they are lying as well?'

'Most certainly so, all of them! In the first instance, they all paint the same thing. Each of us has seen dozens of "cripples" who depict themselves lying under chloroform, their leg being amputated – and all the doctors are arranged in the same order, they all have red faces, and so on. It is obvious that all these pictures were made by the same individual for all of them.'

'Well, I saw a dumb man the other day who was showing everyone his own amputated tongue in a bottle of spirits. Could that be a fraud too?'

'A most brazen one. We had one such dumb man with us recently. He proved a lively talker soon enough, and his tongue turned out to be...'

'What?...'

---

3   According to *The Standard* of 22 September 1900, the man's name was Peter McDermott and he was tried as a 'rogue and vagabond'.

'An ordinary oyster, slightly dyed... Oh, their tricks are beyond count... For instance, recently I encountered this kind of professional: he carries around a jar with some tinted liquid, trying to get into the thick of a crowd so someone bumps into him. The jar falls to the ground and the liquid spills out. He turns to the person who pushed him:
"Recompense the poor man for his medicine!"
'And they pay. They pay a lot...
'And here is another trick – of an entirely innocent kind. A poor woman, ragged in the extreme, goes with a sealed envelope from one post office to another. Everywhere she asks for a stamp and offers money – but who would think of taking money from a poor woman! Everywhere they give her the stamp for free, and that's precisely what she is angling for.'
'So how much can a professional beggar make in a year?'
'Oh, not nearly as much as they say. In my twenty years of "practice", I've only come across one man who could "earn" £300 a year (about 3,000 roubles). The rest by their lying, by their endless vigils in the cold, by their humiliations, barely manage to prolong a hungry and dark existence...'
I have quoted only a part of the conversation with Mr Bosley, but the reader can easily ascertain from it how powerless are bans of any kind in the fight against a whole way of life...

Korney Chukovsky, 'Buterbrodnie Lyudi' ['Sandwich Men']
Odesskie Novosti, 24 December 1903

London
(From our own correspondent)
28 December

At Christmas everything here froze over: no post, no horse trams, no people. The whole of London was eating pudding and singing:

God bless all merry English[men]!
May nothing them dismay.[1]

This deliberate merrymaking, conscientiously timed for the 25th, was very tedious, which is why I was genuinely delighted to get the opportunity on the third day of Christmas to visit a sandwich dinner.

A sandwich is, basically, bread and butter.[2] But in London slang, this word is used to designate special people who, like bread with butter, are covered with boards for pasting bills. These boards are attached to an iron ring through which the sandwich men put their heads. A third board is attached to the same ring on little metal mounts and placed above the sandwich man's head. All of this is extremely cumbersome, unwieldy and, above all, unnecessary, since all the pavements, house walls, omnibuses and restaurant tablecloths have already been appropriated by advertisers. But the same hidebound resistance to change that prompts the English to install door hammers when there are electric bells, to use wooden staircases when fires and the costliness of wood might have suggested to them the idea of iron ones – that same resistance daily makes them saddle this unnecessary yoke on the necks of many thousands of people.

I could never look at these toilers without pain. They walk past in a long file, one after another, with a slow, funereal pace. They cannot stand still, they must forever keep moving, forever keep shoving their boards in the faces of passers-by. The ring weighs down the shoulders, the head keeps jerking, there is no possibility of straightening out or

---

[1]   Chukovsky provides a Russian translation in parentheses. This is clearly a variation on the traditional Christmas carol 'God rest you merry, gentlemen, / Let nothing you dismay.'

[2]   The original reads, literally, 'a sandwich [transliterated from English] is a sandwich [Russian 'buterbrod' (from German *butterbrot*)]'. The following explanation of the phrase's origin is wrong because Chukovsky's understanding of what a sandwich consists of is Russian/German (a slice of bread topped with butter) rather than English (two pieces of bread with filling). The sandwich man, of course, is the filling in the sandwich, with the boards acting as bread. Contemporary depictions of sandwich men were legion, see the illustration 'Sandwich Man (Trafalgar Square)' in William Nicholson, *London Types* (London: William Heinemann, 1898).

taking any rest throughout the whole day. But the main torment is the humiliating incongruity between the placard-bearer and his placard.

A poster depicts lavish delicacies from a fashionable restaurant – while the sandwich man is hungry and gaunt.

A poster proclaims the virtue of the excellent Peter Robinson lacquered boots – while the sandwich man sports on his feet some kind of sieve instead of shoes.[3] A poster reminds us that *The Merry Wives of Windsor* is on today at the Garrick Theatre – the sandwich man is sullen, wretched, and the word 'merry' on his poster seems like a cruel mockery.[4]

The Liberal Sunday paper *Reynolds's Newspaper* had raised a hue and cry long before the holidays, beseeching its readers to aid these unfortunate souls. The aid was meant to take the form of a Christmas dinner.[5] A Christmas dinner is a sacred thing in England. Suffice it to say that when Englishmen wish to curse someone roundly, they exclaim: 'God grant you are left without a Christmas dinner!'

Many responded to the call. The Queen donated twenty pounds. Several thousand were raised. And *Reynolds's Newspaper* was able to invite 1,500 sandwich men to Lambeth. (Lambeth is the poorest part of London, where nearly all the sandwich men stay.)

When I arrived at the Lambeth Baths building,[6] I found the feast in full swing. Long tables are populated with bent figures. The accommodation in the bathhouse is rather cramped, there is nowhere to take off one's coat, so those who come in their coats keep them on at table.

3   Peter Robinson was a well-known department store in Oxford Street throughout the Victorian and Edwardian periods.
4   A photograph of a similar scene, with a sandwich man carrying bills advertising the play *Cynthia* at Wyndham's Theatre, London, which ran from mid-May to early June 1904, may be seen in Jennifer Newton, 'Life Before the Great War: Incredible Black-and-White Images from a Grand Tour of Europe in 1904', *MailOnline*, 21 September 2018, www.dailymail.co.uk/travel/travel_news/article-6189675/Incredible-black-white-images-grand-tour-Europe-1904.html.
5   For a different take on the *Reynolds's Newspaper* Christmas dinner for sandwich men, see Shklovsky's 'Father Christmas' in part III below. The tradition of putting on Christmas dinners for paupers in workhouses, for instance – and the tradition of criticising and satirising such philanthropy – were both well-established by the time Chukovsky was writing, see e.g. Laura Foster, 'Christmas in the Workhouse: Staging Philanthropy in the Nineteenth-Century Periodical', *Journal of Victorian Culture* 22.4 (December 2017), 553–78.
6   Chukovsky is referring to the Lambeth Corporation Baths built in 1897 at the junction of Lambeth Road and Kennington Road, see the 1898 photograph of 'Lambeth Baths and Washhouses, Kennington Road, Lambeth', Lambeth Archives, *Lambeth Landmark*, https://boroughphotos.org/lambeth/lambeth-baths-and-washhouses-kennington-road-lambeth-2/. There was an older building behind Westminster Bridge Road. The '*Reynolds's* Sandwichmen's Fund' organised a Christmas 'Dinner and Entertainment' at the Prince's Hall, New Lambeth Baths every year.

Fig. 17. 'Reynolds's' Sandwichmen's Fund.

But not many are labouring under this inconvenience, as only two or three per cent possess such a luxury. Each man's hat is under his chair. Behind the chairs are waiters in black tailcoats, fastidiously distributing the steaming victuals to their grubby patrons.

The orchestra is blaring Christmas hymns. Everyone is chewing intently. The organisers of the dinner wish their guests a happy Christmas, shake their hands, praise their hard work – and all of it with such tact and warmth that the initial unease quickly evaporates – and the hum of general conversation soon resounds across the table.

I had taken a seat next to one of the old men, and after exchanging a few general phrases I learned that each sandwich man earns one shilling a day in summer and 1s. 2d. in winter. Which is exactly the price of one pound of meat. The sandwich men are perhaps the most un-organised representatives of labour in England. They have no close-knit cooperative associations or any links to a union. This is because every one of them regards his work as casual and temporary, despite the fact that there were many people among the diners who had been sandwiching for forty years or more. This same atomisation has resulted in the low wages, which are also caused by the supply of sandwich shoulders significantly exceeding the demand for them. This year is particularly bad. The cotton famine has driven hundreds of unemployed here from Manchester.[7] Where can they go? Of course, where else but sandwiching. 'And now all these Jews have swarmed in from Russia in numbers beyond count. They are happy to walk around with posterboards for five pence (twenty kopecks). They are stealing our bread, they are. **That's the devil of it!'** – and the old man started to curse his competitors.

I left him. The dinner was over. Each of the participants was given a florin (one rouble) and a suit of clothes. This was a surprise, and the sandwich men's delight was indescribable. Flushed with ale, they jumped up and down like boys. So when the hall was cleared of tables and a 'smoking concert' began (everyone was given a pipe and some tobacco), they were all so excited that no-one even listened to the music.

My old man grabbed some curly-haired fellow by the buttonhole and, forgetting his erstwhile cursing, proceeded to expound to him at great length that, in fact, all people were brothers, that there should be peace on earth and good will toward men...

But who knows what this same old man will say when his suit grows threadbare and not a farthing is left of his florin.

---

[7] Chukovsky is referring not to the famous Cotton Famine of the 1860s, but to the shortage in the supply of raw cotton from the summer of 1903 that created thousands of unemployed in the northwest of England. For the causes, see Bruce E. Baker and Barbara Hahn, *The Cotton Kings: Capitalism and Corruption in Turn-of-the-Century New York and New Orleans* (Oxford: Oxford University Press, 2016).

Korney Chukovsky, 'Godovschina Kolledzha' ['The College Anniversary'] *Odesskie Novosti*, 8 July 1904

London
(From our own correspondent)
16 July

I am writing in haste. In half an hour, Mr Torrington will pick me up and we will set off for somewhere called Crowndale Road, where the Prince of Wales will officially lay the first foundation stone of the new building of the Working Men's College.[1] Mr Torrington, my College colleague, is by occupation a cobbler. The moment he meets you, he takes a sheet of paper out of his side pocket, hands it to you and asks you to 'take note'. The sheet is covered with drawings of all kinds of shoes which Mr Torrington makes very deftly 'for the lowest prices' in his dark workshop.

But if you were to look into this side pocket of Mr Torrington's, you would see to your amazement, next to the drawings of shoes, Haeckel's 'The Riddle of the Universe', or Clodd's 'Pioneers of Evolution', or Stephen's 'An Agnostic's Apology' – in short, something that in no way resembles shoes.[2]

Upon further acquaintance, your astonishment would continue to grow.

---

[1] The College did not begin the move to its new site in Crowndale Road until 1905 (the laying of the foundation stone by the Prince of Wales did indeed take place on 16 July 1904). Chukovsky's descriptions in this article refer to the old College building in Great Ormond Street (where he had lived at one point). The Working Men's College was a famous London adult education institution for skilled artisans founded in 1854 by F. D. Maurice and other Christian Socialists. See J. F. C. Harrison, *A History of the Working Men's College 1854–1954* (London: Routledge and Kegan Paul, 1954) and J. Llewelyn Davies, ed. *The Working Men's College 1854–1904: Records of Its History and Its Work for Fifty Years, By Members of the College* (London: Macmillan and Co., 1904).

[2] Ernst Haeckel (1834–1919) was a prominent German zoologist and evolutionary biologist whose philosophical treatise *The Riddle of the Universe* (1899) was first published in English translation (by Joseph McCabe) in 1901. Edward Clodd (1840–1930) was an evolutionary anthropologist and president of the Folk-Lore Society; his *Pioneers of Evolution from Thales to Huxley* (London: Grant Richards, 1897) traced the idea of evolution from ancient Greece to modern times. Leslie Stephen (1832–1904) was a prominent Victorian man of letters (and father of Virginia Woolf); his 'An Agnostic's Apology' appeared in the *Fortnightly Review* in 1900 and was republished in the collection *An Agnostic's Apology and Other Essays* (London: Smith, Elder & Co., 1903). See Jonathan Rose, *The Intellectual Life of the British Working Classes* (London: Yale University Press, 2001) for a classic account of autodidact reading in the period.

Fig. 18. Working Men's College, Great Ormond Street: A Debate.

Your interlocutor can, on occasion, freely quote from Voltaire, Goethe and Calderón in their native tongues... He likes to reinforce his contentions in debates with expressions like: 'Huxley told me', or 'I heard that from William Morris', or 'The late Ruskin would often point out to me', and so on.[3]

But your amazement would be fated to grow even more if you were to come into our College 'coffee room' and see at once several dozen such Torringtons, hear similar speeches and receive similar price lists, where you would be asked to 'take note' of the tailoring, joining, or bookbinding talents of your new acquaintances.

You are a newcomer. You have just paid two or three shillings at the office and registered as a student of civil law, or sacred history, or the Italian language. You have been issued with a card which tells you that you have been made a member of the College club and granted the right to borrow books from the College library. You go to the 'coffee room' and ask one of your new colleagues to show you the library. The colleague leaves his game of chess, puts on his coat and willingly climbs with you to the first floor. You are in the library. In the middle is a long table at which students who do not have a room of their own at home are preparing their lessons. There is a portrait of Edgar [Allan] Poe on

---

3   T. H. Huxley (1825–1895) was a famous Victorian evolutionary biologist and public intellectual; William Morris (1834–1896) was a famous Victorian writer, designer and socialist leader; John Ruskin (1819–1900) was a famous Victorian art and social critic.

the wall. Your guide shows you the bookshelves and gives you a cursory overview of their contents. 'How do you know all this?' – 'How could I not: I have been a student here for over seventeen years, I've had time to read this entire library.' There are books on mechanics, on the theory of art, on horse breeding. Behind a separate counter on the left sits a boy of about eleven. In front of him are huge ledgers. He is the librarian. If you wish to take some book home, he asks your name and address with authority. And then he slowly records your responses in separate columns. If you talk too loudly in the library, he will reprimand you and point to a notice enjoining silence.

You descend the staircase decorated with dusty busts of Sir Walter Scott and some other unknown. Before you is a door with a sign reading: 'Common Room'. You enter. The room is full of small tables. Immediately opposite the door is a menu for tonight's dinner and a telephone leading to the kitchen. You order roast beef, tea and jam. You sit down at the first available table, take off your coat and browse the evening papers (the College receives nearly all the English journals and newspapers). An elderly lady with a tray enters the room and asks who ordered what. You have a shilling ready for her, in line with the usual prices, but you find that the order costs only three pence. You want to give her a penny *pour boir*,[4] but one of the students comes up to you and says that this woman is not a servant here, she is a member of the College, like we all are.

Once you feel more at home, you take a look round. One man is drinking beer, reading *Punch* and smirking at the cartoons. Another is ensconced in a large armchair, legs and all, and napping peacefully. A group near the window are arguing about Nonconformists. The majority are buried in their papers and if they tear themselves away, it is only to find on the map of the Far East some Guangdong Province or some Haicheng or another equally strange word.[5]

Notices are hung beside the map: such-and-such a railway is offering students discounted tickets to Cambridge; such-and-such a cycling club wants to recruit students to its membership; some place or other will host a lecture on Carlyle, and so on.[6]

Here is also a large portrait of Frederick Denison Maurice,[7] the founder of the College. An open energetic face – benevolent, but reserved in the English way – looks at you from a gilded frame. And you remember what you read about him in every history of English

---

4   French: 'tip'.
5   Both in China.
6   The famous figures mentioned in this and preceding paragraphs include the American poet and short story writer Edgar Allan Poe (1809–1849), the Scottish poet and historical novelist Walter Scott (1771–1832) and the influential Scottish intellectual and man of letters Thomas Carlyle (1795–1881).
7   Denison is misspelled Davison in the original text.

education. He was a Professor of Theology, this Maurice, and lived nearby, just around the corner, in **Queen Square**. In the fifties, caught up in the broader populist movement,[8] he and his disciples took up charitable work amongst the poor folk of the surrounding quarters... Soon, he noticed the appalling ignorance of his neighbours. (It is true that popular education had already become universal, but in practice, only two out of five children attended school – and this was in the seventies, i.e. twenty years after Maurice's endeavours.)[9] So he started gathering a few poor people at his home and telling them about astronomy, divinity, mathematics... Then he found some teachers; then rented a large space; and finally, in 1857, he donated five thousand roubles for the establishment of the present College. When he heard about this venture, John Ruskin, who was then at the height of his fame thanks to his *Modern Painters*, offered himself as a drawing teacher. Rossetti and Burne-Jones volunteered to teach art,[10] and their fame greatly contributed to the popularity of the College.

This project of Maurice's had one un-English trait. Maurice avoided so-called 'useful knowledge'.[11] 'Knowledge for knowledge's sake' was his motto. He was advised to print in his prospectus that knowledge of French would help clerks earn higher wages, that an acquaintance with mechanics would help a working man procure a better position, and so on. But he saw in all this an insult to learning, and if such an air of intellectual enthusiasm now reigns in the College, such a broad, noble interest in everything great created by the human spirit, it is due precisely to this trait of Maurice's, so rare in an Englishman: the absence of utilitarianism.

More about the internal arrangements next time.

---

[8] The original has 'Going to the People' movement, a reference to the Russian movement of the 1870s which saw revolutionary students travel to the countryside to inspire peasants to political action – the movement was a failure.

[9] This aside seems to demonstrate Chukovsky's confusion: he is talking about the 1850s, but it was only in 1870 that the 1870 Education Act made provision for state elementary education on a national scale. However, as Chukovsky indicates, many children in rural areas and in poor urban districts still fell through the cracks, primarily due to child labour (attendance was not made mandatory until the 1880s and 1890s).

[10] Dante Gabriel Rossetti (1828–1882) and Edward Burne-Jones (1833–1898) were the leading artists of the Pre-Raphaelite movement.

[11] 'Useful knowledge' was an important nineteenth-century concept, popularised by the Society for the Diffusion of Useful Knowledge (1826–1846), but penetrating all areas of Victorian popular print and educational culture. It has generated a large historiography.

Korney Chukovsky, 'Godovschina Kolledzha (Prodolzhenie)' ['The College Anniversary (Continued)']
Odesskie Novosti, 16 July 1904

London
(From our own correspondent)
25 July

Let me return to the College anniversary.

A distinguishing feature of all such English establishments is that they exist for you – and not you for them. In the public gardens, the most gorgeous flowers grow without being in any way fenced in. You can pick them if you want to, but you won't do it because they are yours. Precisely because you have been granted full use of them, you will not do anything to damage them. The same holds for museums and libraries. In the British Museum, books stand on the shelves ready to hand; you take them from the shelf without asking permission of anyone. And this is precisely why you have no intention of tearing any pages out of them; you feel that they are your property.

Our College operates on the same system. The College has been created for my convenience, which means that if I want to, say, dance in the refectory, I have the right – without asking any persons in charge – to move aside the furniture, to drag in the piano from the neighbouring room and to invite the scullery maid from the kitchen for one turn of the cakewalk.[1] It often happened in winter that you'd come into the 'coffee room' only to see a gentleman stretched out on each settee and taking a quiet nap. How surprised they would be if a set of 'rules' appeared in their College forbidding such postures. That would seem to them every bit as strange as a ban on kissing their own wives.

The convictions of all these gentlemen… But, reader, are you familiar with the 'Panama' hat?[2] A good Panama hat costs thirty or forty roubles, which is why you'll find it on the heads of rich mill-owners, fashionable doctors, lords, and so on. But could a poor clerk – who melts with rapture as he observes all these lucky ones on **Rotten Row** in Hyde Park every Sunday – possibly wear anything else on his own head after he has seen Duke **So-and-so** sporting a Panama?[3] Of course

---

[1]   Nineteenth-century American dance of African-American origin, which achieved international popularity at the turn of the twentieth century. See Shklovsky's 'In the Russian Quarter' above.

[2]   The well-known traditional straw hat from Ecuador, distributed internationally via Panama from the middle of the nineteenth century, achieved particular popularity in the early 1900s. However, it is also possible that Chukovsky mistook the widely worn straw boater hat for the Panama. The purpose of this abrupt digression becomes clear two paragraphs down.

[3]   Cf. Chukovsky's 'Public Meetings in Hyde Park'.

not; and so we have hat shops offering 'almost Panama hats' for five to ten roubles.

But a few days later, counterfeits of these counterfeits appear; they cost a shilling apiece. This means that even the working man, instead of standing up for the honour of his crumpled bowler, has discovered in these imitations a better means of upholding his prestige.

Such is also the way with convictions. Mill-owners and bankers back Chamberlain;[4] and no wonder, it is in their direct interest. But a clerk waxes lyrical about protectionism and shouts 'To hell with foreigners!' only because this is the custom in high society. He borrows convictions as he does the 'Panama' hat – out of a complete lack of respect for himself and his own. The working man – for whom protectionism means famine, who is regularly offered such surprises by the Balfour Government as the introduction of Chinese labour into South Africa – will also,[5] in imitation of his greatest enemies, repeat to you ad nauseum: 'Every gentleman in England has been a Conservative since the dawn of time. Chamberlain is the number one gentleman in Britain. I like gentlemen', and so on. Not everyone, of course, is like that, but I am speaking of the majority.

And nothing can persuade him otherwise. Having no opportunity of *setting himself against* that which he considers fashionable, he copies that which is fashionable on a smaller scale, like that defenceless weed which, so as not to be devoured by cattle, mimics the stinging nettle...

Out of the various College activities, I personally love the meetings of the Home Reading League the most.

This is how it goes. One of the students writes on a scrap of paper: 'Gentlemen! I have read Bacon's **essay** *Of Death*.[6] Very interesting. Get this book and read it'.

---

4   See previous notes. Chamberlain's campaign for tariff reform was spearheaded by the Tariff Reform League, founded in 1903 to lobby for protectionism and the support of British industry against foreign competition.

5   After the end of the Boer War, the Unionist government under Balfour imported Chinese labourers to work in the Transvaal gold mines. This policy provoked extreme controversy and elicited a mass TUC demonstration in Hyde Park in March 1904 as described by David Glover in 'London, Liberalism, and the Chinese Labour Question', in Paolo Cardullo, Rahila Gupta and Jamie Hakim, eds. *London: City of Paradox*, 3–5 April 2012, University of East London (London, 2012), 66–73, https://repository.uel.ac.uk/download/95e3f053437f9fbfbeb6a808a7fb446f4f9a438 698102a91812945d6ede1e570/1256564/LondonCityofParadox.pdf. See also Rachel Bright, *Chinese Labour in South Africa, 1902–10: Race, Violence and Global Spectacle* (Basingstoke: Palgrave Macmillan, 2013) and the rest of the extensive historiography on this topic, and the *LSE Digital Library* 'Political and Tariff Reform Posters' for 'Chinese Labour' posters.

6   'Of Death' is one of the philosopher Francis Bacon's (1561–1626) collection of *Essays*. Bacon was widely regarded as one of the originators of the essay form.

And he hangs the paper up in the Common Room. About eight people willing to read Bacon's essay are found; each of them reads it *separately*. Then they gather in the College under the chairmanship of some professor and begin picking apart every word. At first, it is all rather forced. We arrive, sit down around the table, take out our books – and fall silent. Everyone puffs at his pipe, the professor is new and ill at ease, and no-one knows what to do with himself. Then things improve, and now our circle numbers 105 permanent members.

The professors neither hold themselves aloof from the workmen, nor fawn on them or curry favour. Personal relations are very straight-forward, not studiedly fixed, but natural. The professors are not averse to partaking in a game of draughts with their students or splitting a pot of ale with them – but when it comes to exams, neither are they averse to failing their erstwhile partner.

The visionary element that Maurice brought to the College enterprise is gradually withering away. It is the applied sciences that are being increasingly studied, and of the arts, the ones that flourish are bookkeeping and shorthand.[7] Instead of the workers who once upon a time listened enthusiastically to Ruskin and Rossetti – with their dreams of a beautiful, high-minded life – the walls of the College are crowded with scrofulous youths only interested in getting the knack of some clerical trade as quickly as possible in order to grab a lucrative position in some **Home Office** department. The new spirit of England is penetrating into all possible recesses…

[7]   Chukovsky is clearly being ironic in calling these 'arts'.

Isaak Shklovsky [Dioneo], from 'Whitechapel'
Sketches of Contemporary England (St Petersburg, 1903): 507–31[1]

I.

'Whitechapel.' This word is always associated with the idea of incredible squalor and incredible suffering – the total antithesis of the lavishly wealthy West End of London. One need only mention Whitechapel and scenes of astonishing mental torpor and savagery sketched by Taine, Louis Blanc and others appear before the mind's eye.[2] These scenes are very popular in Russia. Whenever one of our compatriots finds himself in London, he immediately inquires how to make his way to Whitechapel. He expects to see those 'white savages' about whom the German economist reported such horrific facts. 'Their degree of culture may be seen from the following dialogues', the above-mentioned author wrote: '**Jeremiah Haynes**, a boy aged twelve, asserted that four times four is eight. The king, in his words, **is him, that has all the money and gold**. Told we have a king, and that king is a queen, and that they call him the Princess Alexandra. Told that she married the King's son. A Princess is a man.' A thirteen-year-old boy explained: 'I don't live in England. Think it is a country, but didn't know before'. John Morris, age fourteen, explained: 'Have heard say that God made the world, and that all the people was drownded but one; heard say that one was a little bird.' A girl aged ten, who said instead of '**God – Dog**', had an idiosyncratic notion of the devil: '**The devil is a good person. I don't**

---

[1]   Originally published as a Letter 'From England' under the pseudonym Dioneo in the monthly journal *Russkoe Bogatstvo*, February 1897, 102–24. NB. *Russkoe Bogatstvo* issues were divided into two halves for pagination purposes, with page numbering beginning anew in the second half, which is where Shklovsky's Letters were always found. The *Sketches of Contemporary England* collection included an introductory section entitled 'Change of Currents' and sections on: 'The New Phase', with Letters devoted to imperialism, industry, the stock market, and so on ('Imperialism' is excerpted in this anthology); 'Political Life and Public Figures', with Letters on the House of Commons, the House of Lords, 'Queen Victoria' and 'An Election' (the latter two excerpted here); 'Literature and the Press', with individual Letters devoted to reviews, quarterlies, the 'popular' and 'street' press, Grant Allen, Oscar Wilde and Walt Whitman; and 'The People', including Letters on 'The Life of the Poor in Cities', 'Sects', 'The Working Quarter', 'Whitechapel' and 'Frankie' (all but the first excerpted here).

[2]   Hippolyte Taine (1828–1893) was an influential French critic and intellectual whose *Notes sur l'Angleterre [Notes on England]* appeared in 1872. Louis Blanc (1811–1882) was a French socialist politician and historian who spent many years in England as an exile after the revolution of 1848. Shklovsky quotes from Blanc's *Lettres sur l'Angleterre [Letters on England]* (1866) in his other Letters.

know where he lives', and so on.[3] So when they get to Whitechapel, our compatriots are liable to be slightly disappointed. It is not what they expected. They overlook the fact that Marx collected his evidence about forty years ago, and since then certain changes have taken place. Let us start with the fact that in 1841–48, 32.6% of the men and 48.9% of the women in England signed the marriage register with a cross due to illiteracy. In 1840, 40% of Londoners were illiterate, while in 1896 only 1½% were. In 1850, there were only 1844 schools in the whole of England, with 197,578 pupils, whereas in 1896, there were over six million pupils. In Whitechapel, that kingdom of torpor and savagery, there are now two free people's universities, several lecture halls where a few thousand students gather to follow courses in the social sciences, a huge concert hall where Mendelssohn oratorios attract three to four thousand listeners, many libraries, and so on.[4] True, an observer in Whitechapel may even now find strikingly grim scenes at every step; but those grim impressions won't be the only ones he will come away with. The observer, in a sense, becomes like Voltaire's Babouc, sent by

3   Shklovsky's note: *K. Marx*, 'Capital', vol. I.
    Editor's note: Shklovsky is quoting (with some inaccuracies) from footnote 66 to Section 4: 'Day and Night Work. The Relay System' of Chapter 10: 'The Working-Day' of Volume 1 of Karl Marx's *Capital* (1867). He was probably using the 1887 English edition: 'The degree of culture of these "labour-powers" must naturally be such as appears in the following dialogues with one of the commissioners: Jeremiah Haynes, age 12 – "Four times four is 8; 4 fours are 16. A king is him that has all the money and gold. We have a king (told it is a Queen), they call her the Princess Alexandra. Told that she married the Queen's son. The Queen's son is the Princess Alexandra. A Princess is a man." William Turner, age 12 – "Don't live in England. Think it is a country, but didn't know before." John Morris, age 14 – "Have heard say that God made the world, and that all the people was drownded but one, heard say that one was a little bird." William Smith age 15 – "God made man, man made woman." Edward Taylor, age 15 – "Do not know of London." Henry Matthewman, age 17 – "Had been to chapel, but missed a good many times lately. One name that they preached about was Jesus Christ, but I cannot say any others, and I cannot tell anything about him. He was not killed, but died like other people. He was not the same as other people in some ways, because he was religious in some ways and others isn't." (l.c., p. xv.) "The devil is a good person. I don't know where he lives." "Christ was a wicked man." "This girl spelt God as dog, and did not know the name of the queen." ("Ch. Employment Comm. V. Report, 1866" p. 55, n. 278.).' See Karl Marx, *Capital: A Critique of Political Economy*, trans. Samuel Moore and Edward Aveling, vol. 1 (London: Swan Sonnenschein, 1887) in *Marx/Engels Internet Archive*: www.marxists.org/archive/marx/works/1867-c1/.
4   Shklovsky probably procured his statistics from some of the nineteenth-century literature of social investigation he goes on to summarise in this Letter. The modern historiography of the Victorian and Edwardian East End (academic and popular, not to mention memoirs and studies of 'slum fiction'), is very extensive. To begin with, see the publications of Peter Keating, Gareth Stedman Jones, William Fishman and, more recently, Sarah Wise and John Marriott listed in the Bibliography.

Ituriel to find out whether Babylon should be destroyed.[5] Just like the virtuous brahmin, the observer meets now pleasing, now melancholy sights with every step he takes.

[Shklovsky proceeds to offer an extensive social history of East End exploration. He begins with the conventional West End attitudes to this 'unknown world', the social fears it evoked and the awakening of the 'familiar to us type' of the young social missionary and settler, beginning with Edward Denison in 1867. He refers to the publications of observers and researchers, such as Henry Mayhew's London Labour and the London Poor *and John Hollingshead's* Ragged London *in 1861, and then offers the familiar narrative ranging from Arnold Toynbee in the 1870s and his followers in the settlement house movement of the 1880s – specifically, the establishment of Toynbee Hall in 1884, Mayfield House, the Women's University Settlement and Walter Besant's People's Palace – all the way to Charles Booth's* Life and Labour of the People in London *(maps included). Shklovsky emphasises the educational and cultural activities of the above-named institutions and provides lots of details on their operation. He then devotes several pages to the life and work of Edward Carpenter, Beatrice Webb and Clara Collet. He concludes his overview with an account of the reading habits of the 'masses', including the 'penny dreadful' and attempts to counteract its baneful influence by the publication of cheap classics series and the establishment of public libraries. The judgements Shklovsky expresses here are carbon copies of those found in late-Victorian reviews.]*

In the poor quarters, the libraries are organised on the principle of general trust. No deposits are required. And, as far as I know, the organisers have had no cause yet to repent of their belief in elementary human decency.[6] Admittedly, there is on the whole more trust in people in England than on the Continent. You hand in your parcel at the post office, and you get no receipt. At the railway station, a label with the name of the station of origin is stuck on your case, and then it is taken to the luggage car without any receipt. When you arrive, you pick out your case yourself from the luggage car.

In Paris, you have to make a **déclaration** to the police on the third day after arrival. In Berlin, it is not so easy to stay for a long time with a Russian passport. In England, no-one is interested in you; no-one

5 Shklovsky is referring to Voltaire's *conte philosophique Le Monde Comme Il Va: Vision de Babouc écrite par lui-même* (1748) in which the angel Ituriel sends Babouc on a mission to observe Persepolis in order to decide whether the corruption of the city's inhabitants merits celestial punishment.
6 Shklovsky is presumably referring to the free libraries brought into existence by the Public Libraries Act 1850, which enabled boroughs to fund them out of local rates, in conjunction with philanthropic donations. There were several hundred such libraries across Britain by the turn of the twentieth century.

inquires who you are, why you are here or how long you plan to stay.[7] When you head to the bank to receive some money or to the post office, you can leave your passport at home. Your word is sufficient 'proof of identity'. Until you have yourself given some cause for concern, you are regarded as a gentleman. On the Continent, it is the other way about. There, every man is regarded as a swindler and must provide certification that he is in fact an honest person. This leads to endless (and useless) red tape which, without guaranteeing anything to those who make the inquiries, annoys and offends those from whom such proof is demanded.

II.

Perhaps the most characteristic spot not just in Whitechapel but in the whole of London is the famous docks, those stores of colossal riches, and at the same time, those 'gutters' where society's outcasts end up, sometimes having suffered shipwreck in life's dreadful storms. The docks, it seems to me, may serve us as an object lesson in the slow yet incessant process of change unfolding in that world which seems to us an inescapable hell.[8]

As we approach the docks, we see an abrupt change in the character of the street. The shops here sell exclusively things necessary for long sea voyages. Compasses, nautical spyglasses and sextants peek out of every shop window. Beyond them are heaped chains, anchors, cables coiled like huge snakes. Above the doors dangle striped sailor shirts, canvas shoes, etc. You find pubs on every corner. Their names also point to the kind of customers who frequent them. Everywhere are dotted colourful signs like 'The Jack',[9] 'Mother's', the 'Jolly Sailor'. Interspersed between the pubs are brothels, pawnbroker shops marked with the three golden balls above their doors, and opium dens. The latter were originally set up for the Chinese; but there are many Europeans among their clientele, primarily sailors who have acquired the habit

---

[7]   This juxtaposition between the Continental 'police states' and England's more liberal environment was a convention of nineteenth-century Russian accounts. It was also part of Britain's self-image in the nineteenth century, which was being severely challenged by new developments in police surveillance, anti-immigrant legislation, etc., by the turn of the twentieth century.

[8]   For a history of the London docks, see Fiona Rule's *London's Docklands: A History of the Lost Quarter* (Hersham: Ian Allan Publishing, 2009). It is worth noting that Shklovsky is letting 'Whitechapel' stand for the inner East End; the docks he refers to were in Wapping and Limehouse, districts to the south and east of Whitechapel. The following paragraphs include numerous errors of fact and repeat the clichés of the least reflective of contemporary sensational journalism. However, their purpose is clearly to furnish a contrast with the improvements that Shklovsky traces in the conclusion of the section, illustrating the 'process of change', so they may be read as an example of his rhetorical strategy.

[9]   Shklovsky's note: English sailors are nicknamed 'Jack Tar', i.e. Van'ka Tar.

of smoking opium during their voyages to the Far East. There is no furniture of any kind in these houses. They are gloomy, dank lairs. The smokers lie on the floor, in empty rooms, on straw mattresses. Some lie without moving, and their faces are frozen to stone. Others toss violently, grit their teeth, wail and swear in divers tongues. The keepers of the houses have to watch over such people especially closely, because sometimes they jump out into the street and attack the nearest passer-by with a knife.[10]

Occasionally, one sees lighted signs above the entrance doors of some houses reading: 'Good and comfortable beds for gentlemen. Price two pence per night'. By day, these streets hardly differ from any other London streets. Perhaps they're just a little dirtier. But at night, they turn into a proper hell. For policing purposes, London is divided into districts marked with different alphabetical characters. This district is marked with the letter F and is considered to be the most dangerous and violent.[11] Only veritable athletes are appointed as policemen here. For serving in district F, they receive their pensions considerably earlier. The policemen are assigned to their posts in pairs. Beginning at eight o'clock in the evening, the streets become very busy. Sailors from every country move in a solid mass: a Negro next to a German, a Brazilian next to a Swede, etc. Everything that is most obscene, repulsive and filthy in the languages of the world washes in a wave over these streets and alleyways. For the most part, the crowd is dead drunk. Here and there, the oaths boom more forcefully, furious screams are heard, then a commotion begins; they are probably pulling apart two men who have attacked each other with knives. Wretched, half-drunken women, some with black eyes, prowl about among the sailors. This maze of dark alleyways where no policemen dare to show themselves, these gloomy dens are the nests of unnatural, repulsive vices brought here by sailors from far-off lands. On occasion, the rich denizens of the West End turn up here in disguise to titillate their dulled nerves.[12]

---

[10]   Shklovsky would have encountered depictions of opium addicts in the fiction of his favourite English writer Charles Dickens, not to mention another writer he clearly read attentively: Oscar Wilde. But opium dens were a favourite motif of many *fin de siècle* writers and East End social commentators. See, to begin with, Ross G. Forman, *China and the Victorian Imagination: Empires Entwined* (Cambridge: Cambridge University Press, 2013).

[11]   Shklovsky gets this wrong: London Metropolitan Police F Division was Paddington (previously Covent Garden); this whole area was H Division. See the 'Metropolitan Police Historical Timeline: Events Between 1829 and 1899', *Friends of the Metropolitan Police Heritage Charity*, https://fomphc.com/timeline-1829-to-1899/.

[12]   Editor's paragraph break. On slumming, see Seth Koven, *Slumming: Sexual and Social Politics in Victorian London* (Princeton, NJ: Princeton University Press, 2004). However, Shklovsky's cliché-ridden rhetoric here bespeaks not so much eye-witness testimony as his wide reading in the contemporary literature on the subject of East End depravity.

A tall, huge wall separates the dockside from these streets. The London docks are an engineering marvel. [...] All that is most refined, luxurious and expensive in the world is stored in the colossal warehouses and cellars of the dockside. At the same time, the docks house all that is most wretched in the whole of London. Instead of 'go to the devil!', the English say **go to the docks!** What a wonderful place it must be that has earned such an honourable reputation! All kinds of labourers are required in the docks, but most in demand is brute physical strength. A man is valued here only as an animal. No brainpower is required at all. This means that almost anyone can find employment in the docks. The plight of the 'dockers' had until recently been, in every sense of the word, desperate.

[Shklovsky goes on to explain the difference between 'permanent' dock labourers and those employed 'on a temporary basis', who 'end up in the street' if there is no 'shipment to load'. He quotes 'historical' descriptions of casual labourers fighting for work at the dock gates from Henry Mayhew's London Labour and the London Poor *and from Charles Booth's* Life and Labour of the People of London, *including Beatrice Potter's class analysis, and then offers a history of the New Unionism, giving potted biographies of John Burns, Tom Mann and Ben Tillett and their agitation among the dockers in the late 1880s and 90s, thus tracing the dockers' transformation from 'homeless tramps' to self-respecting and confident 'workers'.]*

Anyone who had seen the deputation from the dockers' union at the huge rally in support of the Armenians held in Hyde Park in the autumn of 1896,[13] could hardly believe that those were the very same 'tramps' who ten years ago spent every day literally fighting over a slice of bread. Every evening in the Whitechapel libraries you can meet with lots of dockers; not a few of them attend concerts held at the People's Palace where their children study.[14] Of course, their situation still leaves very much to be desired; but the awful sights one would have witnessed just a few years ago are no more. The dockers now have their own political clubs, their own organisations, when recently their only gathering place was the pub.

[13]   The 11 October 1896 demonstration in Hyde Park to protest against the 'Armenian atrocities' – massacres carried out by the Ottomans from 1894 to 1896 – was organised by various trade unions and other bodies. The procession marched from the Thames Embankment to the Park, with speakers, including the Radical MP and former docker leader John Burns, addressing the crowd from '12 platforms'. See 'The Eastern Crisis: Hyde Park Demonstration', *South Wales Daily News*, 12 October 1896, 6.

[14]   The People's Palace, inspired by Walter Besant's *All Sorts and Conditions of Men* (1882), was built in 1887 to provide culture, entertainment and education to the people of the East End. It included a concert hall, a library and various other facilities.

III.

Let us pay a visit to Whitechapel, a quarter that numbers some two hundred thousand most diverse inhabitants.[15] You could say that all countries have their representatives here. A twenty-minute ride on the underground railroad and we find ourselves in an entirely different world. At first, we feel disappointed. What, is this really Whitechapel? We had expected to see dirty winding streets, half-ruined hovels and other attributes of destitution. Meanwhile, before us is a wide, well-paved street, large shops, tall buildings. The street traffic is remarkably busy. Heavily laden wagons, 'buses' (omnibuses), horse-tram cars, cabs, etc. move in a continuous line. It is not until you've taken a closer look at the passers-by that you are convinced that you've ended up in a different city, separated from London by a span of several centuries. It is Saturday night. All the workshops are closed. The workers have received their wages and everyone is expecting them. Numerous stalls and booths have been hastily set up along the wide pavements of the main street, Whitechapel Road. Everywhere resound the shouts and cries of the touts. In one spot, a gentleman in a dress coat, buttoned up tightly to conceal any defects of linen, is offering miraculous pills that cure any ailment for a penny a box. He is 'The Court Physician of His Majesty King of Dahomey and Cavalier of the Order of the Nile Crocodile',[16] as his placard proclaims. Further on is a whole range of shooting galleries where bottles, dolls and wondrous beasts are arranged in rows.[17] Here is a tent where some beauty named Beatrice is being displayed 'for gentlemen only'; over there, 'hawkers' are crying the merits of their trousers, shirts, purses and cheap, popular books and prints until they go hoarse. A mass of ragged boys shivering from the cold are crowding near stands bearing cups with eels of a disgustingly green hue.[18] The numerous pubs are being taken by storm. The oath which the English consider to be the height of obscenity washes over in wave after wave. Englishmen blush when they hear it in the streets. The oath in question is **bloody**, i.e. 'bloodstained'. The London proletariat make use of this swearword at every opportunity.

---

[15]   The population of Stepney, of which Whitechapel was part, was 298,000 in 1901.

[16]   The Kingdom of Dahomey, known for its role in the Atlantic slave trade, existed in West Africa for several hundred years before becoming a French colony at the turn of the twentieth century. *In Dahomey: A Negro Musical Comedy* was also an immensely popular American all-Black vaudeville musical that toured the United Kingdom in 1903, premiering at the Shaftesbury Theatre (it featured the famous cakewalk).

[17]   On shooting galleries and various other kinds of 'sideshow' attractions (with photographs), though none as gruesome as the ones Shklovsky describes later in the Letter, see 'Sideshow London' in Sims, *Living London* 2, 281–85. 'Saturday Night in Whitechapel Road' received an illustration to itself.

[18]   The original has 'snails'.

'Tell your **bloody** land-lord that if he's going to serve such **bloody** gin, then I'll be a **bloody** man if even one **bloody** docker comes to his **bloody** pub',[19] a ragged man shouts hoarsely.

This word, which strikes such terror into the well-bred Englishman, is in essence an abbreviated blasphemous oath, **byour Lady**, by which Cromwell's men-at-arms used to swear.[20]

From the main street, a knot of dark winding alleys leads in both directions. They are so narrow that if neighbours living opposite each other took it into their heads to shake hands, they would be able to do so without leaving their rooms: they would just need to lean out of their windows. One's foot sinks deep into the 'kitchen waste' that covers the pavement.

Fig. 19. Saturday Night in Whitechapel Road.

One recalls a philosophical comment about Whitechapel made by Mr Weller Jr (Pickwick's servant): 'poverty and oysters always seem to go together'. Indeed, at every step, whole heaps of oysters crunch unpleasantly under one's feet, as if one were walking along the seashore rather than Osborn Street. As Mr Weller noted sagaciously, 'Blessed if I don't think that ven a man's wery poor, he rushes out of his lodgings, and eats oysters in reg'lar desperation'.[21] As for poverty, there is no

---

[19] '**Bloody** man' appears to be a euphemism, but it is impossible to tell what Shklovsky means to refer to here.

[20] This is one of many existing theories for the origin of the profanity. The contraction 'by'r Lady' (by Our Lady) does indeed go back to the seventeenth century. At the turn of the twentieth century, it was considered a shocking obscenity and its use was associated with the lower classes of society.

[21] Osborn Street in Whitechapel is associated with, among other things, Jack the Ripper. Shklovsky is quoting from chapter 22 of Charles Dickens's *The Posthumous Papers of the Pickwick Club* (1837; London: Hazell, Watson & Viney, Ltd, 1933): 'And away went the coach up Whitechapel, to the admiration of the whole

lack of it here. The houses are low and lopsided, the windows have
no curtains. The panes have been smashed and replaced with paper. In
one spot, a thick crowd has blocked the pavement in front of a wide
and brightly lit window with a garishly painted sign which reads: 'The
Rivals! An astonishing and entertaining play about two brother-dukes,
the fair Monimia and the fool Littlefool. The most entertaining in all
of London'.[22] On a step at the open doors stands a woman of about
thirty-five years, her face whitened with chalk and crudely rouged with
some paint. The woman is wearing only a short knee-length petticoat,
dirty and tattered, and a corset. On her head is an enormous old hat
which looks like it has just been fished out of a rubbish heap. Next to
her is an old man in Scottish costume, with bare knees. He does not
require any rouge because his puffy, sickly face is already greyish-red
in colour. His nose is of a particularly vivid shade. Further inside, one
more face can be discerned: a tall, broad-shouldered man in a colourful
shirt sewn with sequins and representing, apparently, a coat of mail. On
his head is a torn and battered felt hat. His trousers are tucked inside his
gaiters. The knees are ripped, and his big toe can be seen sticking out
of his right boot. Apart from me, about fifty other people wish to see
the play. They are standing in single file. Next to me is a gentleman in
a jacket but, apparently, no undergarments; his cap is pulled low over
his brows. Deep-seated eyes glare from under a cracked peak, beneath
one of them is a huge dark-blue bruise. I reflect that my wallet is not,
perhaps, entirely safe and look around to see if I can find a neighbour
with a more reassuring physiognomy. But the faces all about are the
same. At last, our entrance fees are wrested from us, one penny apiece,
the inner doors swing open, and I am propelled into the theatre together
with the crowd.[23]

---

population of that pretty densely populated quarter. "Not a very nice neighbourhood
this, sir," said Sam, with a touch of the hat, which always preceded his entering
into conversation with his master. "It is not indeed, Sam," replied Mr. Pickwick,
surveying the crowded and filthy street through which they were passing. "It's a
wery remarkable circumstance, sir," said Sam, "that poverty and oysters always
seems to go together." "I don't understand you, Sam," said Mr. Pickwick. "What
I mean, sir," said Sam, "is that the poorer a place is, the greater call there seems
to be for oysters. Look here, sir; here's a oyster stall to every half-dozen houses.
The street's lined vith 'em. Blessed if I don't think that ven a man's wery poor,
he rushes out of his lodgings, and eats oysters in reg'lar desperation." "To be sure
he does," said Mr. Weller senior; "and it's just the same vith pickled salmon!"
"Those are two very remarkable facts, which never occurred to me before," said
Mr. Pickwick. "The very first place we stop at, I'll make a note of them.'" (245).

22   This seems to be a version of Thomas Otway's tragedy *The Orphan; or The
      Unhappy Marriage* (1680), which features Monimia (the eponymous orphan), and
      the two noble brothers Castalio and Polydore, who vie for her love.
23   Editor's paragraph break. Shklovsky is describing a so-called 'penny gaff' or cheap
      theatre, common in working-class London. There are many similar descriptions

The 'auditorium' is low-ceilinged and unimaginably filthy. The stage is small, and some knight's castle is depicted on the curtain. There are no seats or boxes. There are only the stalls – the 'pit' in English – where everyone stands. The **pit** is packed to the rafters. Behind me, someone is bobbing up and down, grabbing me by the shoulders and evidently trying to find a more comfortable position. I dare not look behind because I have heard how the gentlemen of Whitechapel can deftly and silently unbutton one's coat. The 'orchestra' is fenced off by a low barrier. There, a small bare-footed boy in rags is turning the handle of a broken barrel-organ. From time to time, he stops and warms his little hands, blue with cold, at the gas jet. An old, evidently ill monkey sits all huddled up on top of the organ; the expression on her wrinkled old-womanish face is singularly piteous. In the pit, the crowd starts to show its impatience. There are whistles, catcalls, shouts. Now the woman in the petticoat, the Scotsman and the man in the coat of mail have shouldered their way through the crowd and mounted the stage, the barrel-organ has stopped screeching, and the small boy who was turning the handle has run up to the gas jet and almost thrust his little hands into the flames. The audience begins to stir. The gentleman behind me jumps up once more and leans heavily onto my shoulders. Only the monkey remains motionless. The curtain is up. The woman in the petticoat has now thrown on a soiled, incredibly worn loose satin robe. She is the fair Monimia. She is courted by two brothers, the Duke's sons: MacCastel, the gentleman in Scottish costume, and Polydore, the knight in armour. Monimia loves MacCastel and marries him secretly for fear of her enemies. Polydore offers Monimia all his riches, but the beauty proudly refuses to love him. And one's heart sinks painfully when an actor whose toe sticks out of his boot talks of thousands of guineas. It is likely that the poor man has had no dinner today and will probably have no dinner tomorrow or for the rest of the week, because performances in this paupers' theatre are only given on Saturdays.

[Shklovsky offers a brief summary of the play's plot.]

The audience applauds wildly; they call Polydore out only to drive him away with whistles. The entire play lasts no more than three-quarters of an hour. I try to recall the author of the familiar play, and finally the name comes back to me. This is in fact a drama by the unfortunate Otway, who grew up and died in this quarter. How dreadful and tragic was the author's fate!

---

of penny gaffs in the writings of Victorian social investigators such as Henry Mayhew, James Greenwood and others. See the primary documents on 'Penny Gaffs' reproduced in Lee Jackson, *A Dictionary of Victorian London: An A–Z of the Great Metropolis* (London: Anthem Press, 2006) and the online version at *The Dictionary of Victorian London*, www.victorianlondon.org/entertainment/pennygaffs.htm.

[Shklovsky gives a brief account of Otway's tragic life and legend.]

I find myself in the main street again. The kerosene torches are burning with a smoky yellowish flame. It seems that even more tents than before are now pitched along the pavement. On one platform a field church has been set up. Some bearded gentleman is waving his arms and inviting the public to repent. Next to him, the owner of a cart filled with old clothes is praising the quality of the fabric of some trousers.

'Three shillings, gentlemen, only three shillings. What could you buy for such a sum? You couldn't even have a nice chat with your friends. And for such a pittance, I am offering you a real treasure. Look, the Prince of Wales himself wouldn't say no to such a pair of trousers.'

He is interrupted by his neighbour, a seller of braces:

'Gentlemen! Just look at the length: enough to stretch from your fingers to your shoulder. And the strength! You'll wear them for fifty years, and then pass them on to your children. But that's nothing! If a gentleman from the West End is consumed by spleen and decides to hang himself, offer him these braces without fear – they'll hold 'im!'

There is a real crush by the pubs. Men and women go in and out all the time. A dozen barrel-organs squeal shrilly. Drunken women and girls are dancing on the pavement, their broken boots smacking the ground. Drunken men, their brows furrowed fiercely, are muttering oaths. The English are, for the most part, dismal and very riotous drunks. The police news informs us that the majority of crimes are committed in a drunken state. The streets are growing even more gloomy: a fog saturated with the smoke of a million chimneys creeps out of the dark alleys and spreads everywhere. The penetrating damp sends shivers down one's spine. A light but persistent drizzle starts up. Near one of the pubs, a ragged consumptive lad with a red moustache, most likely an Irishman, stops and strikes up a song in a cracked and quavering voice. Every now and then, he has to pause, choked by a dull cough that seems about to tear his breast apart.

'Ah, this is our song, the very one they sing in Dungarvan', says an old woman who has just emerged from the pub. Her hair is dishevelled; on her shoulders is a long and formerly green cloak with a hood; in her shrivelled lips is a pipe.

'Oh, we sing lots of good songs in Ireland. Wait, listen to this one: "Oh Bethuma! would you like to come with me to a wondrous land"', she intones, smiling sweetly. And strange, coming from the mouth of an old crone, sound the words of a song about a wondrous land where 'the maidens' hair shines like cut sheaves and their bodies are as white as the mountain snow; the land where everyone is happy'.[24] How madly discordant do these words of happiness sound!

---

[24] I have been unable to locate the original song. Dungarvan is a town on the south-east coast of Ireland.

'Save my soul! That's not how you dance the jig!' the old woman breaks off abruptly. 'Only English asses tread the pasture like that. You just wait, auntie Edith is going to show you how they dance in Dungarvan.' With arms akimbo, she begins to kick her legs up in the air almost an arshin high.[25]

'That's how a baptised man should dance if he believes in St Patrick.'

A thick crowd is milling about on the pavements. A panorama – the sign above reading: 'All Kinds of Executions Here: The Guillotine, the Gallows and the Spanish Garrotte' – is being stampeded by children and adolescents. They have glued themselves to the glass. The air is abuzz with the cries of 'hawkers' (pedlars), the crackling of bullets in the shooting ranges, the pounding of great hammers used to try one's strength, the drunken songs and the screeching of barrel-organs. Once again, a dense crowd has flooded the pavement. Everyone is looking at a lit window where a bill has been pasted on the glass: 'Victorina, The Greatest Fist Fighter of Our Time!'. With difficulty, I push my way towards the entrance, curtained off with a dirty, faded horsecloth which is lifted before me by a negro – ragged, half-naked, every muscle in his body shivering with the cold and damp. The negro's skin has turned soot-coloured from the cold. And to judge by its folds, he does not get to eat every day, that much is clear. I am in the 'salon'. Obviously, on regular days, this is just a shed. Here is the staircase leading to the attic. They have tried to drape it with a pile of rags. A drunken, tattered man with a swollen face exhibits to the public 'The Wonder of the XIX Century', the beautiful Victorina. In two fingers of one hand, stretched out in a characteristic lackey's gesture, the exhibitor holds a fag end; with the other, he pokes at Victorina's bare arms, shoulders and breast, which are covered all over with bruises. She is dressed in some russet rag sewn with twisted and blackened braid. I look at the 'wonder's' face and feel my throat constrict spasmodically and a lump 'rise' in it. Victorina is about thirty years old. It is hard to discern her facial features because of the enormous blue bruises under her eyes, on her forehead and cheeks. Only the eyes are visible, which reflect the fear of an animal who knows that it is about to be thrashed but at the same time submits itself to the inevitable affliction. Victorina lifts the rags that swathe her legs; it turns out that they are bare above the knee and also covered with a mass of bruises.

'Gentlemen!' the man urges, 'who wants to try their strength? Victorina challenges everyone: dockers, sailors, professional boxers.'

The 'gentlemen' stand motionless. I look around. In vain does the exhibitor call out the sailors: there are none here. They obviously consider this place too low for them. All about are tattered jackets buttoned up to the neck and peak caps pulled low over mostly blackened

---

[25]   An 'arshin' is an old Russian unit of length equal to 28 inches or 71 centimetres.

eyes. These are, evidently, down and outs, as well as gentlemen whose business begins after midnight and involves dark alleyways. Until a willing person can be found, the exhibitor shows the public another attraction.

'My friend, Professor Lister,[26] yesterday sent me another wonder of our age', he begins and takes out from under a rag a dried-up, dissected little corpse of some freak baby with an enormous head. The audience stretch their hands, touch and smell the cadaver. With a heavy heart, I leave the shed.

A woman comes out of a neighbouring pub, staggering; her shawl has slid off her shoulders, her broken straw hat is askew. She is singing an obscene song in a hoarse, raspy voice.

Girls, small and scrofulous, are standing at the pub doors, evidently awaiting their parents. Now a man comes out, burly, broad-shouldered, with a rough, ferocious face; he looks around, as if searching for someone, and then sees a skinny boy of about seven with a jug in his hand. The little fellow was, apparently, sent on some errand, but could not resist the temptation of stopping to gaze at the garishly painted sign proclaiming that 'Count Ivan Orloff', he of the completely transparent legs, is on display here.[27] The man begins to beat the boy.

'**Shame!**', rings out, all of a sudden, a calm, stern voice, belonging to a passing sailor. He stops, and then silently proceeds to remove his jacket. This is a formal challenge to a fight. The man lets the boy be. Volunteers scatter round to keep watch at the crossroads for any 'bobbies' (policemen) that might show up. After a minute, the sailor, with whom the public's sympathies obviously lie, has turned his adversary's face into a bloody pulp. The public appears to conclude that the retribution is complete.

'Enough!', voices are heard. The sailor stops immediately, puts on his jacket, pats the little boy on the head and disappears in the direction of the docks. A few tender-hearted people lead the beaten man to a fountain and help him to wash himself off. New faces are now noticeable in the crowd: women in black straw hats with turned down brims, bound around with red ribbon. In the women's hands are stacks of newspapers and brochures. These are the 'soldiers' and 'officers' of the Salvation Army, who have come out to 'reclaim lost souls from the devil'. The

---

[26] Possibly a reference to the famous Joseph Lister (1827–1912), the surgeon who introduced the use of antiseptics.

[27] 'Count Orloff' (1864–1904) was a real 'freak show' star and contemporary posters did indeed depict him with transparent legs. See *The Life of Count Ivan D. Orloff: The Only Living Transparent and Ossified Man* (Liverpool: Nicol, Kendrick, 1900). Contemporary accounts of the East End, such as those found in Sims's *Living London* volumes, corroborate how commonplace the exhibition of 'freaks' for public entertainment still was in this period; the most famous Whitechapel 'freak' of all was, of course, the Elephant Man.

Fig. 20. A Salvation Army 'Dedication'.

'outpost soldiers' have their barracks, their 'salvation stations' and night shelters right here in Whitechapel.[28]
One of the 'officers' thrusts a 'manifesto' into my hands.

[Shklovsky summarises the contents of the manifesto in a few sentences.]

Around the corner, in one of the alleyways, is the Army's 'barracks'. There is a meeting today, so I set off there. An enormous hall is hung with fantastic flags. These are all banners of countries that the Army has conquered. One part of the hall is occupied by a platform, upon which benches rise stepwise up to the very ceiling. Musicians, 'soldiers', 'officers', and the recently 'saved' are seated on the platform. Below and in the front, the 'captain' strolls back and forth in his tailless red jacket with a white crown embroidered on the breast. The captain rubs his hands and from time to time twirls his long, military-style moustache. The public benches are crowded, though the majority are wearing the 'Army's' uniform hats. There are not many sinners to speak of: a few soldiers, who with their bright-red tunics, caps worn aslant and riding

---

[28] On the Salvation Army's shelters and barracks in Whitechapel and elsewhere, including many illustrations, see London's *The People of the Abyss* and Peter Higginbotham, 'Salvation Army Establishments', *The Workhouse: The Story of an Institution*, www.workhouses.org.uk/SA/. There were shelters in Hanbury Street, Commercial Street and Whitechapel Road. The Salvation Army's Men's Social Work Headquarters was at 20 and 22 Whitechapel Road.

crops in hand look like characters from an operetta,[29] two or three sailors and a few homeless tramps who have come in because it is warm here and there is no dripping rain.

'Brothers! strike up our victory hymn!' the captain commands. On the platform they begin to sing to a dancing tune. The musicians' cheeks puff out, their eyes grow bloodshot. The brass trumpets roar, the pipes squeak shrilly; but it is the drums that are working the hardest. The longer it goes on, the more fervent the drummers get. Soon everything is drowned out by the rattling sounds: 'boom! boom! boom!'.

The captain waves his hand. The musicians stop. Just one drummer boy continues to bang a solo for a few more seconds.

'Sister Margaret Routledge, tell us how you were saved', the captain suggests.

A small, wizened, shrivelled old lady with grey, prickly little eyes stands up.

'I was a menace to my neighbours. My wicked mouth spouted blasphemies continually.'

'O-o!' the captain moans.

'O-o!' everyone moans on the platform.

'Not a day went by without me picking a fight with someone.'

Once again, moans erupt on cue.

'But I got to know the "brothers" and have renounced the devil.'

A broad grin appears on the captain's face. By the movement of his shoulders, the rubbing of his hands and the twisting of his legs he expresses how happy he is that Margaret Routledge has renounced the devil.

'William Collier! – it is now your turn to repent.'

A tall, lean man of about forty-five years, with a pointed red nose, rises. He walks up to the barrier, staggering slightly. If the captain had looked more attentively at Collier and seen his suspiciously moist eyes, he would never, of course, have called him up.

'Gentlemen... nay, brothers', Collier begins, 'I was a lost man. My soul belonged to the devil. I drank and drank – you know what? that horrible Irish whiskey. But now, now... mm!' the orator lows, staggers slightly and clutches the barrier.

'Bill's done with the whiskey now and has moved on to gin!', remarks one of the 'sinners' in the audience. There is a burst of laughter.

'Bill is now saved', the captain swoops in. 'Quickly, a hymn to God! Let us praise his salvation!' Again, the pipes squeak; again, the brass trumpets roar; again the rolling of the drums drowns everything out. Some negro from among the 'saved' jumps down from the bench and dances on the platform, singing wildly and baring his white teeth.

---

[29] 'Riding crops': Shklovsky is referring to the so-called 'swagger stick' – a short cane or riding crop carried by soldiers when off duty as part of their uniform.

With an unpleasant aftertaste lingering in my heart, I leave the 'barracks'.

A few steps from the entrance is one of the libraries set up by the younger generation. All the rooms are packed with readers. Here are the same ragged coats, the same peak caps as everywhere; but the faces are more animated, more intelligent. A huge chart shows which exact books have been borrowed today. I can see that, aside from the English classics, also in circulation today are a course in popular astronomy, lectures on applied mechanics, Rogers's 'The Economic Interpretation of English History', Mill's 'On Liberty', Hallam's 'The Constitutional History of England', etc.[30] Some of the readers are copying out extracts from the books. In front of others lie notebooks with hand-drawn diagrams and calculations. In the 'newspaper room', among a mass of publications in the English language, I come across two Russian newspapers and several journals in the Polish-Jewish jargon.[31] There are up to thirty thousand Russian Jews in Whitechapel, immigrants from the Northwestern Krai. For the most part, they are 'sweated' workers, cobblers and tailors.[32]

Next to the library is a museum.[33] Its collection is rather a motley one. Apparently, those who established it did not have any specific idea in mind; but even in its current form, it can do some definite good.

It is not very late; in all likelihood, the first act of the melodrama has only just finished at the 'Pavilion', 'Whitechapel's Main Theatre'.[34] To visit Whitechapel and not to see the latest show is absolutely out

---

[30]   James E. Thorold Rogers, *The Economic Interpretation of History* (London: T. Fisher Unwin, 1898); John Stuart Mill, *On Liberty* (London: John W. Parker & Son, 1859); Henry Hallam, *The Constitutional History of England* (Paris: A. & W. Galignani, 1827). These kinds of books were staples of working-class autodidact historical reading at the turn of the century. Compare this positive description of working-class Englishmen in a library with Chukovsky's contemptuous judgements in his 'Whitechapel' Letter.

[31]   Yiddish.

[32]   Shklovsky's note: In early 1899, a free Russian library was set up for them in Whitechapel.
        Editor's note: see the 'Foreigners in London' section.

[33]   Shklovsky is almost certainly referring to the Whitechapel Free Library founded by Samuel Barnett of Toynbee Hall and renamed Passmore Edwards Library in 1897, and adjoining museum, whose collections included natural history, antiquities and colonial artefacts. See 'Whitechapel Gallery, former Whitechapel Library', *The Survey of London: Histories of Whitechapel*, https://surveyoflondon.org/map/feature/396/detail/.

[34]   The Pavilion Theatre, 191–193 Whitechapel Road, rebuilt several times over the course of the nineteenth century, was indeed the East End's main theatre, seating several thousand people and known for staging melodramas of the kind Shklovsky describes next, as well as pantomimes and farces. At the turn of the twentieth century, it also began presenting a Yiddish programme, although Shklovsky makes no mention of this. For a history of the theatre see '191–193 Whitechapel Road',

of the question. Sixpence gets us our seats. The huge theatre is packed with people. There are absolutely no hats in sight: only workmen's, soldiers' and sailors' caps all around; but this audience is undoubtedly 'cleaner' than those who frequent the abovementioned spectacles. The sailors are sitting next to the so-called **sailors' women**, their temporary wives, who put one in mind of Japan. When a steamer docks after a long voyage, the sailor immediately, as soon as he sets foot on shore, takes up with a **sailor's woman**. The sailor gives all his wages to his temporary wife, which usually amount to twenty-five or thirty pounds. The 'spouses' move in together, and together attend the theatre and other **amusements**. The 'wife' keeps house, mends her 'husband's' linen, restrains him from drinking excessively, and so on. The sailor's leave usually lasts six weeks. In this time, the wages are all spent. The moment of parting arrives. The 'spouses' bid each other a tender farewell, and then the sailor sets sail for Rio de Janeiro, Botany Bay or Shanghai. The **sailor's woman** takes up with another. On the whole, the couples live in harmony with each other and fight comparatively rarely.

On the stage, they are performing the drama 'It Is Never Too Late to Mend'.[35] I arrive at the moment when the hero is bidding farewell to his motherland. The villain of the piece has ruined him, and he is forced to emigrate to Australia. The actor is perfectly mediocre; but the theme is very familiar to the audience, and they follow the play with all-absorbing interest. Now the musical accompaniment starts up a touching song, full of pathos, of the emigrants' leave-taking of home.[36] You can hear deep sighs in the auditorium; tears glisten in women's eyes. The residents of Whitechapel know all too well the emotion felt by the emigrants. A girl in a white dress, the hero's beloved, swears to wait for him and presses her hand to her heart pathetically. The audience rewards her for this with applause. The curtain falls. The villain is recalled for the sole purpose of being driven away again with deafening whistles. Now for the next act.

[Shklovsky proceeds to offer a detailed summary of the melodrama, including scenes in Portland Prison, whose realism in the depiction

---

The Survey of London: Histories of Whitechapel, https://surveyoflondon.org/map/feature/1468/detail/.

35 A play based on Charles Reade's eponymous 1856 novel; the dramatisation had been performed on stage since the mid-Victorian period.

36 There were countless songs (and paintings) in the nineteenth century on the theme of 'the emigrant's farewell', mostly originating in Scotland and Ireland, though some were English. A search of *Broadside Ballads Online*, http://ballads.bodleian.ox.ac.uk/, yields over thirty hits. Some were printed at the time in collections such as Alexander Whitelaw's *The Book of Scottish Song* (Glasgow: Blackie & Son, 1843); some have been reprinted since with music and lyrics in volumes such as Dan Milner and Paul Kaplan, *Songs of England, Ireland and Scotland: A Bonnie Bunch of Roses* (New York: Oak Publications, 1983).

*of 'hard labour' and brutality he admires (the prisoners' round in
the exercise yard, picking oakum, straitjackets, the **'black hole'** (i.e.
solitary confinement), etc.). He describes the audience's outraged
reactions to the abuse of a boy convict by the prison warden (whistles,
cries of **'shame'** and **'Bloody Hero!'** from the 'gallery', storms of
curses, brandishings of fists and sticks and thrown missiles including
'coconut shells' and 'apple cores'). He wonders how actors dare to
play villains before such a 'lynch' mob and recalls the audience's
ancestors who hanged Judas during a performance of the Lord's
Passion. Finally, he describes the part of a 'pastor' who 'appeals to*

Fig. 21. Leaving the Pavilion Theatre, Whitechapel.

the people', Bible in hand, and is met with thunderous applause. The play concludes with the hero striking it rich in Australia and returning home to his waiting girl. Shklovsky remarks on the 'crude', 'weak', black-and-white portrayal of good and evil in the drama, but judges that there is nothing in it liable to 'corrupt' the audience, since the author evidently had 'the best of intentions'.]

And when one recalls the words of an observer who had seen the Whitechapel theatres a quarter of a century ago, one has to conclude that here too significant progress is in evidence. Then, the public had at their disposal either fist fights, rat-baiting or, at best, fantastic performances 'with pyrotechnic tricks, with devils of various colours, and with Satan emerging from the trap door'.[37]

Midnight. To remain in Whitechapel at this hour is no longer entirely safe. It is time to return to the West End.

[37]   I have not been able to locate the source of the quotation.

Isaak Shklovsky [Dioneo], from 'Rabochiy Kvartal' ['The Working Quarter']
Sketches of Contemporary England (St Petersburg, 1903): 483–507[1]

I.

I wanted to get acquainted a bit more closely with the London masses, to study not *abstract* man as he figures in the columns of statistical tables, not the 'hands' bringing a known portion of their labour power to market, but rather Smith, Jones, Clark and Robinson, who have their own private joys and their own private sorrows. I wanted to see what this Smith was like in himself: the one who is clocking his 'hours', getting his wage on Saturdays and… has such high chances of becoming the pensioner of a workhouse in his old age. In a word, I was interested in *'living* numbers', to use Gleb Uspensky's expression.[2] 'Facts by themselves do not say anything; they teach nothing until interpreted by reason', says Marshall.[3] And in order to interpret correctly, we need to reckon not with an abstract Smith, but with a live one who has his own individuality. But how could I make my wish come true? Of course, by following the example of a hundred other English observers and settling

---

[1] Originally published as a Letter 'From England' under the pseudonym Dioneo in the monthly journal *Russkoe Bogatstvo*, January 1899, 119–42. The January issue also included translations of two Rudyard Kipling stories and a 'Letter' from Moscow entitled 'The Moscow Whitechapel and the Plan for Its Abolition'. Shklovsky prefaces the collected volume in which this Letter was reprinted with the following words: 'This book consists of articles published in *Russkoe Bogatstvo* since 1897 […] A few chapters of this book, such as, for instance, "The Working Quarter", "Frankie" and others, are semi-belletristic [fictional] in form. I wanted to provide some adequate illustrations for the "living numbers"' (v, viii). 'The Working Quarter' is indeed preceded by a long section, 'The Life of the Poor in Cities', composed almost entirely of statistics from Charles Booth, Seebohm Rowntree and other contemporary sources. This Letter thus puts some semi-imaginary flesh on the dry bones of sociological fact; furthermore, in the opening paragraph, Shklovsky clearly states his intent to humanise and individualise the 'economic man' of the political economists.

[2] Gleb Uspensky was a major narodnik writer whose cycle of sketches *Living Numbers* (1888) described the impact of capitalism on the lives of countryside workers. This may have provided a formal model for Shklovsky's own journalistic practice in terms of its combination of factual research, opinion, portraiture, humour and use of idiomatic direct speech. See Gleb Uspensky, *Zhivie Tsifri [Living Numbers] in Sobranie Sochineniy v Devyati Tomakh [Collected Works in Nine Volumes]*, vol. 7 (Moscow, GIHL, 1957).

[3] This is Shklovsky's version of the influential neoclassical economist Alfred Marshall's words in *Principles of Economics*, 3rd ed., vol. 1 (London: Macmillan, 1895): 'The economist must be greedy of facts; but facts by themselves teach nothing. History tells of sequences and coincidences; but reason alone can interpret and draw lessons from them' (113).

135

down myself for a time in some poor quarter of the huge metropolis. I had often made short forays there; but they have the disadvantage of not revealing to the investigator a picture of *everyday* life. It is quite another matter to live oneself within the field of observation, if one can put it like this. But which quarter to choose? Whitechapel? North Pancras? Lambeth?[4] All these are centres of the utmost destitution. They are interesting in their way, but firstly, there already exists a large literature dealing with them. Dozens of researchers have worked and are currently working there. Secondly, although these quarters may present a striking and vivid picture, it will not illustrate the life of *young* England, called into civic life by the latest reforms; and it was precisely this that interested me. In view of this, I decided to take up residence in a quarter with a mixed population, where alongside the *Slums* there would also live people with regular earnings.[5]

I had a friend called Haufen, a good-natured old crank, originally a Westphalian German, cast away in England about twenty-five years previously. A tiny fortune and very modest needs allowed him to live in retirement without worrying about the future. In his youth, Haufen had wandered all over the world: he had been to the Balkan states, France, Italy, and had spent many years in North and South America. As a result, Haufen had learned to babble a little and to swear perfectly in every language. His distinguishing features also included highly developed social instincts and a complete nihilism when it came to dressing and washing. According to a strong expression of Haufen's, the habit of washing every day and watching one's language was '**die Dummheit und der Unsinn der Ferkelcivilisation**' (the stupidity and nonsense of a hoggish civilisation). As a result of his strongly developed instincts of 'sociability', Haufen attached himself to the society in which he moved as if it were his own family. This society at present was the workingmen's club to which he belonged and on whose committee he served. Often, in the middle of a conversation, Haufen would take out his watch and then spring up like a shot. 'I need to run to the club; we are having a soiree there', he would say anxiously. I knew that Haufen had many friends amongst the people and so I asked whether he knew a working family that would agree to let me a room for about three or four weeks. Haufen looked at me sullenly, somehow sideways from under his large round wobbly spectacles wound about with string and clicked his false teeth. This was always his way of expressing surprise.

'**Sacrebleu!**[6] Ha! What do you want that for?'

I explained.

---

4   'North Pancras' is probably a reference to the Somers Town district, east of Euston Station; 'Lambeth' refers to north Lambeth.
5   Editor's paragraph break.
6   French: old-fashioned interjection akin to 'good God!'.

'Hm!' he mumbled, scratched his bristly beard, which had probably never been brushed since the day it first grew, and again clicked his false teeth. '**Sie sind doch ein Beobachter**',[7] the old bachelor grumbled. 'You probably want to discover some new laws. As it is, **ventre gris!**,[8] it's hard to know where to hide from formulas!'

I replied that I had no far-reaching plans and was not intending to invent any formulas, but simply wanted to live for four weeks in the home of some Smith or Clark.

Two days later, I was installed in a room on the first floor of a little house in Dalling Road occupied by the carpenter Randle.[9]

I had acquainted myself with the local topography beforehand. Dalling Road is a very long and very dirty street with two rows of little old blackened houses. Landlords let them out on conditions quite

---

[7] German: 'You are an observer.'

[8] French: old-fashioned interjection *ventre-saint-gris* meaning 'begad!' or 'gadzooks!'.

[9] Dalling Road is in Hammersmith, less than half a mile away from Kelmscott House, the headquarters of the Socialist League and residence of William Morris until his death in 1896 (see below for Morris). Shklovsky's choice of this street is not coincidental: the Russian Free Press Fund with which he was closely associated in the 1890s (see the Introduction) was based in 15 Augustus Road, just off the north end of Dalling Road, so Shklovsky clearly knew the area well (it should also be recalled that at some point Shklovsky lived in Shepherd's Bush). The Fund was presided over by L. B. Goldenberg, whose looks and international travels (though nothing else) Shklovsky used for the almost certainly fictional Haufen (see Shklovsky, 'The Old London Emigration', 42–44; the 1901 London census does not list anyone named Haufen). The Free Press Fund was established by revolutionary émigrés and published books, pamphlets and newspapers; see John Slatter, 'The Russian *Émigré* Press in Britain, 1853–1917', *The Slavonic and East European Review* 73.4 (October 1995), 716–47. It was a magnet for Russian revolutionaries visiting London and was under the surveillance of both Russian and British police spies. George H. Duckworth's 'Notebook' in the LSE Library Charles Booth Archive, which covers, amongst others, 'Police District 30 [Hammersmith]', describes a walk with Sergeant Hopkins on 17 February 1899, which took in Dalling Road and Augustus Road. In the latter, Duckworth saw 'a Russian with window open & study full of books'; this is almost certainly Goldenberg, because Hopkins identifies him as 'a revolutionary, nihilist editor, paper used to be printed in the Godolphin Rd & circulated abroad, police watch kept upon them, but they are very quiet & don't cause any trouble over here' (Booth/B/361, 13, https://booth.lse.ac.uk/notebooks/b361). Duckworth describes Dalling Road itself as 'mixed: shops above let out often to poor tenants: N[orth] end better than South […] Dalling Rd is much poorer on the S[outh] side' (61); see also other references to the street on pages 13, 63, as well as Booth/B/268, 'Notebook: Nonconformist District 30 [Hammersmith]' from 1899, which gives interviews with Primitive Methodist and Congregationalist ministers from the street. The coloured map in Charles Booth, *Life and Labour of the People in London*, series 3, vol. 3 (London: Macmillan, 1902), 162–63, classes Dalling Road as 'poverty and comfort mixed', which backs up Shklovsky's description of it. See Map 2 in this anthology.

different from those in the more affluent areas. There, the term of rent is three years, and tenants pay in thirds as the term expires. There is no such trust in the inhabitants of Dalling Road: the carpenters, bricklayers, draymen, dyers,[10] and other folk who get a weekly wage. They pay their rent every Saturday. Failure to pay for two weeks running leads to an order to vacate the property. The result of this payment system, as it happens, is as follows. Those who rent a house by the year also pay the city rates and so have the right to participate in municipal elections. But it is the landlord who pays the city rates on behalf of those who rent lodgings by the week. He, of course, charges this expense to the tenant; but the latter is deprived of the right to vote, while the landlord gets several votes. It was this particular phenomenon that the drafters of the Newcastle Programme had in mind when they brought forward the 'one man, one vote' principle.[11]

At the centre of the quarter stands the large but rather awkward building of the Board school, around which hundreds of boys and girls buzz like bees every morning and noon.[12] The inhabitants of the little houses are poor but earn a regular wage; there are no pubs to be seen, nor drunken, brawling ruffians or tear-stained blowsy women with huge bruises under their eyes. The children messing about on the pavements do not produce the same kind of dispiriting impression, like kittens thrown in the gutter, as in the Lambeth quarter, for instance. For all this, statistical reports list the local school under the category of **'special difficulty school'**. The meaning of this term is as follows. School statistics divide the population of London into three classes: 'lower', 'middle', and 'upper', based on the regularity of their wages. The 'lower' class includes the semi-criminal population consisting of

[10]   The exact translation of the occupations listed here and below is a matter of inter-pretation. Randle might be a joiner or cabinet-maker rather than a carpenter; and similarly, Shklovsky might mean stonemason instead of bricklayer; carter, carrier, carman or even cabby, instead of drayman.

[11]   Shklovsky's note: Every voter pays the following rates: for the relief of the poor, for the maintenance of the **county council**, police, museums, and local libraries for popular education, after which come lighting and street drainage, and the maintenance of pavements. The rate is allocated in proportion to the rent. In total, municipal rates amount to one third of the rent. Moreover, there exists also a small house rate, the so-called 'crown tax', which is used for the benefit of the state. The greatest amount has to be paid for the relief of the poor. In my borough, we annually pay 1s. 6d. 1/8 per each pound of rent to the **'Relief of the Poor'** fund. Editor's note: The Newcastle Programme was a statement of the policies of the Liberal Party issued in 1891, which included a number of reforms, among them the abolition of plural voting. However, Shklovsky's account of the franchise here is incorrect: lodgers, i.e. subtenants, had the right to vote after twelve months' residence in a borough; plural voting was not finally abolished in the UK until 1948 for parliamentary elections and 1969 for local elections.

[12]   This is most likely the Board School at the northern end of Dalling Road, which may be seen on Booth's map and Ordnance Survey maps of the period.

Fig. 22. Board School: Playtime.

tramps, beggars, thieves, etc. The 'middle' class are those who do not possess a regular wage or trade, such as porters, dockworkers, apprentice masons, etc. The 'upper' class includes labourers on good regular wages who earn over 25s. per week. In the Board schools, children from the three groups present a different appearance. The children belonging to the 'upper' class come to school clean and well-fed; they find it easier to follow the instruction. Other children come hungry and exhausted by work, which makes them dull. The job of the teacher is especially gruelling in the quarters inhabited by the semi-criminal population. The perennial poverty, the chronic hunger across several generations, the degradation and drunkenness have all left their mark on the children. 'The class presents a sad picture', says the researcher. 'Only two or three pupils look tidy. Their faces are washed and there are clean collars around their necks. The rest are a group of ragamuffins who seem to be vying with one another for the worst rags. Many look positively sickly,

Fig. 23. Swinging.

their eyes red and festering… The marks of destitution, grief, hunger, drunkenness and intimidation stand out in sharp relief… A quarter of all children in the classes are complete dunces. Grown-up boys with the faces of cowed and frightened sheep sit in the lower forms trying to learn; but they cannot do it. In the girls' forms it is the same. The girls are broken by the hardships of a life that has placed untimely burdens on their shoulders. Here is an old woman, twelve years of age, who has to keep house because her mother is in prison and her father drinks.'[13] These schools are known as **special difficulty schools**, that

---

[13]   Shklovsky's note: **Ch. Booth, Life and Labour of the People. v. III, p. 219**. Editor's note: this is not so much a direct quotation as a rephrasing and condensation of fragments from pages 215–220 of the 'Elementary Education' chapter in volume 3 of the 1892 edition of *Life and Labour of the People in London*. The entire paragraph is heavily indebted to this chapter (especially pages 208–11),

is, those where teaching presents special difficulties. And this is the category to which the Dalling Road school belongs. One only needs to turn the corner to see the reason. The character of the quarter changes abruptly. The streets are dirty and poorly drained, which makes them smell strongly of sewage. Winding alleys crawl in every direction like spiders. The houses are old, blackened, their windowpanes shattered and replaced by newspapers. Many doors are boarded up: these houses have been pronounced unsuitable for occupation by the sanitary inspectors. We are in a typical London **Slum**. Few families here occupy a flat consisting of more than one room. Aside from the owner, such flats also contain a tenant. Children for the most part roam the streets, returning home only when the countless pubs shut. One comes across the pubs at every step. Shivering people in rags, gone livid with whisky, crowd beside their doors, especially towards the evening. They are weaker and shorter than the rest of the population. They appear to be a completely different tribe.[14] Aside from pubs, one also meets with an abundance of three gold balls, the sign of the pawnbroker. They accept any rag in pawn and issue loans of 1½d.

How drastically the home of the carpenter Randle that I had chosen as my observation point differed from these dens![15] The little house consisted of two floors. The lower had two rooms: a parlour and a dining room that also served as the kitchen. The upper floor also had two rooms. The Randles paid eleven shillings a week for the house. In order to have a known sum secured at all times, the Randles, like most of the workers here, let one room to a lodger for 3½ shillings a week. The house was rather dark and smelled slightly of damp; the wallpaper, especially in the entrance hall, had frayed at the bottom and was hanging in tatters; but everything was spotlessly clean.[16] The doormats had been scrubbed – not a stain on them; the oilcloth that covered the stairs was positively gleaming. The missus washed it with soap every day. There were soft

---

and other observations from it make their way into Shklovsky's account later on. The description of the Board school catchment area that follows is not entirely accurate: although there are indeed 'light blue', i.e. 'poor' streets nearby, there are no 'winding alleys'.

[14] Shklovsky is probably adopting the anthropological classification of the poor as a distinct 'tribe' that was typical of Victorian social investigators like Mayhew.

[15] Although Shklovsky's Preface implies that the characters in this Letter are fictional, there are three likely carpenters listed as living in the parish of Hammersmith in 1901: Samuel Randle, b. 1842; George Randle, b. 1869; William Randall, b. 1862, as well as 'Mrs Randles' of suitable ages. As for the children Shklovsky names below, the census lists the siblings Florence Randall, b. 1891 and May Randall, b. 1896, and there is also a Flora Rendell, b. 1892 and May Rundle, b. 1894. Unsurprisingly, though, none live in Dalling Road and none are found all together in the same family.

[16] Cleanliness is one of the key markers of the 'respectable' working class in Victorian and Edwardian social commentary and fiction.

furnishings in the parlour and in every corner some kind of little shelf with little cups, photographs, small porcelain jars, etc. Pride of place on the wall was given to a photographic group depicting a cricket match in which my host had taken part and a large meerschaum pipe – the victory trophy.[17] In the place of honour near the fireplace stood a handmade bookcase. Aside from a pile of reports produced by the carpenters' union, to which my landlord belongs and in one of whose branches he serves as secretary, and a few pamphlets, there were a couple of dozen books: the Bible, Shakespeare, Blatchford's 'Merrie England', 'Fabian' publications, Sherard's 'The White Slaves of England', a volume of Green's 'History of the English People', the poems of Walt Whitman, Hobson's 'The Evolution of Modern Capitalism', etc.[18] Above the books, in a large frame, hung the diploma issued to Randle by his trade union. I already knew something about my hosts from Haufen's account. I knew that Randle was the son of a 'Hodge' (an agricultural labourer), that he earns about thirty-five shillings a week, that he is a member of one of the richest 'unions' in England numbering around fifty-four thousand members.[19] It was known to me that Randle paid one shilling a week in union membership fees, plus another shilling per year to the emergency fund. This gives him the following rights: in case of illness

---

[17] The original text has 'croquet' instead of cricket, but it is almost certain that Shklovsky means the latter when he says the former throughout his correspondence. This is confirmed in his translation from Thomas Hughes's *Tom Brown's School Days* in 'Frankie', where the English 'cricket' is rendered 'croquet' in Russian. I have therefore used 'cricket' throughout.

[18] This is a typical list of books consumed by socialistically inclined working-class autodidacts. As a starting point, see Jonathan Rose's *The Intellectual Life of the British Working Classes*. Robert Blatchford's *Merrie England* (London: Walter Scott, 1894) was a wildly successful book of socialist propaganda that sold millions of copies; Fabian Society pamphlets dealt with a variety of topics; Robert Sherard's *The White Slaves of England* (London: James Bowden, 1897) was the fruit of undercover social investigation among the poor; J. R. Green's multi-volume *A History of the English People* (1880) was a pioneering work of social history whose original popular one-volume version (London: Macmillan & Co., 1874) was widely consumed in radical circles; and J. A. Hobson's *The Evolution of Modern Capitalism* (London: Walter Scott, 1894) dealt with the development of machine industry and the economics of capitalism.

[19] Shklovsky most likely has in mind the Amalgamated Society of Carpenters and Joiners, whose membership figures match the ones listed here most closely (unlike, for instance, the General Union of Carpenters and Joiners, the Alliance Cabinet Makers Association or its successor National Amalgamated Furnishing Trades Association [from 1902], or the Amalgamated Union of Cabinet Makers – memberships of all of which were under ten thousand). Interestingly, a J. Randle was an executive council member of the ASC&J in the 1890s. See the materials on 'Furniture and Timber Unions' held by the Working Class Movement Library, www.wcml.org.uk/our-collections/working-lives/furniture-and-timber/furniture-and-timber-unions/ and also 'Amalgamated Society of Woodworkers', *Trade Union Ancestors*, www.unionancestors.co.uk/amalgamated-society-of-woodworkers/.

to get (for the duration of three months) twelve shillings a week; if he loses his job, he will be supported for six months (at ten shillings per week). If he is injured at work: e.g. loses an arm, the union will pay him £50, and in the event of his death his family will receive £100. He is also, to a certain extent, provided for in old age. If he remains a union member for twenty-five years, he will receive five shillings per week; if for thirty years, then seven shillings. In the event of an industrial dispute, all members of the union get fifteen shillings per week. The Randles have two children, both girls, six and four years of age. Since education is compulsory in England from the age of five, the older girl, Florrie, goes to school every day. The younger, May, is still at home.

I am installed in my room. Evening falls. Fog envelops the melancholy street ever closer in its milky shroud. I can see from my window neighbouring women, wearing men's caps instead of headscarves, running to the shop or chatting as they wait for their heads of household, who are due to return from work soon. Children are standing on the doorsteps or on the pavement looking out for their fathers. I can hear May and Florrie messing about downstairs, and Mrs Randle clinking the cups as she prepares tea for her husband. She is singing; at first, I cannot make out the words, but soon I manage to catch the following:

> 'The night is dark,
> We are not afraid:
> The dawn is near.'[20]

I have heard this song many times at meetings. Now a door bangs. The children squeal with delight. A weary male voice sounds. The head of the house must be back from work. The fog and the dark together seep into the open window of my tiny room. It seems to me that this is a special kind of darkness, replete with the poverty and grief of the neighbouring quarter. It seems that the darkness is something formless but alive, entangling a person in its cold, black tentacles. A nervous shiver runs down my entire body. I have just returned from the Continent, and the wonderful mountain landscapes still stand out with striking clearness in my imagination. That may be why this gloomy quarter makes such a strong impression. I go out to wander down the neighbouring shopping street.[21] It comes alive in the evening, when people return from work. The gas lamps give out a dim and hazy light in the fog. There is a horrible crush on the slippery pavements, but this is not a Whitechapel crowd: no drunken sailors or painted women

---

[20]   This may be Shklovsky's rendition of the opening words of Edward Carpenter's popular 'England, Arise!' in *Chants of Labour: A Song Book of the People* (London: Swan Sonnenschein & Co., 1888): 'The long, long night is over, / Faint in the East behold the dawn appear', or any number of other contemporary socialist chants featuring the passing of the night and the advent of dawn.

[21]   Shklovsky is probably referring to Goldhawk Road.

are to be seen; no booming oaths are to be heard. The crowd consists of workers and their wives. All have crawled out to do their shopping. One constantly meets with groups such as the following: the husband pulling a little cart where a child dozes with a dummy in its mouth, the wife carrying a parcel from which poke a celery stalk, several potatoes, a packet of tea and some butter wrapped in paper. If it were not for the wild cries of the butchers, shouting across each other to advertise the excellence of their products, the street would be perfectly quiet, despite the mass of people. There are many shops, but all of them cater for very slim wallets. If any semi-expensive items are sold in them at all, such as crockery or furniture, the buyers are lured in by the instalment system. 'Just one shilling a week for a magnificent bed', one window signals. 'A sofa and six armchairs for just half a crown a week', another beckons. Young people engaged to be married walk from one window to another hand-in-hand, discussing the details of their future household. I have to return home. It seems that the air of the street is even more replete with the breath of poverty and grief than the darkness that had penetrated my room. The fog has thickened. It is already nearly eleven o'clock.

It's best to try and fall asleep. That is the best way to get acclimatised in a new place.

Drunken voices waft in from the street. They are raging and swearing near 'The Seven Stars' pub at the first corner.[22] Snatches of beery songs can be heard, but most often crude oaths, meaningless combinations of the word **'bloody'** and female weeping. But now the drunkards have fallen silent. Someone begins singing a rousing popular comic song. The singer's voice is hoarse but pleasant. It has been well trained. One can guess from the singer's pronunciation of words that he has been on the stage. It is undoubtedly a 'fallen' one, come down, perhaps, all the way from the aristocratic music hall to the pub doors.[23] I can imagine the singer's figure: he must be standing now at the entrance, smiling timidly every time the doors open, and gesticulating theatrically ('for laughs') with his arms. He is wearing a worn little old jacket with its collar raised so as to better protect the body lacking in undergarments.

[22] According to the 'Post Office London County Suburbs Directory, 1911 [Part I: Street & Commercial Directories]', 126, available at *University of Leicester Special Collections Online*, http://specialcollections.le.ac.uk/digital/collection/p16445coll4/id/25458, there was a pub named 'The Seven Stars' at the corner of Goldhawk Road and Paddenswick Road (ordnance survey maps of the period also show a 'Public House' at that intersection) – near enough to Dalling Road, but definitely not within hearing distance. There was a pub called 'Prince of Wales' in Dalling Road itself.

[23] Of course, the music hall originated in pubs earlier in the nineteenth century. On pubs, see Mark Girouard, *Victorian Pubs* (London: Studio Vista, 1975).

Perhaps it is also 'for laughs' that the singer has smeared his face with soot, livid as it is with the cold and the vodka.[24]

[Shklovsky proceeds to compare this singer with another one he has seen during his recent trip to France while observing the Paris crowd along with other foreigners seated in the Café Américain on the Boulevard des Capucines.]

II.

'Would you like to come to the club with us?' my landlady proposed the next day, when the children had been put to bed. 'Today we're having a lecture, dancing and tableaux vivants.'

Mr Randle had not yet returned from work; there was some urgent job to finish, and they were kept on at the workshop longer than usual. The two of us set off together. On the way, I learned the history of the **'John Ball'** club, so named in honour of one of William Morris's characters.[25] A group of about forty people rented the house for £42 per annum; the ladies came after finishing their housework and washed and scrubbed the building clean. Then it was the men's turn. The house had been let relatively cheaply because it was in a rather dilapidated state. The 'gentlemen' came there after work, repaired the floors, adjusted the ill-fitting sash frames, mended the creaking doors, pasted back the tattered wallpaper and gave an extra lick of paint where defects were most likely to catch the eye. The house turned out a picture! The rent was covered by membership fees, a shilling a month; but since there happened to be a deficit of £5 in the first year, a bazaar was organised to cover it. One member contributed an old jacket, another long-super-annuated boots, another a hat that had served him well many a year. The ladies gathered all of these in the club, cleaned and mended them, turned them inside out if necessary, and mounted a jumble sale. The buyers included street pedlars, newspaper sellers and all those who, in the characteristic words of the English economist, 'are caught in the maelstrom of work that does not require any technical training'.[26] Was it possible to resist the temptation and refrain from buying, when boots were going for five pence, hats for a penny, and when one could flaunt a sound pair of trousers after stumping up just eight pence? The soiree for which we had set out today was intended to cover once and for all the part of the deficit not entirely made up by the sale.

---

[24]   Shklovsky routinely uses 'vodka' in his Letters to refer to gin.
[25]   The reference is to William Morris's socialist story of the 1381 Peasants' Revolt, *A Dream of John Ball* (1888). On Morris and late-Victorian socialist culture, see Anna Vaninskaya, *William Morris and the Idea of Community: Romance, History and Propaganda, 1880–1914* (Edinburgh: Edinburgh University Press, 2010).
[26]   I have not been able to locate the source of the quotation.

The lower 'reception' room of the club could not boast an abundance of furniture. The décor consisted of a simple kitchen table, rather ancient of days (its legs had buckled from age and it wheezed and creaked at every careless move), and some assorted chairs. The furniture had been assembled piecemeal from donations. Just one framed print hung on the wall – a symbolic depiction of the triumph of labour.[27] It seemed that we had been hasty and had arrived too early. There were two bicycles in the corner, but no visitors were to be seen. While waiting for the start of proceedings, I began leafing through the newspapers lying on the table: 'Justice', 'The Labour Leader', the inevitable 'Clarion' and 'Reynolds's Newspaper'.[28] Among these publications, I came across a small, postal-paper-sized copybook about fifty pages long: the club magazine **'The Searchlight'** of which Haufen had already told me. Quite a few of the numerous English workers' clubs have their own magazines.[29] For the most part, these publications appear monthly. They can be divided into three groups. First of all, there are the trade journals. If the club consists of mechanics, carpenters, electricians and other specialists, they like to keep up with developments in their trade. For the most part, these magazines are published by clubs associated with one of the large propagators of technical knowledge among the populace: the London Polytechnic or the People's Palace.[30] The second type includes magazines published by self-improvement clubs. They are usually produced from one of the 'centres' of the **University Extension movement**.[31] These magazines print abstracts, reports of debates, new

[27] Almost certainly a print of Walter Crane's 'The Triumph of Labour' (1891), see the print at the British Museum: www.britishmuseum.org/collection/object/P_1955-0420-7.

[28] *Justice* was the newspaper of the Marxist Social Democratic Federation (its leader H. M. Hyndman was Shklovsky's acquaintance); the *Labour Leader* was the organ of the Independent Labour Party, edited by its leader Keir Hardie (1856–1915); the *Clarion* was the best-selling socialist newspaper of the period, edited by Robert Blatchford (1851–1943), and the focal point of the popular socialist Clarion movement; and *Reynolds's Newspaper*, the longest-running publication of the lot, was originally a Radical, but by the late 1890s Liberal Sunday paper. The selection is absolutely typical of the reading matter of turn-of-the-century working-class socialists.

[29] 'Workers' clubs': the word 'narodnie' in the original text literally means 'popular' or 'people's', as in Narodnaya Volya or 'People's Will' revolutionary organisation, so Shklovsky has in mind a much broader category than 'workingmen's clubs' narrowly defined.

[30] The London Polytechnic was founded in 1838 to provide technical instruction, though its actual remit by the end of the century was much broader and it hosted many different clubs and societies. It was relaunched under different names several times in the nineteenth century.

[31] The University Extension movement was founded in the 1870s by Cambridge and Oxford Universities to reach sections of the adult population, such as women and artisans, who were traditionally barred from higher education. By the turn of

course prospectuses, etc. Sometimes, a magazine is devoted entirely to the topic currently being investigated by the club. For instance, in 1896 forty young carpenters and founders in Glasgow organised a 'Marx Club' for studying 'Kapital'. The study was completed in twenty readings. Each member in turn took a chapter or several paragraphs and paraphrased them as clearly as possible; then the synopsis was read at the club and discussed. The debates were then jointly summarised, the clearest and most concise version was chosen, and the synopsis was printed in the magazine. When the study of 'Kapital' had been completed, the club published all the summaries as a 2d. pamphlet (**'A Short Exposition of Marx's Capital, by W. S. Murphy**). According to Glasgow University professor Smart,[32] this pamphlet represents the best exposition of Marx's teachings in English. Magazines of the third type are handwritten humorous publications, which offer unpretentious imitations of second-rate English comic papers. Local concerns and veiled references to club affairs loom large in them.[33]

Turning several pages of the *Searchlight* was sufficient to ascertain that the publication of the 'John Ball Club' belonged to the third type of magazine. I happened to pick up the third issue. In the opening article, entitled 'The Editor's Expertise', the editor says: 'the success of our *magazine* has exceeded all expectations. The club is in a state of ferment. Fleet Street (the London street where nearly all the newspaper offices are located) is quaking with fear. The editors are very proud of this success: but it has also caused us a lot of worry and bother. A few individuals are for some reason convinced that only certain known persons are fully responsible for that wisdom which is found in such abundance in the *Searchlight*; they look askance at the suspects and lower their voices when these pass by. Why these precautions? The individuals are afraid that the pearls of their eloquence and political wisdom will be reproduced in the pages of the *Searchlight*.'

'What are you doing here, **Kamerad**? Eh?' someone spoke in German.[34] I recognised Haufen by his voice and even more so by the inevitable accompaniment of his clicking dentures. 'Reading the **Searchlight**. Well then? Ha-ha! **Sacramento de Dios!**[35] Do you like it?'

---

the century there were numerous Extension 'Centres' across the land delivering programmes of lectures and classes.

[32] I have not been able to identify this person. The original periodical version of the Letter says: 'see details about this club in the *Labour Leader*'.

[33] This was a style typical of the socialist press more generally – see the tone of columns in the *Clarion* in particular, which were full of in-jokes – not to mention other types of 'club' publications. See Alan Argent, ed. *The Angels' Voice: A Magazine for Young Men in Brixton, London, 1910–1913* (London: London Record Society, 2016).

[34] German: 'comrade' or 'mate'.

[35] Spanish: 'Sacrament of God'.

'N-not quite', I drawled indecisively. As was his custom, Haufen bristled at once and sprang to the defence of his club, an assault upon which he detected in my comment about the magazine.

'Ha! Damn it! And how, pray tell, is *Scraps* better?'[36] The dentures clicked so vigorously, and oaths in all languages poured forth in such abundance that I did not consider it necessary to present my views in detail to the good-natured old bachelor for whom the club had become a surrogate family.

People were starting to gather. There was a sound of laughter and joking. I could not determine the social status of those who surrounded me by their dress and faces; and as for their language, that other measure of class in England, it also did not turn out to be an entirely accurate index. Admittedly, some of those present, especially the ladies, spoke with a strong 'Cockney' accent, pronouncing **'baby'** as 'biby', **'lady'** as 'lidy' and misplacing the letter *h*; but the majority spoke correctly and formally. My mentor was Mrs Randle, who joined me at that moment.

'Do you see that tall young gentleman, the quite handsome one, with curled moustaches – that is a mechanic, Mr Neville, the editor of our magazine. And that clean-shaven, broad-shouldered one, burly as a porter (he is our best cricketer), is a carpenter, Mr Snellgrove. And there in the corner, by the fireplace, is a clerk. He works at a large jewellery store. Now do you see that girl?' She pointed at a pretty young woman in a grey dress with a pink sash, who was leafing through a newspaper. 'That is Miss Clark, a maid. She has completed all six standards of the Board school, can play the piano and even knows some French. She learned all that in the evening school.'

'Gentlemen', Neville spoke up cheerfully. 'I saw such a scene on my way here! it would be fit for **Punch**! There were two ladies sitting in our carriage discussing where they had spent their **holiday**. "I spent all my time in Llandudno", says one, a shrivelled old thing, with thin, pursed, mean lips, a perfect Miss Murdstone,[37] "but I'm never going there again. There was such a mass of Irishmen there, I simply couldn't bear to go out onto the promenade." And just at this moment our carriage stops at the station. A fat woman in a battered hat with a green shawl over her shoulders, who had been sitting on the same bench as the ladies, disembarks and then yells in a thick Irish accent for the whole train to hear: "Missus! If you decide to take your **holiday** next year, go straight to the devil in hell. You probably won't meet any Irishmen there."'

The general laughter drowned out the voice of the storyteller. A bell rang somewhere: the lecture was about to begin. 'Let's go', Mrs Randle told me. We all moved to another room, which had a platform.

---

[36] Shklovsky's note: A third-rate London comic magazine.
      Editor's note: *Scraps* was launched in 1883 by the publisher of *Funny Folks* and was a kind of early comic.

[37] Shklovsky's note: The sister of the hero's stepfather in 'David Copperfield'.

As was customary, before starting, everyone sang **'England Arise!'** in unison.[38] But presently the song, whose droning, somewhat monotonous tune was reminiscent of a church hymn, was over. The chairman went up onto the platform and, according to English custom, introduced the lecturer to the audience, although, by all accounts, the latter already knew him perfectly well. The lecturer had an interesting face: not handsome but energetic, with a broad forehead and square chin. Such faces seem to say: 'I will achieve whatever I set out to do'! The lecturer was at most twenty-six or twenty-seven years old. His shaven moustache and beard and curled tuft of fair hair (a fashion very popular among English workers and clerks) imparted to MacMillan (for so the lecturer was called) an even more youthful aspect.

'MacMillan is a carpenter', Mrs Randle whispered in my ear. 'He lives next to us. His landlady told me that he sits poring over his books until two or three in the morning. The things he knows! The union to which he belongs long ago proposed that he leave his job and become a secretary. And they were offering a good wage, too! But Mr MacMillan doesn't want to hear of it and keeps refusing; he says: "I can understand things better when I sit down with my books after work." We put him forward as a candidate for the School Board at the last election; he was just eleven votes short of winning.[39] I heard that if the general election were to happen tomorrow, we'd nominate MacMillan as a parliamentary candidate.'

Meanwhile, the chairman had finished. The lecturer started to read a paper about wages and the '**Truck Acts**'.[40] 'They say that the good Caliph Harun al-Rashid was wont to leave his splendid palace on occasion and walk around Baghdad in disguise', the lecturer began in a slightly sing-song voice, as is typical of most public speakers here, especially those with little experience.

[Shklovsky proceeds to give an account of the opening of the lecture, which takes the form of a conversation with a personified John Bull – self-satisfied but with an awakening conscience.]

The lecture was interesting. It seemed that the lecturer had a limited store of ideas, but he had mastered them perfectly, had selected the

---

[38] See note 20 above. 'England, Arise!' was the unofficial hymn of the early socialist movement, sung at socialist gatherings across the land in the late nineteenth and early twentieth centuries.

[39] The School Board for London, established in 1870 to equip London with elementary schools, was abolished by the London Education Act 1903, its functions transferred to the Education Committee of the London County Council from 1904.

[40] Shklovsky's note: Laws outlawing payments in kind. Such payments are no longer offered in factories; but they have persisted in some workshops.
Editor's note: the most recent Truck Acts were passed in 1887 (extending the Truck Act 1831) and 1896.

relevant figures and used them well. Like all English public speakers, MacMillan had a weakness for witticisms, which the audience greeted with laughter and applause every time. The speaker finished. Everyone sang once more, a different hymn this time...

Then the audience moved back to the first room, from which all the furniture had been removed and a piano wheeled in. The dancing started. The young people danced with enthusiasm. First, waltzes and polkas, then the purely English **barn-dance**, which is a somewhat disciplined type of jig.

I was very interested in MacMillan's character. I asked Haufen to introduce me to the lecturer. It was not so easy to extricate the German. He kept trying to show the dancers how to dance a 'real' Grossvatertanz.[41] The figure of the dancing Haufen, in a short cutaway, with back bent, was a curious sight to behold. He accompanied every step with a click of his false teeth. '**That is the real German** *Grossvater*', he kept repeating with a good-natured smile. He himself seemed to derive as much pleasure from the dancing as the people around him.

III.

Saturday. Our street has an unaccustomed look. At 2 p.m., I see from my window the workmen hurrying home, carpetbags full of tools slung over their shoulders.[42] Everywhere, little children are keeping watch at the windows. As soon as father appears, the children dash out to meet him. Today is payday. Every father has something in his pocket for his child. From my window I can see a workman hand over his bag of tools to a little lad of six and lift a two-year-old girl up on his shoulders. The girl squeals with delight and shouts for the whole street to hear:

'Gee-gee! Gee-gee! Giddyup! giddyup, gee-gee!'[43]

The boy carrying the tools marches along with uncommon solemnity and gravitas, as behoves a person entrusted with such an important task. Across the street is a sweet shop. Horrible English sweets, meant for a strong stomach, peek from the only window: candied rhubarb, ginger in treacle, coconut flesh mixed with sugar, 'Scottish rock cakes', which live up to their name honourably, etc. Amongst these delicacies can be seen symmetrically arranged bottles of ginger beer, the children's favourite drink. These shops located in the poor quarters, for the most part near the Board schools, fulfil the same function for children as pubs do for adults. Children are always crowding near the shop doors. Today, there

---

[41] The Grossvatertanz is a traditional German folk dance dating from the seventeenth century.

[42] This underlines the identity of the street as a home of respectable artisans rather than a slum. The bag of tools (its possession or its lack) is a key marker of class status from Arthur Morrison's fiction to George Orwell's documentaries.

[43] Shklovsky's note: That is what English children call a hobbyhorse.

are especially many of them: the fathers, having received their wages, have provided their offspring with pennies and ha'pennies. The happy age of childhood! I have been observing one little gentleman, about six years of age, in a red cap with a tassel, for over twenty minutes. The boy must be having a feast today. He has eaten countless numbers of apples, gnawed through a huge piece of 'Scottish rock', drunk two bottles of ginger beer, eaten, despite the cold, a huge portion of ice-cream which contains everything except milk – obtained from an Italian in the street,[44] and after all that, and none the worse for it, he has started playing 'frogs' (a variety of the leapfrog game) with the other little Luculluses.[45]

Around the corner, near 'The Seven Stars', one can already hear the drunken voices. I see women in rags walking up and down the pavement there. Some are carrying children in their arms. The women are not yet looking in through the windows. They are still waiting for their husbands to arrive and hoping that they might be able to preserve the whole of their wages...

I remembered that I had promised to pay a visit to MacMillan. He lived two houses away, so I did not have far to go. The organ-grinders, who do not stop by our street on weekdays, have also remembered that it's the Sabbath day when money is stirring in everyone's pocket. A dirty, ragged Italian grinds the barrel-organ set on his wheelbarrow. A woman wrapped in a shawl is harnessed into the shafts. Next to the barrel-organ on the wheelbarrow stands a basket with a shade. An infant is fidgeting in it. Dozens of little girls are dancing to the sounds of the organ on the pavement and in the street. The fathers, who have already changed their clothes, are all hastening in one direction, towards the savings bank, to lay aside a shilling or two.

MacMillan occupied a top floor back. It was the usual type of room: the same carpets, the same wide bed in the middle of the room and the same prize fighters next to the racehorses on the walls; but there was something singular in it too. In a corner stood a handmade bookcase. There were about fifty books in it, if not more. Papers and pamphlets were stacked tidily on a plain table. I had to wait for a short while: MacMillan was eating downstairs, in the landlady's dining room. On the table lay an issue of Cassell's **'Popular Educator'**,[46] opened at a German lesson.

---

44   Italian ice-cream sellers were a staple of London street life in the late nineteenth century – recognised as such by contemporary observers, see the photograph of the 'Italian ice man' in John Thomson and Adolphe Smith, *Street Life in London* (London: Sampson Low, 1877). Ice-cream making and selling was monopolised by Italian immigrants.

45   The Roman general Lucullus was so renowned for his banquets that he became a byword for lavish eating. Sims includes a photograph of boys playing leapfrog in the street in his anthology.

46   Shklovsky's note: **Cassell's Popular Educator** is a series of self-education textbooks for different subjects, published in separate numbers for 4½d. each.

Fig. 24. Girls in a London Street Dance to the Music of a Barrel Organ, Circa 1900.

I went up to the bookcase. There was a curious selection there: the Bible, Shakespeare, Adam Smith's 'Wealth of Nations', Rogers's 'Six Centuries of Work and Wages', Gibbon, Henry George's 'Progress and Poverty', Karl Marx's 'Kapital' in English translation, Sidney Webb's 'History of Trade Unionism', Thomas More's 'Utopia', Shelley's poems, 'Pickwick', Walter Scott's 'Ivanhoe', Bellamy's **'Looking Backward'**, Blatchford's 'Merrie England', 'Robinson Crusoe' (the favourite book of the English; and in my opinion, the best reflection of the English character), Disraeli's 'Sybil', Holyoake's 'History of Co-operation', Green's 'History of the English People', Jevons's 'Money and [The Mechanism of] Exchange', 'On the Origin of Species', Booth's 'Life and Labour of the People [in London]', etc.[47] This library appeared to

---

It includes courses in four modern languages, lectures on mathematics, music, shorthand, history, etc. The textbooks are intended for persons who embark on their studies equipped with the most elementary knowledge. Overall, the series is intended to prepare individuals to sit exams for the degree of **bachelor of science**. Cassell's series, prepared by the best specialists, is considered a classic of its kind in England.

[47] Again, this list is absolutely typical of the reading, circa 1900, of the class of person being described (see Rose). It includes political economy (Smith, Jevons, George, Marx), socialist best-sellers (Bellamy, Blatchford), social, economic and labour history and sociology (Green, Rogers, the Webbs, Holyoake, Booth), classic working-class reading matter (the Bible, Shakespeare, Gibbon, Defoe, Scott, Dickens) and 'radical' or 'condition of England' literature (More, Shelley, Disraeli). Shklovsky might almost be echoing George Gissing's description of the study of a socialist artisan in *Demos: A Story of English Socialism*, vol. 1 (London: Smith,

be the product of long-term savings: some of the books – for instance, Sidney Webb or Booth – are expensive, and even a person with a more capacious wallet than a workman would hesitate before acquiring them.

MacMillan entered. Having noticed on his table a stack of pamphlets published by the **'English Land Restoration League'**,[48] I asked him whether he was now specifically studying the land question.

'No. Last year, I was part of a corps organised by the **"Clarion"** newspaper. The corps was supposed to operate according to the programme developed by the "League": our main task was to gather as much material as possible on the situation of the country labourers. We left London in proper military formation: with tents, cauldrons and music. By and by, we would come to a riverbank or the edge of a wood, pitch our tents, put out our flag, and then the music would start playing. Country labourers would come running from all directions. Then we would hold a meeting, question those present, distribute our publications, etc. A portion of the material we collected was printed by the "League", another portion was issued by the **Clarion** press, and part still remains in manuscript.'[49]

We fell into a conversation. The impression that MacMillan had made on me at the club was now reinforced even more strongly. A remarkable energy could be felt in his every word and gesture. The outlook of my interlocutor was not particularly broad, but MacMillan had an excellent understanding of the significance of every phenomenon that occurred within his field of vision.

'We will not allow ourselves to be carried away by an abstract ideal', he told me. 'We must put forward something positive and real that we could aim for immediately via the parliamentary route. My comrades will not accept an abstract ideal. We must express everything in concrete terms, and if we see that it is not mere **"dreaming"** (my interlocutor used this word frequently, investing it with his own meaning) but real life, we will be able to achieve what we desire. For we are tenacious; it is not for nothing that the English are called bulldogs. ("You, at least,

---

Elder, 1886), 78: 'The one singular feature of the room was a small, glass-doored bookcase, full of volumes. They were all of Richard's purchasing; to survey them was to understand the man, at all events on his intellectual side.'

48   The English Land Restoration League was an organisation established in the 1880s to promulgate the land reform proposals of the American economist Henry George (1839–1897).

49   This is a representative depiction of the activities of the Clarion Scouts and similar socialist organisations devoted to education and propaganda. See e.g. the Working Class Movement Library 'Clarion Movement' collections at www.wcml. org.uk/our-collections/creativity-and-culture/leisure/clarion-movement/ and Denis Pye, *Fellowship is Life: The National Clarion Cycling Club, 1895–1995* (Bolton: Clarion Publishing, 1995), 27–33. The Clarion Press, earlier the Clarion Newspaper Company, based in London, published Robert Blatchford's books as well as other socialist material.

won't back down!" flashed across my mind as I glanced at MacMillan's broad brow with its slight transverse crease and at his heavy lower jaw and square chin.) We are moving forward slowly, groping every step of the way; but, on the other hand, we will never turn back or let go of what we have achieved.'

'And who, in your opinion, is doing otherwise?'

'Well, the French, for instance.'[50]

It turned out that my interlocutor had some knowledge of French. He was self-taught and pronounced the language entirely in the English manner: 'Ow rivoyr' (**Au revoir**), he said to me when we parted. The meeting made a most positive impression on me. The 'living numbers' were taking on the aspect of flesh and blood more and more before my eyes, and their significance was growing clearer and clearer.

IV.

I had settled in a bit and got acquainted with the quarter.

I knew that next to us, on the other side of the partition wall, lived a family whose head had been without a job for four months. As he did not belong to a union, the family would probably have starved to death if their female neighbour had not helped them out. The children were fed, their old breeches and jackets were altered, and they were given new shirts. I knew that the family had sold and pawned everything of any value. Everyone around understood very well why the starving family did not turn to the workhouse for help. Aside from professional beggars and tramps, the needy would prefer to die of hunger rather than go to the workhouse. With what triumph did Mrs Randle announce to me one day that Mr Springfield – that was the neighbour's surname – had found a job! It was a place at a brewery in Brixton, about four versts from us. The shifts were at night. Springfield set out in the evening and returned at three in the morning. He had to walk back on foot because omnibuses do not run at that ungodly hour; but how his whole family rejoiced!

The four weeks were drawing to a close. My departure loomed. On its eve, I decided to have a longer chat with Mr Randle. In the evening, I took a bottle of wine and went downstairs to the parlour where my host was sitting in an armchair beside the fire, his pipe between his teeth. He had just washed and eaten after returning from work. I proposed that we share a glass of wine. Mr Randle is a handsome, somewhat pale man, about thirty-five years of age. He has a strong provincial accent

---

[50]   The juxtaposition of utopian dreaming and practical parliamentary campaigning was a commonplace of the socialist discourse of the period. The distinction between English pragmatism (and common sense, empirical compromise) and Continental, especially French, abstract theorising was also a typical cultural cliché.

and though his speech is, on the whole, correct, it does have defects.[51] Gradually, our conversation warmed up.

'Please tell me, what is your opinion of the causes contributing to the exodus from the countryside?' I asked Mr Randle, pouring him another glass of wine. I was interested to know which conditions my interlocutor would point out first.

'Oh!', drawled Mr Randle in the English manner, 'hunger, before all else. Just wait a minute, I will show you the budget of a "Hodge"'. Randle rummaged on his shelf and took out a pile of pamphlets in red covers: the reports of the researchers who travel around England every year 'in red vans' to study the conditions of the agricultural labourers.[52] Their reports contain a mass of precious raw material. Here is what I read in one of the pamphlets.

[Shklovsky proceeds to quote at length from several English Land Restoration League illustrated pamphlets, including Among the Agricultural Labourers with the Red Vans *(1894), adducing lots of statistics, including those dealing with workhouses. He transcribes the budget and diet of a 'hodge' – remarking how much more lavish it is than that of a Russian peasant – and the social investigators' descriptions of and Randle's commentary on the living conditions in the countryside (rural cottages) and the evils of landlordism, including Lady Scott's 1896 case, exploitative rents and the allotments and small holdings system (with lots of detailed statistics). Shklovsky concludes by quoting Cardinal Manning on the 'land question'.]*

'Mr Randle is too fond of the countryside', his wife began. 'He cannot abide noise; he hates cities. His greatest happiness is to sit in the garden after work. Fine, if there were something there! But there are just a few sunflowers! Who can spot a country bumpkin! I, on the other hand, would die of boredom in the country!'

I had already had the opportunity to ascertain that the Randle spouses were representatives of two different trends: he was a 'hodge', despite the fact that he must have, to all appearances, left the country a long time ago. Mr Randle did not like the club. He spent most of his evenings at home. If he was not occupied with the affairs of his 'union' (by all accounts, he found the process of writing a much harder task than overtime labour on a hot day), he liked to play with his children or to sit and smoke his pipe on the kitchen doorstep which gave onto the little garden. He could stay in this position for a very long time. Only the five sunflowers and a tree swayed in front of him – and not even in his little garden but in the neighbouring one.

---

[51] Note how here and elsewhere in this piece Shklovsky presumes to assess the quality of his interlocutor's English, as if from the point of view of an educated native speaker.

[52] The red vans belonged to the English Land Restoration League.

Mrs Randle, on the other hand, was a typical townswoman. She would hasten to the club as soon as she had put the children to bed. She loved dancing to distraction and could probably dance until morning, provided there was any music playing. Mrs Randle took the affairs of the club even more closely to heart than Haufen and was very flattered when she was elected to the committee. But though the spouses represented two different trends, they lived in peace and harmony with one another.

[Shklovsky now asks Randle how he ended up in the city and Randle gives a biographical account of his boyhood migration from the country to an Oldham textile factory, which provides an occasion for a long digression on child labour in cotton mills earlier in the nineteenth century, as Randle describes his life as a 'half-timer' and 'piecer'. Shklovsky concludes with an allusion to the Trades Union Congress resolutions on the 'abolition of child labour'.]

My interlocutor was getting tired. Tomorrow he would have to get up at six o'clock to go to work. We exchanged firm **handshakes**. Tomorrow we would not have a chance to see each other; today was our last meeting. We parted. I returned upstairs to my room and reflected that the four weeks did not pass without leaving a trace; that in this time I managed to become acquainted with the 'living numbers' and to better understand the young, burgeoning England, so rich in strength and energy...

Isaak Shklovsky [Dioneo], from 'Buduschie Kommoneri' ['Future MPs']: II. 'Richard Kelly'
On the Themes of Liberty: An Article Collection, vol. 1 (St Petersburg, 1908): 28–60[1]

I.

One of the most savage and destitute places in London is, of course, the St Saviour Parish in Southwark, on the south bank of the Thames.[2] The train bringing the tourist from Dover speeds over the roofs of this part of the city. The traveller sees only a thicket of round red chimneys that Heine once compared to teeth torn out by the roots.[3] If it is a Monday, the eye is also struck by the motley rags hung out to dry on the roofs and in the courtyards. Southwark is a historic seat of poverty. Other districts of London, such as, for example, Bethnal Green, had once seen better days, or, like Park Lane, had a dark past and have only now become a holding pen for millionaires. But Southwark has *always* been a poor and savage quarter. In the time of Elizabeth, i.e. three centuries ago, the quarter's reputation was exactly the same as today. Only the scenery has changed a little. Once, for instance, Blackfriars Bridge, which leads from the north to the south bank, was covered with pikes on which were impaled the heads and arms of criminals and rebels.[4] At the southern end of the bridge there once stood a gallows, upon which swayed always the tarred corpse of a man executed for taking part in strikes or secret labour unions. Here too could be seen in all its glory a huge unwieldy machine that resembled a well sweep, the **ducking stool**. A chair was attached to the arm of a lever suspended over the river. They used to tie cheating bakers to it and, to the crowd's general

---

1   Originally published as 'Profiles: Letter From England' under the pseudonym Dioneo in the monthly journal *Russkoe Bogatstvo*, February 1905, 1–27. This is clearly another fictional 'portrait' like that of the Randles. In the Preface to the first volume of *On the Themes of Liberty*, collecting *Russkoe Bogatstvo* articles written up to 1907, Shklovsky explains the title and unifying theme of the collection: the meaning of 'liberty, based in respect for oneself and for the individuality of others [...] I had lived in Russia too long to forget the manifold manifestations of despotism and contempt for human dignity. I have lived in England too long not to appreciate Feuerbach's remarkable aphorism: "**Homo homini Deus est**". The comparison of England with Russia, i.e. the juxtaposition of respect for the individual with contempt for him, emerged unbidden' (iii–iv).
2   A parish formed in the sixteenth century and abolished in 1930.
3   The German poet Heinrich Heine (1797–1856) visited London in 1827. See his *English Fragments* (1828/31), which included 'A German Poet's View of London', published in English in a translation by Sarah Norris in 1880. See also S. S. Prawer, *Frankenstein's Island: England and the English in the Writings of Heinrich Heine* (Cambridge: Cambridge University Press, 1986).
4   Shklovsky has confused Blackfriars Bridge with London Bridge, where the famous heads on spikes were located.

amusement, duck them three times over in the river. All this, of course, has long ago become the stuff of legends. In the sixteenth century, there also stood on the south bank near the bridge a tall round building without a roof, the famous *Globe* theatre, where Londoners gathered to watch, perhaps, a tragedy by Marlowe or Shakespeare or a comedy by the learned Ben Jonson. With equal pleasure, they came here to watch the bearbaiting or some good fight.[5] Then the *Globe* vanished without a trace and another building appeared in its place, which also exists no longer but which left a profound mark on English literature. Here stood the historic dismal debtors' prison, the *Marshalsea*, described by Smollett and especially by Dickens (*David Copperfield*, *Little Dorrit*).

Present-day Southwark is a long labyrinth of alleys and little streets to which the London County Council has only recently turned its attention,[6] cutting a massive, broad avenue through the slums. The oldest and gloomiest houses have remained along the river, where it forms a giant curve. Here huddle the destitute riffraff, who crawl daily into the city to earn their bread. They have no money for fares, so they do not abandon their damp, dark, dilapidated houses, which are a stone's throw from the centre. The workers who earn decent wages have long ago moved to the new suburbs on the outskirts of the city, where the County Council has built comfortable, handsome cottages and connected them to the centre with a network of cheap tram routes. The great unwashed, who have neither a profession nor a regular wage, can only count on their own two feet, so they crowd nearer to the river.[7]

In Southwark, in a dark blind alley with the completely undeserved name of *Sun Parade*,[8] was born the current trade unionist parliamentary candidate Richard Kelly, or Dick for short. His father, Ginger Dan, was a costermonger, i.e. he sold flowers, eels and oysters from a stall.[9] Learned men say that the costermongers of Southwark are the descendants of gypsies who settled here in the twelfth or thirteenth centuries. In evidence, they cite certain words and customs of the costermongers, and their love of bright colours. They also refer to their skulls, which are supposedly different from those of other Englishmen, although Southwark has as many blond, red-haired, snub-nosed people as any

5   Nearly every element of Shklovsky's travel-guide-like account is still reproduced in contemporary tourist sightseeing lists.
6   The original here and below has 'municipality' for LCC.
7   It is ironic that everything Shklovsky describes in this paragraph Orwell was still describing thirty years later in *The Road to Wigan Pier* – in relation to towns in the North of England.
8   Sun Parade appears to be fictional (it is not found on nineteenth-century maps of London), but there was a Sun Street in Shoreditch and in Woolwich.
9   Here and below Shklovsky has 'snails' for 'eels'.

Fig. 25. Grooming Costers' Donkeys.

other district.[10] Many are hereditary costermongers, who have pursued the profession across a number of generations, at least to the extent that family legends of it have been preserved. But there are also not a few newcomers and outsiders amongst the costermongers. To sell flowers or eels from a stall is such a simple matter that ruined shopkeepers, actors ruined by drink and lawyers who have been expelled from their corporation for some misdeed (it is called **to be struck off the rolls**) all attempt it. A costermonger's job is the penultimate rung of the social ladder. Below it are the docks, and further down the quagmire of crime and pauperism. Every day, when the large bell on the tower of Parliament strikes four, sixty thousand costermongers wake up in Southwark and Lambeth and ask themselves, where is today's dinner coming from?[11]

Ginger Dan, Dick's father, was a hereditary coster. His wife had died long ago. Nannie, the adult daughter, helped her father. The family also owned a donkey named Neddy,[12] whose stabling cost a shilling a

---

[10] As mentioned above, these kinds of anthropological accounts of costers and other denizens of the London streets were popular with social investigators like Henry Mayhew.

[11] Editor's paragraph break.

[12] 'Neddy' is slang for 'donkey'. See Morrison's *A Child of the Jago* for a slum donkey character of this sort, or Charles Welsh, *Neddy: The Autobiography of a*

week. He was a tried and loyal friend who had succoured the family many times. At four o'clock in the morning, Ginger Dan would harness Neddy to a two-wheeled cart and set off with Nannie to the Covent Garden market, where he would use all his operating capital to buy up apples, cabbages, turnips, carrots or flowers. Then everyone would return to South London, to a large pub called *The Elephant and Castle*.[13] Here, Ginger Dan would get in line alongside the other costers. On Saturdays, this was and is the site of a battle royal with fortune. If the weather is relatively nice, the buyers who have just drawn their wages mill around the stalls, eating oysters and purchasing herbs and flowers. So that by midnight, a coster can earn back his working capital and a surplus to acquire some Australian mutton. If the weather is bad, the customers spare their clothes and remain at home. Perishable goods such as flowers cannot last until Monday, and then the costermongers experience a terrible crisis. And if it were not for their remarkable mutual aid, hundreds of costers would starve to death after every serious incidence of black fog. Other costers come to help during the crisis. One gives his comrade a bunch of flowers, another a head of cabbage, a third a bundle of carrots. And so the stall fills up. Dick's first memories were connected to just such an industrial crisis. His father had invested all his capital, about seven shillings, in daffodils. But that Saturday there was a blizzard. Neddy, wet through, stood patiently, his ears drooping. He was used to everything. Ginger Dan watched in despair as his white flowers perished under the snow. At midnight, Ginger Dan carted all his wares home. By Monday, the daffodils were ruined. It was a desperate time. Ginger Dan, Nannie, Dick and Neddy went hungry on Sunday; they went hungry on Monday and on Tuesday. The blizzard had brought all the costers to their knees. On Wednesday, Ginger Dan met his sister Margery, who was married to a fat, burly, boorish and heavy-handed navvy called Bill. The navvy had fallen out with Ginger Dan long ago and had forbidden his wife to see her brother. The coster told his sister about his misfortune. She had no money but offered to pawn her husband's best suit until Saturday,[14] without his knowledge, of course. Ginger Dan got seven shillings and bought his wares.

Donkey (Boston, MA, 1905), which is partially based on an account of a trial in the London *Times*.

13 Shklovsky is referring to one of the many incarnations of the famous coaching inn and public house of that name in Southwark, which was a local shopping and socialising hub in the early 1900s. According to D. Pasquet in *Londres et les Ouvriers de Londres [London and the Workers of London]* (Paris: Librairie Armand Colin, 1914): 'le monument central de Londres-Sud [...] est un vulgaire cabaret, l'*Elephant and Castle*' (413) ['the central monument of South London [...] is the vulgar cabaret, the Elephant and Castle'].

14 The husband's 'Sunday best' would presumably not be missed until Sunday.

Muse! you have sung of many heroes who have won fame by their great villainies! Now sing how Ginger Dan rushed around London on Saturday in search of money to buy back the suit and save his sister Margery from Bill the navvy's heavy fists. But the poet will probably disdain such a subject. Ginger Dan's misery and despair are too prosaic a theme. At six in the evening, the coster still lacked half a crown. Nannie and her father separated in order to gather the money more quickly. At ten in the evening, they were still a sixpence short. By eleven o'clock in the evening, all seven shillings had been collected. Since Nannie was nowhere to be seen, Ginger Dan left Neddy and the cart in the street, risking the loss of his donkey, and bolted quickly to the pawnbroker's, who locked up his shop at midnight on Saturdays. The suit was recovered and returned to Margery. The navvy had been sitting in the pub all this time, so he never knew anything. Such was Dick's first memory.

In the summers it was better. Since the weather was more settled, industrial crises were put off for a while. Besides, summers meant extra earnings. By two or three o'clock Neddy would be brushed and saddled, and then Ginger Dan with the donkey would take his position beside some school. Children could ride the donkey for a penny, while the coster ran after them and whooped. The summer was also good because towards the end of it, the whole of Southwark removed to the hop fields of Kent. There they set up a gigantic gypsy encampment. Hops are picked by young and old, by seventy-year-old crones and ten-year-old children. So there was work for everyone. And on Sundays, when there was no work to be done, the **hop-pickers** played games: they raced each other with a dozen empty baskets on their heads, or they knocked coconuts off posts with bowling pins, etc.[15] At hop-picking time, the population of Southwark lived in the midst of nature.

II.

Dick was six years old when his family was struck by a whole series of misfortunes. It began late in autumn. One morning before dawn Ginger Dan entered the stable to lead Neddy out and found him lying with his legs stretched out like sticks. He was dead. This was a disaster of such magnitude that Ginger Dan, for the first time since his wife's death, got

---

[15] Shklovsky is describing a strange version of skittles. On hop-picking, see oral histories like Hilary Heffernan's *Voices of Kent Hop Pickers* (Stroud: Tempus, 1999) and *Hop Pickers of Kent and Sussex* (Stroud: History Press, 2008), Gilda O'Neill's *Lost Voices: Memories of a Vanished Way of Life* (London: Arrow Books, 2006), Melanie McGrath's *Hopping: The Hidden Lives of an East End Hop Picking Family* (London: Fourth Estate, 2009) and, of course, George Orwell's accounts of his hop-picking experiences in his essays and (in fictionalised form) the novel *A Clergyman's Daughter*.

drunk, fought with a *bobby* and was arrested. The magistrate ordered him to pay two pounds in fines, and since the coster did not have any money, he was sent to prison for two weeks. The neighbours helped Nannie and little Dick to get by during this time.[16] Ginger Dan came out of prison wretched, dejected and ailing. He took some bundles of ferns to sell, spent the whole day wandering in the heavy rain and returned wet, shivery and ill. By the morning, the coster was feverish and delirious. He kept reminiscing about his 'missus', i.e. his dead wife, and every now and then fell to singing:

> **'Come along, my Annie,**
> **Fetch all your money;**
> **Put on your Sunday clothes,**
> **Come along with me.'**[17]

It was the same favourite ditty that Ginger Dan, then a young fellow, used to sing to his future wife twenty-two years ago, when he met her hop picking. The song alternated with questions about the price of oranges and carrots. Then followed tears and exclamations about 'the poor kids!'.[18] The coster was thinking of his children. Faithful Neddy also figured in the delirium. After two days, Ginger Dan passed away.

The neighbouring women from Sun Parade washed Ginger Dan's shrivelled corpse and took little Dick away with them.[19] The entire household's funds amounted to no more than five pennies and one farthing. However, according to ancient custom, costermongers consider that their dead comrades ought to have 'a respectable send-off'. I truly do not know why such incredible pomp is necessary to declare to the whole world that a pauper has left the stage, who in life, so to speak, was always huddling against fences. The fact of the matter is that the London poor spend all the money received from friendly or insurance societies on funerals. Ginger Dan did not belong to a friendly society, so there was no money to pay for his burial. But the entire male population of Sun Parade and the neighbouring alley gathered in the *Green Cow* pub. A large plate was placed on the table, and then everyone who

16 There are many 1890s fictional analogues for these events: the death of the horse (the family's breadwinner) in Thomas Hardy's *Tess of the D'Urbervilles* (London: James R. Osgood, McIlvaine & Co., 1891); the neighbours' help when father is imprisoned in Morrison's *A Child of the Jago*, etc.
17 Shklovsky supplies a Russian translation. I have not been able to locate the original song, but it bears an uncanny resemblance to 'Put on Your Sunday Clothes' from the musical *Hello, Dolly!*.
18 Here and below Shklovsky translates the English 'kid' into Russian literally – as 'baby goat'.
19 On all the aspects of working-class death and burial that Shklovsky describes here (including the care of the corpse, burial insurance and the notorious 'respectable' [i.e. extravagant] funeral), see Julie-Marie Strange, *Death, Grief and Poverty in Britain, 1870–1914* (Cambridge: Cambridge University Press, 2005).

believed he could please the company with his voice rose and asked for 'a few seconds' from the elected chairman. When the chairman nodded and said: '**go on**', the coster would begin to sing a sentimental ballad or a comic song. Then everyone would put on the plate as much as he could in accordance with how highly he rated the singer's art. In the language of the costers, such a concert is called a '**brick**'. When the greater part of the company had already succeeded in singing twice, the doors of the pub were flung open, and in came Bill the navvy, Margery's husband – burly, fat, bloodshot and full of beer. He had come straight from work, judging by his clay-stained striped corduroy trousers tied up with straps under the knees. Floundering and not finding the right words, Bill informed the company that although he was quarrelsome at times, he was not at all the lost cause people took him for. He, Bill, might take a drop on occasion and get into fights; but when you have spent the whole week mucking about in wet clay and are chilled to the bone, you'd have to be one of those saints drawn on church windows not to get drunk and come to blows. Bill declared that he pitied Ginger Dan. Even more he regretted that they had been at odds. He, the navvy, had his heart in the same place as other people.

Fat Bill, who was used to expressing himself exclusively by the short oath *bloody*, even broke a sweat while giving such a long speech. He had feeling enough for another speech, but he'd run out of words. He grunted and placed a large silver coin on the plate, a crown that he had been clutching in his fist all along. The chairman invited the gentlemen to shout hooray three times in honour of Bill the navvy.

A COSTER'S FUNERAL (WALWORTH).

Fig. 26. A Coster's Funeral.

They raised so much money that they managed to give Ginger Dan a splendid send-off. A hearse drawn by four horses, torch bearers in black suits and ruffled-up top hats, six coaches carrying the black-garbed denizens of Sun Parade – in a word, everything was '**highly respectable**'. Nannie, Dick's sister, was then nineteen years of age. In the cemetery, as the neighbours bent over the open grave to see how deep Ginger Dan had been lowered, the girl suddenly began to weep loudly and grabbed little Dick by the hand.

'Listen, **daddy**!' she shouted. 'You can rest in peace! I, Anna Jane Kelly, will let myself be skinned like a rabbit but I shall be a mother to the kid and won't let him go into the workhouse! He will be a good man. I, Anna Jane, swear this to you, **daddy**!'

Nannie kept her word as best she could. She gave up selling flowers and went to work at a pickles and preserves factory. Twelve shillings a week is not a large sum of money for two; but Dick went to school well-fed, in well-mended clothes. In school, he was the best pupil, and at the age of twelve he left it with distinction.

Now Nannie had a helper. In any case, Dick had already started earning a shilling or two a week by selling newspapers when he was nine years old. The boy liked to tear along the streets with a bundle of freshly printed papers under his arm, a huge eye-catching placard in his hand, and yell, holding his free hand as a megaphone: '**Special!**' '**Paper!**'.[20]

Dick knew which news to bring to which district. When a paper tells, for instance, of scandalous divorce proceedings, one must rush immediately to the prosperous streets. They love that kind of story there. And the more scandalous revelations and testimonies by peeping chambermaids, private detectives and shady furnished-room domestics there are in the newspaper, the more guarantee there is of sales in a rich quarter. But if the evening paper writes of a 'terrible tragedy', i.e. a murder, then most issues are sold in the poor and feral districts. Your little London newspaper boy is a profound psychologist. A quick skim of the latest news column, and the boys know with certainty to which street it is most profitable to hasten at any given moment.[21]

At the age of thirteen, Dick started work in the same factory as Nannie. Now the two of them found it significantly easier to manage. And it got better still when chance helped the boy get a job at a printing house. As Dick began to earn more and more, he tried to persuade Nannie to leave the factory for good, but the girl would not agree to it. At nineteen, Dick was making thirty shillings a week. Together with the fifteen his sister earned, it was enough to live in a style poor Ginger

---

[20] Dick's Cockney pronunciation of 'Paper' is rendered phonetically in Russian in parentheses as 'pipa'.
[21] Cf. the description of a newspaper boy and his customers in Sims, 'Off the Track in London: V. In the Shadow of St. Stephen's', 152.

Fig. 27. 'Paper!'.

Dan would have deemed suitable for royalty. The brother and sister rented three comfortable rooms, ate and dressed well, and on Saturdays frequented the music hall together. They had long ago opened an account at a savings bank, which they also visited routinely on Saturdays.[22]

[22] On Victorian savings banks for working-class people, see Paul Johnson, *Saving and Spending: The Working-Class Economy in Britain 1870–1939* (Oxford: Clarendon Press, 1985), as well as more recent work by Josephine Maltby, '"To Bind the Humbler to the More Influential and Wealthy Classes": Reporting by Savings Banks in Nineteenth Century Britain', *Accounting History Review* 22.3 (November 2012),

Fig. 28. Socialism in London: A Sketch in Hyde Park on Sunday Afternoon.

Like thousands of other young English workers, Dick was a member of a sports club and regularly attended a **dancing-academy**, or simply speaking, dance classes. Dick went there together with his sister.[23]

The mind of the young labourer was as yet asleep. He merely felt an animal contentment in the contrast between his warm and well-fed present and his cold and hungry past. Dick was just waiting until the years were ripe for him to join a trade union.

But, at last, the young man's intellect was awakened by an accidental jolt. His thoughts began to work and to lead Dick down an entirely different path. And now, after seven years have passed, all the young man's acquaintances, as well as Nannie, know that the time is nigh when the workers will show Kelly the great honour of sending him as their representative to Parliament. This is how the awakening happened. Seven years ago, on a Sunday in July, Dick curled his forelock in the young workman's fashion, put on his best, carefully ironed suit, stuck a rose in his buttonhole, and went for a stroll in Hyde Park. He was used

---

199–225 and Linda Perriton and Josephine Maltby, 'Working-Class Households and Savings in England, 1850–1880', *Enterprise & Society* 16.2 (2015), 413–45.

[23] The increasing prosperity and rise in living standards of the skilled working class in the late nineteenth century (due to increasing wages and falling prices) is a commonplace of economic history.

to seeing dozens of religious speakers among the trees near Marble Arch, whom he regarded as something amusing. But today, Kelly noticed an orator who was not screaming the word '**Lord**' in divers tones. He was a thickset man, seemingly a labourer, without a frock coat and with a neckerchief instead of a collar around his neck. (It was very hot.) The speaker had climbed onto an overturned box. Beside the coatless man stood his comrades, apparently also workers. One of them held in his hands an enormous red banner. All of this greatly interested Dick, and he came up to listen to what the coatless man was saying.

III.

[There follows a many-pages-long account of the man's speech, his interaction with the audience, and his reading (verbatim) from Robert Blatchford's pamphlet The Tramp and Bob's Fairy *(London: Clarion Newspaper Co., 1898), the first of the 'Clarion Tales for the People' series.]*

The speech produced a particularly strong effect on Dick Kelly. A whole new world opened up before him. He saw now a range of questions he had never thought about before. When the speaker had finished and climbed down from his box, Dick approached him and asked where one could learn more about the things he had just spoken of. The speaker pulled from his bag a whole bundle of books. Here were the Fabian Society penny tracts: 'Why Are The Many Poor?', 'Facts from the Political Economists and Statisticians', 'An Eight Hours Bill', 'Land Nationalisation', etc. Then followed Robert Blatchford's famous book 'Merrie England', the same author's pamphlet 'Britain for the British', and publications of the *Clarion* newspaper: 'Collectivism', 'The Independent Labour Party Programme and the Unemployed', 'The Coming Fight with Famine', etc. For a shilling, Dick acquired a small library.[24] Until that moment, Dick had never interested himself in economic questions. Now they absorbed him wholly.

[24] Cf. the carpenter's bookcase in 'In the Working Quarter'. On socialist agitational literature (Fabian and Clarion) handed out at open-air meetings, see Vaninskaya, *William Morris and the Idea of Community*. Shklovsky is referencing the following works: W. L. Phillips, *Why Are the Many Poor?* Fabian Society Tract 1 (London: Fabian Society, 1884); Sidney Webb, *Facts for Socialists from the Political Economists and Statisticians*, 2nd ed., Fabian Society Tract 5 (London: Fabian Society, 1891); Sidney Webb, *An Eight Hours Bill*, Fabian Society Tract 9 (London: Fabian Society, 1889); Sidney Webb, *Practicable Land Nationalisation*, Fabian Society Tract 12 (London: Fabian Society, 1890). See the *LSE Digital Library* collection of 'Fabian Tracts: 1884–1901', https://digital.library.lse.ac.uk/collections/fabiansociety/tracts1884-1901. Blatchford's *Britain for the British* (London: Clarion Press, 1902) was his second most famous book of socialist propaganda after *Merrie England*. Tom Mann, *The Independent Labour Party Programme and the Unemployed*, Clarion Pamphlet 6 (London: Clarion Newspaper Company, 1895);

His awakened intellect demanded answers. Generalisations presented themselves which needed to be supported by facts. Every time Dick was brought up short before a dark expanse, and he understood that he knew very little. And so, the music hall and the dance classes lost all their appeal to him. He signed up for lectures at the neighbouring 'Polytechnic' and began to borrow books from the free library. Now Dick was depositing a lot less in the savings bank than he used to. Not because his wages had been reduced, but because the young man spent his spare money on books. The English are not just persistent but systematic in their work. Dick began with the ABCs, using Cassell's 'People's Library' as his guide. In a year's time, the homemade bookshelves in Dick's room were filled with a series of classic volumes.[25]

[There follows a series of quotations from Dick's notebook of **'McCulloch's Principles of Political Economy'***,* **'Henry Fawcett's Manual of Political Economy'** *and* **'J. S. Mill's Political Economy'***.]*

In England, whenever anyone arrives at what he considers to be the truth, he can no longer sit still. He has to spread the word to others, to his **'fellow citizens'**.[26] The truth, in the opinion of the English, is only good when it can be shared with those who have not yet learned it. Furthermore, such an exchange is indispensable because it enables people to object and to make suggestions which had not entered one's own head. In this fashion, a notion is subjected to universal criticism, and the person who has thought of it can see for himself whether he is in possession of the truth or a mere delusion. And so Dick began to go to the Forum every Sunday for a couple of hours, in order to share with his fellow citizens under the Constitution Tree the conclusions that he had arrived at. The London Forum and the Constitution Tree are a school of eloquence for many aspiring political and religious leaders.[27]

Alex M. Thompson, trans. *Collectivism. A Speech Delivered by Jules Guesde to the French Chamber of Deputies*, Clarion Pamphlet 5 (London: Clarion Newspaper Company, 1895); William Jameson, *The Coming Fight with Famine*, Clarion Pamphlet 13 (London: Clarion Newspaper Company, 1896).

[25] Again, cf. 'In the Working Quarter'. On polytechnics, free libraries and Cassell's series, see notes above.

[26] Shklovsky provides a Russian translation.

[27] Shklovsky is almost certainly referring to the so-called 'Forum' at Victoria Park in the East End, 'the most heavily patronized [park] in the metropolitan area' in the 1890s. See James Winter, *London's Teeming Streets, 1830–1914* (London: Routledge, 1993), 165: 'Although speakers had been in the habit of holding forth on Sunday afternoons from the 1860s on, it was in the late Victorian and Edwardian periods that Victoria Park became London's main outdoor forum, or as some contemporaries put it, "forum and agin 'em." Hyndman, Mann, Tillett, Morris, Shaw, and Burns spread the socialist gospel there under trees called the Six Sisters, secularists challenged evangelicals, and preachers from Anglican missions took on Roman Catholic theorists in fervent but apparently disciplined debate. Participants

Here, they learn in actual practice to respect the opinion of others, to quickly come up with rejoinders, and to understand the psychology of large audiences whom they must excite and carry along with them. The traditional formal declamatory style of the Commoners and the famous English church orators was conceived, in effect, in the open forum.[28] Dick soon acquired a reputation. Various workingmen's clubs began to invite him to speak on this or that issue of the day. It was in one such North London club that I first heard Dick Kelly four years ago at the height of the South African War.

[There follows a general discussion of imperial propaganda, an English-language quotation from 'Britannia Rules the Waves', remarks on the Fabians' and Blatchford's support for the war, a description of jingoist violence at anti-war rallies, and a several-page-long transcript of an anti-war speech given by Dick, including an exchange with a pro-war worker in the audience.]

V.

Dick Kelly proved to be a prophet. The war ended, leaving a huge debt and a horrible mess in South Africa. In England, there followed a crisis instead of a business revival. The factories closed. Thousands of workers were left without bread. And when the winter came, processions of the unemployed filled the streets. The imperialists, who had hitherto extolled the beneficial effects of war, now explained to the masses that unemployment arises from two causes: free trade and the influx into England of foreign migrants who stole the bread of the native

---

of all persuasions testified to the high level of the exchanges between audiences and speakers as well as between speakers themselves. [...] performers needed to have done their homework [...] the place that had been intended by its sponsors to be a Hyde Park for the East End had become something more: a reconstruction [...] of a public space in the traditional sense.' See also Charles Poulsen, *Victoria Park: A Study in the History of East London* (London: Stepney Books and the Journeyman Press, 1976); John James Sexby, 'Victoria Park – Meath Gardens' in *The Municipal Parks, Gardens, and Open Spaces of London: Their History and Associations* (London: E. Stock, 1898), 552–74: 'No account of Victoria Park would be complete without some reference to the position it occupies as the forum of the East End' (563). Shklovsky's 'Constitution Tree' may be a reference to an actual tree (perhaps one of the Six Sisters) or just to the proverbial Shire Oak, under which Anglo-Saxon folkmotes were held in the open air according to popular Victorian (especially radical) historiography. Compare Shklovsky's admiring description of the level of oratory in Victoria Park to his and Chukovsky's (in 'Public Meetings in Hyde Park') scoffing accounts of Speaker's Corner in Hyde Park. Shklovsky's many detailed transcriptions of exchanges between audiences and speakers at public meetings of various sorts were clearly based on extensive acquaintance with the real dynamics.

28   'Commoners': Shklovsky means members of the House of Commons.

Fig. 29. Tariff Reform League Poster.

population.[29] Dick Kelly now had a lot of work on his hands. Not a day went by without him speaking at one or even two meetings.

[There follows a long account of Dick's speeches dealing with protectionism, immigration, the Aliens bill and the real causes of unemployment, with explanations of monopoly capitalism and boom and bust cycles.]

This is how Kelly explained it all. And not just he alone, but hundreds of other speakers. The unemployed, in the meantime, held demonstrations in the streets to draw the country's attention to their plight. These demonstrations sometimes consisted of three or four dozen workers with a single banner. At other times, hundreds or even thousands took part. On these occasions, the demonstrators carried several flags, followed by trade union and friendly society banners. There were also processions with music. It sometimes happened that the demonstrators sang: either the old songs composed by their forebears during the 'hungry years', when a strike could lead to transportation to Australia or even execution, or new ones such as 'No Master', 'The long, long night is over: faint in

---

[29]   See the 'Foreigners in London' section and the Tariff Reform League London posters blaming unemployment on foreign competition in the *LSE Digital Library* 'Political and Tariff Reform Posters' collection.

the east behold the dawn appear'.[30] They also sang a sad ballad about three fishermen who sailed out to sea despite the stormy weather.

[Shklovsky proceeds to summarise 'The Three Fishers' ballad, which was written by Charles Kingsley in 1851 and later set to music.]

The refrain is even sadder than the ballad itself:

'For men must work, and women must weep,
And there's little to earn, and many to keep.' [31]

In midwinter, the unemployed decided to hold a large demonstration on an upcoming Sunday, and this is when something happened which kept all of London occupied for three days running. As is usual in such cases, the plan of the demonstration was most thoroughly worked out by the organising committee. Separate detachments of a hundred to a hundred-and-fifty people were to start with their banners at a given hour from various quarters of the gigantic capital, march down certain streets and then congregate by two o'clock at the Hyde Park forum.[32] And indeed, this is what transpired. But the detachment of two hundred people that was meant to start from Southwark, cross the bridge and march past St Paul's Cathedral came to the forum very late, in dreadful disarray and without its leader, Richard Kelly. And the London forum began to buzz like a giant beehive when it emerged that Dick had been taken by the police. In another hour, the newspaper boys were crying everywhere: 'Outrage at the Cathedral. Clash with the unemployed. Police use their truncheons. Leaders arrested.' This was such an important incident that special telegrams were printed, even though English newspapers are not published on Sundays.[33]

---

[30]   Presumably a reference to the Hungry Forties, and also possibly to the Tolpuddle Martyrs, trade unionists transported to Australia in 1834. 'No Master' is one of William Morris's *Chants for Socialists* (London: Socialist League Office, 1885). 'The long, long night': the first two lines of Edward Carpenter's popular socialist hymn 'England, Arise!'. Shklovsky's Russian is a loose, not a literal translation (cf. 'In the Working Quarter'). Both songs were staples of radical working-class gatherings in the late nineteenth and early twentieth centuries.

[31]   The refrain is translated directly into Russian in parentheses. This ballad was popular throughout the nineteenth century, and so well-known in Shklovsky's time that it was routinely – and sarcastically – quoted by the child protagonists of Edith Nesbit's books, from *The Story of the Treasure Seekers* (London: T. Fisher Unwin, 1899) to *The Wonderful Garden* (London: Macmillan & Co., 1911) and *Five of Us, and Madeline* (London: T. Fisher Unwin, 1925).

[32]   Speaker's Corner.

[33]   It is not clear what Shklovsky means by this, given the existence of the Sunday papers. Newspapers had relied on telegraphic dispatches since the 1850s and regularly printed 'special telegrams'. Reuter's was known as Reuter's Telegram Company Limited. See also Andrew Hobbs, 'Local Newspapers in the Victorian Era: Early "Rolling News" and Reading as Pub Activity', *Press Gazette: The Future of Media*, 27 December 2018, www.pressgazette.co.uk/

So what had happened at the Cathedral? A party of the unemployed headed by Richard Kelly had crossed the bridge in perfect order, entered the sleepy City and rounded the corner of the vast Cathedral whose walls have been blackened not by time, but by the thick coal-imbued fogs. Right before the main entrance, facing Fleet Street and with its back to the Cathedral, stands a marble statue of Queen Anne – '**Brandy Annie**', as her subjects nicknamed her in her own lifetime due to her fondness for the bottle.[34] A popular couplet reproaches the Queen for standing with 'her face to the gin-shop, her back to the church'.[35] In the direction where *Brandy Annie* gazes one can still find the historic public house 'The Bell Savage', mentioned by Fielding, Smollett and Dickens.[36]

Two workers carrying a huge banner reading: 'We give the strength of our muscles; let us have bread' came level with *Brandy Annie*. In the church, a service was about to begin. Well-dressed, well-fed, sleek gentlemen in glossy top hats, with huge gilt-edged prayer books in their hands, and ladies in rustling silk gowns were walking up the stairs. The worshippers in English churches belong exclusively to the middle classes (mostly the lower-middle). One never sees any workingmen or commoners.[37] In England, the church is one of the attributes of 'respectability'. The congregation proceeded to church with facial expressions most suitable to the occasion. But at the sight of the unemployed, their kindly or pompous demeanour changed into something else: a feeling of offence, as if the churchgoers had seen something shocking and

---

local-newspapers-in-victorian-times-early-rolling-news-and-reading-as-a-pub-activity/: 'Wars, elections and other newsworthy events […] along with election or sporting results, attracted crowds to the newspaper offices, to read the telegrams and posters stuck on the windows or shutters, and to buy ad hoc supplements with verbatim reports of election speeches or special editions, the Victorian version of "rolling news".'

34 The original Russian gives '**Anny Brandy**' throughout – a typical error. The statue faces Ludgate Hill, which Shklovsky must have considered an extension of Fleet Street. Queen Anne was generally known as 'Brandy Nan', but 'Brandy Annie' does occasionally occur as well.

35 See E. Cobham Brewer, 'Brandy Nan', *Dictionary of Phrase and Fable* (Philadelphia, PA: Henry Altemus, 1898), www.bartleby.com/81/2413.html: 'On the statue of Queen Anne in St. Paul's Churchyard a wit wrote –
"Brandy Nan, Brandy Nan, left in the lurch,
Her face to the gin-shop, her back to the church."
A "gin palace" used to stand at the south corner of St. Paul's Churchyard.'

36 The Bell Savage Inn, a former playhouse and coaching inn dating from Shakespeare's time, stood on Ludgate Hill until 1873 – Shklovsky clearly identifies it with the 'gin palace' of the rhyme. See Herbert Berry, 'The Bell Savage Inn and Playhouse in London', *Medieval and Renaissance Drama in England* 19 (2006), 121–43.

37 'Commoners': Shklovsky actually says 'black people' (in quotation marks) which is a Russian technical term dating from the Middle Ages designating the common people, or more specifically, free peasants and artisans.

indecent. The gentlemen in top hats looked askance and scowled. The ladies in rustling dresses pursed their lips. Noting this, the unemployed began to sing '**The Starving Poor of Old England**', which refers to hypocrites.[38] One of the unemployed offered a collection box to the clergyman who was looking with a particularly unfavourable eye on the procession, requesting him to drop in a penny.

'Idlers!' shouted the clergyman.

'Look who is reproaching us with idleness!' exclaimed Dick. 'Comrades, do you know who this clergyman is? This is the Reverend Somerville, author of 'Impressions of Mission Work in the Far East'.[39] In his book, he extols the system of slavery in South Africa. And this

---

[38] The song may be found in the *Social Democratic Federation Song Book* (Shklovsky had close connections with the SDF, so could easily have picked up the song from their meetings) and appears in a number of publications of the 1890s and 1900s, including J. Ellis Barker's *British Socialism: An Examination of Its Doctrines, Policy, Aims and Practical Proposals* (London: Smith, Elder, & Co., 1908), which reproduces several verses, and John Henry Mackay's *The Anarchists: A Picture of Civilization at the Close of the Nineteenth Century*, trans. George Schumm (Boston, MA: Benjamin R. Tucker, 1891). The latter also contains a scene uncannily similar to the one Shklovsky describes here. In a chapter entitled 'The Unemployed' (set in 1887, the year of Bloody Sunday), a German anarchist revolutionary finds himself in a procession of the unemployed that enters Westminster Abbey. Disgusted by the clergyman's sermon, the unemployed leave the Abbey – the worshippers sighing with relief after 'the impious' have gone – and 'the immense procession' heads back to Trafalgar Square. 'They followed the waving of the red flag. They crowded together in closed ranks as if so to feel their hunger less, their power more. [...] And out of this procession rose as by premeditation a song. Low, sombre, sad, and defiant, it burst from a thousand throats to the sky [...] They sang the old immortal song of "The Starving Poor of Old England": "Let them bray, until in the face they are black, / That over oceans they hold their sway, / Of the flag of Old England, the Union Jack, / About which I have something to say: / 'Tis said that it floats o'er the free, but it waves / Over thousands of hard-worked, ill-paid British slaves, / Who are driven to pauper and suicide graves – / The starving poor of Old England! [...] / 'Tis the poor, the poor, the taxes have to pay, / The poor who are starving every day, / Who starve and die on the Queen's highway – / The starving poor of Old England! [...] / But not much longer these evils we'll endure, / We, the workingmen of Old England!" (83–84). Mackay was an egoist (individualist) anarchist – a current of anarchism that Shklovsky covered in another Letter, so it is not inconceivable that he had seen Mackay's book in its original German, in English translation or perhaps even in the Yiddish translation published by London anarchists in 1908.

[39] The Rev. W. J. Somerville, *Impressions of Mission Work in the Far East* (London: T. Cornell, 1904). The book is not listed in the British Library Catalogue but was referenced or reviewed in 1904 in *The Church Missionary Review*, vol. 55, *Luzac's Oriental List and Book Review*, vol. 15 and in *The Bookseller*, and in 1905 in *Revue d'histoire ecclésiastique*, vol. 6. It is unlikely that Shklovsky had actually seen the man; he was probably following his usual practice of providing a fictional persona for a name encountered during his surveys of the periodical press.

man, who dances on his hind legs before the African magnates, rebukes us for our unwillingness to work!'

The fat clergyman hastily retreated into the church.

'See what the **aliens** have done!' came some indignant voices from the crowd of gentlemen in top hats.

'**Aliens**!!' one of the workers – an unusually tall, wiry fellow with a bowler hat on his conical head – exclaimed suddenly and violently (he was none other than Alfred Watson, the defender of imperialism).[40] 'If there had existed a law against **aliens** two hundred years ago, even the Hanover dynasty would not have come here.'

'Let's go, Alfie', Dick pulled him by the hand.

'No, I won't go!' Alfie (i.e. Alfred) hollered. 'I have to tell them that if they go on treating us like this, the workers will start speaking a different tongue: like they do in Russia – with bullets and bombs. Yes!'

Several dozen *bobbies* were hurrying to the Cathedral as fast as they could.

'Move on! Move on!' a police inspector cried out. But Alfie had flown into a rage, he was gesticulating and shouting something. Many of the workers and gentlemen in top hats were also gesticulating and shouting. And now something happened which the magistrate failed to clear up: whether it was the enraged workmen who hit the 'bobbies' first, or the 'bobbies' who lost their usual composure – either way, a fight broke out. The English police are not armed, but 'bobbies' carry a short truncheon in their back pockets, which they have the right to take out only in the most extreme circumstances. Now, the truncheons were not just out but put squarely to use. The workers, in their turn, responded with sticks and fists. The ladies fled, to spread the news of an outrage at the Cathedral. But the usual English calm prevailed both among the workers and the 'bobbies'. The fracas ended after several minutes. The workers departed for the forum, leaving behind two captives in the hands of the police: Dick and Alfie.[41]

The following day, the morning papers were full of yesterday's 'outrage'. The tabloid press resorted to astounding flights of imagination. According to the '**Daily Mail**', Richard Kelly was a dreadful anarchist who had formed a special detachment of desperadoes in order to attack St Paul's Cathedral, cut the throats of the congregation and plunder the golden vessels. The '**Daily Express**' reported that on Saturday a large conclave of anarchists met in a cellar. All 'swore on a dagger' to execute their leader's plan, i.e. to pillage the Cathedral. But detective (sleuth) Pinkerton infiltrated the secret meeting 'by disguising

---

40   This is the same – formerly pro-Boer War – workman who had challenged Dick in the section omitted above.
41   On interactions between policemen and crowds, see Peter K. Andersson, *Streetlife in Late Victorian London: The Constable and the Crowd* (Basingstoke: Palgrave Macmillan, 2013).

himself as an anarchist'. Thus, all was revealed, and 'the anarchists were ambushed on Sunday, when they turned up at the Cathedral'. The level-headed press demanded to know how it happened that the police came to use their truncheons.[42]

At eleven o'clock in the morning on Monday, the arrested men appeared before the magistrate, and the 'outrage case' assumed the proportions of an ordinary fight. The magistrate released Dick on the spot. But he had some questions for his comrade.

'Did you say that the workers will use weapons?' the magistrate asked.

'Yes!' Alfie replied.

'Were you drunk?'

'No.'

'Have you ever been admitted to a lunatic asylum?'

'No.'

'Well, if you are not drunk or ill, how do you not know that no-one may infringe on the right to freedom of assembly and speech in England. Go. You are free if you promise to conduct yourself quietly, to wit, not to get into fights for six months.'

Thus ended the case of the outrage at the Cathedral. The magistrate reprimanded the police severely for taking out their truncheons without need. From that day, the name of Richard Kelly attained wide renown far beyond the bounds of the workingmen's clubs.

VI.

Now Dick Kelly is standing for Parliament. His candidacy was put forward by the **Labour Representation Committee**, which is dedicated to ensuring that English workers have their own party in Parliament after the general election. Now Dick devotes all his free time to agitation among his voters in South London.[43]

[There follow many pages of transcripts from William Cobbett's Letter to the Journeymen and Labourers of England, Wales, Scotland and Ireland *(1816) and Kelly's election manifesto, in order to compare*

---

[42] I have been unable to find any reference to the incident in the *Daily Express* or the press more widely; however, similar accounts of anarchist plots and outrages peppered the pages of the national and local newspapers throughout the 1900s. The descriptions attributed to the *Daily Express* also echo typical elements of contemporary anarchist potboilers, the best known (and most idiosyncratic) of which was G. K. Chesterton's undercover-policemen-as-anarchists caper *The Man Who Was Thursday* (London: J. W. Arrowsmith, 1908). A 'Pinkerton' was, of course, a private detective.

[43] The Labour Representation Committee (LRC) was established in 1900 to push for labour representation in Parliament. It was a coalition of trade unions and various socialist groups and the forerunner of the modern Labour Party.

*what 'the people's tribunes' told 'English workers a hundred years
ago and now'.]*

Dick is by no means the main representative of the new party that
will appear in Parliament after the coming election. He is overshadowed
by such fighters as, for example, John Burns. But when all is said and
done, any movement, when it becomes broad-based, stands in equal
need of talented leaders with striking personalities and of rank-and-file,
ordinary men, among whom one can number Richard Kelly.[44]

[44] On John Burns, see 'An Election' in part IV below. It is a curious coincidence
that a Richard Kelley, a trade unionist born in 1904, did indeed become a Labour
Party MP after the Second World War. However, Shklovsky most likely based his
character on George Davy Kelley (1848–1911), who was not from London, but was
a prominent trade unionist who worked as a printer and was selected by the LRC
in 1906 as a candidate, becoming a Labour MP for Manchester South West.

III

LONDON AT HOME
AND AT LEISURE

Fig. 30. Postcard, 1908: 'Much Better Than Cycling'.

Semyon Rapoport, Summary of 'Angliyskie Rabochie na Dosuge: Ocherk Razvlecheniy Rabochikh v Londone' ['English Workmen at Leisure: A Sketch of Working-Class Amusements in London'] *Vestnik Evropi*, September 1898, 219–46

In this article, Rapoport gives a detailed account of the uses to which London workers put their increased leisure time, juxtaposing the mid-Victorian attitude to 'popular recreation' with the variety of entertainments that characterised late nineteenth-century Sundays and bank holidays. He begins with extensive descriptions of the fundraising street processions of the temperance and friendly societies; the political rallies in Hyde Park and Trafalgar Square, which he regards as serving primarily a recreational rather than a political function; and outdoor religious gatherings – all of which provide musical entertainment for onlookers. He proceeds to the massive Nonconformist choir competitions at the Crystal Palace and other festivals and concerts involving members of cooperative societies, sports societies, etc. He discusses the LCC's support for public parks and orchestras; working-class 'club' sports such as football and cricket; the popularity of cycling, including designated cycling lanes and bicycle rental schemes in the London parks. Working-class women (unlike their middle-class counterparts), he notes, almost never take part in sports, though they do occasionally play lawn tennis in the park or enjoy themselves on Hampstead Heath on a bank holiday. Military drill for volunteer detachments is described in detail, and a long section is dedicated to excursions. These include 'cooperative' trips abroad arranged by Toynbee Hall, the Regent Street Polytechnic and other institutions; local employer-organised 'bean feasts' (Rapoport describes the famous excursions organised annually by the Bass Brewery in Burton-upon-Trent, which in 1898 laid on fifteen special trains, as well as steamships and sailing boats, to take nine thousand workers for a day's worth of entertainment at Scarborough); week-long family trips; caravan excursions to the countryside or seaside organised by clubs, choirs or friendly societies, with Rye House and Southend being particularly popular destinations for London workers; and railway or steamship excursions further afield organised by, for instance, the Pleasant Sunday Afternoon Society or offered as promotions by commercial enterprises such as the tea firm Tee-To-Tum. Of course, no account of popular amusements would be complete without a long description of the stage, and Rapoport provides a detailed overview of the audience, furnishings and variety entertainments at a Mile End music hall (complete with an assessment of the differences and similarities between East and West End theatres). He concludes the article with a downbeat evaluation of working-men's clubs (both political and social) – an institution which, he believes, has failed of its promise and is in any case mostly dependent on middle-class sponsorship, though it does fulfil a recreational purpose. Rapoport promises his reader that on another occasion he will show the English worker at home and in the bosom of his family.

179

Semyon Rapoport, Summary of 'Istoriya Odnoy Ulitsi: Iz Domashney
Zhizni Bedneyshego Sloya Londonskogo Naseleniya' ['The Story of
One Street: The Domestic Life of the Poorest Stratum of the London
Population']
Vestnik Evropi, November 1899, 121–58

The subject of this article is the downward trajectory of a street called
Garden Terrace, between Notting Hill and Fulham, as it sinks from an
upper-middle-class street of prim and respectable family houses all
the way down to a slum. Although there is no such street on contemporary London maps, the real Palace Gardens Terrace in Kensington,
as pictured in photographs of the period, certainly lives up to the grand
appearance of the street as Rapoport first sees it. Rapoport describes
how, over time, the outward look of the street changes to match the
changing nature of its inhabitants, as the well-to-do occupants flee and
the family houses are taken over by 'house farmers' and divided up into
individual flats, with an ever-increasing rate of tenant turnover, driven
partly by the constantly rising rents.[1] The street becomes visibly dirtier;
glass door panels and cast-iron grilles are broken; the live-in maids
and lace in the windows give place to bedraggled visiting charwomen,
faded calico curtains, and eventually rags. The regal silence and closely
guarded privacy of the street's heyday are superseded by the sounds of
piano tunes and singing coming from open windows, the knocking of
knocker-ups, the shouts of milkmen, greengrocers, rag-and-bone men,
knife grinders and pedlars of all kinds. The street fills with children
playing outside and its very smell changes, as it is permeated with
the odours of fried fish and damp washing. Coal is now bought by the
half-hundredweight rather than the half-ton, or not bought at all. And as
for the inhabitants of the street, they too change out of all recognition.
The solicitors and businessmen are replaced first by the 'aristocracy of
labour', the comparatively well-off families of carpenters, mechanics
and postmen, whose wives had formerly been in service and whose
children are clean and not too numerous. This is the point at which
Rapoport himself moves into one of the Garden Terrace flats, and the
narrative of his interactions with his upstairs and downstairs neighbours
traces the declining fortunes of the street. Readers are given detailed
glimpses into the neighbours' lives and professions and the births and
deaths of their babies (which leads into an explanation of the workings

---

[1] Compare George R. Sims in 'Off the Track in London: II. In the Royal Borough
of Kensington', *Strand Magazine* 27 (May 1904), 545–51, which describes (with
illustrations) a very similar street: 'This is a street of black and battered doors, of
damaged railings, and of broken windows. On the doorsteps here and there stand
groups of slatternly, unkempt women. [...] Many of the houses here are common
lodging-houses; but some of them are in the hands of the house-farmers, who let
them out in furnished rooms at a shilling a day' (547).

Fig. 31. One or Two Women Standing on the Doorsteps Watch the Proceedings.

of life and medical insurance for the poor). Through the walls Rapoport hears the sounds of banjo playing, hymn singing and the weeping of the postman's young wife. Despite the postman's occasional bouts of drinking, there is no physical abuse and a divorce is amicably arranged.[2] But these people too desert the street and the unsuccessful German artist with whom Rapoport shares his flat commits suicide. The original neighbours are replaced by others: a tailor, a footman, a carman, a cabbie, wives who take in mangling, and a destitute cobbler – a Polish-Russian Jew with a Protestant English wife and numerous kids who fantasises about owning his own workshop. A succession of prostitutes posing as seamstresses move into the basement flat (providing a piquant contrast with the daughter of an upstairs family who works at an ABC tea shop), but their eviction cannot stop the street's downward slide. By now, battered, untidy and drunken women can be seen standing around in knots gossiping and bickering; after school, children fetch mugs of beers for their mothers from the pub; and crimes committed in the street

[2]   Compare the wife-beating that Chukovsky hears coming from upstairs in his description of his lodgings in Gloucester Street in his diary (*CW* II, 86).

make it into the newspapers. At this point Rapoport decides to leave, but before the street is completely overwhelmed by the rising waves of 'slumdom' all the houses are demolished – to be replaced by new ones intended for people in a higher income bracket.

Isaak Shklovsky [Dioneo], from 'Frankie'
Sketches of Contemporary England (St Petersburg, 1903): 531–58[1]

I.

I met Frankie's father, Mr Hartnell, at the 'Logos' Club soon after my arrival in England.[2] When I first heard this pretentious name, I was for some reason immediately reminded of a scene from 'The Learned Ladies' in which Trissotin introduces Vadius to the ladies and thrills them with his announcement that the latter knows Greek. I thought the 'Logos' was something like the academy of pedants proposed by Philaminte and Armande.[3] **'Nul n'aura de l'esprit, hors nous et nos amis!'**[4]

I was mistaken. The 'Logos' proved to be a regular English club: not the 'Carlton', which represents the fondest dream of every nouveau-riche brewer or brace manufacturer; not the 'Athenaeum' – a conclave of literary and political cardinals; not the 'Savage Club', where millionaires dressed up as for a ball turn up to play at bohemianism. No, the 'Logos' turned out to be a middle-of-the-road club with nothing pedantic about it except its name. One could occasionally meet a ruddy-cheeked lord there who for some reason considered himself a radical and was forever laughing at his own jokes, or a couple of politicians who had dropped by 'for the connections', just in case. But these were not the usual kind of visitors. The club's habitués were artists whose paintings had not yet begun to sell (this explains why such a mass of paintings adorned the club's walls), young novelists just spreading their wings, journalists, people of modest independent means, etc. These people were at times a bit too original and overdid their paradoxes a little; but on the whole they were an amiable set, not constrained by a worship of convention and therefore more akin in spirit to us Continentals. This is why the 'Logos' could boast such a motley collection of foreigners, ranging from

---

[1] Originally published as 'Frankie (Letter from England)' under the pseudonym Dioneo in the monthly journal *Russkoe Bogatstvo*, March 1902, 69–95.

[2] Shklovsky arrived in England in 1896. This was not the only time he described the club he frequented – another long account of the club appeared in 'The Crank'. In that article, the club is not identified and includes among its patrons not just a lord and various lawyers, but a Hindu scholar from Calcutta who works at the British Museum, a Japanophile lady in an Eastern-style dress, and assorted feminists, including Rational Dress Society lecturers. I have been unable to identify this club – it is probably fictionalised to some extent.

[3] *Les Femmes Savantes [The Learned Ladies]* is a comedy by Molière (1672). See *Œuvres Complètes de Molière [The Complete Works of Molière]*, vol. 3 (Paris: Charpentier, 1910), 505–81. Trissotin and Vadius are caricature scholars and versifiers. Philaminte and Armande are the eponymous 'learned ladies'. All are satirised.

[4] French: 'Except our friends and us, none shall have wit!'.

the inhabitants of Ecuador to Norwegians. But if the 'Logos' differed from other clubs in its patrons, it did possess two things without which no Englishman would acknowledge such an establishment: soft, thick carpets and an abundance of deep armchairs to climb into and either pull your legs up or stretch them out to the brightly blazing fire – indeed, to climb into and adopt any position, even curl up into a ball. These armchairs are of such a character that, once there, you can observe the other patrons in peace, study their physiognomies, the shape of their foreheads, the square, energetic chins; or, last but not least, you can cover yourself with a copy of *The Times* and doze sweetly, while to the others it appears that you are studying the leading article on the two-penny increase of income tax. The English prize such armchairs highly and refer to them as **my growlery**, i.e., my den where I can grumble in private. After living in England for some time, you too will, at last, begin to acquire a taste for such a **growlery**, in which no-one can disturb you until you have changed your spleen for a favourable disposition and emerged into the light of day a sociable and optimistic being.[5] The 'Logos', like other English clubs, sometimes hosted, in addition to musical soirees (**at homes**), conferences and discussions that touched upon the most burning contemporary questions. At these conferences, I always came across a gentleman whom I never saw at the club at any other time. He was a man of about fifty-five, already beginning to grow stout, but still in his prime, with a fresh, handsome face, clear eyes and the broad shoulders one only meets with among Englishmen who, until they reach extreme old age, spend an hour every morning after a cold bath dancing about with a dozen weights and clubs of various types. His slightly greying moustache did not conceal the energetic, sharply delineated mouth. His clean-shaven face revealed a prominent, taut **musculus masseter** and a massive, square, perfectly British chin which spoke of extraordinary tenacity.[6] I became even more interested in this gentleman when he took part in the debates. I was struck by the lucidity, precision and force of the speaker's argumentation, by his point of view, then by his rare erudition. He had, it seemed, an excellent familiarity with many authors other than English ones.

'Who is this?' I asked.

'Mr Hartnell, a civil servant.'

Subsequently, I obtained even more detailed information.

[There follows a biographical sketch of the prototypical Victorian Mr Hartnell, an Oxford graduate who intended to become a deacon but, having lost his faith after reading Feuerbach's Wesen des Christentums, *instead decided to become a civil servant. Shklovsky*

5   Shklovsky is using 'spleen' in the sense of 'depression' or 'melancholy' – known as 'the English disease' in the nineteenth century.

6   'Masseter muscle': Shklovsky is clearly aiming for the British bulldog look.

gives a detailed overview of the reform of civil service appointments after 1855 from a system of patronage to one of competitive merito-cratic civil service examinations akin to China's.]

Mr Hartnell passed the examination for 'Civil Servant First Class' (i.e. most senior). He began his service at the government accounts department in the City. Now, after twenty-five years of service, Mr Hartnell was earning 1,200 pounds per annum, which is a great deal by Continental standards. In the English context, this is just an 'average' salary.[7] Governmental mores have changed a lot since 1855: a Tory Government now is not at all concerned about the extreme radicalism of one of its prominent civil servants.

Mr Hartnell and I met and grew close. At this time, Andrée's expedition was just being prepared.[8] It was rumoured that the travellers might end up in north-east Siberia, somewhere near Chaun. Since I have some knowledge of this region, I shared my own reflections with Mr Hartnell.[9]

'If only my boy could hear the tale of a polar explorer!' Mr Hartnell exclaimed jokingly.

In early June 1897, I finally decided to keep the promise given long ago to Mr Hartnell and pay him a visit. It was Sunday. Everywhere, bells were ringing the changes melodiously. Gaudily attired ladies and gentlemen were on their way to church, sporting solemnly pious expressions on their faces and enormous gilt-edged prayerbooks in their hands. Dozens of cyclists of both sexes were speeding along the empty streets out from the city. The 'bike' (i.e. the bicycle) has revolutionised the English Sunday, the preachers are complaining. Young people, instead of dozing in church as before, now hurry to the countryside in their spare time. Huge charabancs filled with all manner of folk were rolling the same way. It was a mass exodus from the boring city.[10]

---

7   This figure appears to be in the right order of magnitude. According to Guy Routh, 'Civil Service Pay, 1875–1950', *Economica* 21.83 (August 1954), 201–23, in 1876 (i.e. twenty years before 1896), the average pay of a Permanent Head of Department, such as the Treasury or the Inland Revenue, was £1,920 per year and that of the Administrative Class of civil servants (next in seniority) was £530 per year.

8   Andrée's Arctic balloon expedition of 1897 was an unsuccessful Swedish attempt to reach the North Pole, which ended in tragedy.

9   The Chaun is a river in the far east of Siberia. See Shklovsky's collection of sketches, *In Far North-East Siberia* (1895), translated into English and published by Macmillan in 1916, and his earlier work for the Russian Geographical Society based on his observations at the time of his Siberian exile for his narodnik activities (1886–1892).

10   The cycling craze of the 1890s has received a lot of attention from academic and popular historians.

Fig. 32. In Birdcage Walk.

Hartnell lived outside London, near Richmond. By the magnificent 'Kew', a park which takes up several hundred desyatins,[II] stretch some quiet, fashionable streets. There are no noisy, dirty slums here, nor endless rows of 'card houses', all identical like a handful of newly minted coins – the favourite haunt of clerks. In the streets near Kew, each house has a special character of its own. The walls are thickly overgrown with ivy, which hangs in beautiful festoons over the front doors. In front of the houses are little gardens which invariably feature some rare curiosity of the plant kingdom imported from far-off colonies. In the mild, humid English climate, all plants of the subtropical zone thrive wonderfully. Each house has its own name. You pass by the 'Dwelling among the Cedars', the 'Rose Alley', the 'Lohengrin', the 'Pamir', the 'Eucalyptus', the 'Velasquez': names which already give some notion of the tastes of their owners or the places where they served. The inhabitants of these houses are fashionable artists, successful novelists, well-to-do civil servants and so on. They closely guard the 'fashionableness' of their street and keep an eagle eye out for any pub, junk shop or greengrocer's shop, etc. that might intrude into their midst.

[II] Russian unit of land measure equivalent to 2.7 acres. For Victorian Richmond, see 'A Walk Down Hill Street', *London Borough of Richmond Upon Thames*, www. richmond.gov.uk/a_walk_down_hill_street and recall that according to Chukovsky, Shklovsky himself lived somewhere near Richmond and Kew in the early 1900s. There is no doubt that Hartnell and his son had real-life prototypes.

II.

The door was opened by a boy of about ten, remarkably tall for his age, ruddy-cheeked, with large red hands that stuck out awkwardly from the sleeves of a child's jacket.

'Here, let me present my boy to you', Mr Hartnell said to me as he emerged into the entrance hall. 'Frankie, here is that Russian gentleman I told you about, who has visited the north-eastern shore of Asia.'

'Did you fight with any savages there?' Frankie asked eagerly. My reply in the negative seemed to disappoint the boy somewhat.

Every corner of the house, every square arshin of the wall bore a stark imprint of the owner's individuality. Frankie volunteered to be my cicerone. Noticing that I was looking at an old model of a small sailing frigate above the bookcase, the boy explained:

'This is "The Success", a merchant ship that my great-great-grand-father commanded. The ship disappeared without a trace between Valparaiso and Sydney in 1794. And that comes later than great-great-grandfather', he pointed respectfully to a tall, ancient lacquered sailor hat that was hanging under the glass beside the model. 'That is great-grandfather's umbrella; he was a village vicar. There is a long family story connected with this umbrella. And here is a little bag my father brought from Tangiers; they are woven by the prisoners there.'

It appeared that this family, belonging exclusively to the middle classes, had preserved traditions about a whole set of ancestors who had lived in accordance with principles that they believed to be right. They lived, they made plans for the far future for themselves and for their sons, without fearing any unforeseen force that, like a **deus ex machina**, could interfere suddenly and upset all their calculations. The boy was relishing his role of cicerone. He led me to his father's study where I saw cases full of books, including a most excellent selection of works by Montesquieu, Rousseau, Voltaire, Holbach, Helvetius, Condorcet and other authors of the eighteenth century.[12] Then I found myself in a small room where I noticed, before all else, a large jar in which three crested newts were swimming restlessly. Nearby, in another jar, a huge green frog was sitting forlornly on a small ladder made of sticks. Something was rustling in a cardboard box. 'I've got a grass-snake there. I caught it yesterday. I haven't yet made a terrarium', Frankie explained calmly. On the floor, among the boots, were scattered some tools, a butterfly net and a green botanic capsule on a broad ribbon. 'This is my room!' Frankie explained with pride. I could see the neighbouring gardens from its windows. In one of them, a gigantic broad-shouldered gentleman with a mop of black hair on his round head was lying sprawled in a

---

[12]   Compare this selection of French Enlightenment *philosophes* with the reading matter of the working classes described in part II.

long bamboo deckchair. In another, I descried a small, exceptionally upright old man.

'The black-haired gentleman is Mr Ridley, a pioneer who has just returned from Australia', the boy told me. 'And that old gentleman is a retired general. Their boys are great friends of mine.'

We soon finished surveying the house.

'Would you like me to show you "Falcon's Nest"?' Frankie offered. I thought at first this had something to do with birds and could only wonder where they could have come from so near to London. But, in fact, it turned out to be something rather different. We came down into the little garden, which is an obligatory appendage of all English houses. Aside from the usual lilac bushes, prickly holly and strange Australian 'monkey puzzle tree', there were several poplars growing in the garden, as well as a huge horse chestnut tree at the back. Low walls separated the garden from the neighbouring yards. From one of them, a boy leapt over deftly to our side; he was the same age as Frankie, but a little heavier set, with a dark complexion, black hair and huge jaws. This was the son of the Australian pioneer. In the other garden, a short wizened old man with a grey moustache so thick it looked like he was holding a sparrow with outstretched wings in his mouth was marching with a measured military step down its sole alley lined with hollies. As he walked, the old man kept jerking his head, shrugging his shoulders and muttering something. His tread was light and quick, although he seemed advanced in years.

'Hola! Frankie! Up the ladder!' he shouted when he spotted us.

'Yes, General.'

'My Harold still can't do it: head spins. Still too weak', the old man barked out the short phrases and marched on.

'He is a retired general of the Indian army', Mr Hartnell explained to me. 'He is finding retirement very boring, so much so that he has even taken to keeping chickens for entertainment. Harold is his son, a very sickly boy. He cannot seem to recover from the "yellow jack" he was ill with in Calcutta.[13] Even the stairs make his head spin.'

High up above the ground, in the sturdy branches of the chestnut tree, a platform had been erected, and upon it a sort of hut or round booth. A rope ladder of a kind that can still be seen on small sailing vessels came down from the platform to the ground.

'And here is "Falcon's Nest"', Frankie told me with some pride.

The idea for the structure and the name itself were borrowed from *The Swiss Family Robinson*, which had Frankie wholly under its spell now, it seemed.

---

[13] 'Yellow jack' is one of the names of yellow fever. Harold is clearly suffering from post-viral fatigue syndrome.

'Frankie is always begging me to show him on the map what group of islands New Switzerland might belong to, where his friends Fritz, Ernest, Jean and François ended up',[14] Mr Hartnell said with a good-natured smile. 'Like the little Englishman he is, he likes precision in all things. Could you perhaps help him?'

'That would be rather difficult', I replied. 'Wyss wrote, without a doubt, one of the best children's books, one that our grandfathers devoured and that our grandchildren will probably savour as well. But as for geography, it does not look like the author reckoned with it. There is such a mixture of animals from different zones and continents on the island as would only be possible in a zoological garden. In a small space, the shipwrecked family meet with penguins, birds of the Arctic seas and monkeys, they fight brown bears and lions, shoot kangaroos, walruses and pythons. The same may be said of the flora. Plants from different latitudes appear together as in a botanic garden.'

Frankie took my comment very much to heart and began to argue passionately for the reality of New Switzerland. I must confess, I felt sorry that I had destroyed the boy's illusion, so I limited myself to repeating that the book was very good.

Nimbly, like a monkey, Frankie climbed up the ladder to the platform, and the Australian clambered after him.

'Are you not concerned about this ladder and the rather risky structure?' I asked Hartnell.

'I have inspected the one and the other. They are sound. Of course, there is always a modicum of risk, but it is just as insignificant as when riding a bicycle. Having weighed everything, I believe I am right not to forbid my boy to build a somewhat risky dwelling. He must not grow up a coward. There is nothing worse than that. It is more bitter than death. A coward is an unreliable man in life. Most cowards are liars. And all liars are cowards.'

'Come up here!' shouted Frankie from above. 'You can see far from here. Climb up. The ladder is strong.'

It was indeed stretched so taut by means of large rocks that it hardly even swayed. The platform was well constructed from sturdy boards attached to branches by ropes let through specially drilled holes. On the platform stood a hut of woven boughs, covered, in case of rain, with an old oilcloth and a rug which had seen long service, judging by the holes. Up above, the webbed, wrinkled chestnut leaves were whispering softly. With each breath of wind, orange dust rained down onto the platform from the enormous flower panicles which stuck up like candles on a Christmas tree. Frankie showed off his domain and

[14] The main boy characters in Johann David Wyss's children's classic, *The Swiss Family Robinson* (1812). Shklovsky's version of the names differs from the commonly used English ones: the younger boys are called Jack and Franz (Francis). Frankie probably read W. H. G. Kingston's popular 1879 version of the book.

his possessions with inordinate pride. Above the entrance hung an old rusty cap pistol bought for a few pennies; here, I also noticed a map of the London suburbs, a small compass, a hatchet, a saw – in a word, the full Robinsonian kit.

You could indeed see very far from that platform. On one side, shrouded in a whitish mist despite the sunny day, spread the colossal city. The countless factories resembled resting elephants squatting to the ground with their broad, heavy bellies, their trunks stretched up very high.[15] In honour of Sunday, no clouds of smoke came bursting from them today. Huge steam cranes, like the talons of gigantic griffons, stood frozen motionless in the air beside the factories. The city of many millions was dozing, it seemed, sprawling in the sun and covering itself against its rays with a white sheet of fog. Tomorrow, this monster will awake, the trunks will begin to puff and blow, the towering talons will start to swing smoothly, lifting like feathers stones measuring a cubic fathom each, the steel centipedes of trains will crawl in all directions – boundless energy will once again be expended in the pursuit of money and bread; the crash and roar, like to the noise of colossal breakers, will resound above the city. But at that moment, I could only occasionally hear the rumble of a steam engine or the rattling wheels of a lone omnibus. If one closed one's eyes, one could imagine that it was the sleeping city-giant snoring. To the right spread the bright-green fields of the county of Surrey, cut across by regular rows of poplars and beech trees. Here and there among those fields one could see the red roofs of 'villas'.[16] The sprawling city, like a turbulent sea, had splashed its stone spray – solitary streets – far and wide across the neighbouring counties. The English landscape has a special charm. Its colours are as bright as the cheeks of English women. Everything in it speaks of power, of an excessive abundance of strength... Sheep wandering about the enclosed fields appeared from that treetop like beetles that a boy had gathered into a box and then emptied out onto the green cloth of a card-table.

Frankie climbed into his hut, rummaged about in a corner, where I noticed a spirit lamp, an iron tripod and a frying pan, and returned with

---

[15] Charles Dickens famously compared factory machinery to 'melancholy mad elephants' in *Hard Times* (1854; Oxford: Oxford University Press, 2006), 69, 106, 237. Shklovsky must be facing roughly south-east.

[16] These 'villas' and the encroaching suburbanisation of the countryside they represented were a frequent target of criticism in late nineteenth and early twentieth-century British literature centred on London, from William Morris's *News from Nowhere* (1890; London: Penguin, 1998): 169 ('the hideous vulgarity of the cockney villas of the well-to-do, stockbrokers and other such, which [...] marred the beauty of the [Thames'] bough-hung banks') to E. M. Forster's *Howard's End* (1910; London: Penguin, 2000): 329 ('"All the same, London's creeping." She pointed over the meadow – over eight or nine meadows, but at the end of them was a red rust. "You see that in Surrey and even Hampshire now," she continued.').

Fig. 33. Boating on the Thames at Richmond, Early 1900s.

a spyglass which, judging by its battered sides, had seen better days before it had found its way to 'Falcon's Nest'.

'Look N.N.W. by the compass', the boy recommended. 'Not there. Further west, past that tree there. What do you see?' (Frankie had, it seemed, recollected Stevenson's *Treasure Island*.)

'Something white.'

'Those are the Chiltern Hills', the boy explained to me. I began to study with curiosity the white chalk hills that play such a prominent role in the parliamentary history of England.

[In the following paragraph Shklovsky offers a brief history of the office of the Bailiff of the Chiltern Hundreds, from the Middle Ages to the present day, to illustrate the conservatism of English institutions (a common theme – cf. Chukovsky): 'England manages to preserve the shadow when the object which used to cast it has long ago disappeared'.]

'Now look at the river', the boy suggested, demonstrating everything like a conscientious guide. The curve of the Thames near Richmond could be seen as clearly as on a map. The tide did not reach here; the river was much narrower, but also much cleaner. Both banks were overgrown with trees. Willows stooped over the water, bathing their boughs in it. A hubbub of laughter floated over the river. One after another, ancient steamboats crawled along, filled to the brim with crowds of holidaymakers. The discordant sounds of string instruments rose from the decks. Thousands of gaily attired men and women were resting and making merry to the best of their ability, having left behind in the slumbering city till Monday all their troubles and affairs. Hundreds of boats of all descriptions darted about the river.[17] Here, an elegant Canadian canoe glided by like a swan, propelled by an elderly gentleman without a coat and with a double-bladed paddle in his hands. Next, an ungainly black barge crawled slowly past, full of factory girls in huge hats with colourful feathers, all screaming with laughter. They would burst out laughing on the least pretext: when the boat started to roll in the wake left by a steam launch, when an inexperienced friend began to back water instead of sculling, when someone's oar splashed, etc. The ungainly barge, which resembled a mud-covered pig, was overtaken by a stylish gig rowed by young gentlemen in picturesque flannel suits. Well-dressed ladies reclined on the benches, propped up on silk cushions under multi-coloured parasols. A long and very narrow boat shot by like an arrow; its six oarsmen, all sporting jerseys, short trousers and bare knees, swung the oars rhythmically, like automatons. These were students preparing for the 'Regatta' (a large racing event in July).[18] Along the banks stretched rows of houseboats: one saw singularly ornate little villas on top of great barges. Now a small, stylish steam launch puffed past, towing just such a houseboat after it. A tent of blue, red, yellow and green silk strips was pitched on the deck. Its raised flaps laid open to view a peculiar company. On a carpet, in a deep armchair, sat a fat mulatto with a trimmed grey beard (it looked like his lips and chin were daubed with soapy lather) and diamond earrings in his ears. Around the mulatto on the carpet reposed some gaily and brightly dressed ladies, also coloured. Their eyes and teeth flashed, the whole company was laughing loudly and trying to sing something. By the looks of it, this was some nabob from the West Indian isles.[19] They prefer to leave their hot native land and settle down in damp London because in England there is no colour prejudice of the kind that exists in its colonies or in America.

But the loudest laughter, songs and music came from the place where the Thames splits into two branches and forms a little island

[17] Boating on the Thames near Richmond was one of the most popular pastimes at the turn of the century, with hundreds of pleasure boats available for hire. Shklovsky's 'thousands' is not an exaggeration.

[18] The reference is to the Henley Regatta, established in 1839.

[19] Shklovsky is obviously using the term 'nabob' in its general sense of 'wealthy person', rather than the particular sense associated with India (not the West Indies). His use of dated vocabulary now considered racially offensive, such as 'mulatto', has been retained.

overgrown with willows and birches, the favourite spot of the London factory workers.[20] Musicians blew their trumpets with all their might and whistled with their clarinets. Young people were dancing 'till they dropped' to these discordant sounds. Soldiers in red coats, their caps askew, strutted about like ducks, barrel-chested and flourishing swagger sticks. But it was not fated that they should attract the attention of the parlour and kitchen maids. The heroes of the day were sailors from a man-of-war who had, by all appearances, just returned from a long voyage with an endless supply of stories to tell.

The din rising from the river was not the drunken seething of a wretched and cowed people who drink themselves into a stupor in their free minutes in order to escape, if only for a moment, their grey, stultifying existence. No, one heard the joyful laughter of a free people *at rest*, gathering strength for the new day. In these hours of leisure on the river, everyone feels equal: the factory girls, giggling as they splash about with their oars, and the smartly dressed titled lady in a captain's cap skilfully steering her little yacht with purple sails; the 'coster' (a type of wandering pedlar) and the elegant gentleman standing in a gleaming skiff with a pole in his hands. Everyone's human dignity is acknowledged equally. And it is for this reason that an exemplary order prevails everywhere. Merrymaking never turns into the kind of wild riot of which only the cowed man is capable, in whom intoxication awakens the long-seething resentment against the continual suppression of his human dignity.

'Listen, you should come visit us when "the Battle of the Blues" (i.e. a river race between Oxford and Cambridge Universities) is on', Frankie began.[21] 'You can see everything from "Falcon's Nest".'

The boy was rooting for Cambridge, so during the race he flew a large dark-blue flag, the University's colour, over his domain.

Apart from the weapons and cooking utensils, I also noticed several books in the treehouse (Frankie called it 'my *wigwam*'): a thick battered volume of 'The Boy's Own Paper', White's 'The Natural History of Selborne', a pocket plant guide, Stanley's 'In Darkest Africa', and several volumes of Ballantyne, the author most beloved of English boys. All of Ballantyne's works are a series of adventures in South America and Australia.[22]

---

20 Shklovsky is referring to Eel Pie Island, a popular pleasure ground since the 1700s which was featured on postcards at the turn of the twentieth century.

21 The Oxford and Cambridge Boat Race took place on the Thames annually since the mid-nineteenth century.

22 All typical middle-class boys' reading: the *Boy's Own Paper*, a popular story paper which featured adventures in imperial locales, was published from 1879; Gilbert White's *The Natural History and Antiquities of Selborne* (London, 1789) remained popular throughout the nineteenth century; Henry Morton Stanley's *In Darkest Africa* (London: Sampson Low, 1890) recounts the expedition he led in the late

'Do you like Jules Verne, Frankie?'
'No', the boy retorted categorically.
'Why not?'
'Well, there isn't a single battle in it!'

When we came down from the tree, Frankie showed me his other projects. First of all, a deep pit which the three of them had dug together. A sort of crank was spinning above it. Since water was seeping into the pit, the boys had constructed a crude but very ingenious pump.

'It's a mine', Frankie explained. 'Do you see the opening at the bottom there? We are excavating a tunnel from it to the pioneer's garden.'

'Are you not afraid that the earth will cave in and crush you?'

'No, that's impossible', Frankie replied confidently. 'We have constructed a framework out of bottomless barrels there and placed supports where necessary. Branson is an expert at that kind of job', Frankie pointed to the dark-complexioned boy with large jaws, who nodded his head affirmatively. Near the mine, in the shadow of a hornbeam, stood a large boat on rollers, crudely knocked together but fully rigged. The father did not interfere with the boy's aspirations to be now a navvy, now a prospector, now a shipwright. In Mr Hartnell's view, boys benefit greatly from undertaking such projects. There was just one thing he insisted on: that the job, once started, was finished without fail, otherwise – he said – one would not develop the perseverance so necessary in life.

III.

I no longer frequented the 'Logos' and did not see Mr Hartnell for three years. There is nothing surprising about this when one considers London distances and living conditions. No other city 'weans one off people' like this sad endless plain of stone houses, **'d'une longueur telle qu'il faut pour la franchir un jour à l'hirondelle'** ('which takes a day to cross as the swallow flies', a verse by Barbier from the poem **'Londres'**).[23] In that time, Frankie had lived through some important changes. He had left his private school and moved to a **Public school**, one of the few large secondary educational establishments. St Paul's School,[24] which

---

1880s; R. M. Ballantyne was an extremely prolific author of boys' adventure fiction set in 'exotic' locations across the globe from 'the wilds of Africa' to 'Eskimo Land'; his most famous book was *The Coral Island* (London: T. Nelson & Sons, 1857). Jules Verne's books were very popular adventure reading in Russia.

[23]   French: 'of such a length that it takes a swallow one day to cross it'. Auguste Barbier's 'Londres' ['London'] in *Iambes et Poèmes [Iambics and Poems]* (Paris: Paul Masgana, 1841) describes London as a dark, immense, hellish city inhabited by crowds of silent, blackened people who spend their lives chasing after gold.

[24]   St Paul's School, founded in 1509, was one of the public schools investigated by the Clarendon Commission; at the turn of the century, it had its own prep school as

Fig. 34. St Paul's School at the Present Day [1909].

my little friend attended, shares many features in common with other well-known English educational establishments of the same type, such as Eton, Rugby, Harrow, etc. All of them place the greatest emphasis on character building and the preparation of the future British citizen, who must be aware of his responsibilities but also stand upon his rights. In all of these schools, great care is taken, before all else, to establish a system of total trust between the headmaster, the teachers and the 'bulldogs' (form masters) on the one hand, and the boys on the other. This is achieved, first of all, by the teachers recognising the boys as *human beings* who have their own individuality, instead of regarding them as shapeless, pliant living clay that can be moulded at will. All of these schools, unfortunately, are only accessible to the affluent classes because their fees are very high. But all of them offer innumerable bursaries which are awarded to *everyone* who passes the requisite exam. These bursaries range from six hundred to one thousand roubles per annum.

St Paul's School differs from Eton and Harrow in some respects. Latin and Greek have been largely displaced here by the natural sciences. Furthermore, St Paul's is a day school, so it lacks one antipathetic trait that has rooted itself firmly in English boarding schools – the '**fagging**' system. This consists in the new boys and the younger boys becoming the servants of the senior 'sixth-form' (final-year) pupils. The little 'fag' sweeps his 'master's' room, boils his kettle, toasts his bread, serves him during games, runs errands for him, and so on. If a 'fag' is insufficiently diligent, he is sometimes beaten by his cruel 'master'. A special

---

well. It was originally located in the City of London, then moved to Hammersmith in 1884 and then to Barnes in 1968. The Hammersmith building was subsequently demolished.

parliamentary commission was even set up to eradicate the 'fagging' system. It sat for a long time and collected a mass of deplorable facts,[25] but in the end, custom proved the stronger, and 'fags' remained a fixture of large boarding schools, although their situation is better now, perhaps, than it was thirty years ago.

Frankie's first day at school was memorable both for himself and for his family.

[Shklovsky goes on to describe how Frankie is bullied on his first day at school by some older pupils and is challenged to a fight, which the 'bulldog' intentionally fails to observe in the interests of character-building and (pupil-enforced) discipline. Frankie adheres to the rules of a 'fair fight', makes peace with the older boy and is accepted into the 'school family on equal terms'. Frankie's mother's and father's contrasting reactions to the boy's black eye are described and Shklovsky concludes with a reference to T. H. Huxley's recollection of a school fight in his autobiography.]

Another fight, eulogised at the time in *The School Argus*, followed several months later, and its consequences were such that Mrs Hartnell spent two days trying to persuade her husband to take Frankie out of that 'breeding ground for savages'. It happened like this. The South African War had just started.[26] Parsons and teachers were strenuously inculcating warlike patriotism in the schools. Schoolchildren sang 'The Soldiers of the Queen', learnt the martial verses of the poet laureate and Kipling

---

[25] Shklovsky's note: The book 'Tom Brown's School Days' describes how a 'master', desiring to punish a 'fag' for disobedience, began to 'roast' him before the fire. The parliamentary commission for the investigation of the fagging system says: 'Boxed ears, kicks and socks on the jaw are regarded not as punishments but as signs of affection. The "masters" have invented a whole system of tortures for the "fags": these include beating with a stick, birching, and so on; some "fags" were so cruelly flogged by the senior pupils that they could not take part in games for a long time.'
Editor's note: The incident Shklovsky cites in his footnote concerns the eponymous Tom in chapter 8 of Thomas Hughes's *Tom Brown's School Days* (London: Macmillan, 1857), who questions the right of the fifth-form boys to fag him and rebels against their 'tyranny'. In the main text, Shklovsky is probably referring to the report of the Royal Commission on the Public Schools (Clarendon Commission, 1861–1864), published in 1864, which addressed fagging among other things and concluded that, despite abuses at certain schools, the fagging system was, on the whole, sound and in no need of substantial reform. I have not been able to locate the specific quote above. The text of the *Clarendon Report*, vol. 1 (1864) is available in *Education in England: The History of Our Schools*, www.educationengland.org.uk/documents/clarendon1864/clarendon1.html; see also 'Public Schools Commission', Debated on Friday, 6 May 1864, *Hansard*, vol. 175, https://hansard.parliament.uk/Commons/1864-05-06/debates/8bde32a8-df93-4980-9afd-bda8def8ecd4/PublicSchoolsCommission.
[26] This places the action in October 1899.

by heart, and had their vocabulary enriched with new words such as 'veld', 'kopje', 'pom-pom', 'Long Tom', etc.[27] The Canon Knox-Little, who taught at the school, wrote in *The Times*: 'We have been fighting *the greatest war of modern times. We have fought not only against Boers, but against the trained adventurers of the world. We have fought them and beaten them. Thanks to the wisdom of our colonial secretary, we have also bested the slander that poured on us from the gold-bought newspapers of all the world.*'[28]

Is it any wonder that the only thing the schoolboys could think of now was 'how to shoot down the enemy in the field', as that same canon proclaimed in *The Times*? Mr Hartnell himself did not sympathise with the war, even considered it England's greatest disgrace and, despite

[27] The poet laureate was Alfred Austin. 'The Soldiers of the Queen' was a popular patriotic music hall song composed by Leslie Stuart in 1895, and also one of 'over a dozen plays specifically concerned with the war [which] [...] used pantomime conventions to elicit audience response; the Boer President Paul Kruger would be represented as the villain, treacherous and antagonistic towards the audience, quickly followed by the entrance of dashing "heroes", such as Dr. Jameson. *The Era*'s review of *The Soldiers of the Queen* stated that "the references that continually crop up concerning British pluck and Boer treachery generate a sort of electricity in the air, and the Hoxton Britons are swayed accordingly"', in Stephen Attridge, 'The Soldier in Late Victorian Society: Images and Ambiguities', PhD thesis, University of Warwick, 1993, 37. The popularity of Afrikaans words like 'veld' and 'kopje' is reflected in contemporary poetry, such as Thomas Hardy's 'Drummer Hodge' (1899): 'They throw in Drummer Hodge, to rest / Uncoffined— just as found: / His landmark is a kopje-crest / That breaks the veldt around', see *Poems of Thomas Hardy*, ed. Claire Tomalin (London: Penguin, 2006). 'Long Tom' is a cannon.

[28] Shklovsky is quoting selectively from the Letter to the Editor of *The Times* of 15 January 1902 by the Rev. William John Knox-Little (1839–1918), author of *Sketches and Studies in South Africa* (London: Isbister & Co, 1899). The actual text reads: 'We have been fighting the greatest war of modern times. [...] We have fought not only against Boers, but against the trained adventurers of the world. [...] We have fought them and beaten them. [...] As well as the campaign of arms we have had to meet the campaign of slander, paid for by gold, and organized by craft.' Knox-Little was a Church of England clergyman who served as a chaplain during the South African War. According to the *Oxford Dictionary of National Biography*, he was never a teacher at St Paul's, nor lived in London, though he did preach at St Paul's Cathedral. This is a typical example of Shklovsky's conflation of fact and fiction. In a Letter to the Editor of *The Times* published 22 December 1899, Knox-Little described the South African War as 'one of the most righteous wars – as most of us believe – ever waged'. This followed on from numerous letters earlier in the year calling for war in the most strident of terms and fulminating against Kruger 'propaganda' and was succeeded by many others over the next three years defending the war, the government's use of 'concentration camps' ('humane and unexampled efforts of kindness' – 31 October 1901) and popular expressions of jingoism against their 'hysterical' 'traitor' critics (misguided 'Radicals' and Christian 'philanthropists', and even Kipling!).

the many claims on his time, joined the '**Stop the War**' league.[29] But Frankie came home from school so electrified by the general patriotic atmosphere that prevailed there, that his father's 'pro-Boerism' had no influence on him.

Meanwhile, the Fifth of November arrived.

[Shklovsky gives a brief history of the Gunpowder Plot.]

From early in the morning on the fifth of November, processions of mumming pub regulars wander the streets: chalk-soiled clowns hobble in the van, followed by donkey-drawn carts; in the carts are several 'Guy Fawkes' effigies with enormous noses and even bigger mouths. The 'Guy Fawkeses' are made to look like the most unpopular individuals of the moment. One year, 'Guy Fawkes' appears in a paper Papal tiara, then in a Turkish fez, then in a Prussian helmet, etc. That year, the 'Guy Fawkeses' were Kruger, Botha and other Boer leaders.[30] The procession makes the rounds of all the streets. The clowns shout: 'Gentlemen! Don't forget, today is Guy Fawkes Day!' and thrust their caps at the passers-by, who (not too generously) drop in their pennies and ha'pennies. In the evening, all the earnings congregate in one place – the pub, and the 'Guy Fawkeses' are burned in a bonfire right there on the pavement before the pub entrance. The 'bobbies' know not to interfere until the bonfire has completely burnt out.

Similar illuminations are organised in the gardens of all the houses that contain boys from eight to fifteen years of age. On Guy Fawkes Day, five or six friends gathered at Frankie's. The sickly son of the 'General' was there, as was the big-boned, daring son of the Australian pioneer who thrilled his companions with tales of the pleasures of life in 'the bush' (Australian woods) in Mouramba, New South Wales.[31] After these tales, it was decided that they should without fail remove to Mouramba and become either prospectors or 'cowboys' (herdsmen) or kangaroo hunters. Presently, the boys put together a Guy Fawkes out of a sack filled with straw, pulled an old frockcoat and a broken top hat on him, placed a book in his hands and stuck a pipe in his mouth. In a

29   The Stop-the-War Committee, founded by W. T. Stead, was at the 'extreme' end of the anti-war, pro-Boer organisations. Its president was John Clifford, about whom Shklovsky writes in 'An Election' (see part IV below). See Jodie N. Mader, 'W. T. Stead and the Pro-Boer Response to the South African War: Dissent Through Visual Culture', *Victorian Institute Journal Annex* 40 (2012): https://nines.org/exhibits/_W_T_Stead_and_the_Pro-Boer_Re and John Davis, 'Pro-Boers', *Oxford Dictionary of National Biography*, 24 May 2008, https://doi.org/10.1093/ref:odnb/95545.

30   Paul Kruger (1825–1904), the President of the South African Republic (Transvaal); Louis Botha (1862–1919), Transvaal politician and Boer general during the war. A photograph of a 'Guy' may be seen in Thomson and Smith, *Street Life in London*.

31   Mouramba County in the colony of New South Wales, which became part of the Commonwealth of Australia in 1901.

word, they made 'Kroojer',[32] as he is portrayed in English caricatures. The boys messed about with this effigy the whole day: they shot at it with a bow, they fired at it from an old gun, they hung it up or they beat it with a stick. And when it got dark, 'Kroojer' was thrown into the bonfire. The children joined hands and danced around the blazing straw, singing at the top of their lungs a ditty of their own making:

> 'Oom Paul the villain
> Burning bright,
> Stinks to high heaven
> In the night.'[33]

In the darkness, the group reminded one of a picture from *Robinson Crusoe* depicting savages dancing wildly around a spit on which their captives were being roasted alive.

At this moment, Mr Hartnell returned from the City. Already at the station he could hear the savage song and see the glow of the bonfire.

Fig. 35. 'Oom Paul'.

He frowned and for a time reflected on something intently, apparently anticipating and weighing everything up. The bonfire burnt itself out. The boys departed. Frankie burst into the room with flaming cheeks.

'Hello, dad (papa)!' he shouted cheerfully in great excitement.

'Let us go upstairs, my boy', Hartnell said gravely. 'I would like to talk with you.'

In his study, the father began to explain to the boy why one's sympathies could not be with the English in this war. Frankie objected. He could not, of course, refute the facts adduced by his father and polemicised more, so to speak, from the heart.

'Dad, as patriots we cannot be for the Boers', said the boy.

---

32 Kruger. Shklovsky spells the name phonetically as it was pronounced at the time (this pronunciation has been preserved in contemporary newspaper accounts).

33 'Oom Paul' or 'Uncle Paul' was Kruger's nickname. The literal translation of the Russian words of the song is: 'Burns, burns / the villain Oom, / Stinks, stinks / All around.'

'It is precisely as patriots that we must not allow our motherland to commit a crime. True patriotism in this case consists in not fearing the majority.'[34]

[Mr Hartnell proceeds to enumerate various exempla from English history of now venerated individuals being punished and scorned for standing up for 'minority' views such as freedom of conscience and freedom of speech: Latimer, More, Hampden, Prynne, Defoe.]

'England is the freest country in the world. She wishes to give the Boers good laws', Frankie repeated an overheard argument.

'Yes, but you cannot force another to accept what you believe to be good. Besides, as a man, you cannot be a proponent of this war', his father concluded.

'Why not?' the boy asked, perplexed.

'Here is why. Imagine that a big grown-up professional boxer is fighting a ten-year-old boy. Can you sympathise with the brawler? Of course not. Can the big fellow take pride in finally felling the boy? No again. This is the state of affairs we see in South Africa.'

The father spent a long time talking with Frankie; the latter did not give up, raised objections, but finally fell silent. All evening he remained quiet and thought hard about something. The next day, upon returning from school, he asked his father for some books about the war and began to study them attentively. As an Englishman, albeit a small one, Frankie did not wish to accept anything on faith. He needed facts which would lead to conclusions as clear as those of Euclid's theorems. Even in matters of religion, one must *prove* to an Englishman that it is *unprofitable* to be a sinner.[35] So it continued for about two weeks. Then, after a few more days, Frankie came home from school with two big black eyes, a split and swollen lip, and a shirt torn to shreds, but excited in the extreme.

Mrs Hartnell got a real fright, gasped and proposed to call the doctor because Frankie refused his dinner in his state of nervous excitement. For the same reason, he was also unable to give a coherent account of the origin of his bruised eye and swollen lip. It was not until the evening, when his father came back from the City, that the matter was explained. Frankie had suffered for his convictions. The newly converted opponent of the war decided to persuade his comrades. He was deluged with shouts of 'traitor! coward! pro-Boer!'.

---

34 This is typical of the pro-Boer arguments of the time. See G. K. Chesterton's 'A Defence of Patriotism' in *The Speaker* (4 May 1901), a periodical that embodied the Liberal anti-war stance: '"My country, right or wrong", is a thing that no patriot would think of saying except in a desperate case. It is like saying, "My mother, drunk or sober".'

35 Compare this and other similar descriptions of English national character in Shklovsky's Letters ('In the Working Quarter', 'Richard Kelly') with Chukovsky's.

'I am not a traitor!' Frankie proclaimed proudly. 'I love free England no less than you do. I would rather be a "traitor" like Latimer and Prynne than a patriot like Cecil Rhodes. And if you call me a coward, you lie. Come forward who dares.'

So Frankie fought in succession with three little patriots, and the arbitrators found that he had conducted himself 'like a gentleman and an Englishman'. A general shaking of hands followed. The 'bulldogs' found it convenient not to notice that four boys had returned to class with black eyes. The school valued Frankie's readiness to defend his views, and the fight elevated the boy considerably in the eyes of his comrades. Only his mother kept sighing and repeating that Frankie had to be removed from that 'breeding ground for savages'. Mr Hartnell remained silent, but a pleased light glowed in his eye. When the evening after the fight the boy was saying goodnight to his father, Mr Hartnell looked at the little Prynne, patted him on the shoulder and uttered his invariable 'all right, son'. And Frankie, proud and content, ran upstairs to his room.

Not all of his school subjects came equally easily to Frankie. He really loved physics and mathematics, and especially chemistry, to which he devoted himself with zeal. The boy even set up a whole laboratory in the hut in his garden, from which he once jumped out with singed eyebrows and hair – he had put a match too soon to the neck of a Woulfe bottle in which he was purifying hydrogen and an explosion followed. Frankie had done so well in chemistry and mathematics that he was allowed to study the subjects together with the senior form. But when it came to classical languages, the boy could not have fared worse. He had to study them with the fifth form. With us, such a boy would have been 'failed' in Latin, made to repeat the year, 'failed' again with a clear conscience and expelled as 'incapable', notwithstanding his brilliant successes in other subjects. In England, the matter was settled very simply. Here, they have a deep-rooted conviction that there are no absolutely 'incapable' pupils (idiots aside), though there are absolutely incapable teachers.

Frankie's brilliant successes in mathematics and chemistry did not win him any laurels in school, just as his feeble record in the classical languages did not bring any disgrace or punishments upon him. Both the one and the other are considered normal occurrences. The teachers attentively observed each boy's character and cultivated any noted affection for a particular subject.

In the eyes of his peers, Frankie excelled thanks to his talents in sport. The school has an enormous swimming pool in which water is maintained at a constant temperature in winter and summer. Every morning, all the year round, the pupils swim and tumble about in it. And it turned out that Frankie could swim faster and more easily than anyone else in the school. Then a competition was organised between two large schools. Frankie emerged as the winner; now his peers began to regard him as the glory of the school. He was nicknamed *The Water Rat*. Judging by the tone in which Frankie informed me of this, I suspect that my young friend was no less proud of his new nickname than of his successes in chemistry.

Before I speak of the school clubs and journal that prepared Frankie to become a citizen, I must recount a sad episode from his life which will also shed some light on one trait of an English boy's character.

[A long section on football follows, including a detailed description of a match between St Paul's and Christ's Hospital (with a digression on the famous uniform) in which Frankie breaks his leg.]

V.

'Frankie, what are you reading?' I asked him recently. The boy handed me a small book called 'The Citizen Reader' by Arnold-Forster, which forms part of the Modern School Series published by the firm 'Cassell and Co'. 'The Citizen Reader' is intended for English elementary schools and seems to be widely disseminated. I had in my hands the 335th edition issued in 1900.[36] The Foreword to the book is written by Forster, a Conservative Member of Parliament. The author, Arnold-Forster, is also a Member of Parliament and an ally of the governing party. Thus, from an English point of view, there is nothing radical about 'The Citizen Reader'. That is why I was particularly curious to find out what kind of alphabet of civic consciousness was being hammered into little Englishmen.

[Shklovsky proceeds to give an extensive, chapter-by-chapter account, with many long quotations, of the contents of the Reader.]

Frankie did not just read the book attentively; from a young age he also learned to put its principles into practice. He read that organisations are an inalienable right of the free-born Englishman. And so a whole range of 'clubs' sprang up at his school. Before all else, of course, come the sports clubs: 'athletic', 'cricket', 'football', etc. Alongside these there is the miniature school parliament or ***Debating Society***. Each club has its elected representatives, secretaries and treasurers. Neither the 'bulldogs' nor the teachers, nor even the **headmaster** have the right to interfere

---

[36] Shklovsky's note: The first edition was printed in January 1886.
Editor's note: H. O. Arnold-Forster's *The Citizen Reader* was extremely popular and was reprinted countless times many decades into the twentieth century. The ideological uses of school reader series have been widely studied: see, to begin with, Stephen Heathorn's *For Home, Country, and Race: Constructing Gender, Class and Englishness in the Elementary School, 1880–1914* (Toronto: Toronto University Press, 2000) and Peter Yeandle's *Citizenship, Nation, Empire: The Politics of History Teaching in England* (Manchester: Manchester University Press, 2015).

with these clubs (nor do they think to do so). Sometimes, if the boys feel a particular love and respect for the **headmaster** (i.e. the director), they elect him as an honorary chairman. All these clubs together constitute a kind of **self-government** by the pupils. The 'parliament' addresses various questions: literary, political, philosophical; bills are introduced and discussed, speeches are made. The secretary keeps minutes, which are read out at the following session.

In these clubs, Frankie learns to deal conscientiously with real life. He becomes aware that a boy is not a pale, withered sprig covered with a flowerpot so as to be entirely cut off from all light, but a young shoot that needs lots of freedom, light and air to grow into a strong, healthy plant. Frankie is already capable of expounding his thoughts concisely and figuratively, without digressing or waffling.

The boys remember well that the expression of one's thoughts in print constitutes another inalienable right of the Englishman. And so in 'sixth form', i.e. in the senior class, an elected editorial board publishes a school journal, 'The Argus'. At first, the journal was lithographed, but now it is printed in three hundred copies.[37] 'The Argus' is read not just in the school. Former pupils, or '**old boys**' as they are known, also receive the journal. Some of them are already advanced in years, and with sadness they might recite the beginning of Piron's quatrain:

> '**Pas à pas j'arrive au trou**
> **Que n'échappe, fou ni sage.**'[38]

But despite their advanced age, they still recall their school with delight and take a keen interest in everything that happens there.

[Shklovsky again alludes to the author of Tom Brown's Schooldays to exemplify 'the love of an "old boy" for his school' and contrast it with the hatred felt for their schools by pupils on the Continent.]

Frankie is now an assiduous contributor to 'The Argus'. Like all beginner writers, he still has a weakness for quotations, but he expresses his thoughts in writing quite well already. In the latest issue of 'The Argus', my young friend published a lengthy article the spirit of which is evident from the epigraph borrowed from the 'Magna Carta Libertatum': 'No free man shall be seized or imprisoned, or stripped of his rights or

---

[37]   Lithography is a process for producing prints that involves pressing inks by hand onto a tablet; mechanical printing has a much higher capacity for reproduction.

[38]   Alexis Piron (1689–1773) was French epigrammatist and dramatist; the quotation is from one of his burlesque epitaphs on himself: 'Dernière épitaphe' ['Last Epitaph']. The full quatrain reads: 'Pas à pas j'arrive au trou / Que n'échappe fou ni sage, / Pour aller je ne sais où: / Adieu, Piron; bon voyage!' [Step by step I arrive at the pit / that neither the mad nor the wise escapes, / To go I don't know where: / Farewell, Piron; bon voyage!] in L. E. Kastner, ed. *A Book of French Verse: From Marot to Mallarmé* (Cambridge University Press, 1936), 132.

possessions, or **outlawed** or exiled, except by the lawful judgment of his equals or by the law of the land'.[39] In his article, Frankie tried to prove that the English government had committed a crime in executing the Boer commander Scheepers.[40] When I saw the conclusion of the article, I understood why Frankie had been so busy lately rummaging in his father's library: 'When I travel in a country', it said, 'I don't inquire whether it has good laws but whether those that it has are *applied*, for there are good laws everywhere.' **'Oeuvres Complètes de Montesquieu', tome V, p. 286, Paris, 1820**.[41]

'The Argus' supports the war, but it gave space to its 'respected friend's' article in the form of a letter to the editors. 'Freedom of expression above all else', the editors proclaim on this head in the leading article, which also concludes with a quotation from the 'Magna Carta': 'To no-one will we sell, to no-one deny or delay right or justice'. The quotation from Montesquieu had made an impression and elicited a counter-quotation.

Frankie will finish school in two years' time.

[Shklovsky adduces some more quotations from Tom Brown's Schooldays *and Darwin's* Autobiography *and reflects on the way the 'classical languages are yielding their place to the natural sciences and modern languages' in English schools.]*

The tenacity acquired in school serves as a guarantee that at the age of sixty Frankie will still be working with the same intense vigour as at thirty.[42] From the age of twelve, Frankie has understood that he possesses, as a member of society, not just responsibilities but also rights, to defend which is the citizen's highest duty. That is already a major advantage. For when I think of certain of Frankie's Continental

---

[39] Shklovsky does not quote exactly and omits the clauses: 'or deprived of his standing in any way, nor will we proceed with force against him, or send others to do so'. See the transcript of the *Magna Carta*, 1215 in *The National Archives*, www.nationalarchives.gov.uk/education/resources/magna-carta/british-library-magna-carta-1215-runnymede/.

[40] Commandant Gideon Scheepers was a young Boer officer court-martialled and executed by a British firing squad in 1902 for war crimes. The execution aroused protests not just from Frankie but from Winston Churchill.

[41] The quotation is, appropriately enough, from Montesquieu's *Notes on England* *[Notes sur l'Angleterre]*. Shklovsky liked to quote from this work – he adduces another quote in French from page 284 of the referenced volume in 'The Crank', 108. See Iain Stewart, *Montesquieu in England: His 'Notes on England', with Commentary and Translation Commentary*, 2002, Oxford University Comparative Law Forum 6, https://ouclf.law.ox.ac.uk/montesquieu-in-england-his-notes-on-england-with-commentary-and-translation-commentary/.

[42] As this and the preceding paragraphs show, Frankie is growing up to be just like his father, as described at the beginning of the piece.

colleagues who will leave school as young bankrupts with a profound hatred for it, without any character, any knowledge, any health, with the beginnings of neurasthenia already in place, with the fearful prospect of sharing the fate of those youths whom the Athenians once sent to Pasiphae's monstrous offspring, I cannot help but exclaim with envy: 'Frankie, you are fortunate!'. You will not be cast into the labyrinth of Knossos, the abode of the Minotaur! In school and at university, you are protected, cherished, doted upon, and the awakening in you of civic self-consciousness is greeted with joy. You are considered the flower of England, its only hope. You are fortunate, Frankie! And woe to the Minotaur's victims![43]

---

[43] Ironically, Frankie is of the right age to have fought (and, as an officer, probably died) in the Great War. The classical allusions in this paragraph are to the ancient Greek myth of the Minotaur (part-man, part-bull – son of Pasiphae, Queen of Crete), who lived in the Labyrinth at Knossos and devoured Athenian youths and maidens sent to him as sacrifice. The monster was eventually killed by the hero Theseus.

Isaak Shklovsky [Dioneo], 'Father Christmas'
English Silhouettes (St Petersburg, 1905): 101–23[1]

I.

[The opening paragraphs invoke the stereotypes of the Dickensian Christmas of Pickwick and Scrooge and contrast them with the meaning of Christmas in 'contemporary England'. The role of food is emphasised: St Valentine's Day is forgotten because no special dish is associated with it, but not so Shrove Tuesday.]

In this sketch, I will try to give my readers some notion of the merriest and most revered holiday in England, of '**Father Christmas**'. There are special publications and special performances associated with this day that Dickens never said a word about anywhere. The performances, as the reader shall see, have now become a propaganda vehicle for economic doctrines.

In London, the first signs of the approach of Christmas may be seen initially in the poor quarters, and very early on at that: at the very beginning of September. This is the time when notices appear in pub windows announcing the formation of 'Goose Clubs'. Apart from the plum pudding (**Real, honest, substantial British plum pudding**, as the English call it), the centrepiece of a Christmas dinner is a turkey or, failing that, a goose. Without it, Christmas is not Christmas. And in the poor districts, they begin to dream of a goose from the end of summer. The purpose of the 'Goose Club' is to provide people who have to get by on a day labourer's wage not just with a bird, but with many other things besides. 'Club' members pay a sixpence (a quarter) every week to the pub owner and, come Christmas, they receive a basket containing a goose, some tinned goods, a bottle of wine and two bottles of 'Old Tom' (vodka).[2] Only in rare cases does the 'Goose Club' provide a plum pudding, because making it is a kind of sacrament for the wife of a labourer or clerk. They spend three whole weeks chopping the innumerable ingredients of the plum pudding, stirring, boiling, cooling, worrying, fretting, boiling again.

---

[1]   Originally published as a Letter 'From England' under the pseudonym Dioneo in the monthly journal *Russkoe Bogatstvo*, January 1904, 55–76. Compare with Chukovsky's view of the English Christmas in 'Sandwich Men'.

[2]   A 'quarter' was a Russian silver coin worth twenty-five kopecks. 'Old Tom' is gin. Goose Clubs were a Victorian working-class Christmas institution. See the mid-Victorian description of 'Goose-Clubs' in *A Holiday Book for Christmas and the New Year* (London: Ingram, Cooke & Co., 1852): 23; see also the photograph of 'A Christmas Eve Distribution of Turkeys, Geese, Etc. (Aldenham Institute)' in Sims, *Living London* 2, 259. For a quick introduction to the Victorian Christmas, see Simon Callow, 'Charles Dickens and the Victorian Christmas Feast', *British Library*, 8 December 2017, www.bl.uk/romantics-and-victorians/articles/a-victorian-christmas-feast.

For the wife of a junior clerk or labourer, cooking a plum pudding is a sort of transubstantiation of 'home'. And what can be more important for an Englishman than his 'home'?[3] At the same time as the Goose Clubs, i.e. in late August or early September, appear the lavishly illustrated Christmas issues of 'magazines' and weekly literary journals. The illustrations have been in preparation since spring. Since countless numbers of copies are printed, the issue has to be put together at the height of summer. According to tradition, of course, the illustrations depict London covered in snow, i.e. with an aspect that the vast capital never takes on in real life. Winters here are sullen and gloomy, but mild. It hardly ever snows; at any rate, the snow never stays on the ground for more than an hour.

[Shklovsky proceeds to describe the illustrations that appear in the 'Christmas extra' issues of magazines such as Pearson's, *specifically Lawson Wood's well-known 'The Stage Coach in Prehistoric Times', in connection with British humour. He then reflects on the British love of Christmas 'ghost stories', from Dickens via Hawthorne's* Twice-Told Tales *to the 'real' ghost stories of the 'theosophists and spiritualists', as represented by William Stead. He references Taine's* History of English Literature *on the national character trait that accounts for the British predilection for 'supernatural adventures', and remarks on Kipling's and Wells's new experiments in the genre of the fantastic.]*

II.

'A merry day is coming', an old English ballad says. '"Tis the season to be jolly. Deck the halls with mistletoe and the posts with sacred **holly**... All the neighbours' chimneys are smoking. The smell of roast beef is everywhere. Leave misfortune at the door, and if it freezes there, we'll bury it in the plum pudding.'[4]

These days, the coming of Christmas is marked not so much by an increase in traffic in the streets of London as by the appearance of a phenomenal number of beggars. They come in all shapes and sizes![5] Here is an unreconstructed beggar, so to speak: a bearded blind man with a fiddle in his hand, or an armless one led by a dog. You can see them in the streets of any city. But here are some characteristic beggars typical

---

3   The opening of the article is dedicated to Dickens, so the whole stereotypical discourse of the Englishman's home as his castle is invoked by implication from the outset.

4   I have been unable to locate the original of this 'old ballad', but given the resemblance of some of the lines to Christmas carols like 'Deck the Hall' and a variety of traditional Victorian 'Plum Pudding' Christmas songs, it is conceivable that Shklovsky spliced several songs together.

5   Cf. Chukovsky's 'Beggars in London'.

A BUSY CRIPPLE (STROUD GREEN ROAD).

BLIND (REGENT STREET).

BLIND (REGENT STREET).

PARALYSED (VICTORIA STREET).

"MATCHES AND LACES!"

BLIND (ST. MARTIN'S CHURCH STEPS).

CRIPPLED (REGENT STREET).

Fig. 36. London Street Characters.

of London: an elderly man of very respectable appearance, wearing a pince-nez, clean-shaven, in an old but clean black frockcoat and top hat, offers you a box of matches. A lady in a bonnet and black mantle walks down the street and sings psalms or church hymns. On the Continent, especially in Paris, people sing in the streets when they are happy. In London, only beggars sing in the street. And if you hear someone sing, then however respectable their attire might be, feel free to offer them a penny if you are kind-hearted. Here is another typical London beggar: a presentably and neatly dressed lady in hat and gloves is drawing family scenes, landscapes, galloping generals, etc. in chalks on the pavement slabs.[6] There is a portrait of *Joe*,[7] because though the lady might be a beggar, she reads the newspapers and follows politics. Next to the drawings stands a little bowl into which the passers-by can toss a copper coin.[8] And since the hearts of the English are compassionate towards the poor, especially before Christmas, the pennies fall thick and fast. Beggars of this type may be met with, for the most part, in the affluent quarters. They rely on touching people's hearts by their respectability. In the poor and working districts, the beggars are of a different type. Here is a whole company, about five strong. One young fellow in a long coat, a tweed cap and an enormous scarf wrapped around his neck is turning the handle of a huge barrel organ. It is so heavy that it has to be dragged by a long-suffering scruffy donkey. Another young fellow is playing the pipe; nearby an old man is striking a triangle, and another man, somewhat younger, is dancing a jig and stomping heavily in the mud with his broken boots. And in the cart next to the barrel organ sits a legless man with stumps instead of arms. A sign on the barrel organ reads: 'Good people and friends! You find before you unemployed men who wish, in this manner, to **"turn an honest penny"**.[9] The legless and the armless whom you see have been crippled in a factory.'

*[Shklovsky then speculates that though unemployment has indeed increased because of the Boer War, the people with the barrel organ are probably 'professional **tramps**' rather than real workingmen, who are too proud to publicly advertise their destitution. Trade unionists would receive help from their unions, Shklovsky explains, while un-unionised unskilled labourers would rather become sandwich men than resort to beggary or go into the workhouse.]*

The nearer it gets to Christmas, the more frequently do the so-called 'minstrels' appear on the streets of London's poorer districts. They walk about in parties of about five people. One sees men made up like

---

6   'Chalks': the original Russian has literally 'dry coloured pencils'.
7   Joseph Chamberlain.
8   The lady is a screever or pavement artist – see Orwell's description of London
     pavement artists in *Down and Out in Paris and London*.
9   A Russian translation in parentheses is also provided.

negroes, in top hats, green tails and red waistcoats, and women in short skirts and broad crimson 'bergère' hats with coloured ribbons.[10] The men play mandolins and the women dance.[11] In such itinerant troupes one can often meet with real, professional actors and dancers who have lost their engagement at the music hall. It is difficult to imagine a more melancholy spectacle than the sight of these wretched, painted women dancing in their 'shabby-gay' costumes outside pub doors, in the black fog or beneath the penetrating rain. This spectacle haunts one later like a nightmare. One begins to see something symbolic in it. Further on from the 'minstrels', a Scotsman in picturesque national costume is playing the bagpipes, while a woman, also wearing national costume, performs the Caledonian 'sword dance', i.e. with two old soldiers' swords.[12] The sound of the bagpipes, which has a meaning in the mountains of Scotland where its echoes resound in otherworldly tones, causes nothing but a painful irritation in the streets of a big city, especially in the fog – and at the same time drives one to tears. The woman is dancing, brandishing her swords spiritedly, crying out the refrain of an ancient song in the Celtic language, all the while glancing anxiously now and then to see if anyone has tossed a copper coin from the pub doors. And here is a universally familiar figure: an Italian boy is turning the handle of a barrel organ, on top of which, shivering in the damp, sits a forlorn monkey in a greasy red jacket and fez. The barrel organ is spewing into the fog the incongruous sounds of a popular music hall song. Dozens of children are dancing to its music on the pavements and in the street, right in the mud.[13] Here are girls in mantles, with dirty hair falling loose from under their straw hats; here are the young **laundry girls** in curlpapers and spangled pleated dresses with tattered, muddy hems. The **laundry girls**, like the London flower girls, astound one equally by their passion for gaudy feathers and curlpapers, their eternally dishevelled appearance and the array of old and new bruises they sport under their eyes.

The main streets of the poor quarters are flooded with light, and you cannot move for the crowds. Entire families walk down the pavements and the streets together. Here is one, for example. The husband, a labourer in a bowler and with a pipe between his teeth, pushes a perambulator in which lies a baby in a red cap with a dummy in its mouth.

---

10   'Bergère' hat: a shepherdess-style hat popular in the eighteenth century and used in entertainment costumes in the nineteenth. For background on female blackface, see Laura Vorachek, 'Whitewashing Blackface Minstrelsy in Nineteenth-Century England: Female Banjo Players in *Punch*', *Victorians: A Journal of Culture and Literature* 123 (Spring 2013), 31–51.

11   By 'mandolin', Shklovsky almost certainly means the banjo.

12   Shklovsky is describing a type of Highland dancing.

13   This is one of the most frequently recurring street scenes in Shklovsky's Letters, alongside Salvation Army bands, costers and drunken pub-goers.

Fig. 37. Waiting to Buy 'Trimmings' of Meat.

The baby has opened its eyes wide and is staring at the bright lights. The perambulator also contains bundles and parcels of purchases wrapped in paper. Next to it walks the 'missus', the labourer's wife, in a bonnet and a mantle over her shoulders. A little girl clutches at her mother's skirts. A boy of about five sits on his father's shoulders.

The goose is already laid by. It has been sent from the Club; but there is still meat to buy. And now a difficult question arises: what to choose – beef, mutton or rabbit? Dozens of butchers are crying the merits of their mutton and beef to the whole street. The rabbits are sold from stalls by mysterious, unshaven, sullen-looking characters. Family councils are held on the pavements, in which even the children sitting on their fathers' shoulders get to take part with full right to a casting vote. Somebody is crying out the merits of old trousers and jackets. Further down, a gentleman in a top hat is selling pills that cure all diseases.

'Ladies and gentlemen', the seller exclaims, 'I offer a sovereign to anyone who can prove that my pills cause any harm. They are worth a gold coin sight unseen, and all I'm asking is a penny for a packet!'.

In a side alley, the soldiers of the Salvation Army are straining their voices. Somewhere in the fog, a hammer clicks: those are passers-by trying out their strength. The pubs are full. The doors keep opening, and at the bar one can see red-coated soldiers, vagabonds, men of uncertain professions, blowsy women in battered hats and chequered shawls thrown on instead of mantles. By about eleven o'clock at night, it becomes impossible to jostle one's way through the crowds in front of the butchers' shops. The shoppers are very poorly dressed, mostly elderly women with weary, anxious faces. At this hour, the butchers sell trimmings, bones and offal – all that is scorned by the more well-to-do customers of the working districts – to the paupers.

I have already mentioned that the English have a compassionate heart when it comes to the destitute, especially on the eve of Christmas. It is probable that in no other country is charity so widespread as it is here. Take, to begin with, the fact that all the English hospitals are maintained on private donations. Just before Christmas, charity can take on particularly original forms. Such are, for instance, the banquets for 'sandwich men' put on annually by the editors of **Reynolds's Newspaper**, the most popular of the Sunday papers, extremely Radical in outlook.[14] It had its origins in the days of the Chartist movement and has retained its 'republican' colouring since that period. Readers will presently see why I have stressed the latter circumstance. The newspaper organises the banquet for sandwich men on the principle that these people should feel themselves to be the editor's *guests* at the soiree, and not 'favoured' paupers. The banquet is held in some large restaurant. The newspaper readers, male and female, sit at tables interspersed with the ragged sandwich men, numbering about two thousand. And you should see with what dignity these sandwich men conduct themselves at table! It's true that many of them have seen better days. Among these sad, unkempt and shabby men there are former priests, solicitors, officers, representatives of the middle classes, etc. Each one of them could reveal some private drama; but they are all an exceedingly reserved people. However, many more of the sandwich men are those who were born and bred and will likely die in the slums. Yet all without exception bear themselves with dignity at the banquet, like real gentlemen. You should see with what grave courtesy a sandwich man offers a jug of water or a salt cellar to his splendidly dressed female neighbour at table! The editor of **Reynolds's Newspaper**, a solicitor called Thompson,[15] presides at the dinner and gives a speech, to which one of the sandwich men responds. The best English actors, singers, and musicians offer their services to entertain the sandwich men after dinner. When the guests disperse, each of them is handed a bundle containing some clothes, tobacco, a new pipe and a half crown in cash (a rouble and a quarter).[16] Such an entertainment for the sandwich men costs several thousand roubles. And all this money is collected by subscription in a few days. The **Reynolds** is a very democratic and republican paper, yet the King and Queen are always among the first to send in their contribution to the editors (usually, one hundred roubles each). Such is the singularity of

[14] Cf. Chukovsky's description of these banquets in 'Sandwich Men'. *Reynolds's Newspaper* began organising its Christmas Dinner for sandwich men in 1895 and Shklovsky's account is probably drawn at least partly from the newspaper's own columns.
[15] William Thompson was editor from 1894 until 1907.
[16] A half crown was equivalent to two shillings and sixpence.

Fig. 38. 'Truth' Toy Show at the Royal Albert Hall.

English customs. Such is the deep and *mutual* respect for the *individual*.
In issue after issue, **Reynolds's** argues that the crown is a superfluous
element in the English mechanism of state; but the newspaper also
acknowledges that Edward VII is an ideal constitutional monarch and,
before all else, a gentleman, which constitutes the highest praise in the
mouth of an Englishman. For their part, every year the King and Queen
send a telegram with Christmas greetings to the sandwich men, care of
Thompson. These annual banquets are one of the most characteristic
features of the Christmas holidays in London.[17]

No less curious are the toy exhibitions organised before Christmas by
Labouchère, the editor of the Radical journal **Truth**.[18] The vast halls of
the **Albert Hall** turn, for three days, into the kingdom of 'Santa Claus'.
Here are thousands of dolls, whole cities of toy houses, countless herds

[17]   Editor's paragraph break.
[18]   *Truth* was a periodical founded by Liberal MP Henry Labouchère in 1877, known
for its exposés of frauds and libel suits. Labouchère was an opponent of the Boer
War. For more details on the 'Truth' Doll and Toy Show, which was mounted
annually at the Royal Albert Hall from the 1890s to 1913, see Jacky Cowdrey,
'1890–1913: The Truth Toy and Doll Show', *Royal Albert Hall*, 12 December 2013,
www.royalalberthall.com/about-the-hall/news/2013/december/the-truth-toy-and-
doll-show/. Cf. Marshak's article 'At the Children's Exhibition'.

of horses and colts, arsenals of toy guns, swords and cannon. The dolls are dressed artistically. All this is owing to the care of the subscribers. One astounding section of the exhibition features a huge collection of mechanical – in some cases remarkably ingenious – toys. In the same section, behind glass, is kept a gift that an anonymous donor has sent in every time for fourteen years running: twenty thousand newly minted sixpence silver coins (the size of a quarter). All the toys and coins are distributed after the end of the exhibition to children who are patients in London hospitals.

III.

Christmastime is here. Let us see how the average English family celebrates it.

[The next section offers a double portrait of Christmas in the home of a middle-class and a working-class family. Shklovsky begins by remarking how much has changed since the Dickensian Christmas of The Pickwick Papers *and then paints the home of a hereditary physician with eight children. He describes its colonial connections; its traditional decorations (kissing under the mistletoe is now considered 'improper'); the guests in paper caps from the Christmas crackers, including a Scottish industrialist and a doctor from Georgetown in British Guiana; the maid; the dinner of turkey with chestnut stuffing, roast beef, plum pudding decorated with a national flag and twig of holly and with silver coins and other souvenirs in every slice, and champagne; the Christmas games like musical chairs in the parlour, the reading of ghost stories from the Christmas almanacs. He ends by quoting Thomas Browne's* Religio Medici. *This is followed by a description of Christmas in a respectable workingman's (trade unionist's) flat, which is similar in many respects, except that the daughters are either in service or at the factory and the sons wear soldiers' or sailors' uniforms or are labourers like their father. In both homes the daughters play piano: classical music in the middle-class home, music hall songs in the working-class one. The section concludes with a peroration on the contrast between the uplifting holiday celebrations of a free people who are aware of their rights and their and others' individual dignity, and the bestial holiday rioting of drunken slaves who turn to bloodletting and the working off on those weaker than themselves of their own humiliation. The implicit contrast between Britain and Russia is clear.]*

IV.

The first day of Christmas, with its nightmares brought on by the heavy plum puddings and the thick Spanish wines, is over. Now comes **Boxing-day**, the second day, for which entrepreneurs prepare from the very beginning of autumn. Most theatres arrange for their new plays to open on this day. But the most characteristic feature of **Boxing-day** are the so-called pantomimes. The English, as one Frenchman discovered, do everything not like on the Continent, but in reverse: coachmen keep to the *right* side of the road; in his letters, the Englishman writes *I* with a capital letter and *you* in lower case; when greeting an acquaintance, a Frenchman removes his hat, whereas an Englishman pulls it lower down over his ears, etc. It is probably in this spirit of contradiction that the English have given the name 'pantomime' to performances during which not only do the actors not communicate with gestures but, on the contrary, actually talk too much, much more than the plot requires. 'Pantomimes' are staged with remarkable opulence. As many as three to four hundred people are involved in the production. The costumes and sets astound by their beauty. Especially splendid is the set design of the last act, the 'metamorphosis' scene: a forest is transformed at one stroke, without the curtain being dropped, into a magical palace; a street becomes a fairy grotto sparkling with lights and festooned with roses, etc. On **Boxing-day**, more than fifty out of one hundred London theatres stage 'pantomimes'. Such performances were originally intended for children. Indeed, from Boxing-day and almost until Shrove Tuesday,[19] you can see the rosy cheerful faces, exuding health and happiness, of little English boys and girls at matinee performances in the theatres. It is a real pleasure to look at those healthy faces. You see a strong, assertive, intelligent nation in embryo, possessed of an immense energy and capacity for work. How wretched in comparison with these children do our own pale little gymnasium pupils seem, worn out by excessive and meaningless cramming, almost all of them already showing premonitory signs of the 'Russian disease', as they call neurasthenia here![20] And they have dressed our boys up in uniforms, like soldiers, as if intentionally to deprive them even more of their individuality.

Small children aside, many adult and even elderly English people attend pantomimes at the theatre. It is hard to tell who is enjoying themselves more: the children or the adults. An Englishman at work is completely engrossed in his affairs. In order to keep his mind better focused on **business**, he reads almost nothing. But when it comes to his hours of leisure, the Englishman makes merry like a child. Important judges, members of Parliament and the Cabinet, serious university professors, all laugh themselves into stitches at the theatre at a well-placed pun or a clown's whimsical high jinks. In this regard, the adults can hold their own with the children. But what are the pantomime

[19] The original has 'pancake week', the Slavic holiday celebrated before Lent.

[20] Shklovsky's description takes on an unintentional irony when one recalls the national panics about school overwork and cramming that gripped Britain from the 1880s onwards. See J. Middleton, 'The Overpressure Epidemic of 1884 and the Culture of Nineteenth-Century Schooling', *History of Education* 33.4 (July 2004), 419–35.

Fig. 39. A Pantomime Rehearsal.

plots? They can be divided into three groups. The plots of some of the plays are inspired by well-loved fairy tales and stories: these include Aladdin, Little Red Riding Hood, Bluebeard, Sindbad the Sailor, Jack the Giant Killer, Puss in Boots, Cinderella, Babes in the Wood, Robinson

Crusoe, etc. The authors give free rein to their imagination. When it comes to the plot, they do not stand on ceremony, but introduce new scenes or move the action to countries that lend themselves to more beautiful stage decorations. The play is embellished with music, singing, dancing and even acrobatic performances. Let us take, for instance, the tale of Bluebeard, which provides the basis for the pantomime that is currently running at the **Coronet Theatre**.[21] The action has been moved to Persia.[22]

[Shklovsky gives a summary of the plot, complete with the 'Persian' characters, caricature English trial and Scottish solicitor, clown-gymnasts 'Hookit and Crookit', musical comedy stars instead of Bluebeard's dead wives, etc.]

Another example I can give is the pantomime 'Babes in the Wood'. It is worth knowing that the same plot is reworked simultaneously in two or even three theatres by different authors and composers. Thus, every Christmas in London you can watch no fewer than three 'Little Red Riding Hoods' or 'Dick Whittingtons'. Everyone knows the story of Little Red Riding Hood. Dick Whittington is the hero of a London legend.

[Shklovsky proceeds to summarise the plots of Dick Whittington *and* Babes in the Wood, *both the ballad and the pantomime (which changes the grim ending and introduces Robin Hood). He then offers 'an anatomy of the pantomime', explaining the main roles of the 'principal boy', 'principal girl', 'second boy', 'second girl', first and second 'comic women' [dames] and 'comical beasts', and describes the clown costumes, the dance and chorus acts, comic scenes from* The Forty Thieves, *etc. He also introduces Dan Leno (1860–1904), probably the best known late-Victorian music hall comedian, 'without whom the pantomime at the Drury Lane Theatre would be completely unthinkable' (Leno starred in the pantomimes from 1888 until his death).]*

Such are the pantomimes of the first category, i.e. those whose plots are borrowed from fairy tales and legends.

To the second category belong pantomimes inspired by popular children's songs, the so-called '**nursery rhymes**'. All these songs are very short, with almost no content. This is probably why they are so tempting to authors, since they leave a lot of scope for the imagination.

---

[21] Shklovsky's note: Written in 1903.
    Editor's note: The Coronet Theatre in Notting Hill Gate opened in 1898.
[22] See Peter Yeandle, 'Exotic People and Exotic Places in Victorian Pantomime', in Tiziana Morosetti, ed. *Staging the Other in Nineteenth-Century British Drama* (Oxford: Peter Lang, 2015), 125–51.

For instance, the pantomime *Humpty Dumpty*, currently playing with great success at the Drury Lane Theatre, is of this kind.[23]

[Shklovsky explains how a whole play in fourteen acts has been spun out of a short nursery rhyme and gives a very detailed description of this popular pantomime, starring Dan Leno. In his account of the plot, Shklovsky emphasises the elements of blatant anti-free trade and pro-Chamberlain/protectionist propaganda that are woven into the action and songs, and the amazing scenery, technical wizardry of the scene changes, and interludes with clowns, acrobats and magicians.]

In pantomimes of both the first and second type – i.e. performances based on fairy tales and on children's songs – the dramatis personae, especially the clowns, constantly allude to current affairs. A free-born Englishman, even a clown, is not prohibited from criticising whatever he pleases. But because English theatres are for the most part capitalist enterprises and are wholly owned by joint-stock companies, the clowns, chorus girls and satirical ballad singers who make 'lunges' at the burning issues of the day must usually defer to the interests of the 'owners'. The pantomimes used to preach 'real' imperialism.[24] Now nearly all of them sing Chamberlain's praises and propagandise the necessity of a bread tax and protectionism.

[Shklovsky now digresses to give an extended analysis of the protectionist platform.]

This year, **'Comical Women'**, **'Principal Boys'** and ordinary clowns have become prophets of protectionism in their pantomimes. In *Humpty Dumpty*, the **Principal Boy** sings patriotic verses in the enchanted forest that are now being played by all the barrel organs in the London streets. 'When our Nelson kept the British flag a-flying', the **Principal Boy** begins,[25]

---

[23] The pantomime was so popular that it was even used to advertise products like 'Cork Lino' in papers such as the *Daily Express*, which also reviewed it.

[24] For recent takes on this very well-studied topic, see Jane Pritchard and Peter Yeandle, '"Executed with remarkable care and artistic feeling": Music Hall Ballet and Popular Imperialism' and Jeffrey Richards, 'Drury Lane Imperialism' in Peter Yeandle, Katherine Newey and Jeffrey Richards, eds. *Politics, Performance and Popular Culture* (Manchester: Manchester University Press, 2016), 152–73 and 174–94. Richards gives an excellent primary account and overview of the scholarship on imperialism in London pantomimes in particular.

[25] Shklovsky offers a loose translation into Russian prose of the song 'The John Bull Store', also 'performed at the Alhambra in 1903 with Chamberlain's portrait as a backdrop on stage. Themes of national decline, xenophobia and patriotic rebirth were combined in its verses', see Peter Gurney, *The Making of Consumer Culture in Modern Britain* (London: Bloomsbury, 2017), 127. Instead of back-translating Shklovsky's prose, I have given the original verse version from the *Daily Express*, which printed the song in full (with an illustration in the vein of the protectionist

'When we hammered Boney on the shore,
There were traders coming hat in hand a-buying
At the counter of the John Bull Store.
When we'd beaten all our foes, then, as everybody knows,
They were begging for the things we made,
For the German, Yank, and Russ, tho' they liked to sneer at us,
Weren't a patch upon John Bull at trade.'

'Buy! buy! buy! at the John Bull Store', the chorus of girls in tights takes up the song, waving national flags,

'The Deutscher and the Yank we shall want no more;
And the money that we gain will in British hands remain
If we buy at the John Bull Store.'

'But an altered tale our present day is telling', the Principal Boy begins again,

'For the Empire's glory seemed to fade;
We're buying where we used to go a-selling,
And the foreigner has grabbed our trade.
Just when things are looking black and the orders getting slack
Comes a champion leaping to the fore —[26]

With an eyeglass in his eye,
That the quicker he can spy
What is wanting in the John Bull Store.'

'Buy! buy! buy! at the John Bull Store, etc.' the chorus picks up the song again, waving national flags.
'And he made a plan to draw our lads together', the **Principal Boy** strikes up,

'All the Empire standing hand in hand,
That our trade may grow in good and evil weather,
And Fortune smile upon our land.
Now our "Joe" is straight and square, and he's always played us fair
When we've trusted him with jobs before;
So let's help him all we can,

And we'll find that Joey's plan,
Is the saving of the John Bull Store.'

The note of protectionism can be heard in almost all the pantomimes staged this year. In *Bluebeard*, sister Anna (a clown) looks out from

---

posters Shklovsky describes elsewhere) on 15 October 1903 and again in 1906 before the general election.

[26]   The loose Russian prose translation here yields to a verbatim quotation in English, which Shklovsky translates into Russian in parentheses. Ditto below. I have left Shklovsky's exact phrasing here, while silently correcting typographical errors.

a tower to see if Prince Selim's band is galloping up the road to the rescue.

'Look there!' Anna cries, 'dust is swirling in the road. Could that be Selim?'

'No. The dust is moving away towards the seashore.'

'Excellent! That means all the foreigners are clearing the hell out of England.'

In *The Forty Thieves*, Herbert Campbell, no less famous a clown than Dan Leno, sings a hymn to 'Good Old Joe'.[27] Almost the whole troupe comes out on stage with flags bearing portraits of Chamberlain.

'Gone are the days', the clown begins, 'when our trade was brisk and gay;[28]
Gone are the days when we held commercial sway.
Taxed are our goods in foreign lands, but, oh!
We're going to get our own back soon thro' "Good old Joe!"'

'He's going, he's going', the chorus takes up the song, 'to give them blow for blow;
He'll take a bit of knocking out, will "Good old Joe!".'

'With that old blade, "Free Trade," our throats we've cut', the clown begins again,
'Look at our mills and fact'ries that are shut!

[27]   The Sixpenny Popular Edition song sheet of 'Good Old Joe!' (London: Francis, Day & Hunter, 1903), written by Arthur Seldon, may be seen in the Gonzaga University Digital Archives: https://digital.gonzaga.edu/digital/collection/p15486coll3/id/14010. Herbert Campbell (1844–1904) was a famous Victorian music hall comedian and singer, who starred in the lavish Drury Lane Christmas pantomimes from the 1880s until his death, in partnership with Dan Leno. These included most of the pantomimes that Shklovsky enumerates above. The 1903–1904 pantomime, where Shklovsky saw him, was his last. The *Daily Express* advertised Herbert Campbell's 'Good Old Joe' in October and December (for Christmas) 1903 along with other songs for sale at 6d. each under the rubric 'Music for the People. A Public Want Supplied. Sixpenny Popular Editions of Francis and Day's Musical Copyrights' (30 October 1903, 2). 'Good Old Joe' was no. 31. On 30 January 1904, in a review of acts at the Drury Lane pantomime (a 'colossal show, which is now in the height of its success'), the *Express* remarked: 'It is pleasant to note that Mr. Herbert Campbell's Protection song, "Good Old Joe," is received with thunderous applause and without a single dissenting voice' ('Miss Love at the "Lane"', 5). Cf. Shklovsky's comment below. 'Good old Joe! He's all right!' was how a member of the public greeted Chamberlain, 'the great pioneer of Tariff Reform', on his return to England in April 1904, see 'Home Again. Mr. Chamberlain Returned Quietly to London Yesterday', *The Daily Illustrated Mirror* (16 April 1904), 2.

[28]   As above, I have replaced Shklovsky's loose Russian prose translation with the original lyrics (in a departure from the usual practice throughout, the formatting is that of the English original); but Shklovsky's English quotations (which he translates in parentheses) are given using the Russian formatting.

When you've to *loaf*, you can't buy *bread*, you know;
"Let charity begin at home!" says "Good old Joe."'

'He's going, he's going, etc.', the chorus comes in.

'Lib'rals say *they're* "The working-man's best friend"', the clown strikes up.
'Why don't they try our dwindling trade to mend?
Fine words won't fill your "Little Mary," no!
"Protection," tho', will do the trick, says "Good old Joe".' [Let's believe him.]

He's going, he's going to buck trade up, what-oh!
We'll soon be multi-millionaires through Good old Joe!

'Joe's battle-ship, "Protection," soon will be
Launched on the waves of the **"Phiscalpolli Sea."**
She's got a splendid pilot, and, I trow,
He'll steer her safely into port, will "Good old Joe!".'

I cannot vouch that the audience consists entirely of protectionists. Loud voices are also sometimes raised in protest from the auditorium during the singing; but at the end of the day, **Christmas is Christmas**, as the English say. The public has arrived at the theatre in a cheerful mood, to enjoy itself, and not to trouble its head about economic questions. It hears out the clowns in their role of professors of political economy, and even applauds them, chiefly because they are amusing.

[Shklovsky then digresses into an analysis of Chamberlain's politics, the economic situation in the metropole and the colonies and the publications of the Tariff Reform League, and then returns to the subject of pantomimes, covering the third category of 'fantastic' rather than 'political' pantomimes and focusing on the popular Blue Bell in Fairy-Land. *The final section of the piece is devoted to a description of the music hall (Shklovsky mentions various acts including clowns, a 'one-legged cyclist' who jumps from on-high into a pool together with his cycle, and Theodore Hardeen, magician, escape artist and Harry Houdini's younger brother) and the music hall's various lower-, middle- and upper-class audiences in the gallery, pit, etc. Costers, butchers' errand boys, flower and laundry girls who shriek, whistle and laugh loudly and get their opinions from publications like* Ally Sloper *are contrasted with clerks, 'bookmakers' and shopkeepers on the one hand and with stockbrokers and the jeunesse dorée on the other. Shklovsky briefly examines the role of protectionist and patriotic propaganda in popular music hall songs, such as 'The Soldiers of the Queen'; and the rivalry (including litigation) between music halls and theatres. The Letter concludes with an ironic account of a pre-Christmas notice from 'the provincial newspaper* Barrow News' *of a 'Wesleyan' church seeking 'phonograph' recordings, for every week of the year, of sermons and church services to be played to its congregation.]*

Isaak Shklovsky [Dioneo], from 'Buduschie Kommoneri' ['Future MPs']: I. 'Mr Muir'

On the Themes of Liberty: An Article Collection, vol. 1 (St Petersburg, 1908): 1–28[1]

[Shklovsky announces his intention to provide a series of 'profiles' of unknown Parliament back-benchers who never figure in the news reports and are only just beginning their public careers. He opens with a list of internationally well-known Members of Parliament, and then gives a detailed overview of Dickens's fictional portrayals of contemptible MP types. He ends the first section by promising to acquaint his reader with a 'young candidate' standing for election in Malvern, Mr Muir.]

II.

It happened eight years ago, when I had just arrived in London and was living at a pension or **boarding house**.[2] These boarding houses, or, more precisely, the colourful personages who inhabit them, merit a few words. A most curious company gathers in the evenings in the **drawing rooms**, with their stereotypical and cheerless furnishings. Most are foreigners. First and foremost, without fail, there is a ruddy-cheeked German, a commercial traveller or bank clerk.[3] He tries his hardest to anglicise his appearance: wears very high turndown collars which cause his head to resemble a whorl of red cabbage with its stalk wrapped in white paper, talks about sport, and even shaves off his curled-up Wilhelm moustache.[4] In his free time, the German clerk talks to the other guests about Germany's military strength. If there are any young ladies living in the boarding house, the German will not fail to declaim to them, rolling his eyes, some sentimental verses of this kind:

> **Träum'ich? ist mein Auge trüber?**
> **Nebelt's mir ums Angesicht?**
> **Meine Minna geht vorüber?**
> **Meine Minna kennt mich nicht?**[5]

---

[1] Originally published as 'Profiles: Letter from England' under the pseudonym Dioneo in the monthly journal *Russkoe Bogatstvo*, November 1904, 25–48.

[2] Shklovsky arrived in London in 1896.

[3] For background, see 'German Immigrants in Britain, 1818–1914' in Panikos Panayi, ed. *Germans in Britain since 1500* (London: The Hambledon Press, 1996).

[4] Variously known as the Kaiser or Imperial or *Es-ist-erreicht* moustache, named after Kaiser Wilhelm II. Its ends are turned up sharply.

[5] German: 'Am I dreaming? Is my eye clouded? / Is it making my vision misty? / Is my Minna walking past?/ Does my Minna not know me?'. These are the opening lines of Friedrich Schiller's poem 'An Minna' ['To Minna'] in *Anthologie auf das Jahr 1782 [Anthology of the Year 1782]* (Stuttgart: J. B. Metzler, 1782), 190–92.

The young man explains to the uncomprehending young ladies that this is very good poetry, though far from the best in German literature. The English **misses** purse their lips and reply with the stock phrase: **'Is it? Very nice indeed!'** If the boarding house is located in the quarter bounded by Montague Street, [New] Oxford Street and Tottenham Court Road, some of the lodgers will inevitably be Russians who have come 'to the British Museum': for the most part young Master's students, awkward, clumsy, and possessing only a theoretical knowledge of the English language.[6] They find it easier to quote a verse from Byron than to ask a smart-looking parlourmaid for a glass of water. They are a hard-working, extremely absent-minded folk, absorbed entirely by the *Domesday Book* and medieval charters on agrarian relations.[7] They continue to astonish the English public by their clumsiness, diffidence and learning. On Sundays, when the Museum is shut, the Russians who work there either go to hear the magnificent music at **Queen's Hall** or set out to 'study Whitechapel'.[8] I do not know why, but Russians who find themselves in London seek out this district before all else.[9] In a **boarding house**, you will inevitably find a vivacious Frenchman: an irrepressible prattler and first-rate salesman. Frenchmen always know how to combine these qualities to perfection. The Frenchman invents for himself a special kind of sport. He soon discovers that the English **misses** do not understand French, though they sometimes pretend to knowledge of the language. So under the guise of compliments, the Frenchman says the most impossible things to the overripe Englishwomen, up to and including '**chèvre anglaise**'.[10]

---

6   Ironically, this could pass for a fairly accurate depiction of Marshak, a student who lived in just such a boarding house in Bloomsbury, or Chukovsky (minus the student status) and some of his circle of acquaintance. Russians in the British Museum have received their fair share of scholarly attention, see Robert Henderson's (himself former Russian Curator at the British Library) *The Spark that Lit the Revolution: Lenin in London and the Politics that Changed the World* (London: I. B. Tauris, 2020) for background information on this period, as well as for one of the few English-language engagements with Shklovsky's Letters.

7   By the turn of the century, Russians had made a name for themselves as specialists in English medieval history – see the biography of Shklovsky's acquaintance Paul Vinogradoff (1854–1925), Professor of Jurisprudence at Oxford from 1903 and the leading specialist on feudal England after F. W. Maitland, in Peter Stein, 'Vinogradoff, Sir Paul Gavrilovitch', *Oxford Dictionary of National Biography*, 23 September 2004, https://doi.org/10.1093/ref:odnb/36664.

8   'Queen's Hall': London's premier concert hall in Langham Place, not far from the British Museum. It was opened in 1893 and hosted the Proms and performances by leading international composers and musicians of the period. It was destroyed by enemy action on the night of 10–11 May 1941.

9   Both Chukovsky and Shklovsky himself did the same! See the Whitechapel pieces in this anthology.

10   French: 'English goat'. Editor's paragraph break.

The English people one meets with in a **boarding house** are generally uninteresting. They are ordinary provincials who have come to see the capital. If this is the case, they will tell anyone who will or will not listen, at meals and in the drawing room, that they have stood for three hours by **Rotten Row** in Hyde Park but did in the end manage to see the Duchess of Devonshire riding past.[11] There is one point on which the provincials disagree. Some of them aver that the Duchess was wearing her famous earrings with rubies the colour of doves' blood that *Tit Bits* wrote about, while others maintain that Lady Devonshire was in fact wearing different earrings with *Joujou* diamonds. Intelligence about these is also gleaned from the same periodical.[12] There is always some retired shopkeeper living in a **boarding house**. Boredom drives him to become a **one book reader**. Here is what this means. The man takes a fancy to one particular book, for instance, **'History of the War in the Peninsula'** by Major General Napier, and proceeds to read that one book alone.[13] Having finished the sixth volume, he starts again from the first one. This kind of **one book reader** will not only tell you in minute detail about the battle of Badajoz or the siege of Zaragoza but will recite by heart where the French Grenadiers were stationed at Barrosa.[14] Military history and memoirs are the favourite object of study with such readers. One might say all their knowledge is contained within the walls of Tarragona and Zaragoza. Next to the **one book reader**, there sits perhaps a little grey-haired, well-fed clergyman who devotes his leisure time to literature: he is writing a tract in which he seeks to prove that the Tempter invented the bicycle in order to revolutionise the Church. In former times, young people went out on Sundays to listen to sermons. Now that Satan has invented the *bike*, young people have forsaken the church and instead ride off in the mornings to the countryside with their sweethearts.[15] In a **boarding house** one can also

---

[11] Louisa Cavendish was Duchess of Devonshire from 1892 to 1908. Cf. Chukovsky's 'Public Meetings in Hyde Park' and 'The College Anniversary – Continued'.

[12] *Tit Bits* was a popular weekly founded by the press baron George Newnes in the 1880s which contained, as per its name, snippets of interesting information. Chukovsky reserved some scathing words for it in his correspondence.

[13] Sir William Francis Patrick Napier, *History of the War in the Peninsula and in the South of France from the year 1807 to the year 1814*, 6 vols (London, 1828–1840). Napier was a soldier and military historian still famous in the early twentieth century.

[14] These are battles of the Napoleonic Wars: Wellington's siege of Badajoz in 1812, the sieges of Zaragoza by the French in 1808–1809 and the Battle of Barrosa in 1811.

[15] The romantic implications of the cycling craze of the 1890s were reflected throughout popular culture, from music hall songs such as Harry Dacre's 'Daisy Bell (Bicycle Built for Two)' (1892) to fiction such as H. G. Wells's *The Wheels of Chance* (London: J. M. Dent & Co, 1896), not to mention numerous postcards, posters and depictions in the periodical press. Cf. Shklovsky's 'Frankie' above.

Fig. 40. In a Boarding-House: Dinner.

meet people who have grown tired of battling with their servants and left home for a '**change**' (for rest). They will turn every conversation to the unruliness, impudence, exactingness and expense of the modern chambermaid and cook.[16]

A Russian, who usually arrives in England equipped only with a book-learned knowledge of the language and who does not understand the spoken word, finds himself in the first two or three months in the same situation as Vakula the blacksmith in St Petersburg.[17] "'Gracious Lord! What a number of nobility one sees here!" thought the blacksmith; "I suppose every one here, who goes in a fur cloak, can be no less than a magistrate!"'.[18] Had Vakula lived longer in St Petersburg, he would have discovered that not all passers-by were as distinguished as he imagined. In the first few weeks, the **boarding house** guests impress the Russian by their outward appearance of culture, and he gains a most exaggerated opinion of their education. Then 'Vakula' realises, to his

[16] Editor's paragraph break.
[17] The main character of Nikolay Gogol's story 'Christmas Eve' (1832), who is taken from Ukraine to St Petersburg by the devil. See also Tchaikovsky's 1874 opera *Vakula the Smith*.
[18] I have used George Tolstoy's 1860 translation of Gogol's story. See Nicholas Gogol, 'The Night of Christmas Eve: A Legend of Little Russia', in *Cossack Tales* (London: James Blackwood, 1860), 1–67.

great surprise, that the 'magistrates' are among the dullest of people, for the most part extremely parochial and exceptionally ignorant. Only later does the Russian understand the import of his discovery. The people one meets in a **boarding house** belong in the main to the 'lower middle class'. In our country, such people amuse themselves by gathering in a body and 'going to drown the priest's cur'.[19] That is, perhaps, worse than spending one's life reading Napier's history of the Spanish war. Sometimes, though, one meets very interesting people in a **boarding house**. The Muir family, whose acquaintance I made eight years ago, belonged to their number.[20]

At that time, everything in England was a novelty to me. I had come equipped with a knowledge of the country derived from books, on whose basis I had formed a certain notion of what England was like. The more I came to know the reality, the more convinced I became that my understanding was extremely outdated, that in consequence of the law of evolution and under the influence of new factors, contemporary England was no longer the country I had studied in books. My ideas of the English people proved to be even more one-sided. I remember what a strong impression was produced by a trivial fact I was told about in the boarding-house drawing room. The subject was '**Ragging**', the brutal custom of taking the law into one's own hands, which is practised in English officers' barracks and among the student youth of both sexes. The newspapers at the time were discussing an incident that took place in a lunatic asylum (**Tooting Bec Asylum**, if I am not mistaken).[21] The female nurses grew angry with their friend for some reason, held a 'court-martial' and sentenced the guilty party to a dunking in a cold-water bath. Eight young women (the nurses all belonged to the middle classes) took it upon themselves to carry out the sentence. They broke into their friend's room at night, snatched her from her bed and carried her to the bath. A vicious fight ensued, which ended in bruises and broken noses. The one who was to be flung into the bath was cruelly beaten. In the **boarding house**, this incident was recounted as a witty joke.

---

[19]   I have been unable to locate the source of the expression.

[20]   Editor's paragraph break.

[21]   Tooting Bec Asylum in Tooting Graveney admitted its first patients in 1903, and in 1904 the press, such as *The British Journal of Nursing*, did indeed carry stories and letters about 'Ragging by Nurses' there who were dismissed for assaulting junior nurses. So Shklovsky is referring to an incident that took place eight years later to illustrate his first impressions of London. For general background, see Peter Higginbotham, 'Tooting Bec Asylum, Tooting Bec', *The Workhouse: The Story of an Institution*, www.workhouses.org.uk/MAB-TootingBec/ and Niall McCrae and Peter Nolan, *The Story of Nursing in British Mental Hospitals: Echoes from the Corridors* (London: Routledge, 2016).

'In our college at Oxford,' the little grey-haired clergyman who had been denouncing cyclists informed me, 'in my time, there was constant **"ragging"**. Students would give a ragging to their fellows for a whole range of offences: for having a provincial accent, for wearing patent-leather shoes, for studying too assiduously, for having a light purse (at the ancient English universities, the sons of rich people look down on their poor comrades), etc.'.

At the time, facts such as these astonished me immensely. I can just about understand how Ben Allen or Bob Sawyer (students in the *Pickwick [Papers]*) could give somebody a 'ragging', but I could not imagine Dickens's young ladies Kate, Dora, Arabella Allen or Ruth dragging Agnes Wickfield to the bath.[22]

[The rest of the Letter is devoted to a life portrait of the 'young Mr Muir' – a kind of 'energetic middle-class' Radical counterpart to the 'proletarian' Richard Kelly – whom Shklovsky supposedly met in the boarding house in 1896 (when Muir was still an unsuc-cessful 'machine inventor'), and again in Venice in 1904. There are detailed descriptions of Muir's travels and work in South America in the interval, his political platform as he stands for election, and the usual political-historical digressions (e.g. on Thomas Paine).]

---

[22]   Ben Allen and Bob Sawyer are, appropriately enough, medical students. Arabella is Ben's sister, who ends up marrying one of the Pickwickians. The other 'young ladies' are from different Dickens novels: Agnes is David Copperfield's second wife and Dora his first in *The Personal History of David Copperfield* (London: Bradbury & Evans, 1850); Kate is Nicholas Nickleby's younger sister in *The Life and Adventures of Nicholas Nickleby* (London: Chapman & Hall, 1839); and Ruth is Tom Pinch's sister in *The Life and Adventures of Martin Chuzzlewit* (London: Chapman & Hall, 1844). Most of these characters are typical sweet and passive Dickensian women.

Samuil Marshak, 'Na Detskoy Vistavke' ['At the Children's Exhibition']

Birzhevie Vedomosti, evening edition, 10 January 1913, 3[1]

A Letter from London

For two weeks only, a children's exhibition was held at the huge Olympia hall – home to exhibitions and grand theatrical performances. This exhibition was meant to have been unprecedented in terms of its aims and preliminary plans. It was called the '**Children's Welfare Exhibition**'. It was to be an encyclopaedic compendium of everything directly and indirectly related to a child's life and welfare. The idea for such an exhibition could only have been conceived in a country where family values and love of children are paramount, the country of Charles Dickens.[2]

As the first experiment of its kind, the exhibition could not possibly have lived up to all the exalted hopes placed upon it. The famous 'Children's Floor' that so much had been written about and that was supposed to present a number of model nurseries (a boy's room, a girl's room, a classroom, etc.) turned out to be a display of the products of some furniture company, like those that can be seen in City shop windows.[3] There was nothing new in the way of nursery furnishings, apart perhaps from the fact that a comfortable nursery could be fitted out without much luxury or pretentiousness, using chintz curtains, unpainted furniture, and so on.

One circumstance was a disappointment (especially for us Russians): the clearly commercial nature of the exhibition. Every lecture given there, every bit of children's entertainment carried a separate fee, the traditional 'sixpence' (24 kopecks).[4]

---

[1] The article was signed D-r F-n, a shortened version of Doctor Frieken, Marshak's press pseudonym throughout the 1910s. Digitisations of the St Petersburg paper *Birzhevie Vedomosti* are available via the Russian National Library: http://nlr.ru/res/inv/ukazat55/record_full.php?record_ID=152303.

[2] There were two Children's Welfare Exhibitions organised at Olympia, West Kensington (a Victorian-era hall) by the *Daily News*: the one that Marshak attended, from 31 December 1912 to 11 January 1913, and a second one from 11 to 30 April 1914. The first one was opened by Mrs Winston Churchill and included the world's largest Christmas tree illuminated with a thousand electric lights, according to contemporary press coverage. Similar exhibitions were held almost contemporaneously in the United States and in Australia, so *pace* Marshak, the idea was hardly unique to Britain.

[3] Marshak may be referring to the Heal & Sons 'model nurseries' display on the 'Children's Floor' of the exhibition, a photograph of which has been preserved in the Archive of Art and Design, Blythe House.

[4] The 'commercial nature of the exhibition' (also noted by historians of the event) caused a minor controversy at the time when a group of doctors who had been

228

One Russian lady, a graduate of the Bestuzhev Courses and a teacher,[5] wrote an impassioned letter to the exhibition organisers, offering her services gratis and her support for the beautiful and lofty cause. The organisers wrote back expressing their sincerest gratitude, although in the tone of the letter one could discern a certain puzzlement at the Russian lady's selflessness and idealism.

Be that as it may, no parent left the exhibition without absorbing some new detail of nursery decoration, some new ideas about child upbringing, whether concerned with gymnastics, music or children's dances. Children's creative work and amateur dramatics were superbly represented at the exhibition.

Here are the 'Boy Scouts' at work. As the reader probably knows, the 'Boy Scouts' are a boys' military and sporting organisation. The children are trained to carry out scouting operations for the army, as well as the duties of 'brothers of mercy' in wartime,[6] while at the same time learning crafts and various types of labour. At the exhibition, a large, fenced area was allocated to them, covered in greenery to imitate a summer lawn. In it were pitched camp tents, a camp kitchen and a little field hospital with Red Cross vans. The boys spent the whole two weeks at the exhibition, demonstrating to the public their sports exercises, first aid skills, and labouring from dawn till dusk as blacksmiths, carpenters, cobblers, tailors, cooks, photographers, mechanics, etc.

Beyond their fence, a small steam engine chugged by regularly, pulling behind it lots of little platforms with benches for child passengers.[7] The train would stop at the end of the hall, at a miniature station. There the engine driver, a grown man, would disembark from the front car platform, open the lid of the coal box, and having deposited a handful of coal with a small shovel into the furnace of his 'steam engine', would give a whistle, and the train would whirl on.

It looked for all the world like the Boy Scout camp really was pitched somewhere among the fields, with the trains rushing by.

---

solicited to become patrons of the exhibition condemned the organisers for allowing the Antivaccination League to take a paid stall. See 'Antivaccination at the Children's Welfare Exhibition', *The British Medical Journal*, 11 January 1913, 97.

5   The Bestuzhev Courses at St Petersburg University provided higher education for women, especially those who wished to teach in secondary schools, and were named after Prof. Konstantin Bestuzhev-Ryumin (1829–1897), their first Director. Bedford College in London was an approximate analogue. A decade earlier, Chukovsky had used exactly the same image (the selfless idealism of the Russian lady teacher) to berate English middle-class women for their pettiness and materialism.

6   'Brothers of mercy': male nurses – by analogy with the sisters of mercy.

7   According to Peter Scott, 'Early Public Miniature Railways in Great Britain (1901–1918)', *Minor Railways – Histories*, April 2021, www.minorrailways.co.uk/history1.php, eight thousand people rode on the model railway during the exhibition.

Fig. 41. Bassett-Lowke Model Railway, 1913 Children's Welfare Exhibition, Olympia.

A similar camp was organised by a girls' organisation, the Girl Guides: the future sisters of mercy and army cooks.[8] A prominent place at the exhibition was given over to children's drawings specially made by the children for the exhibition competition. But there was also a separate solo exhibition of drawings by the twelve-year-old artist Daphne Allen. Her watercolours of Gospel subjects have an extraordinary air of harmony and mildness about them. Some are bizarre fantasies: 'Spirits of the Wind', 'Spirits of the Storm' (a dark wave brings forth a heap of strange, dimly glimpsed infants). There is also one landscape of a river flowing under a bridge that is amazingly full of impulse and movement; this landscape is called 'Rivers Hastening to the Sea'.[9]

The exhibition also contained some adult creative work, but it spoke directly to the child's imagination. The children's author Miss Nesbit erected an entire '**Magic City**' on a large table in her pavilion.[10] Lit from the inside by red lanterns, the city did indeed produce a magical impression. White Grecian colonnades, Egyptian obelisks, Hindu pagodas, cathedrals, mosques and buildings in an unfamiliar style with

---

8   Photographs of the exhibition which appeared on page 19 of *The Penny Illustrated Paper* on 11 January 1913 featured the Girl Guides section, as well as a Peter Robinson stand, a picture of 'the oldest doll' in the exhibition, a fairy pageant and the giant Christmas tree.

9   On the child artist Daphne Constance Allen, see Victoria Ford Smith, 'Exhibiting Children: The Young Artist as Construct and Creator', *Journal of Juvenilia Studies* 1 (2018), 62–81. Allen's paintings and drawings are still sold at auction today.

10   Edith Nesbit attended the first exhibition to publicise her novel *The Magic City* (London: Macmillan & Co., 1910) and reproduced the eponymous city there as Marshak describes. See Jenny Bavidge, 'Exhibiting Childhood: E. Nesbit and the Children's Welfare Exhibitions', in A. E. Gavin and A. F. Humphries, eds. *Childhood in Edwardian Fiction* (Basingstoke: Palgrave Macmillan, 2009), 125–42.

bronze elephants on their roofs loomed in the distance… The 'city' lost none of its integrity or 'stylishness' because of this mixture of styles. But the most wondrous thing of all was that the objects which served for construction materials in this city were as follows: candlesticks, bound books, writing implements, bronze inkstand lids, lotto, dominoes, chess figures, draughts, lead acetate paper, bronze figurines 'from father's desk' (that's where the elephants, horses and dogs had come from!), drawing-room china figurines, etc.

Of course, if a child were to follow Miss Nesbit's example to construct such a 'magic city', he would have to strip his parents' house to the bone!… By the way, a certain lady (possibly from the Froebel school) demonstrated at this same exhibition those modest objects which serve as playthings to the poor children of London.[11] Here was everything from an old horseshoe to a broken piece of a pistol or a doll. In order to imagine this collection, one should recall Tom Sawyer's famous pocket with all of its contents![12]

The doll museum at the exhibition was of some interest. It displayed European dolls of all periods and nations, wearing bonnets, hoods, hoop skirts, crinolines. There were Chinese dolls: the men in yellow robes, the women in trousers and red jackets. There were richly dressed dolls from India: red and gold turbans, diaphanous golden scarves, rings, bracelets, necklaces. There was a doll from the Sudan with eyes of pearl. There were savage dolls, dolls from Greenland wrapped in thick furs, etc.

As for entertainment, the most popular kind at the exhibition was dancing. A society dedicated to resurrecting English folk dances mounted a 'country fling' at Olympia.[13] On a wide green carpet, children whirled endlessly in roundelays and in couples, dressed in quaint peasant attire. A single violin hummed; and the good-humoured dance tune reminded one of the freedom of the fields and the quiet of a country sunset.

The only dark spot marring the light of the children's exhibition was the pavilion of the Child Protection Society.[14] The Society displayed

---

[11] German educator Friedrich Froebel (1782–1852) developed a child-centred system of pre-school pedagogy. Marshak may be referring to the Froebel Demonstration School at Colet Gardens, Kensington or the Practising School in Challoner Street. See Jane Read, 'The Froebel Movement in Britain, 1900–1939', PhD thesis, University of Roehampton, 2012 and 'Bringing Froebel into London's Infant Schools: The Reforming Practice of Two Head Teachers, Elizabeth Shaw and Frances Roe, from the 1890s to the 1930s', *History of Education* 42.6 (2013), 745–64.

[12] Marshak is referring to Mark Twain's *The Adventures of Tom Sawyer* (Hartford, CT: American Publishing Co., 1876). The boy hero's pocket does indeed contain all sorts of useful bits and bobs.

[13] Probably the English Folk Dance Society founded in 1911 by Cecil Sharp. The 'meadow [i.e. folk] dances', as Marshak literally calls them, might be Morris dances.

[14] Probably a reference to the National Society for the Prevention of Cruelty to Children.

lashes, whips, iron rods, boots with nails driven into their soles, chains with and without padlocks... All these instruments of torture, used on children by their bestial parents, had already figured once as material evidence in London courts.

It is clear that children's welfare and well-being are not yet adequately provided for even in the most civilised European countries.

Samuil Marshak, 'Pod Zheleznodorozhnim Mostom' ['Under the Railway Bridge']
Nedelya 'Sovremennogo Slova', 1 April 1913, 2222–23[1]

From a London Diary

My favourite 'Picture Palace' (as the cinematograph is called in London) is situated in the gloomiest part of the East End. Its auditorium is located under an urban railway bridge.[2] Unaccustomed viewers go stiff with horror when trains thunder over their heads, making double the usual racket. The place is reminiscent of some colossal and gloomy stable. The dirt is incredible! In tribute to Dante, one could trace the following inscription above the doors of the 'Palace': 'Abandon squeamishness all ye who enter here'. But instead of this inscription, someone has daubed the following words over the entrance in bold paint: 'Entrance fee 1d.'.

It is Sunday. The twilight comes early. At four o'clock or even earlier, the day begins to die. Factory girls go out in groups and pairs 'for a promenade' along the pavements of a damp and dirty East End street. One hears snatches of conversation and hysterical laughter. The gas lights are turned on.

Near the entrance to the cinema, where shines the '1d.' inscription, there is an incredible crush of people. The crowd is largely made up of children, mostly boys. All of them are wearing white turndown collars – though looking rather black now – and grey caps on their heads. Hands are thrust inside the pockets of their trousers. Lips are pursed for whistling. While waiting their turn, they cheerily whistle popular East End tunes and in general behave in an entirely nonchalant and independent manner.

---

1   *Nedelya 'Sovremennogo Slova'* was a free weekly supplement to the St Petersburg paper *Sovremennoe Slovo [The Contemporary Word]* published from 1908 to 1917.
2   See Luke McKernan, 'Diverting Time: London's Cinemas and Their Audiences, 1906–1914', *The London Journal* 32.2 (July 2007), 125–44 for an excellent account of the context for Marshak's article, including the significance of the cinema as a mode of entertainment in the East End in this period, cinema venues, the prevalence of child audiences, the penny price, the 'continuous show' policy, etc. See also *The London Project: The Birth of the Film Business in London* website of the AHRB Centre for British Film and Television Studies, which offers a searchable database of film businesses and venues, 1894–1914: http://londonfilm.bbk.ac.uk/. On the early British film industry, see Rachael Low's and Roger Manvell's seminal *The History of British Film*, 7 vols (London: George Allen, 1948–1985). For more recent case studies, see Simon Brown, *Cecil Hepworth and the Rise of the British Film Industry 1899–1911* (Exeter: Exeter University Press, 2015) and Vanessa Toulmin, *Electric Edwardians: The Story of the Mitchell and Kenyon Collection* (London: British Film Institute, 2006). The cockerel that Marshak references in this article was the logo of Pathé, which presumably produced the reels described.

Some among them are just tiny tots. They wait for the doors to open with their index finger in their mouth, looking pensively to the side. Only the infants brought here by mothers who could not possibly leave them at home betray their impatience. Some whine plaintively, and others scream until they are hoarse.

The doors finally open. Three quarters of the huge auditorium are filled with children. The piano starts its jingling, the soles of someone's feet flicker at the top of the screen, then disappear, and finally, the entire picture, shaking and wobbling like jelly, takes its proper place across the length and breadth of the screen.

The picture is set in the jungle... Oh, the children know and love the jungle and are expecting a lot from this film.

A cottage stands amidst some short undergrowth. An old man and woman live there with their young daughter and their hired hand. The labourer and the daughter are in love. But some rich rider in a pith helmet arrives and asks for the daughter's hand in marriage. Having learned from the young lady about her love for another, the noble rider puts his foot in the stirrup, swings the other leg over the saddle, and – in an instant disappears in the far-off thicket.

A burst of loud applause from the children's benches thunders in the wake of the departed rider. I believe this is the only cinema in London where applause is customary.

The young people on the screen are now married. They live in their own house, though not entirely in peace and quiet – among the tigers, lions, wild boars and other charming neighbours.

Like small fish darting in a shallow river on a clear day, the shadows of ferocious beasts prowl through the depths of the thicket. The children greet and see them off with a united show of jubilation.

So, the young couple have made a nice life for themselves. But that same rider in the pith helmet comes to visit and kisses the young woman by right of old acquaintance. Her jealous husband grabs his gun and runs into the jungle. There is indescribable agitation on the children's benches of the cinema... To think what can drive two good people to quarrel!

As a result, the young wife returns to her parents. Lions get into the couple's cabin and turn it into their den. And the gentleman in the pith helmet goes off in search of the affronted husband.

They meet and make up.

Already prepared by the preceding applause, I expect the greatest bursts of delight at this moment. And indeed, the auditorium is engulfed in a tumult that only the rumbling of the train passing overhead can drown out.

Only one thing remains unclear to me. What or whom do these excited spectators applaud? Is it the director who has produced such good pictures? Or the actors who perform their parts in the cinemato-graphic film? Oh no! The applause is a spontaneous celebration of the highest human values and virtues: magnanimity, nobility, selflessness, self-sacrifice, bravery...

But the final picture of the endless Sunday programme has now gone dim. A cockerel – the logo of the production company – flashes brightly on the screen. The cheerful audience replies with a chorus of 'Cock-a-doodle-doo!'.

The lights go on. The show is over and will be repeated five or six more times in the course of one day. The adult viewers walk away, but a revolt breaks out on the children's benches. The boys do not want to leave. The ushers chase them away from the benches, but having run around the auditorium, they return to their habitual seats clattering and whistling.

English street urchins are a free-spirited and independent tribe. In the streets, they are not prohibited from singing, whistling, whooping, putting on garishly coloured masks or even fighting. In the company of their friends, each of them is perfectly indomitable and fearless. When they are on their own, it is a different matter. Parental hidings must have taught the East End children to start abruptly and shield themselves convulsively in response to an unexpected question addressed to them by a chance passer-by.

But under the railway bridge they are out in great force. So they decide to stand their ground.

Voices call:

'Bill, don't go!'

'Here, Tom!'

'Come back, Jimmy!'

The ushers, who have clearly never served in the army or taken part in quelling Indian mutinies, are in complete disarray. The director's gleaming top hat appears in the auditorium. Having learned what is toward, he addresses the rebels with a soothing speech.

'Gentlemen, you have seen all the promised pictures. Why should you wish to watch them once more?...'

'Then again, you might as well stay!' he adds, resigned.

The children have won.

And once again, the screen flickers with thickets, lions, tigers, castles, palaces, marble staircases and colonnades – and much else, so far removed from the dark and dismal existence in the poorest quarters of the East End.

In the semi-darkness, several boys stand up and drag their feet dejectedly towards the exit.

'Bill!'

'Joe!'

It is the adults, come to collect their children.

The street is quiet. The fog and the damp have caused the Sunday crowd to disperse earlier than usual.

IV

LONDON STREETS
AND PUBLIC LIFE

Fig. 42. Ladysmith Day in London: How the News Was Received in the City.

Korney Chukovsky, 'Sobachiy Protsess' ['The Dog Trial']
Odesskie Novosti, 6 November 1903

London
(From our own correspondent)
14 November

You need to know about the school-missish tenderness of the English towards every kitten, you need to recall the hundreds of pet names they lavish on ducklings, puppies and canaries, to understand their feverish interest in court proceedings where some runty mongrel figures as the hero.[1]

Forget ducklings! I saw a most respectable gentleman finding compliments even for a crocodile in the zoological gardens, although I believe there are many people spending the night on the damp grass of Hyde Park who would gladly exchange places with this reptile.

'**Poor fellow!**', whispers a gangly Miss at the cage of a snarling lion, and the Animal Protection League in its notices begs street urchins in the name of Christ not to destroy birds' nests or to hitch rides on carriages. And although you could not find a nest in London in a hundred years and the carriages here are such that there is no possibility of attaching oneself to them, it is nevertheless still customary for the League's instructions to elicit expressions of admiration and emotion.

Suddenly comes a sensational piece of news: Mr Coleridge, Secretary of the Anti-Vivisection Society,[2] has announced at a public meeting that Professor Bayliss, who lectures in Physiology at University College, tortured and tormented a dog in front of his students without any apparent need, and cut open its maw though it struggled and trembled continuously in his hands. 'The Professor did not even trouble to anaesthetise his unfortunate victim', Coleridge said, and one can easily picture how many tears fell to the floor of the club where the speech was made.

Meanwhile, Mr Bayliss was not aware of anything. Only a newspaper report of Coleridge's speech alerted him to the accusation levelled against him. He is in court. And yesterday I had an opportunity to witness the formalities of a case of 'libel and defamation of a good name'.

---

[1] The subject of this article – the so-called Brown Dog Affair (1903–1910) – was a landmark moment in the history of anti-vivisection and animal welfare, see Coral Lansbury, *The Old Brown Dog: Women, Workers and Vivisection in Edwardian England* (Madison, WI: Wisconsin University Press, 1985). The various stages of the trial were widely covered in the British press, which reported on the repartee just as Chukovsky does here. The origin of the affair was the infiltration by two female Swedish medical students and anti-vivisectionists of William Bayliss's (1860–1924) lecture theatre during an experimental demonstration in February 1903, when a brown terrier dog was anaesthetised, vivisected and killed. The publication of their account led Bayliss to bring a libel case, which he won in November 1903.

[2] The National Anti-Vivisection Society (still active) was founded by Frances Power Cobbe in 1875.

Coleridge's thin lips, tightly pursed in disdain, never once parted during the whole time. Pale, with arms crossed on his chest, he listened attentively to everything that was said in the courtroom. And what was said there was of a kind not calculated to please him at all.

From the very first words it becomes clear that anaesthesia had been administered and that 'the victim's trembling' was a figment of Coleridge's imagination. Two or three deft replies from Dr Bayliss quickly change the public's attitude to the whole case. He – the murderer – becomes the favourite, and a loud approving laughter accompanies almost his every word.

The Professor is on provocatively good form, and his replies are not entirely deferential, as if the main culprit in this case were not himself but the judge.

'Cannot Physiology do without bloody sacrifices?' he is asked.

'Do you not know that Physiology is the dynamics of a living organism? How am I supposed to demonstrate dynamics – using pictures?!' he replies.

'Would you say your operation belongs to the class of simple ones?'

'That depends upon the surgeon.'

'Do not your moral feelings revolt at operations of this kind?'

'They revolt when you kill animals – and kill them so inhumanely – to fill your bellies. But my moral feelings allow me these operations for scientific purposes, especially as the animal was anaesthetised.'

The public applauds. Coleridge smiles enigmatically. The presiding judge says that the trial is not a theatrical performance.

'Do you not think that such operations blunt the students' sensitivity?'

'Let them. I am glad they do. What kind of doctors would they be if they set much store by sensitivity! And moreover, should we, in your view, oppose operations on live humans? They surely blunt sensitivity as well!'

Loud laughter. The presiding judge shouts over it:

'But such operations are performed for humane purposes...'

'And do you think I was conducting experiments on the dog for my own pleasure?'

The face under the powdered wig melts into a wide grin.

Scores of male and female students speak out in court, assuring the judges by various expressions and in various voices that the dog died for the glory of science and humanity.

'An honourable death!' says the voice from under the wig, and the case is adjourned until Tuesday.

Straight from the court I went to **Essex Hall**,[3] where the anti-vivisectionists were holding their meeting. An unpleasant sight. I only caught the middle of it. Loud phrases, bombastic sententia – all of it just about suited to the abilities of the audience gathered there: old maids and churchwardens.

'They used to send children to seminaries and we had a magnificent clergy, but now medicine is all the fashion. So we have neither clergymen nor doctors', said a **Mr Shaw** – for which they gave him an ovation.

Afterwards they undertook a collection for the Society. And from among several hundred people they did not manage to take in even *two shillings*.

I will let you be the judge of these gentlemen's sincerity.

---

[3] Essex Hall, in Essex Street, was the historical home of the London Unitarian congregation. See Mortimer Rowe, *The Story of Essex Hall* (London: Lindsey Press, 1959).

Korney Chukovsky, 'Kazarmennaya Filantropiya' ['Barrack-Room Philanthropy']
Odesskie Novosti, 8 November 1903

London
(From our own correspondent)
16 November

'Boom, boom, boom', resounds the huge drum, and the windows of nearby houses tremble.

The trombone players are a pitiful sight, their eyes about to pop out with the strain.

One bleats the droning tune of a hymn; another shouts out in meaningless combinations: 'repent'... 'save yourselves'... 'doom is nigh'... 'eternity'... 'the Lord'...; another, in a fit of some kind of frenzy, points to the skies, menacingly demanding something from the public.

The people gaze at the cold, foggy sky, see nothing there, and slowly turn away from the speaker.

It starts to rain. Dirty jets of water begin drumming on the horn players' instruments. Umbrellas rise like innumerable scales over this whole clamorous, agitated, crazed mass of humanity – and soon it seems as if some huge, unknown beast is roaring and raging and howling, ready to fly in powerless fury at anyone calm and indifferent, who passes by at a steady pace...

I come nearer. The men's faces are feverish, red from the vodka,[1] the yelling, the ecstatic gestures... They are dressed in ordinary soldiers' uniforms with braid, epaulettes and chevrons.

The women – flat-chested, sallow, with billowing, dishevelled hair – do not lack for military distinctions either. Encircling their black hats is a red ribbon with the words:

'The Salvation Army!'

Yes, these strange people, decked out like jesters, with the antics and gambols of holy fools, with the deafening clangour of their drums, pretend to the role of saviours and leaders of errant humanity.[2] Drums and salvation! Clownish buffoonery and the holy tears of repentance! Military ranks and appeals to the God of equality and justice! What a wild combination of ideas! What blasphemy! Try to imagine more jarring, more mutually exclusive extremes! You couldn't.

Such absurd conjunctions of the exalted and the offensively sordid, of worship and clowning, are not possible anywhere except the country of

---

[1] Chukovsky creates familiarity for the Russian reader by attributing English drunkenness to vodka (gin), just as Shklovsky does.

[2] Cf. the reaction of Shklovsky's characters to the Salvation Army in 'In the Russian Quarter'.

Darwin, Mill and Ruskin. Only the English are capable of this kind of cynicism: the cynicism that is entailed in the union of repentance – that most intimate, most bashful of spiritual acts – with theatrical gestures and military chevrons.

One might think that such a sober nation, so lucid, so mathematically precise in every type of knowledge, could never have created this fantastical, ludicrous and, above all, impractical scheme, but the fact is there for all to see. The brass braying of the horns tears at your ears, the drum never for a minute ceases to remind you of eternity, and one soldier's finger jabs repeatedly at the empty sky – and of course, all this din and whooping amounts to nothing. For all the awful masses of energy these people expend, the effect is nil! Here one of the officers proclaims in an unnatural voice:

'Private No. 102! Tell us the story of your salvation.'

Some wretched, colourless woman comes to the centre of the circle and in a voice that sounds as if she were reciting a page of Ilovaysky's History 'from here to there' rather than telling of her own personal life,[3] recounts:

'Before I repented, I led a dissolute life. My thoughts were carnal and my soul was wicked. But since I joined the Salvation Army, I have been reborn. It is now two years since any man has dared to kiss me...'

The crowd roars with laughter... 'Why don't you first find an ass who'd want to kiss such an old mop!' a passing cabby shouts from his perch, but the drum drowns out his voice and the next 'private' steps onto the stage... I was about to leave, when suddenly I saw a magnificent carriage pull up and a thin and pale grey-haired man emerge from it, with cunning, shifty little eyes and a long hawkish nose. My God! what came over these people! They had not even finished singing their song about the vanity of all earthly things and the futility and transience of human laurels when they dropped everything, fell into line, did an eyes-right soldier-fashion, saluted and barked something that sounded for all the world like 'Good morning, Sah!'.[4]

'Booth, Booth', muttered the crowd. The grey-haired man examined everyone with a commanding gaze, made a few remarks of an entirely un-celestial nature, got back into his carriage and left.

This is their leader, General Booth.[5] He has just returned from America, where he spent eight and a half years. In this time, the

---

3   The Russian historian Dmitry Ilovaysky (1832–1920) was the author of popular school history textbooks reprinted many times throughout the nineteenth century.

4   Literally, 'I wish ye good health, Your Honour'. The original Russian phraseology in this sentence intentionally evokes the parade-ground discipline and military salutes of the Czarist army. This produces the surreal effect of Salvation Army 'privates' behaving like Russian soldiers.

5   'General' William Booth (1829–1912) was a Methodist preacher who founded the Salvation Army, a Christian missionary movement organised on a military

Salvation Army has substantially reinforced its troops. Seven years ago, it had two thousand officers in the United States, and now there are 3,280. The General is inclined to see in this an increase in the number of the righteous. But would it not make more sense to count it rather as an increase in the number of lovers of easy pickings? There used to be seven hundred barracks. Now there are nine hundred. They used to snigger at the Army; now Roosevelt and nearly all the senators are its undisguised adepts.[6] The **New York Herald** – that all-powerful master of public opinion in the Western hemisphere – sings the praises of the Salvation Army.

So whom does this Army save? Who among the drowning will stretch his hands to its rose-coloured chevrons and shiny buttons? Whose obdurate soul will soften at the clattering of its drums? Whom will its studied speeches lead away 'from the jubilant ones, the idle gossips, those who stain their hands with blood'?[7] Clearly, no-one. For that, you need neither buffoonery, nor ceremony, nor soldiers' bearing, but a certain something that these raving drummers lack entirely.

And if so, then why does the Army exist?

Because shrieking at the crossroads is easier than doing any other kind of work that these people might be capable of.

And what explains the success of such a hypocritical institution in English society? Surely not the abundance of old maids? In that case, they are all named Miss Grundy.[8]

---

model that by the turn of the twentieth century was operating internationally. Both Chukovsky and Shklovsky depict Booth and the Salvation Army negatively, but the perception was by no means limited to Russian observers. Booth was considered a charlatan by many sections of British society, and served as the butt of satirical criticism in English literature, such as Morrison's *A Child of the Jago*: 'Then about this time there had arisen a sudden quacksalver, a Panjandrum of philanthropy, a mummer of the market-place, who undertook, for a fixed sum, to abolish poverty and sin together; and many, pleased with the new gaudery, poured out before him the money that had gone to maintain hospitals and to feed proved charities' (76).

6   Theodore Roosevelt was President of the United States from 1901 to 1909. Booth met with him in 1903, during one of his tours of the country, and was invited to open the Senate with a prayer. Beginning in 1904, Booth toured the UK with a motorcade and spoke to adepts from a car.

7   This is a quotation from the famous Russian poet Nikolay Nekrasov's (1821–1878) poem 'Ritsar' na Chas' ['Knight for an Hour'] (1862) in *Polnoe Sobranie Sochineniy i Pisem v 15 Tomakh [Complete Collection of Works and Letters in 15 Volumes]*, vol. 2 (Leningrad: Nauka, 1981). Chukovsky later became a noted Nekrasov scholar.

8   A play on Mrs Grundy, the symbol of social convention and propriety.

Korney Chukovsky, 'Spiritizm v Anglii' ['Spiritualism in England']
Odesskie Novosti, 28 May 1904

London
(From our own correspondent)
3 June

The dance master Blackman's piano, accustomed to ringing waltzes
and cakewalks, is now playing a solemn hymn; the mirrored walls
reflect not whirling youths as heretofore, but white-bearded gentlemen,
sallow-faced ladies and scrofulous young men, looking piously in their
prayerbooks. This time, a Spiritualists' meeting is underway in the dance
master Blackman's hall.

In Germany, Spiritualism tries to attach itself to science. In France,
it is rather successfully accessorised with décolletés, chansonettes and
private boudoirs. In England, it has moved on to prayerbooks, psalms
and sallow Misses of an uncertain age. **C'est fatalité.**[1]

I happened on this meeting when it had already started. The attendees
were on their feet and, looking into some books, were singing in unsteady
chorus the praises of those 'spirits' who appear to the medium:

> *Holy* **ministers of light**
> **Hidden from the mortal sight,**
> **But whose presence can impart**
> **Peace and comfort to the heart.**[2]

I don't remember any more, but even these lines are sufficient to
detect that the enigmatic form of energy that manifests at Spiritualist
séances has already had time to become canonised in England.

The medium himself – a squirming, dishevelled, extravagantly
dressed gentleman with a worn-out face and manners pretending to the
mysterious – offers a prayer from the pulpit to the spirit of all spirits,
then blesses us majestically and begins his séance to the sound of music.
He enters a trance. He gnashes his teeth, rolls his eyes and growls like
the hero of a melodrama. From the first minute you know that you are

---

[1] French: 'It's fate.' English Spiritualism has a large historiography. See Logie
Barrow, *Independent Spirits: Spiritualism and English Plebeians, 1850–1910*
(New York: Routledge & Kegan Paul, 1986); Janet Oppenheim, *The Other World:
Spiritualism and Psychical Research in Victorian Britain, 1850–1914* (Cambridge:
Cambridge University Press, 1985); and for an overview of more recent scholarship,
Sarah Willburn and Tatiana Kontou, eds. *The Ashgate Research Companion to
Nineteenth-Century Spiritualism and the Occult* (Farnham: Ashgate Publishing,
2012).

[2] The quatrain is given first in Russian, where 'holy' is italicised. These are in fact
the first four lines of 'Guardian Angels' from the famous American medium Lizzie
Doten's collection of Spiritualist verses *Poems of Progress* (Boston, MA: William
White and Company, Banner of Light Office, 1871).

faced with charlatanism, and of a tasteless, crude and coarse kind at that, calculated to appeal to the most uncivilised and uncouth public. Look around. You'll see knitted brows, pursed lips – you'll see faith and grim delight. More hymns, more prayers, more trances; the voluntary collection plate goes many rounds – and you find yourself back in the street with the impression that someone has mocked and insulted you, deceived you in a childish, unintelligent, ham-fisted way.

There were a lot of people at the séance; I noticed an abundance of gold coins on the collection plate. The majority had solemn faces, which means that there are those who need all this, who consider all this a serious, vital business, who sate their spiritual thirst from this polluted spring.

But who? And why do they not turn to other springs, which are so readily available here? And how has the Englishman managed to turn all these séances into church services? The Englishman, who is so averse to all ritual, all ceremonial, who searches everywhere for essence rather than form, ends rather than means? I could only answer these questions after a close acquaintance with Spiritualists, their literature, lectures, clubs, meetings and so on.

Of course, this cursory letter is no place to answer such questions. Here, I think, it would be sufficient just to note the general idea behind this movement. First, however, let me remark that the movement is extremely broad. The Spiritualists have five specialist periodicals, among which the monthly *Destiny*, which pays particular attention to astrology and chiromancy, *Light*, a weekly publication (I have its twenty-fourth volume in front of me!), *Hypnotist*, *The Herald of Miraculous Sciences* and others enjoy substantial success.[3] Books with occult contents are printed in dozens of editions; London alone has over three hundred Spiritualist societies and unions – in short, we are dealing with a formidable and durable phenomenon. With regard to its general idea, I once happened to read in Stead's *Review of Reviews* that Spiritualism is good if only because it impresses the masses with a conception of the spiritual life,[4] tears them away from crass materialism and opens to them, in an accessible form, the bright vistas of the hereafter, and so on. This view of Spiritualism is extremely widespread – especially among the clergy – hence that broad sympathy for the Spiritualists' sect that one finds among people in cultivated society.

This view, it seems to me, is a complete misconception. English Spiritualism does not deal with spiritualised matter but with *materialised*

---

3   I have been unable to locate the original of *The Herald of Miraculous Sciences* (the title is therefore back-translated). Possible candidates might be *The Herald of Christian Science* or *The Theosophic Messenger*.

4   Chukovsky dedicated a lot of space in his Letters to the famous newspaper editor and campaigning journalist W. T. Stead (1849–1912) and his monthly periodical the *Review of Reviews*, founded in 1890.

spirit. At the May congress of all the adepts of this teaching it was said that 'spirits are offended if they are roughly treated, that they take vengeance on the unbelievers, that they quarrel amongst themselves, that they play various tricks on the mediums', and so on.[5] In a word, what is apparent here is the Spiritualists' firm determination to bring the spirit down to their level, to put themselves on an informal footing with it, to pat it on the shoulder. The particularising British mind could not stand face to face with spirit without furnishing it with these naively material features. What particularly surprised me at that meeting was the tendency to impose upon spirit a quality as seemingly inappropriate as humour. Once, some doctor, a Mr Coxe, demolished the Spiritualists and said that there were no spirits, only a 'psychic energy'. Then he 'saw the light' and began to summon up the spirit of his late wife. The spirit appeared. 'Who are you? Are you Lucy (the wife's name)?', asked the new convert. 'No, I am a "psychic energy",' replied the witty ghost. Spiritualist periodicals tell a great number of such stories, and one thing is clear from them: the only difference between our savage ancestors and the modern-day savage in a top hat is that when our ancestors clothed the idea of spirit in bodily form, the result was something colossal, majestic and poetic. But when the contemporary savage attempts it, all he achieves is something exceedingly flabby, trite and tittering. Both here and there you have impotence, an inability to perceive the spirit in its spirituality. But if this impotence creates a Prometheus, a Buddha or a Mahomet, then there is no need for potency. Whereas now, the highest that the imagination of the average member of the world's most cultivated populace can attain to is a 'merry sprite'…

Another feature of the English mind – its utilitarianism – has also taken a noticeable toll on the local variety of Spiritualism. I have just finished reading a book by Mr **Wallis**, the leader of this sect, entitled **'Let Not Your Heart Be Troubled'**,[6] and it seems to me that this is the most cynical thing I have ever come across in my life. In it, the author, before all else, paints in dark colours the *inexpediency* of unbelief. 'Any thought of the meaning, aim and direction of your being is limited by the grave; you feel that you are confined between the cradle and the

---

[5]   Chukovsky's note: The annual general meeting of the London Spiritualists was held on 18 May at the **South-Place Institute**.
Editor's note: This was the home of the South Place Ethical Society in Finsbury.

[6]   Chukvosky is most likely referring to *Let Not Your Heart Be Troubled and Human Life After Death: Two Addresses Through the Mediumship of E. W. Wallis, in Cavendish Rooms, London* (London, c. 1900), a two-penny pamphlet published c. 1900 by 'spiritualist author and medium' Edward Walter Wallis, reprinted from *Light*, one of the main Spiritualist journals in England. There are no copies in the British Library; the following quotations are therefore back-translated. Digitisations of *Light* are available from the International Association for the Preservation of Spiritualist and Occult Periodicals, *IAPSOP*, http://iapsop.com/archive/materials/light/.

coffin,' and so on. After saying a bit more about 'the eternal gloom of death' and 'the cold of the Awful Terror', he immediately unfolds before you all the conveniences of every possible kind of Spiritualism. Believe – and you shall have 'joy, faith, vigour and strength; you shall have *health*!' (p. 5). And there's more, for by page thirteen he is already hustling you into heaven as if it were his own shop: 'life does not end in the grave, in the next world new **opportunities** await you, pleasant connections, happy meetings', and so on. And what could be more pleasant, according to Wallis, than the Spiritualist faith? Say you have lost a son. You weep. But the Spiritualist will arrange one or two séances and converse with the departed to his heart's content. 'Nay, yet more: Spiritualists know that the denizens of the other world deeply sympathise with the inhabitants of earth, that they have not gone from them to the far-off heavens, that the dweller on earth need not wait for his own death to see once again his deceased near and dear ones – he can e'en meet with them beforehand.'

Without even mentioning the crudely physical characteristics with which the afterlife is endowed in the author's imagination ('earth', 'heavens', 'close', 'see the deceased', and so on), what most offends the eye is this hedonistic attitude to the objects of the finest religious apprehensions...

If the ideals of the leaders are so mean, what can one say about the masses? What can one say? Let me, by way of an answer, adduce the following advertisement from an English newspaper: 'Western astrologist will send anyone his astrological prognostications and a horoscope for 2½ shillings apiece' (*Suppl. to Light*).

Or: 'Mr Towns, clairvoyant. Séances daily (except Saturdays) at the client's home, and at his own. One shilling per séance' (**Ibid.**, p. 5).

The country of Newton, Huxley, Spencer, working men's colleges, tweed suits and savings banks has managed to give the slip to all that and remain to this day, on the whole, a country of savage, benighted, ignorant people who are prevented by the national lack of imagination from preserving in their savagery the rich world of primitive superstitions. Even superstition has become thin and colourless... To see your deceased mother, pay Mr Towns one shilling. You must admit, reader, that this is cheap, too cheap!

Korney Chukovsky, 'Mitingi v Gayd-Parke' ['Public Meetings in Hyde Park'] *Odesskie Novosti*, 28 July 1904

London
(From our own correspondent)

Fig. 43. Green Park – Asleep on the Grass.

Hyde Park does not really conform to our Continental notion of parks. It is a wide glade many miles long, where one occasionally comes across alleys of shady trees. There are hardly any flowers, and everywhere you look you see green, damp English grass. In winter, in the slack season of general unemployment, thousands of people gravitate there and lie – not getting up, not moving, almost without signs of life – for several days on this cold, wet grass.[1] And each and every day the police gather up stiff corpses there – and the magistrates tabulate them under 'accidental deaths'. But in summer, the grass is transformed. Loving couples make themselves comfortable on it, twenty-five per each square fathom, and kiss passionately, to the passers'-by great embarrassment. The embraces take place entirely in the open, for the Englishman has long been accustomed to consider Hyde Park his own property. He is

---

[1]   A somewhat more measured account of what Chukovsky is describing here may be found in Jack London's *The People of the Abyss*, whose numerous photographs are a great contemporary visual source.

master in his own country, and each of his acts takes place in full view of everyone.

Along one of the park's alleys, **Rotten Row**, carriages circulate ceaselessly. Here fashionable London shows off its outfits, its horses and its ale-flushed faces. It is not for nothing that one Thackeray character asks another: 'Why did I not see you in **Rotten Row** last Sunday? Were you ill?'.[2] Only an illness can prevent a high-born Londoner from engaging in this traditional pastime.

At the other end of the park, at the very entrance, something entirely different is taking place. On approaching, you see a well-dressed motley crowd, umbrellas, women with infants, pipes, policemen's blue helmets, top hats, and only when you find yourself inside the crowd do you notice how strictly it has differentiated itself into distinct groups.[3]

Here, at the very edge, near the marble arch, is a dull huddle of people, entirely composed of spinsters of both sexes. Their clothes are every bit as worn as their faces; in vain do they seek to disguise the clothes' venerable age by repeated applications of benzine. All are wearing gloves, even if the gloves are full of holes, and everyone exudes a strange smell of camphor.[4] In their midst, a speaker stands on a portable lectern, demonstrating something – something, it seems, that he must have grown accustomed to demonstrating a thousand times before, from the days when his frock coat had not yet been reversed, and that was very long ago.

Listen carefully.

'It follows from all of the preceding that the ten tribes of Israel scattered by the Lord across the world, were after long wanderings sent by Him to this island, where they have brought forth the great British

---

2   There are many references to Rotten Row in W. M. Thackeray's works, but this particular one may have been invented by Chukovsky. The closest appears to be from *The History of Pendennis*, vol. I (1848; London: Smith, Elder, & Co., 1891): 'Haven't seen your carriage in the Park: why haven't you been there? I missed you; indeed, I did' (377). Chukovsky's diary entry for 16 June 1904 (new style) mentions that he was reading *Pendennis* (*CW* II, 73).

3   Chukovsky is referring to Speakers' Corner at Marble Arch, which appears in Shklovsky's articles (and in Marshak's personal letters) as well. When busy, as here, the 'Corner' stretched westwards almost to Victoria Gate. Compare the following with Chukovsky's 'Barrack-Room Philanthropy' and also Lord Henry's description in Wilde's *The Picture of Dorian Gray*: 'I was going through the Park last Sunday, and close by the Marble Arch there stood a little crowd of shabby-looking people listening to some vulgar street-preacher. [...] London is very rich in curious effects of that kind. A wet Sunday, an uncouth Christian in a mackintosh, a ring of sickly white faces under a broken roof of dripping umbrellas, and a wonderful phrase flung into the air by shrill, hysterical lips' (205).

4   Camphor refers to mothballs, so the smell Chukovsky notices is that of clothes put away and got out for special occasions. Benzine, along with other solvents such as kerosene and petrol, was used for dry cleaning woollen clothes.

nation.[5] Only this can explain the special grace shown by the Heavens towards our people. The Scriptures say: "The fates of your enemies shall be subjected to your hand",[6] this is said about the English', and so on. Then, screwing up his weak eyes, the preacher starts rooting through the Bible for the Prophet Isaiah's predictions concerning the Boer War.

I approach another crowd. Here the mood is entirely different.

An elderly woman with long arms, long teeth and long lips is standing on a folding chair and saying in a plaintive voice:

'And I says to him, you blaggard! you're spoiling my youth and beauty...'

The crowd laughs.

'... Youth and beauty. And he says to me: why you stupid cow! And I says to him: "you use words like these, tyrant of my heart, and I'll be off to the park tomorrow to tell the whole town about your scurvy temper." And he says to me: "you can go to the devil for all I care." So here I am, and I'll tell you all about his impudence...'

I come across such women nearly every day and I still cannot tell whether there are many of them or if it's just the same one over again – they all look so alike. I only know one thing: that by the evening both this woman and the 'tyrant of her heart' will be sitting in some pub under the sign of the 'Nail and Requiem',[7] sharing the takings collected from the susceptible visitors to Hyde Park, along with a bottle of gin.

Further on, a crowd consisting almost entirely of men has coalesced on the grass. They are mostly pale shopwalkers and junior clerks sporting straw hats, walking sticks and gilded watch chains. Their trousers are rolled up, and they are all so alike that it looks like they were turned out by the gross in some factory. Their attention is focused on the verbal

---

5   See Eric Michael Reisenauer, 'Anti-Jewish Philosemitism: British and Hebrew Affinity and Nineteenth Century British Antisemitism', *British Scholar* 1.1 (September 2008), 94–95. Chukovsky's speaker is referring to 'the set of beliefs known as British-Israelism', which held that the British 'were the direct descendants of one or more of the ten lost tribes of Israel'. British-Israelism has a history going back to the sixteenth century and reached 'its height at the turn of the [twentieth] century [when] the belief was held by more than two million persons throughout the English-speaking world. Associations of believers sprang up across the country and public lectures were given frequently. The theory spawned a sizable literature of books, pamphlets and periodicals, and its largely middle-class Protestant supporters included a not insignificant number of the middling to upper ranks of the clergy, military, and professions.' It relied 'on the prophetic passages of the Bible (which British-Israelites interpreted as predicting great success and prosperity for the lost tribes in the latter days)'. 'Even outside British-Israel circles a common theme in much imperial discourse was that Britain comprised a "new Israel" now in possession of Israel's mission to be a blessing and a light to all nations.'

6   There is no exact counterpart to this in the Bible, although variations on the general meaning are found in several different Books.

7   A made-up name based on the Russian expression 'as alike as a nail and a requiem', meaning 'as different as chalk and cheese'.

sparring of two disputants – an agnostic and a theosophist. The back of the agnostic's neck is broad and sweaty, while the theosophist is a nimble, pointy-bearded old fellow, who hops like a sparrow at every word.

The agnostic says in a ponderous bass:

'I only believe what I see. And what I don't see, I don't believe. Anyone who says any different is either a fool or a hypocrite.'

'Allow me, my dear sir, if I were to prove to you that this is exactly what you are doing, would you be willing to accept that you are both a fool and a hypocrite?'

'You will never do anything of the sort...'

'Half a moment. You have just said that you are sure of your opinion.'

'I am.'

'But you have never seen your opinion. Ergo, my dear sir, you are both a fool and a hypocrite.'

The clerks snigger. The broad back of the agnostic's neck becomes even broader, but try as he might to fumble about in his head,

> The desired *mot juste*
> Would not come to the tongue.[8]

Meanwhile, the old fellow is bobbing up and down continuously: 'And have you ever seen Australia? No? So you don't believe in the existence of Australia? And you don't believe in the existence of General Kuropatkin either? Or, perhaps, you have had a personal rendezvous with General Kuropatkin? Perhaps he invited you to his palace (!) to take counsel regarding Port Arthur?[9] If you please, Mr Johnson.'

Further on, the drum of the Salvation Army. Further still, the Spiritualists offering a poetic hymn to the 'omnipresent spirits' of the dead.

'Hey, you', shouts some drunkard at them, 'why do you take your "omnipresent spirits" for such fools? If they are omnipresent, they can listen to an opera in **Covent Garden** for free! And if they can get to the opera, they'll have no appetite for listening to your squealing. So you're praying to them in vain... They're not listening to you.'

Even the policemen smile.

Further. The crowd has spread out into a wide semicircle on the lawn, for the speaker is not standing still but running back and forth. I can hear snatches of what he is saying:

8   A slight misquotation from the poem 'Fields' (1861) by the Russian poet Apollon Maykov (1821–1897).

9   General Aleksey Kuropatkin (1848–1925) was a Minister of War during the Russo-Japanese War. The Battle of Port Arthur in early 1904 began the war.

'That little pickpocket Austen Chamberlain,[10] whose head is every bit as empty as his father's... But that villainous gang, our Cabinet, finds it as hard to refrain from thieving as I do to mount this button...'

But all this is beginning to weary the spectator. The crowd does not keep still for a minute, moving from one speaker to the next, in holiday mood, having come to the park not just to hear about Chamberlain, but to breathe the fresh air, to show off a new necktie to the whole world, and to run about on the grass with the kids. Hence the light-heartedly inconsequential character of this whole 'popular forum'. People will talk and talk some more, others will listen to them and then they will go their separate ways, pleased with each other

Fig. 44. The Denunciatory Loafer.

but without having their worldviews shifted a whit in either direction.

One cannot acknowledge any educational value in these conversations if only because all, or nearly all, of the speakers are as ignorant as their audience. If you wish to comprehend just how low, how hopelessly, incredibly low is the level of consciousness of these 'enlightened savages in top hats', spend a few hours of your Sunday in Hyde Park.

If there is one good thing about this custom, it is the precious awareness that whatever calamity might befall you, you are not alone, not defenceless in your trouble; you can appeal to your people and find compassion, help, support. This is why the Britisher walks with so firm a step, this is why he holds his head so high.

As for any other virtues inherent in these public meetings, they are just 'mirage and make-believe'. Nothing more.

---

[10]   Austen Chamberlain (1863–1937), son of Joseph Chamberlain, was Chancellor of the Exchequer at the time Chukovsky was writing.

Isaak Shklovsky [Dioneo], from 'Sekti' ['Sects']
Sketches of Contemporary England (St Petersburg, 1903): 424–54[1]

I.

A tourist who wishes to see 'the most characteristic' sight in London should go to Marble Arch in Hyde Park on a Sunday. In all weathers – whether it is pouring with rain, or the season of yellow and black fogs, or in summer heat – from three in the afternoon, a tourist will find a large crowd gathered here to listen to the speakers. Some of them stand under banners embroidered with devices and have collected about themselves a sizeable audience; others have simply climbed onto the railings and are speaking 'into empty space'. There is no-one listening to them, but the orators are not discomfited by this – they keep on speaking. Now one passer-by has stopped, then another, and soon a crowd coalesces around the speaker. It listens attentively; occasionally someone interjects a comment. If the orator does not speak with conviction, no-one will listen to him at all. Sometimes, the speaker's words arouse a profound interest – then the audience breaks up into a dozen groups, each centred around some 'scribe' who voluntarily takes upon himself the duties of a commentator.[2] And the kinds of people you can see in that crowd! A workman, wearing his Sunday best, a soldier in his operetta-style red uniform, with a swagger stick under his arm (English soldiers are prohibited from carrying arms in the street), a sailor and his 'sweetheart' in her garish feathers, hand-in-hand, a clerk in a glossy top hat, a stern Dissenting pastor, and so on. The English set great store by their open assemblies: they have paid very dearly for their right to free speech. To this end, it is instructive to peruse the recently published 'Life' of the late Richard **Carlile**.[3] As little as sixty years ago, a speech in Hyde Park could land you in prison for three years.[4]

Even more curious than the orators themselves are the topics on which they speak in Hyde Park. One speaker denounces the latest government bill with figures at his fingertips; another explains how necessary the higher forms of industry are for England. Under one tree, a speaker expounds the meaning of surplus value, while next to him lectures a 'Neo-Malthusian' or a 'Secularist' or George Gaspari, who every Sunday for thirty years now has been explaining to the public

---

[1]   Originally published as a Letter 'From England' under the pseudonym Dioneo in the monthly journal *Russkoe Bogatstvo*, August 1899, 17–41.
[2]   Shklovsky means 'scribe' in the biblical sense – not just a copyist but an interpreter and religious scholar or teacher.
[3]   Richard Carlile (1790–1843) was an early nineteenth-century radical and atheist who was arrested numerous times on charges of blasphemy, libel and sedition.
[4]   Editor's paragraph break.

what true 'humanitarianism' is and what are its benefits.[5] But the most numerous preachers under the trees by Marble Arch are religious ones, representatives of the countless English sects. Some show up with their own music and choir; others limit themselves to a portable organ and three or four singers; still others come in pairs. And the kinds of dogmas you see on display! The sorts of eccentric theories they concoct! The kinds of things those flimsy '**tracts**' – distributed and sold by the sects in such abundance – preach! Why do the sects exist? How does one explain their propagandistic zeal? The simplest and most widely proffered explanation is English sanctimoniousness. But you only need to take a closer look at the speakers and listen to them to realise that this explanation does not remotely account for all the aspects of the phenomenon. A second explanation for the existence of some of the more eccentric sects is the explosion in crude superstitious beliefs that can at present be observed among a part of the English middle classes. But this explanation also, although it is accurate to a large extent, does not account for the entire phenomenon. There must exist some other reasons which compel a humble clerk or a petty pedlar to turn into a street or *corner preacher*, as they are called here. To find these reasons, let us take a closer look at some of the speakers before we get to know the sects. Perhaps some things will become clearer for us.

Sunday. Four o'clock. The main alley which leads from Marble Arch to the naked Wellington is flooded with people.[6] A little old man is sitting on the iron railings and tightly gripping a stick on which flaps a faded banner depicting a lion. The old man looks so miserable, so hungry, especially when the whole of London is shrouded in an impenetrable cloak of black fog, that one yearns to come up to him and offer him a cup of coffee at a nearby restaurant. Meanwhile, this old man believes himself to be the happiest of mortals. God has sent him to proclaim to the English that they are the ten lost tribes of Israel, who had migrated to England, in the time of some king I can't remember, from beyond the

---

5   The 'surplus value' speaker is a Marxist. On Neo-Malthusians (birth-control advocates), see Richard Allen Soloway, 'Neo-Malthusians, Eugenists, and the Declining Birth-Rate in England, 1900–1918', *Albion* 10.3 (Autumn 1978), 264–86. Annie Besant and Charles Bradlaugh founded the Malthusian League in London in 1877 to promote contraception – there is thus a direct link with the Secularists, headed by Bradlaugh and Besant in the late nineteenth century. On Secularists, see Edward Royle, *Victorian Infidels: The Origins of the British Secularist Movement, 1791–1866* (Manchester: Manchester University Press, 1974) and *Radicals, Secularists, and Republicans: Popular Freethought in Britain, 1866–1915* (Manchester: Manchester University Press, 1980); for a recent overview of the historiography see David Nash, 'Secularist History: Past Perspectives and Future Prospects', *Secularism and Nonreligion* 8 (2019), 1–9. I have been unable to locate Gaspari.

6   Shklovsky is referring to the Wellington Monument, which depicts a nude Achilles.

river Sambation, which throws up continuously a hail of stones.[7] The old man has a whole heap of irrefutable evidence in his pocket, in the form of extracts from the Book of Revelation, some figures, mysterious diagrams, etc. There will come a day when the hosts of the 'saved' shall stand under the banner of the lion, but they are not here yet. The old man stammers dreadfully. He has not even managed to deliver a single speech yet, let alone convert anyone. With the very first phrase he attempts, the tongue refuses to serve him and turns entirely in the wrong direction. Meanwhile, the old man is convinced that if only his tongue would obey him, hundreds of thousands would flock to the banner of the lion. And so, every Sunday without fail, the old man comes here with the banner in his hands, an ardent speech in his head, and a pile of material evidence in his pocket. The only stumbling block is his tongue. And every time, the old man realises that today, too, the speech cannot be given. And having waited three hours, he heaves the enormous flagpole onto his narrow, bent shoulders and trudges back to the outskirts of the city. Tomorrow morning, the old man will be at work. He addresses letters at some firm or other. From seven in the morning until eight at night, he traces out the stupefyingly monotonous lines for a consideration of a half crown a day. In the evening, the old man will think to himself: 'one day closer to Sunday! Perhaps this time I will be able to speak!'.

Next to the old man, a young and handsome Indian is preaching and flashing his dazzling teeth and the whites of his eyes. He gesticulates vehemently with his arms, rolls his eyes in ecstasy and bobs up and down. His lithe, slender figure twists like the body of a cobra wagging its head in time to the air whistled by a snake-charmer on his flute. Several women, mostly old and plain, stand behind the speaker transfixed with rapture, catching his every word. He is a Buddhist who is explaining to the crowd the meaning of *karma*. A little further on, upon an overturned crate that used to contain starch, stands a gentleman in a white robe down to his feet and a strange headdress that looks like something between a tiara and a turban. This orator is a missionary from the shores of the Great Salt Lake. He proclaims to the crowd that the end of the world is nigh and speaks of the revelations hidden in the 'Book of Mormon'. The missionary's attire is that of a high priest – according to him. The Mormons have two 'churches' in London. They say that the missionaries have been displaying particular zeal lately because the city of latter-day saints is in need of manual workers. The London **Lumpenproletariat**, which has two alternatives in life – the soldiers' barracks or the gaol – provides not a few of the new Mormon converts.[8]

---

7 Cf. Chukovsky, 'Public Meetings in Hyde Park'. According to rabbinic literature, the ten lost tribes were exiled beyond the River Sambation, which was described as consisting of or throwing up stones.

8 *Lumpenproletariat* is a Marxist term referring to the rabble or 'ragged' proletariat – the poorest, most degraded stratum of the working class (criminals, the

Voices raised in jubilation ring out; one hears a clashing of cymbals, a squeaking of pipes and a clapping of hands. Here comes a detachment of the 'Glazebrook Army' to 'do battle with the devil'. The 'battle' will consist of the reading of a series of sermons and the singing of a dozen hymns. In the language of the army, this is called 'shelling the devil on all fronts'. The sect of 'believers in Joanna Southcott' is doing battle with the same enemy much more energetically. After a few hymns, all the 'Southcottians' begin to jump up and down on the green.[9]

'Jump higher, brothers! Hallelujah!', shouts the 'captain', struggling for breath – he is a fat, asthmatic old man in a short jacket and a peaked service cap decorated with black braid. 'Higher, higher! The devil is on the earth. The higher you jump, the closer will you be to heaven, and the heavier will you fall on the devil.' But the brothers and sisters are falling over themselves as it is.

By four o'clock, if the weather is fair, the Swedenborgians come along, the disciples of the visionary Emanuel Swedenborg. Their banners are decorated with mystical inscriptions and symbolic triangles. The Swedenborgians, who have about a hundred churches in England, expound the enigmatic book of their founder, '**Arcana Coelestia**',[10] or explicate their prophet's view on some obscure parts of Revelation. At all times you will be certain to meet some 'Agapemonites' in Hyde Park, who preach that the Last Judgment is already upon us, that the whole world has been condemned to eternal torment and the only salvation lies with the 'abode of love', of which more anon. In clear weather, an inquisitive tourist will count no fewer than thirty different sects under the trees and on the green: there are the 'Alethians', the 'Zos Perisos', the 'Hosanna Army', the 'Ranters', the 'Revivalists',

---

unemployed, etc.) who lack class consciousness. For an overview of the scholarship on Mormonism in nineteenth-century Britain, see J. Michael Hunter, 'Mormonism in Europe: A Bibliographic Essay', Faculty Publications, 1389, *Brigham Young University ScholarsArchive*, 2014, http://hdl.lib.byu.edu/1877/3270.

9   Shklovsky is describing millennial and other Christian sects, of which there were hundreds in the period according to *Whitaker's Almanack*, which listed them annually under 'Religious Sects' or 'Religious Denominations' – both the 'Glazebrook Army' and 'Believers in Joanna Southcott' appear there. On the Southcottians, see Jane Shaw and Philip Lockley, eds. *The History of a Modern Millennial Movement: The Southcottians* (London: Bloomsbury, 2017). See also Sarah Bartels, *The Devil and the Victorians: Supernatural Evil in Nineteenth-Century English Culture* (London: Routledge, 2021) and J. F. C. Harrison, *The Second Coming: Popular Millenarianism, 1780–1850* (London: Routledge and Kegan Paul, 1979).

10   *Arcana Coelestia [Heavenly Mysteries]* is Emanuel Swedenborg's most important, eight-volume work, published in 1749–56, which explains the Bible according to his doctrine of correspondence.

and so on.[11] But this is just an insignificant portion of all the sects that exist in England. Open Whitaker's Almanack for this year. There you will find a list of English sects. All in all, there are… 292. But these are, so to speak, the officially existing ones. There in Hyde Park, near Marble Arch, preach not a few evangelists who do not belong to any of the above-mentioned sects. Some petty clerk who spends all week scratching in a gigantic ledger, some workman or small shopkeeper arrives, in the few moments free of his duties, at what appears to him to be an irrefutable truth. And he must seek the truth because he cannot live for mammon alone. The conception of that 'truth' depends directly, of course, upon both the intellectual power and the stores of knowledge of the man who arrives at it. And once the truth is discovered, the clerk or shopkeeper cannot keep it for himself alone. The Englishman is by his very nature a propagandist. Having made a certain discovery, he wishes to share it with everybody. And so, sacrificing his leisure time, he makes his way on Sunday to Hyde Park, or indeed to the nearest crossroads, and proclaims what he believes to be the truth to all and sundry. The discoverer of the truth gains nothing whatsoever from the sermon – neither fame nor fortune. The preacher's only reward will likely be the influenza that he catches because the London climate is changeable, the heavens open often and custom demands that orators speak with their heads uncovered. The public will listen; if the speaker somehow manages to tug at their heartstrings, he will gain some followers. If not, he will end up preaching to the trees.

[Shklovsky then reflects on the English dislike of 'dogmatism' (as expressed in 'popery') and the diversity within Anglicanism ('high church, low church and broad church'); then, in a passage inserted for the 1903 collected version of the Letter, he recalls a street preacher he had seen in Glasgow in the summer of 1901. The following section (II) also does not appear in the original 1899 periodical publication – it replaces a different section which Shklovsky chose not to reprint.]

II.

I found a printed card in my letterbox sent by a grey, well-fed, unctuous little clergyman of our parish: 'Was Christ in Clapton on Sunday, the seventh of September (25 August)?[12] An exposure of the Agapemonites' delusions.' There followed a notification of an important sermon. I

---

[11] *Whitaker's* also lists a 'Glory Band', which is another way of translating the Russian original of 'Hosanna Army'. Shklovsky renders 'Ranters' as 'Howlers'. I have not been able to find anything matching 'Zos Perisos'. 'Agapemone' means 'the abode of love' (see below). See digitisations of contemporary issues of Joseph Whitaker's *Whitaker's Almanack* published annually in London at *HathiTrust*: https://babel. hathitrust.org/.

[12] Shklovsky gives the date in the Russian calendar.

258

have lived in this district for many years.[13] Although the English are completely uninterested in their neighbours, the clergyman at any rate knows me to be a foreigner and not of his parish. There must, therefore, have been some exceptional circumstances which caused him to send me the card. My readers should know that Clapton is a suburb of London and that the Agapemonites are an eccentric sect with members recruited from the wealthy classes. In August 1902, there was not a single newspaper that did not write about 'the incident in Clapton', the Agapemonites and the Reverend Pigott.[14] The sect has its own church in Clapton which is called 'The Ark of the Covenant', including a boarding house or 'abode of love'. But all of this was built in Clapton many years ago by the 'Forerunner of the Messiah', a former Anglican pastor called Prince or 'Brother Prince', as the members of the sect refer to him. The sect attracted no interest,[15] just as a hundred other analogous eccentric religious communities attract no interest from the English public, until the 'event of the seventh of September'.[16]

---

[13] Clapton is in the Borough of Hackney in East London. In other articles of this period, Shklovsky implies that he lives in Hammersmith.

[14] On 7 September 1902, the leader of the sect, Rev. John Hugh Smyth-Pigott, proclaimed himself to be the Messiah. Half the congregation pronounced him a heretic and a riot followed. A sample of contemporary international coverage of the incident may be seen in 'The Agapemonites: Further Demonstrations' in *The Sydney Morning Herald*, 16 September 1902, 5: 'the Rev Smythe Piggott [...] announced on Sunday week last that he was the Messiah. Besides Agapemonites 100 persons were admitted into the Ark of the Covenant yesterday, and angrily protested against and jeered at Mr. Piggott's renewed claim that he was the Son of Man come again into the flesh. Three thousand persons who were not admitted into the building followed Mr. Piggott's carriage homewards and indulged in hooting. Mounted police prevented violence being done.' The sect was founded in the 1840s by Henry James Prince, who also claimed to be God's instrument in preparation for the imminent Second Coming of Christ. The sect's church in Rookwood Road, Clapton was built in the 1890s. Materials produced by the sect may be found in 'Books and Sermon Sheets Produced by the Agapemonite Church, Clapton and by the Agapemonite Church in Spaxton, Somerset', 1896–1908, Hackney Archives (D/F/Wood), see catalogue description at *The National Archives*, https://discovery. nationalarchives.gov.uk/details/r/b5427cb4-9ecb-4e74-9125-12e99baa0f94. See also Jacqueline Banerjee, 'Henry James Prince and the Agapemonites', *Victorian Web*, https://victorianweb.org/religion/agape.html for a useful bibliography.

[15] Shklovsky is not entirely correct – in the mid-Victorian period a series of scandals associated with the sect attracted great public attention and even provided incidents for popular sensation fiction. A few pages later in the Letter, Shklovsky actually gives a detailed account of the scandals of the 1860s, using as his source William Hepworth Dixon's *Spiritual Wives*, 2 vols (London: Hurst and Blackett, 1868) (the sect's leaders took 'spiritual brides' from among the wealthy female following). This part of the Letter *was* reprinted from the original periodical publication, which might explain the discrepancy.

[16] Editor's paragraph break.

Two years ago, Alexander Dowie, or 'the Prophet Elijah' as the faithful call him, visited London from America. He came to proclaim a crusade against the doctors (he himself is a faith healer), beer, tobacco, pork and all the reprobates. His meetings were very riotous – the young shouted unflattering compliments at 'the Prophet Elijah' – but this did not prevent blasé rich men and old maids from giving Dowie large sums of money to build his city of believers.[17] Three days after 'Elijah's' departure, he was completely forgotten. Now only the Salvation Army is intensely interested in him because two 'Colonels' from its 'General Staff', including General Booth's daughter, committed treason and defected to the side of the Prophet. The Clapton incident, however, has been captivating the public's attention for much longer than three days, and will probably continue to do so, judging by the scenes which I witnessed in 'The Ark of the Covenant' some days ago.

The whole episode is highly characteristic of English life.

[There follows an encomium to English 'freedom of conscience', which ensures that extreme fanaticism (because not persecuted) peters out in mere 'curiosities' like the insignificant 'eccentric sects', instead of growing into a 'movement' that 'shakes the foundations of society'. Shklovsky then offers a long summary, first, of the newspaper account (from the Morning Leader*) of the 7 September incident in the Ark of the Covenant Church, when John Hugh Smyth-Piggott proclaimed himself the Messiah, and then of the history of the Agapemonites from their founding to his day, including biographies of their two leaders and the connections of Smyth-Piggott (and Dowie) with the Salvation Army.]*

Early on Sunday morning, armed with a ticket which allowed me entry into 'The Ark of the Covenant', I made my way to Clapton. The church of the 'Agapemonites' is built with considerable taste. Its entire exterior is decorated with allegorical figures carved from stone. Here is an ox trampling a human torso with its feet, further on an eagle stretching its wings, then a lion with a human head;[18] fantastic figures reminiscent of the demons of Notre Dame de Paris look down from the cornices. Though it was still early morning, a huge crowd had already collected by the iron railings, attracted by the articles in the papers. I noticed

[17]   John Alexander Dowie (1847–1907) was a notorious faith healer of Scottish origin, active first in Australia and then in the United States, where he made a business empire out of faith-healing and amassed a huge following. At the turn of the century, he received extensive coverage in the international press. He founded the City of Zion in Illinois in 1900 (defrauding his followers of a lot of money in the process) and soon thereafter proclaimed himself to be the prophet Elijah returned.

[18]   The lion represents St Mark, the ox St Luke and the eagle St John. See the description of the '(Former) Agapemonite Church of the Ark of the Covenant, Upper Clapton, London (Exterior)', *Victorian Web*, https://victorianweb.org/art/architecture/churches/77.html.

here the same types that I had grown accustomed to during the war:[19] well-dressed people prepared to defend with fists and clubs anything that has been established and sanctified by custom. Without a doubt, this crowd would have already smashed the railings to pieces if it had not been for the presence of several dozen impassive, burly 'bobbies' (policemen). With great difficulty, I squeezed through the crowd and into the church. I was asked for my ticket at every step. Inside, 'The Ark of the Covenant' hardly differs from an ordinary English church: the same stained-glass windows, the same rows of pews for the congregation. Only instead of biblical subjects, there were allegorical pictures in the windows – a serpent slithering out from a basket full of magnificent clusters of grapes, a serpent showing its head from a pomegranate, and so on. Before me, near the altar, I espied an old-fashioned armchair made of black oak, apparently 'the throne'.[20] There were already many Agapemonites in the church, for the most part well- (a few even richly) dressed women, no longer young.[21] They were sighing and whispering something to one another quietly. Presently, shouts and whistles were heard from the street, then a sound made by the fall of some heavy object; the locked doors were flung open and about two hundred people from the crowd stormed into the church. The 'bobbies' appeared and the doors were shut again. The organ began to play. The respect in which the English hold every kind of cult hushed the troublemakers – who had arrived intent on creating a disturbance – as soon as the service began. They listened to the organ, and then the hymns, patiently. But as soon as the singing had stopped, loud hisses, cries of 'booo!', catcalls, etc., immediately broke out. Pigott appeared by the throne. I had expected to see a face like that of 'the Prophet Elijah'. Dowie is a fat, stocky man with a bloated, puffy face grown over with a shaggy brush and tiny, cunning eyes. Pigott is a slender, lithe, evidently very strong man with a pale, handsome, clean-shaven face. The most striking features of this face are its sadly smiling mouth and wide-open eyes burning with a feverish fire. I saw such flashing eyes many years ago, in extraordinary circumstances, in the face of a friend of mine who woke me up in the middle of the night to announce that he was not Pavel Aleksandrovich but a descendant of the Greek emperors...

'My brothers, my children whom I love', came a resounding, beautiful, sad voice.

Immediately, sobs were audible from one side and restrained whistles from the other.

---

[19]   The Boer War.

[20]   In the notorious 'incident', it was from this 'throne' that Smyth-Pigott proclaimed himself the Messiah.

[21]   This accords with popular descriptions of the sect's main following.

'My children! I stand before you not as the shepherd of this church but as the Son of Man. I have come again to bless my people and to bring them salvation.'

'May I ask you a question: when exactly...', somebody shouted from the crowd. 'Ts-s-s' came from all sides and the question was never finished.

'You do not know me who am here among you', Pigott continued in the same mournful tone. 'I am the Son of Man. I have brought love and salvation from the Evil One, who still holds you in darkness and in chains. But now the days of his power are numbered. I am the last Son of Adam, the Spirit of Life, the Son of Man become flesh.'

'Don't believe him!' someone shouted.

'Impostor!' screamed another at the doors.

'Liar!'

Hearing the shouts inside, the crowd that failed to get into the church began to roar and charge at the doors. I looked at Pigott. He was standing still, smiling sadly, and only his eyes blazed out more brightly. I remembered my friend – how he explained to me in those extraordinary circumstances that the party of the enemies of the people was plotting to destroy him in order to appropriate the fortune bequeathed by the Greek emperors.

'Where are your nail wounds?' someone from the crowd was shouting in the meantime, shaking his fist.

'Throw him in the gutter!'

'Liar!'

But now the organ sounded again, the congregation began to sing a hymn, and once more the English respect for religion gained the upper hand. The crowd calmed down and gave Pigott a chance to make his exit. In the street, things did not work out so well. There, as it turned out, the crowd surrounded Pigott. Someone grabbed him by the collar, someone raised an umbrella, but the impassive 'bobbies' arrived in the nick of time and helped Pigott into a carriage. Let me add another detail. As I was leaving the church, I saw that the surrounding iron railings had been almost completely torn down. There will be no sequel to these displays of public protest. The English have successfully assimilated Voltaire's thesis: '**Toute persécution fait des prosélytes**'.[22] In view of this, Pigott will be allowed to proclaim himself whatever he

---

[22] French: 'All persecution makes proselytes', found in *Siècle de Louis XIV [The Century of Louis XIV]* in *Oeuvres Complètes de Voltaire [Complete Works of Voltaire]*, vol. 15 (Paris: Garnier, 1878), 30. This was a point George R. Sims made as well – see *Living London*, 3, 220, where Sims explains British religious and political 'free speech' to a 'foreign friend' in relation to street demonstrations and mass meetings in parks: 'The good sense of Londoners has long ago seen that prosecution would give the ignorant ranter a widespread renown, and probably lift a bumptious nonentity into temporary popularity.'

pleases. That way, in a week or two the public will forget all about the Agapemonites, 'The Ark of the Covenant' and the new Messiah.

[Section III is devoted to the sect of the 'Immortals' a.k.a. the 'New and Latter House of Israel' a.k.a. the 'Jezreelites', one of whose places of worship in Gray's Inn Road Shklovsky visited;[23] and Section IV to American faith healers in London, with a very long transcript of the trial proceedings following the death of Harold Frederic.[24] Shklovsky also refers to his 'Letter from England' of December 1901 in Russkoe Bogatstvo *which covers the faith healing trial of the 'Horace spouses' (unidentified). Section V begins with an account of Alexander Dowie's arrival in London from America in 1900 and a description of how he made faith healing into a profitable 'business'; his promotion tactics and the City of Zion ('I found Zion (in the United States) circulars as far afield as a hotel in Tangiers, Morocco'); his personal extravagance and assets; his acolytes and donors, etc. – all typical of the international press coverage of Dowie in the early 1900s. All of this was added for the collected volume version of the Letter and does not appear in the original periodical publication.]*

I will describe my visit to a meeting held in St Martin's Hall in Trafalgar Square.[25] Here the American prophet was busy recruiting neophytes. The chairman was a small, thin, dishevelled old man whose little eyes blinked continually – the bishop of the new church. He occupied the same position vis à vis the Doctor as Jan Matthys did with respect to John of Leiden.[26] Next to the bishop was another old man, but he was thickset, sturdy, of incredibly inflated girth. The old man's huge bald round head with its ruddy, plump face was mounted on the broad shoulders of a fairground athlete. The puffy cheeks were overgrown with a ginger shrub up to the very eyes. From this brick-coloured forest protruded a fleshy, upturned nose, which imparted to the whole face a pugnacious, provoking character. If it were not for this snub nose peeking out from the forest of hair, the old man would have been the very picture of that drunken Silenus whom the intoxicated Satyrs in

---

[23]   See Ruth Clayton Windscheffel, 'The Jezreelites and their World, 1875–1922' in Shaw and Lockley.

[24]   See the Introduction.

[25]   In St Martin-in-the-Fields Church. It is worth comparing the following description of Dowie's person and sermon not just with contemporary press caricatures and transcripts but with James Joyce's depiction of Dowie as 'Elijah' in *Ulysses* (Paris: Shakespeare and Company, 1922) – the manner of speaking is recognisably the same. Dowie's public baptisms in London in 1900 were covered by his newspaper *Leaves of Healing*.

[26]   Jan Matthys and John of Leiden were sixteenth-century Anabaptist leaders of the Münster Rebellion, regarded as prophets. John of Leiden was Matthys's disciple. In this section, Shklovsky refers to Dowie interchangeably as 'prophet', 'Doctor' and 'General'.

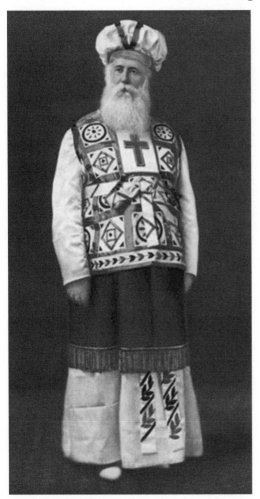

Fig. 45. John Alexander Dowie in His Robes as Elijah the Restorer.

Rubens's famous painting carry along in their arms during the Bacchanalia.[27] The old man rubbed his huge hairy hands which formed remarkably impressive fists. When the prophet – for it was he – stood in profile, his substantial belly was outlined in a vast curve.

I found the sermon already in full swing.

'May I ask one question?' came a thin tenor from the depths of the hall.

'No!' the Doctor cut him short in a thundering bass.

Upon hearing that bass, akin to the roar of a steam-powered foghorn, I immediately believed the tales of one meeting in Chicago where the prophet shouted down six thousand howling 'infidels'.

'No! I will not allow you to ask anything. Hold your tongue. Tie it with a rope if it's itching. And if you don't like this, you can clear out. I won't allow you to interrupt me with questions. I know what I'm teaching and I know where I'm going. No, you won't make a fool out of me. I'm too much of an old hand for that. You're still wet behind the ears, and there you go, sticking your oar in, trying to hoodwink an old bird like me. If anyone wants to gossip about me, you can blab all you want – in the street. It looks like you've read too many shameless newspaper lies and now want to repeat them here. If you don't want me to give you even more of a dressing down, shut your mouth.'

---

[27] Shklovsky must have seen the painting 'Drunken Silenus Supported by Satyrs' in the National Gallery (it is now attributed to Rubens's studio, possibly Anthony van Dyck): www.nationalgallery.org.uk/paintings/possibly-by-anthony-van-dyck-drunken-silenus-supported-by-satyrs.

The voice of the prophet rose and rose, filling the entire hall up to the very roof with its thunderous notes. The prophet accompanied his speech with expressive gestures: he would clench his enormous fists, trace a curve with them as if he were striking someone, or suddenly punch the air in front of him while giving a picturesque kick with his short, fat leg.

[Shklovsky cites an explanation for Dowie's self-presentation given by an American friend of his (being an 'excellent psychologist', Dowie has figured out that only 'rudeness' and 'vulgarity' appeal to 'blasé Yankees'); and goes on to report how he deals with disobedient 'elders' of 'Zion'.]

The sermon began. I have heard my fill of eccentric preachers near Marble Arch, but I had never yet heard anything approaching this in absurdity. The Doctor was threatening with anathema all those who read newspapers, drink strong liquor, smoke tobacco, turn to physicians when ill instead of healing themselves through prayer, and those who belong to secret societies (i.e. masonic lodges). Listening to these ludicrous denunciations, one does not consider the prophet's personality – he is just an ordinary, cunning, ignorant speculator with the natural-born talents of a fairground 'professor' who peddles cure-all pills to the crowd. Rather, it is the 'overfed pessimists' who appear before one, the blasé American dyspeptics surfeited with positively everything, bored and incapable of discovering any as-yet-untasted impression that could titillate their dulled nerves.[28] The Doctor, meanwhile, having finished with the journalists and the smokers, had begun to fulminate against... those who eat eggs and ham, the stock ingredients of an English breakfast since the times of Alfred the Great.

'I can recognise a sinner by his smell!' the prophet thundered. 'I can tell you that here in front of me sits a vessel of the devil.' The General thrust his hairy fist in the direction of the front rows. 'Faugh! How this sinner reeks of beer, vodka,[29] pork and tobacco!' The Doctor crinkled up his stubby nose and furrowed his bushy eyebrows. 'I know that you are the son of a strumpet. I shall smite you with a deadly blow, you vile and filthy offspring of the Whore of Babylon,[30] you Anglican Church, whose bishops and vicars drink beer and eat pork. They live by trading in mysteries in squares and in marketplaces! You, spawn of hell, own

---

[28] It is worth recalling that Shklovsky is writing at the turn of the century and the 'Decadent' clichés of this description are probably intentional. The Paterian and Wildean allusions are oblique, but Joris-Karl Huysmans and his 'novel' *A Rebours [Against Nature]* (Paris: Charpentier, 1884) are mentioned by name in the paragraphs omitted above describing Dowie's American audiences.

[29] As usual, vodka stands in for gin.

[30] The original has 'Roman whore'; 'Whore of Babylon' was frequently used as a metaphor for Rome.

houses rented out to whores, publicans and brewers. You fill your chests with gold received in payment for blood and for dissoluteness. May the Lord curse you as I curse you! And you also I curse, you spawn of the serpent,[31] the periodic press! You are the creation of gamblers, liars, panders, fornicators, tobacco-smokers, drunkards and pork-eaters! Press, you are inspired by Satan! Your spirit is akin to the woodlouse and your body to the slug. Hell alone is more odious than you are. Pray, brothers! Let the Lord of Hosts who destroyed the Amalekites send a hail of stones also on Fleet Street.[32] Let the sulphurous fire that burned Sodom and Gomorrah incinerate the press too! And I shall tell you another thing. Heal yourselves by faith! Send all the doctors to Satan and to his sentinels – to Azazel with his stinking goat, to the three-headed Haborym, to the hairy-winged, bony Astaroth.[33] Brothers, I can name you dozens of cases of miraculous cures from my own practice brought about by the aid of prayer alone. I'll begin with Frank Hopkins, the famous New York football player. On Saturday, he sprained his ankle and was flat on his back. On Sunday, the wretch was tortured by doctors; on Monday morning I healed him with prayer and the same day Frank Hopkins was already kicking the ball nimbly with his foot even higher than before. Here's his card. And the lady from Maidenhead? She had been ill for a long time. All the doctors had refused to treat her. I merely touched her with one finger, said a prayer and the lady was healed. And have you heard about Hastings? No? The young man had twisted his neck. He was brought to me. I said a prayer and all was done. The young man ran off, nodding his head, because he could not believe that it was in place. To hell with chemists! Heal yourselves with prayer!…'

Meanwhile, the entrance doors had been opening more and more often. The blasé dyspeptics and the old maids were joined by an entirely new element: ruddy-cheeked young men in jockey caps – it was the medical students from the London hospitals come to defend their profession.[34]

---

[31]   The original has 'echidna', a reference to the Greek half-woman, half-snake monster.

[32]   Shklovsky's note: A street in London where most of the newspapers are produced. Editor's note: The Amalekites were enemies of the Israelites in the Old Testament (their destruction by the Lord of Hosts is alluded to in the Book of Samuel).

[33]   These are fallen angels and demons (popular in occult circles).

[34]   The rowdy behaviour of London medical students at public meetings was a commonplace of contemporary fiction as well – see Arthur Conan Doyle's *The Lost World* (1912; Oxford: Oxford University Press, 1998): '"Will you come to the meeting?" I asked. […] "If the medical students turn out there will be no end of a rag. I don't want to get into a bear-garden." […] Looking behind me, I could see rows of faces of the familiar medical student type. Apparently the great hospitals had each sent down their contingent. The behaviour of the audience at present was good-humoured, but mischievous. Scraps of popular songs were chorused with an enthusiasm which was a strange prelude to a scientific lecture' (38–39).

'Boo-oo-o!' droned the hundreds of young men who had made their way into the hall.

'I want to say', the General began.

'Boo-oo-o!' the champions of the medical profession intoned even louder. And their voices drowned out even the thunderous bass of the prophet. Presently, several dozen young men started to mew like cats; others howled. In one corner, they began to sing 'The Soldiers of the Queen!'; in another, '**God Save the Queen**'. The singing, mewing, barking and shouts of 'boo-oo-o!' merged into an ear-splitting din.

'I was a medical student myself once', boomed the prophet's powerful bass, overwhelming even that music of a hungry menagerie. 'We could roar even louder when necessary!'

The Bob Sawyers accepted the challenge and immediately proved that they too had a few spare notes still in their range.[35] But now the prophet's brawny bodyguards arrived on stage and, at a sign from the General, made a move on the students. The ladies blanched. The air filled with anticipation of a colossal row complete with broken limbs and bloody noses.

'Hospitals to the rescue!' one of the young men shouted, sticking his head out of the window. Sounds of singing and whistling came from the street. But the bodyguards concluded the fight before the enemy could receive reinforcements. The future doctors were thrown out. The spoils of war littered the floor: ties, collars, torn coats, broken umbrellas, walking sticks, etc. Without a doubt the prophet had seen worse things than this. Not abashed in the least, he continued – when the enemy had been forced out – to denounce the pork-eaters and the tobacco-smokers. I went out. Outside the doors, on the pavement near the entrance, one could see that something was being prepared and that 'the enemy' was not yet willing to admit defeat. A crowd of young people had lined up and were waiting. Presently, the rotund figure of the prophet appeared in the doorway. As if at a signal, an infernal concert began. Some crowed like cocks, some mewed like cats, some sang songs.

'Quack! Impostor!' some shouted.

'To hell with the bearded charlatan!'

'Long live medicine!'

'"Kings",[36] bellow louder!'

'"Guys",[37] praise this fairground mountebank!'

There follow descriptions of the personal comments, shouts, interruptions, etc. addressed from the medical students in the hall to the people on the platform, and the speaker's responses to the heckling.

[35] 'Bob Sawyer': a medical student in Dickens's *Pickwick Papers*.
[36] Shklovsky's note: I.e. students of King's [College] Hospital.
[37] Shklovsky's note: Students of **Guy's Hospital.**

'*Counspay* Dowie!' the 'Guys' responded to the prompting. 'Counspay' is the French verb **conspuez** pronounced in the English manner.[38]

The row had an infectious effect on the crowd. A number of gentlemen appeared out of nowhere, having no obvious relation to medicine but burning with a desire to join the fray.

'Dunk the *Kroojer* in the pond!' suggested some puffy-faced gentleman who had just refreshed himself in a neighbouring pub.[39] But here a **Deus ex machina** arrived in the shape of the burly, impassive 'bobbies'. The row ended in a police court with the judge issuing a small fine and a fatherly counsel not to challenge other people's opinions with fists and howls but with words. The General, like a true Yankee, extracted a not inconsiderable benefit from the scandal by turning it into a splendid advertisement for himself. Three days later, the Doctor baptised no fewer than fifty converts in the pool of a public bathhouse hired especially for the occasion: old ladies, unhinged dyspeptics, etc. The 'newly converted' all wore swimming costumes, black for the men and white for the ladies. The prophet himself, also in a swimming costume, lined the new converts up in a row and led them down the steps into the water, where he immersed each one thrice with his own hands...

[Section VI returns to the original periodical publication and is devoted to Emanuel Swedenborg and the Swedenborgians. Shklovsky appears to have visited their 'book repository in Bloomsbury Street, near the British Museum'. He concludes the Letter with a legend from the Gesta Romanorum.*]*

[38] *Conspuer* means to boo or shout down, to loudly and collectively demonstrate one's disagreement or contempt for something or someone. Shklovsky gives the imperative form.

[39] The scene takes place in 1900, and Paul Kruger's name had become a derogatory moniker during the Anglo-Boer War – see Shklovsky's 'Frankie'.

Isaak Shklovsky [Dioneo], from 'Imperialism'
Sketches of Contemporary England (St Petersburg, 1903): 33–59[1]

I.

Before clarifying the nature of a phenomenon that is celebrated by poets, preached from the church pulpit, discussed in newspapers and in Parliament, extolled in after-dinner speeches, a phenomenon for which rivers of blood have been spilled overseas and many a cheekbone broken in England itself, I shall describe one scene. It occurred in June 1900. I had just ascended from an underground railway station near Mansion House, in the very heart of the City, close to the Stock Exchange and the Bank of England.[2] At three in the afternoon, the traffic here comes to a bit of a lull. The sizeable migratory population sits in its banks and business offices. Suddenly, the cry of the newspaper boys broke the silence. A 'special edition' of the evening papers was out. The boys usually tear along with a bundle of still-damp newspapers under their arms as if the editors had set the dogs on them. Only the huge banner-headlines, which they wave around like flags, flash before the eyes of the passers-by. Now, however, instead of dying down in the distance as always, the cries were getting louder. Hundreds of new voices were joining in the clamour.

'What is it?' asked those who had just emerged from the underground dungeon of the railway, filled with suffocating sulphurous smoke.

'Pretoria is ours! Hip! Hip! Hooray!'[3]

[1] Originally published as 'English Imperialism' under the pseudonym Dioneo in the monthly journal *Russkoe Bogatstvo*, September 1900, 83–107. The periodical publication of the Letter is prefaced with two epigraphs which are omitted from the collected version: a quote from an after-dinner speech at a Chambers of Commerce Congress about 'imperialism and trade' being 'synonyms', and a quote from Cecil Rhodes's speech after the Relief of Kimberley (February 1900) about the 'Union Jack' being a 'precious concession'.

[2] This is the old location of the Stock Exchange (the Royal Exchange) in Threadneedle Street. See the Ordnance Survey map of the area (OS London, 1:1,056, 1893–1895).

[3] The Fall of Pretoria in June 1900, when the British army under Field-Marshal Lord Roberts captured the capital of the independent Boer Transvaal Republic, was a symbolic milestone in the Second Boer War. See H. W. Wilson, *With the Flag to Pretoria: A History of the Boer War of 1899–1900* (London: Harmsworth Brothers, Ltd, 1900). Visual and textual depictions of the earlier jingoist mass street celebrations of the Relief of Mafeking in May 1900 and Ladysmith Day in March 1900 match Shklovsky's descriptions in this article down to the smallest detail, from the songs of black-suited Stock Exchange clerks to the cult of General Baden-Powell. It is possible that Shklovsky conflated them. See, for instance, the images of celebrating London crowds and patriotic paraphernalia in Richard Danes, *Cassell's Illustrated History of the Boer War* (London: Cassell, 1901), *The Graphic History of the South African War, 1899–1900* (London: The Graphic Office, 1900) and *The Graphic* supplement for 26 May 1900.

Fig. 46. The Relief of Mafeking: The Good News Announced at the Mansion House on Friday Night.

Instantly, the square before the Stock Exchange turned into a heaving sea of human heads in top hats, greasy caps and motley-feathered bonnets. Black-suited gentlemen poured out of all the offices, out of all the banks of Lombard Street and Cornhill. 'Hip! Hip! Hooray!' came the shouts from one end of the square. '**God Save the Queen!**' chanted hundreds of people at the other end. '**Rule, Britannia!**' sang the clerks who rushed in a crowd from the huge Parr's Bank.[4] Now cheers rang out. A handsome, thickset old man with rakishly curled moustaches came out onto the Mansion House balcony. This was the Lord Mayor, Newton. He must have been saying something very patriotic, because one could see that he was shaking his fist, pointing at the 'Union Jack' and beating his chest; but his words were impossible to make out in the almighty din. Only disconnected exclamations of '**Pax Britannica!**', 'The Great Empire!', 'A Glorious Day!' wafted over. And who would think that this noble orator, who had not spared even his own chest in

---

[4]   Parr's Bank had a history dating back to the eighteenth century and in 1905 William Howarth called it 'one of the great amalgamating banks in the country' and 'a power in the financial world', see his *The Banks in the Clearing House* (London: Effingham Wilson, 1905), 177, 187. Detailed information may be found in John Orbell and Alison Turton, *British Banking: A Guide to Historical Records* (New York: Routledge, 2017).

the cause of the fatherland, is now being prosecuted for setting up sham publicly traded companies![5]

The square assumed a picturesque aspect. In one place, an engorged gentleman swollen with fat held up the tails of his black suit and, mincing daintily with his yellow-booted legs, performed a **skirt-dance** to the sounds of a street organ turned energetically by an Italian woman in a shawl tied crosswise over her chest.[6] Opposite the gentleman, a young woman with enormous red feathers in her hat was dancing vigorously, holding up her skirts with one hand. In her other hand was a huge peacock's feather with which the young woman tickled the fat gentleman on the nose. The latter was growing hot. His fat stomach, tightly encased in an ornamental silk waistcoat, shook and wobbled at every bounce. The gentleman was puffing and blowing, gasping with the fat and the heat, but still shouting: 'Glory to Bobs' (Roberts)![7] Ragged hawkers rushed to the square from every direction, eager to make use of this moment to dispose of their peacock feathers, rattles, flags, coloured paper caps, pins with portraits of generals and other paraphernalia necessary for the exhibition of patriotic enthusiasm. And here another gentleman in a top hat, also fat but somewhat more youthful, was trying unsuccessfully to climb a streetlamp. A third, young gentleman took something from the hands of the fat one and clambered up the lamppost. He was gripping a rope to whose end was tied a dummy holding a Bible, which was hanged with much applause.[8] The pipes squealed piercingly; the rattles screeched. Thousands of boys were moving in endless procession. Someone fastened a giant flag to a streetlamp. A circle dance formed around the post. Here danced to their heart's content a gaily dressed, quite elderly lady, an old man – to all appearances a labourer, a young gentleman in a top hat and an extremely high collar and a

---

[5]   Editor's paragraph break. Sir Alfred Newton (1845–1921) was elected Lord Mayor of London in 1899 and served until November 1900. He was responsible for raising funds for the City of London Imperial Volunteers who helped to capture Pretoria and his Baronetcy was conferred the same year. See 'Imperial Units: City Imperial Volunteers', *AngloBoerWar.com*, www.angloboerwar.com/unit-infor-mation/imperial-units/542-city-imperial-volunteers and City Imperial Volunteers Catalogue, London Metropolitan Archives (CLA/051), https://search.lma.gov.uk/LMA_DOC/CLA_051.PDF. However, in this period Newton was also involved in shady stock market flotations which came under public scrutiny and were investi-gated by a Chancery judge, as covered in detail in 'The Lord Mayor as Company Promoter', *Daily News*, 29–30 November 1899 and other newspapers.

[6]   See Martie Fellom-McGibboney, 'The Skirt Dance: A Dance Fad of the 1890s', PhD thesis, New York University, 1985. This was a popular dance, originating in the London music halls of the 1870s and still going strong in the 1910s, which involved swirling the fabric of a long, layered skirt.

[7]   Field-Marshal Lord Roberts, pictured as a hero of the Boer War in Wilson's *With the Flag to Pretoria*.

[8]   Probably an effigy of Kruger – see Shklovsky's 'Frankie'.

soldier in a red coat. The atmosphere of the square was growing stifling. In the window of a shop in Cheapside appeared a huge placard depicting a lion tearing apart two boars (*boar* and *Boer* are pronounced the same in English). This image had just been issued by the renegade paper, the *Daily Chronicle*.[9] More and more people were dancing in the street. A carriage passed by. A lady was sitting on top of it – on the roof, dangling her legs, waving an enormous flag and shouting stridently: '**Rule, Britannia!**'. Outside the shopfront of a print seller, an even more eccentric scene: the window displayed a portrait of General Baden-Powell in yellow

Fig. 47. The Relief of Mafeking: An Impromptu Dance in Trafalgar Square on Saturday Evening.

uniform.[10] Some smartly dressed lady shrieked 'my darling!' and fell to kissing the glass opposite the place where the portrait was placed. A dozen other ladies followed suit. And again, a circle dance in the street. The English are ponderous, dignified and prim when outdoors, so these ladies and gentlemen jigging on the pavement produced an especially odd impression. Darkness fell. The streets became even noisier. Thousands of other jubilant patriots poured out of the pubs, with saucepans, pots and frying pans in their hands. The streets resounded

---

9   Shklovsky may be referring to the fact that the proprietors of the newspaper had recently (November 1899) forced the resignation of its anti-Boer War editor Henry Massingham, requiring him to remain silent 'on the policy of the Government in South Africa'. See Jock Macleod, *Literature, Journalism, and the Vocabularies of Liberalism: Politics and Letters, 1886–1916* (Basingstoke: Palgrave 2013).

10   Robert Baden-Powell was the founder of the Scout Movement and a hero of the Siege of Mafeking (1899–1900) in the Boer War, after which he became major-general. His portrait as 'Defender of Mafeking' was also featured on patriotic postcards at this time and was carried aloft in the Mafeking celebrations.

with the infernal din made by the squeaking pipes, the rattling drums, the clanging pots and pans, the shouts of 'hooray!', the snatches of patriotic songs composed in the music halls... Everything merged together into a single roar, continually drowned out by the thunderclap of firecrackers. The new editions of the patriotic evening papers spoke of a 'jubilant imperialism', of the enthusiasm which had gripped the whole of London...

All that remained for the outside observer was to analyse the phenomenon. He had a lot of spare time on his hands, because the noise and the din kept him awake all night. The scenes described are simply the ultimate expression of that 'imperialism' which has been inculcated for about fifteen years, but which has only fully taken its shape in the last five or six. Let us leave aside the spontaneous nature of any mass movement and try to ascertain what 'imperialism' actually is. A close study shows us several currents present within it. There is no doubt that the Lord Mayor of London, the stockbroker, the big industrialist, the old labourer dancing around a streetlamp, and the jingoist bard Rudyard Kipling must have somewhat different notions of 'imperialism'.

[In the rest of the Letter, Shklovsky offers first a cultural ('jingo-poets', etc.) and then an economic (and statistics-heavy) analysis of imperialism, colonial and military policy, modern slavery, etc. He quotes various Blue Books, Statements of Trade and other government sources; newspapers; Chamberlain's and others' speeches; and French and English studies of British imperialism, such as F. W. Hirst's, Gilbert Murray's and J. L. Hammond's Liberalism and the Empire *(1900).*[11]*]*

---

[11] In the Preface to the collected volume where this Letter appears, Shklovsky lists the English anti-war (mostly) Liberal writers whose analysis of imperialism and jingoism particularly influenced him: 'Hobson, Bryce, Robertson, Hammond, Frederic Harrison'.

Isaak Shklovsky [Dioneo], from 'Vibori' ['An Election']
Sketches of Contemporary England (St Petersburg, 1903): 254–83[1]

I.

Since time immemorial, our constituency has been represented in
Parliament by a retired old general.[2] He made his career somewhere
on the western shore of Africa. There, with a small detachment and five
cannon, he spread European culture, i.e. he burned so many villages, cut
down so many fruit trees and exterminated so many negroes and cows
that the land remains barren to this day, although many, many years have
now passed. The general, having finished with the trials of camp life,
settled down in our constituency, which sent him as its representative to
Parliament to uphold 'real' Conservatism there. The old man has only
been to Parliament once or twice, but he made his presence felt. Having
listened to the speeches of the Opposition, the old man announced
that, in point of fact, they should be dealt with 'the African way', i.e.
by letting in a few soldiers, rolling in a small cannon and then: 'One,
two! Thrust to the right and cleave to the left!'.[3] The old general's
speech was met with Homeric laughter from the Opposition benches;
meanwhile, his own side was quite put out and gave the old man some
'friendly' advice not to venture into the unfamiliar field of parliamentary
politics. The old general took offence and has hardly ever made an
appearance in Parliament since. Every day with clockwork regularity,
his grey pointed head held high, his chest sticking out, in a long coat
reaching to the ground, rapping his stout stick and mumbling something
with his drooping lips, the general makes the round of the park. But our
constituency still regularly puts him forward at every election: he is so
respectable, such a 'patriot', and our constituency is ultra-conservative.
Its population consists of three of the most conservative elements in
England, Tories through and through – not because they are in need of
'markets' or the protection of capital invested in foreign enterprises,
but just 'because', because it's '**stylish**'. This population is made up
of clerks, 'cads', and habitual drunkards, the descendants of people
who have lived for two or three centuries in abject poverty. All three
elements, whose views on foreign policy happen to coincide to such

---

[1]   Originally published as a Letter 'From England' under the pseudonym Dioneo in
      the monthly journal *Russkoe Bogatstvo*, October 1900, 100–27.
[2]   Throughout the Letter, Shklovsky uses a Russian word which can be variously
      translated as 'constituency', 'district', 'borough' or 'parish'. All three constitu-
      encies that Shklovsky describes at length: Hammersmith (unnamed here), and later
      Lambeth and Battersea, became metropolitan boroughs in 1900 under the London
      Government Act 1899.
[3]   Shklovsky uses a Russian imperial army command, which also appears in song
      and poetry and is associated with Cossacks.

an extent, inhabit separate quarters which have nothing whatever in common with one another. The clerks reside in neat little houses, with the inevitable colourfully potted palm peeking from behind the white curtains in every window; the 'cads' occupy mansions of twelve or fifteen rooms, overgrown with ivy; the drunkards huddle together in dirty, fetid alleys. There are four churches in the street inhabited by clerks; five or six sports clubs in the 'cad' quarter; and in the dirty labyrinth of the drunkards there are pubs uncountable, which are the hotbeds of the most ardent patriotism.

[Shklovsky goes on to explain who the upper-middle-class sporting 'cads' are by quoting at length the negative description from the popular novelist Ouida's **'Critical Studies'** *(1900).]*

And so, the old African hero represented our constituency in Parliament for almost twenty years.[4] But now the House was dissolved and a new, 'Khaki' election was called.[5] Our constituency displayed even more patriotism than ever during the war. In the churches, the clergy preached patriotic sermons and demonstrated that St George was the first 'Tommy Atkins' and St Stephen the first 'Jack Tar';[6] both the clerks and the cads decorated their homes with flags after every announcement of the success of British arms. The ladies on Sundays no longer played hymns like 'The Holy City' or 'To Heaven Aspire' on their pianofortes,[7] but 'The Soldiers of the Queen', 'Britons, Strike Home!',[8] **'God Save the Queen'** and other patriotic songs. As for the

4　It is probable that Shklovsky is describing Major-General Walter Tuckfield Goldsworthy, Conservative MP for Hammersmith from 1885 until 1900. If so, he is clearly painting a caricature (for one, Goldsworthy's contributions in Parliament were much more extensive, see 'Mr Walter Goldsworthy' in *Hansard*, https://api.parliament.uk/historic-hansard/people/mr-walter-goldsworthy/index.html).

5　Shklovsky actually uses the term 'soldiers' election' to refer to the Khaki election of 1900. On the election specifically and its context more generally, see Jonathan Schneer, *London 1900: The Imperial Metropolis* (London: Yale University Press, 1999).

6　Nicknames for common soldiers and sailors in the British army and navy respectively.

7　The titles in the original Russian are, literally, 'Jerusalem, O Holy City' and 'To Heaven Aspire, O Man'. The former is clearly 'The Holy City', composed in 1892 by Frederick Weatherly and Stephen Adams and a mega-hit at the turn of the century (see Adrian Johns on the sheet music industry in *Piracy: The Intellectual Property Wars from Gutenberg to Gates* (Chicago, IL: Chicago University Press, 2009), 328). I have not been able to locate the second hymn. There are a number of hymns that talk about 'aspiring to heaven', such as the evangelical eighteenth-century hymns 'To heaven, my longing soul aspire' by Simon Browne, Charles Wesley's 'Where shall my wondering soul begin' and various others.

8　On the history of 'Britons, Strike Home!', whose popularity was in decline by 1900, see Martha Vandrei, '"Britons, Strike Home": Politics, Patriotism and Popular Song in British Culture, c. 1695–1900', *Historical Research* 87.238 (November

lumpenproletariat, every victory was celebrated with abundant libations of ale and whisky at the 'Seven Stars', the 'Vineyard', the 'Red Cow', the 'Whistling Oyster' and other patriotic establishments of our district.

And in the midst of all this, the indignant population learned that the 'pro-Boers' were seeking to capture their stronghold of patriotism! Notices inviting them to vote for an unknown candidate put forward by the Liberals appeared on house walls. The general was immediately removed. The voters understood perfectly that the African hero was not suitable and would find it impossible to fight off even the most unimpressive opponent. And the opponent was indeed hardly worth bothering about. The Liberal Federation knows full well that it is impossible to wrest our constituency away from the Conservatives,[9] so it did not at all support its own candidate. He chose to stand at his own risk, knowing that he would be defeated. But he was a young solicitor of ample means, just starting out, and he needed this candidacy as a route to public recognition. The general was no more. Instead, the constituency put forward a typical 'cad', also a solicitor and a true patriot.[10] When the Liberal candidate held his first public meeting, he was able to see for himself – if he still entertained any doubts in the matter – that he had no hope of winning. The public meeting was held in a little square in front of the 'Vineyard', a huge pub where every Saturday some congregation comes together with a beating of drums and a blaring of trumpets 'to shell the devil'. Alas! the devil is invincible.

> *[Shklovsky gives a brief description of one of the sects he mentions in the 'Sects' Letter (above), and of the pub regulars' mocking reception of them.]*

It was in front of this pub that the Liberal candidate addressed himself to 'the gentlemen', condemning the Government's fiscal policy. The meeting was most unsuccessful. The street boys and the drunks from the pub did not let him speak.

I do not intend to offer an analysis of the parties and programmes in this election. I just wish to sketch – in broad brushstrokes at that – a few scenes. Let us journey, therefore, to the place where the electoral battle was fought most doggedly. Such a spot was the south London constituency of Battersea. The Conservatives wanted above all else to win in this district and to vote out the current representative John Burns.

2014), 679–702. It might be another song that Shklovsky has in mind (the original Russian means, literally, 'Smash your enemies, Britannia').

9   The National Liberal Federation was a union of Liberal Associations which represented the opinion of the party membership and in the late nineteenth and early twentieth centuries promoted party policies.

10   In 1900, Goldsworthy was succeeded as MP for Hammersmith by the Tory solicitor William James Bull (1863–1931), who would go on to hold the seat for several more decades.

Fig. 48. John Burns: The Colossus of Battersea.

Such a victory would have proved that labouring London also supported imperialism and that the MP who denounced the war more loudly than anyone else could be voted out by virtue of this fact.[11]

---

[11] John Burns's association with Battersea was legendary: in 1909 a *Punch* cartoon depicted him bestriding the borough as 'The Colossus of Battersea' in a deliberate visual nod to an earlier *Punch* cartoon of his enemy Cecil Rhodes bestriding Africa as 'The Rhodes Colossus'. For more on Burns, see below.

To go to Battersea is to embark on a long voyage. First, we have to traverse the whole of central, fashionable London, proud of its Conservatism, pass the City and catch a tram from the historic London Bridge, which will take us across the Gobi Desert of the vast metropolis, along the endless streets of the borough of Lambeth.

It is hard to imagine anything more melancholy than the 'great brick desert' of South London! From the dirty main street, filled with the reek of stale vodka and stale fish fried in sunflower oil (in London, this mixture of smells enables one to identify from afar, without guide or map, the location of the '**slums**'),[12] narrow, slimy, fetid alleys spread out in both directions. They look like long, gloomy, stifling corridors leading to the palace of the sovereign of this place – Hunger. The little houses stretch out in a single black wall, gone crooked with age. Not a single bush, not one green space! Just the black-soot-covered brick and the cobblestones sticky with stinking mud.

From the narrow corridor-alleyways comes the noisy clamour of children messing about on the pavement and dancing to the sounds of a barrel organ strayed here from God knows where, or why.

The children are of different ages: from those still experimenting with the theory and practice of walking on two legs to five-year-old draggle-tails, green-faced, scrofulous, their noses in a most deplorable state. Hardly any kids older than five years can be seen: they are already busy helping their mothers glue matchboxes or make cheap artificial flowers.[13] The girls are even more ragged than the boys, but their hair is all rolled up in curlpapers, which the London riffraff have a particular weakness for. Today is Saturday. Dirty, ragged women with cracked jugs in their hands are going to the pubs for a pint of ale and to see if their 'man', who was due to get his wage today, is already sitting there – they must salvage at least a few shillings. The women are unspeakably dirty. The old bruises under their eyes, which have not yet healed, will alas! be replaced with new ones this evening, but their hair is rolled up in curlpapers all the same. At the pub doors, their hands tucked under the belts of their corduroy trousers tied around with straps below the knee after the local fashion, stand some lowlifes bloated with vodka and performing all possible variations on the curse '**bloody**' (damned or, properly, bleeding), which seems to be the only adjective in their impoverished lexicon. We are passing through Lambeth – the most savage, rough and poor district of London. The population here consists of unskilled labourers and people belonging to, in the official terminology,

---

[12] 'Vodka': gin.
[13] Typical home-workers' trades in which very young children could be engaged to help. For a fictional depiction of toddlers gluing matchboxes see Morrison's *A Child of the Jago*.

Fig. 49. Outside a Public House.

the 'semi-criminal class'.[14] Once a year, in early autumn, Lambeth is emptied of its residents. All of them, with their wives and children, set off for the hop fields of north Kent in a huge gypsy encampment to harvest that indispensable ingredient which gives its flavour to the 'blood of John Barleycorn, the hero bold'.[15] Temporary pubs grow up

[14] Shklovsky is using Charles Booth's classification of poverty: the 'semi-criminal' or 'vicious' was the lowest classification. He is referring specifically to North Lambeth; Lambeth was a giant borough, much of it middle-class.
[15] Shklovsky is probably quoting Robert Burns's 'John Barleycorn: A Ballad' (1792) – a personification of barley: 'John Barleycorn was a hero bold, / Of noble enterprise; / For if you do but taste his blood, / 'Twill make your courage rise' in *Selected Poems and Songs*, ed. Robert P. Irvine (Oxford: Oxford University Press, 2013). However, there were a number of 'folk', pantomime and music hall variations on the theme of 'the blood of John Barleycorn, the hero bold' in the nineteenth and early twentieth centuries, so it is conceivable that Shklovsky may have had in mind

around the hop fields, where nearly all that is earnt is spent on drink. Parliament has more than once taken up the question of a ban on the sale of spirits in the vicinity of the hop fields. It turns out that the pubs are set up by the very brewers and noble lords who own the hop fields.

One can see shops in the main street. One constantly meets with signs such as: 'Cheap Undertaker', 'Cheap Patented Cures for All Diseases'. Everything speaks of an ailing, destitute, *sickly* – in the Volga men's phrase – population which someone is trying to remove from the face of the earth at the least possible expense.[16] Lambeth often figures in London's criminal news reports. It is interesting to study the names of the criminals who appear in the courts. All these people are English, of course, but their names are not: Darcy (D'Arcy), Deballe (De Balle), etc. They are all descendants of well-born Huguenots who came here after the revocation of the Edict of Nantes. Back then, the Huguenots settled in two villages near London: Bethnal Green and Lambeth. Clockmakers settled in the former, and weavers who manufactured a special patterned fabric in the latter.[17] Several generations prospered; fathers taught their craft to their children. Bethnal Green and Lambeth were wealthy villages with clean, pretty houses, little gardens and schools. But then appeared that insensible but dreadful monster: the machine. First it killed the Lambeth weavers, then came the turn of the Bethnal Green clockmakers. The machine began to produce by the thousand those wheels and screws that had hitherto been manufactured by hand. And the whistle of the steam engine became the funeral hymn of the two villages. The residents found themselves in the street. The neat houses and gardens were no more. The descendants of the Huguenots mixed with the newly arrived English population who were driven from their villages to the suburbs of the colossal capital by the 'death of the land'.[18] After seventy-five years, Lambeth and Bethnal Green have become what they are today, i.e. the most savage districts of London. If I were a poet, I would choose as

---

one of these. See 'John Barleycorn is a Hero Bold', *Folk Song and Music Hall*, 23 October 2020, http://folksongandmusichall.com/index.php/hey-john-barleycorn/.

[16] 'Sickly': Shklovsky uses a dialect word that has no exact English equivalent.

[17] The Edict of Nantes was revoked in 1685 by Louis XIV and Protestantism was outlawed in France, leading to the persecution and emigration of the Huguenots. See Robin D. Gwynne, *Huguenot Heritage: The History and Contribution of the Huguenots in Britain* (London: Routledge & Kegan Paul, 1985) and Debra Kelly and Martyn Cornick, eds. *A History of the French in London: Liberty, Equality, Opportunity* (London: Institute of Historical Research, 2013). Shklovsky gets this history wrong: the weavers were in Spitalfields and Bethnal Green; carpet-makers and dyers were prominent around the River Wandle in Wandsworth, spilling over into Lambeth and Battersea; clock- and watchmakers were to be found more in Soho and nearby. However, the factual inaccuracies do not take away from the rhetorical force of the argument.

[18] Shklovsky covered the topic of the migration from the countryside into the cities in 'The Working Quarter'.

the theme of my epic the fate of the Huguenots in Lambeth, the battle of the dragon-machine with man...

But at least there are a lot of pubs in Lambeth. And like everywhere else in London, all the pubs are hotbeds of the most ardent patriotism. From the roof of the omnibus, I can see several blowsy women bloated with beer and gin sitting in a pub. In the window is a patriotic poster bearing the words: 'Vote for Ridley, a true patriot, not the pro-Boer traitor'. Lambeth is a pillar of Conservatism, one of the Malakoff Redoubts of the fortress of Toryism.[19] In the window of another pub, there is a political caricature (or 'cartoon', as they say here) titled 'A Lesson to Radicals'. Morley, Harcourt, Campbell-Bannerman and other ministers from the last Cabinet are seated on school forms,[20] wearing long faces. 'Joe' (i.e. Chamberlain), in a black teacher's gown and with a birch rod in one hand behind his back, is chalking with the other on the blackboard: 'The Consolidation of Empire', 'A Strong Army', 'A Mighty Navy', 'The Respect of Foreign Powers', 'The Flowering of Trade', and so on. All of these are meant to signify the fruits of imperialist policy. Here is another political cartoon, also in a pub window. Lord Salisbury is standing at a closed door, the inscription on which reads: 'The British Empire'.[21] The artist has imparted an unusually ferocious look to the prime minister's flabby, rotund figure. Lord Salisbury has clenched his fists and is ready to make mincemeat and 'knock the teeth' out of all those enemies who are creeping towards the door.[22] Here is France, contriving to slip on a noose, and Russia, and Kruger, and Germany – in a word, the whole world. Lambeth, browbeaten and feral from destitution, is being indoctrinated with the idea that if it were not for the fist of the flabby prime minister, all of Europe would be coming to ransack the quarter's dirty hovels! ...

Presently, a splendid carriage pulled by a pair of thoroughbreds turns into one of the filthy alleys. A footman wearing a huge fur collar over

[19] An allusion to the French capture of the Russian-held Malakoff Redoubt in 1855 during the siege of Sevastopol in the Crimean War.

[20] William Harcourt and John Morley were Radical Liberals and Henry Campbell-Bannerman was the Party leader and a critic of Chamberlain (Liberal Unionist Colonial Secretary and one of the most prominent figures in the Khaki election of 1900 as an imperialist proponent of the South African War).

[21] Lord Salisbury was the leader of the Conservative Party and Prime Minister in coalition with the Liberal Unionists. For examples of the types of posters Shklovsky is describing see the *LSE Digital Library* 'Political and Tariff Reform Posters' collection and the *LSE Digital Library* 'London County Council Election of 1907' poster collection at https://digital.library.lse.ac.uk/collections/posters/londoncounty councilelection1907#images. On election posters, see James Thompson, '"Pictorial Lies"? Posters and Politics in Britain c. 1880–1914', *Past & Present* 197 (November 2007), 177–210.

[22] 'Knock the teeth': in the original, Shklovsky uses a Russian idiomatic expression associated with seminary students.

his shoulders, which gives him the appearance of a sheared poodle, jumps down from the coach box and unfolds the steps. Out come two gaudily dressed, sweetly smiling ladies with patriotic rosettes pinned to their breasts. Dirty boys and girls with hair coiled in curlpapers rush to the carriage from all directions with noisy shouts. The heads of curious adults peep out from doors and windows. These ladies are members of the 'Primrose League', who propagate true patriotism.[23] They have arrived in the '**slums**' to preach imperialism and Conservatism and to hand out political cartoons to the residents for agitational purposes.

[Shklovsky gives an example, with quotation, of a circular distributed in Londonderry by the wife of a Unionist candidate.]

The great stone desert has come to an end. We have emerged into a flowering oasis. Indeed, after Lambeth, that is precisely what the borough of Battersea (population approx. 165,000) seems like.[24] Clean streets, neat little houses, well-washed children, lots of lawns and little gardens, three free public libraries, a huge popular Polytechnic,[25] several local newspapers, etc. All of this forms a stark contrast to the grime and obscurity of Lambeth. The Battersea Council (the local municipality) is considered the most radical not just in London but in the whole of England. It has set up schools, libraries, public readings and a labour exchange. It has municipalised the trams, built housing for workers on city land and reduced the number of pubs, of which Battersea has fewer than any other area with the same population.[26] Battersea Council tenders public works not to contractors but directly to workers' cooperatives, and it has also introduced an eight-hour working day for all employees and mandated the payment of the minimum wage set by the trade unions. Battersea is the target of unending complaints from brewers and contractors. Finally, for nine years now, Battersea has been

---

[23] The Primrose League was a political organisation dedicated to spreading popular Conservatism, founded in 1883. The prominent role of women in it (the 'Primrose Dames') has been much studied, see Philippe Vervaecke, 'The Primrose League and Women's Suffrage, 1883–1918', in Myriam Boussahba-Bravard, ed. *Suffrage Outside Suffragism: Women's Vote in Britain, 1880–1914* (Basingstoke: Palgrave Macmillan, 2007), 180–201.

[24] Shklovsky is probably referring to the population of the Parish of Battersea in 1896, which was indeed approximately 165,000. The population of the borough formed in 1900 was almost 169,000.

[25] The Battersea Polytechnic Institute, established 1891.

[26] Shklovsky is conflating LCC achievements with those of the Battersea Vestry, forerunner of the Borough Council of 1900. For instance, it was the LCC that had municipalised most of inner London's tramways, not Battersea, and it would have been the main authority for reducing the number of pubs (though the Council played a part by refusing to allow them in its housing estates); nor did the Council build schools, at this time the responsibility of the School Board for London. But the general picture that Shklovsky gives is true enough.

sending John Burns – 'our Jack', born forty-two years ago in this very borough – as its representative to Parliament.[27] In every election, the Conservatives put all their efforts into capturing Battersea, but so far to no avail. The borough also sends the very same Burns as its representative to the London **County Council**. Three years ago, during the last municipal elections, the 'Moderates' (as the Conservative Party on the **County Council** calls itself) pulled out all the stops to force Burns out of Battersea. The *Daily Mail* and the *Pall Mall* [*Gazette*] included his name in their 'blacklist' every day. But it so happened that precisely those who ended up on this fateful list were elected.

The Conservatives have put forward Garton, a rich local brewer and owner of ninety pubs, to stand against Burns.[28] The 'Patriots' want to force Burns out at all costs because, among other things, he is one of the few MPs to speak out sharply and decisively against the war. Burns alone was able to speak against it successfully at public meetings in Battersea, when everywhere else the meetings of the 'pro-Boers' were

[27]   John Burns was a leader of the London Dock Strike and later an independent Radical (Lib-Lab) MP, well known for his opposition to the Boer War. He was born in 1858 and was first elected to represent Battersea as a 'Progressive' in the London County Council in 1889 (the Conservatives were 'Moderates'), and then as an MP from 1892 (until 1918). He was responsible for much of the municipal socialism-style local legislation Shklovsky summarises here, including paying for Council contracts at trade union rates and building a municipal housing estate without the use of sub-contractors. As Shklovsky notes below, he lived on an allowance paid by his constituents instead of profiting from his position. See the John Burns Collection at the University of London.

[28]   The brewer Richard Charles Garton was the Conservative candidate for Battersea during the 1900 general election. He got 48.9 per cent of the vote. Tories dominated the drink trade (and some scholars have argued that the connection of the Tory drink trade with pub and music hall patriotism of the kind Shklovsky describes here was not accidental). For a very detailed account of the Burns vs Garton contest in Battersea in 1900, see Schneer, 248–59. It is fascinating to compare Shklovsky's account with Schneer's. In some respects, the overlap is complete, down to the use of the same words and strikingly similar descriptions of the same scenes (e.g. the interactions between hecklers and speakers at Garton's meetings) – probably due to Shklovsky's reliance on the same periodical sources as Schneer. But there are also many divergences, both in detail and in Shklovsky's ideologically inflected emphases: for instance, his paradoxical insistence on English non-violence, which clashes with the reality of disorder at the election meetings, ending in fights that had to be broken up by the police. Garton ultimately 'gave up public meetings altogether' because he was prevented from speaking so many times (Schneer, 255). For an easily accessible contemporary account of the election campaign, see the *Guardian*'s reprint of its 2 October 1900 article, 'A Bicycle Interview with John Burns, Battersea's Man to Beat', www.theguardian.com/theguardian/2012/oct/02/john-burns-battersea-cycling-archive-1900.

disrupted. A few days ago, Hobson, whom we know so well in Russia, spoke against 'Liberal Imperialism'.²⁹

[Shklovsky quotes from a Hobson article of 28 September 1900 in the Morning Leader *and then describes the dirty means by which the Tories were attempting to dislodge Burns, such as libelling him in the South African press. He then quotes at length from a certain pamphlet No. 1843 which exposed the involvement of the Chamberlain family in five companies that received government contracts for arms and war supplies during the Boer War (see below), giving numerous details of the corruption scandals that plagued Joseph Chamberlain in the late 1890s and the* Morning Leader's *exposés.]*

III.

However, it is time for us to get off the tram to take a stroll through the streets of Battersea. The population of the borough consists of two social types who are disposed towards each other in the least friendly fashion. On the one hand, Battersea is populated by conscientious workers who are for the most part well-paid: machinists, carpenters, joiners,³⁰ and so on. All of them belong to unions. The other part of the population consists of junior clerks, bank employees from the City who have moved over here because the flats are cheaper. In ordinary times, a principal treats his clerk not so much with disdain as simply beneath his notice. For a principal, clerks are just '**Hands**' dressed in uniform black coats and top hats. A clerk goes off to work in the morning, spends all day writing accounts and then returns home, worn out and exhausted. He barely has time to glance through the **Daily Mail** in the mornings and an issue of **Tit-Bits** on Sundays. The former publication provides the clerk with political insights and the latter with scientific and literary ones. Ahead of an election, the principal begins to smile benevolently at the clerk and sometimes even strikes up a conversation to intimate that the two of them, *as gentlemen*, have common interests, patriotic interests, unlike those radicals who pander to the rabble. So the clerk puts on even higher collars and brushes his old top hat even more thoroughly, so as to look even more 'like a gentleman' and to differentiate himself from the labourer. The petty bourgeoisie everywhere are sticks-in-the-mud. But in England, where their level of intellectual development

---

²⁹ J. A. Hobson was an economist and author of *The Psychology of Jingoism* (London: Grant Richards, 1901), which Shklovsky references in 'Imperialism', and the seminal *Imperialism: A Study* (London: James Nisbet & Co., 1902). He was a big influence not just on Shklovsky but also on Lenin, among other prominent Russian figures. Hobson famously argued that the pub and the music hall were key conduits of jingoism.

³⁰ 'Machinist' could also be translated as 'engine-driver', 'engineer' or 'mechanic'; 'cabinet-maker' could be meant instead of 'joiner'.

is extremely low in consequence of the general inaccessibility of a university education, the petty bourgeoisie have ossified completely. In Battersea, the clerks reside separately from the workers, going out of their way to settle in a different street.[31] The houses in this street will inevitably be called 'villas'. If one hears the sounds of a piano coming from the windows of a 'villa', it will surely be 'The Soldiers of the Queen', 'It Was a Glorious Day of Battle' and other patriotic songs taken from the music hall.[32] The clerk will join the 'Primrose League' without fail, mainly with the aim of at least appearing on the same lists as Marquis So-and-so and Viscount This-and-that.[33]

Even a superfluous glance shows us that here in Battersea a bitter fight is looming. The candidates' portraits are displayed in almost every window. Garton can be seen in the 'villas', Burns in the cottages. Under the portraits are short appeals to voters, like the following:

'After such a long and hard-fought war, will you really give in to Kruger and Co.? Of course not. So vote for Garton, the true patriot!'

'Vote for Burns and deliver a guilty verdict to this vile, venal and despicable Government.'

'If you are for God, Queen and patriotism, vote for Garton!'

'Vote for Burns, the enemy of sweaters.'

'Remember Majuba and cast your vote for Garton!'[34]

'Vote for Garton and clear the House of Commons of traitors and pro-Boers!' and so on.

Sometimes, electoral posters are more prolix.[35]

---

[31] The mutual cultural and political antagonism and social separation between lower-middle-class clerks and skilled workers (the aristocracy of labour) are well recognised in the historiography.

[32] I have been unable to locate the original of 'It Was a Glorious Day of Battle'. Patriotic and imperialist songs as popular music hall entertainment have been thoroughly studied. On music hall songs and the Boer War, see, to begin with, chapter 1, 'The Music Hall' in Attridge, 'The Soldier in Late Victorian Society'; Laurence Senelick, 'Politics as Entertainment: Victorian Music Hall Songs', *Victorian Studies* 19 (1975), 85–98; Penny Summerfield, 'Patriotism and Empire: Music Hall Entertainment, 1870–1914', in John M. Mackenzie, ed. *Imperialism and Popular Culture* (Manchester: Manchester University Press, 1986), 17–48. For background, see Yeandle, Newey and Richards; Peter Bailey, ed. *Music Hall: The Business of Pleasure* (Milton Keynes: Open University Press, 1986) and John M. Mackenzie, *Propaganda and Empire: The Manipulation of British Public Opinion, 1880–1960* (Manchester: Manchester University Press, 1984).

[33] Editor's paragraph break.

[34] Presumably a reference to the Battle of Majuba Hill in the First Boer War, which the Boers won in 1881 and which was seen as a humiliating British defeat.

[35] Examples of Liberal election posters from 1900 depicting the kinds of things Shklovsky describes here are held at the National Archives; similar examples from later elections may be seen in the *LSE Digital Library*.

[Shklovsky proceeds to give verbatim transcripts of two Opposition posters: one addressed to 'London workers' and arguing, with lots of arithmetic calculations, that the Tory government could use the money it takes from everyone in taxes to fund old age pensions instead of giving it to landlords as 'bribes' (because of the 'Rating Act' of 1896); the other, even longer and even more bursting with figures, tracing the increase in the cost of living (tea, beer, tobacco, coal) to the Boer War and the 'public money' used to fund it. This poster argues that public spending will only grow if the government remains in power, which will lead to new taxes and a bigger army. It addresses itself to 'farmers', whose agricultural labourers the government takes away and sends to their deaths in 'tropical lands'; to industrialists, who will lose their workforce to Chamberlain's proposed conscript militia; and to workers, who are enjoined to 'vote against militarism' and 'imperialism' to ensure that their sons remain 'free citizens'.]

Political cartoons and drawings have been put up everywhere they could possibly have been pasted. An enormous drawing titled 'External and Internal Enemies' catches the eye. A Boer is aiming his gun point-blank at a huge John Bull, while a Chinaman is raising his sword. Russia and France stand at a distance, also poised to attack, but a multitude of pygmies are clutching at John Bull's arms and legs and preventing him from defending himself. On the pygmies' sleeves are labels: 'Home Rulers', 'Pro-Boers', 'Disparagers of England'. The pygmies are members of the Opposition. Some of them have drawn their bows and are preparing to shoot arrows labelled 'Slander' at John Bull. And here is a drawing by the brilliant modern caricaturist Gould.[36]

[Shklovsky proceeds to give detailed descriptions of several F. C. Gould cartoons used in the 1900 election campaign, such as a caricature of members of the Cabinet 'hiding behind a doll dressed in a soldier's uniform and raising a flag with the word "Khaki"'; and two caricatures of 'Joe' Chamberlain.]

These drawings aim to give a pictorial representation of the current state of affairs to the most unsophisticated readers.

---

[36] Francis Carruthers Gould (1844–1924) was a prolific Liberal political cartoonist and journalist. His caricatures of Westminster politicians may be found in 'Caricatures of Politicians by Sir Francis Carruthers Gould, circa 1889–1912', *National Portrait Gallery*, www.npg.org.uk/collections/search/set/90/Caricatures+of+politicians+by +Carruthers+Gould. The preface to a volume published for the 'Khaki Campaign' of 1900 asserted that 'At no previous General Election have political cartoons been used so freely, both as leaflets and posters, than during the one just concluded. The fact that both sides have made so large a use of pictorial attacks, arguments and appeals, shows that the picture has come to have a practical value in political warfare', quoted in John Percy, 'Political Cartoons of Sir Francis Carruthers Gould', *Working Class Movement Library*, www.wcml.org.uk/blogs/Lynette-Cawthra/ Political-Cartoons-of-Sir-Francis-Carruthers-Gould/.

Fig. 50. Liberal Election Poster.

Fig. 51. Liberal Party Poster.

This was clearly the task set for themselves by the designers of an enormous poster which is meant to give the common reader an immediate idea of the results of the Government's fiscal policies.

[A detailed description follows of an infographic with explanatory text depicting the reduction in lower-class London voters' purchasing power with reference to a basket of common food staples.]

The English are great masters at putting together a graphic course of political economy and presenting a budget in pictures rather than figures.

And here is a drawing by the above-mentioned Gould which is meant to give the electorate an idea of the Government's broken promises. John Bull is raising the 'Union Jack' (the national flag), under which Chamberlain is carefully trying to hide some piece of paper. It is Chamberlain's electoral manifesto from 1895, promising a range of social reforms: an old age state pension, an eight-hour working day, a reduction in the sale of spirits, etc. 'Wait a minute, Joe', says John Bull, 'I'd like to see what it is that you're hiding there under the *Union Jack*. I am determined to investigate everything.'[37]

IV.

Dusk is falling. The dark, damp, cold, autumnal London night slips down over Battersea. In the distance, the whistles, the droning and groaning of the huge factories, have fallen silent. Young people, workers by the look of them, are hurrying to the libraries and to the 'Polytechnic'. And what have the gentlemen in top hats inhabiting the 'villas' whose windows display Garton's portrait created for themselves? Next to the handsome new building of the town hall is an ugly 'music hall', brightly illuminated with electricity, on whose doors is pasted a gaudy playbill depicting a girlie in a mask and short skirt reaching to the knees. The playbill announces that today the music hall, known as 'The Shakespeare Theatre', is presenting an operetta called 'The Gay

---

[37]   See Percy, 'Political Cartoons of Sir Francis Carruthers Gould': 'Chamberlain, was one of the most frequent targets of Gould's satire and the subject of some of his most memorable images. [...] Gould's attacks reveal the compromises he thought Chamberlain had made in becoming a Minister (Colonial Secretary) in the Salisbury government. In the cartoon "Juggler Joe and his vanishing programme" of 1895, Chamberlain holds up a list of the progressive causes he had been identified with; Salisbury says "I'm not going to swallow all that" and Chamberlain whispers "I'll manage all the vanishing business". The 1900 election took place against the backdrop of the Boer War, and Chamberlain had become an attack dog against those Liberal "doves" who were accused of being pro-Boer. "Pasting them over" shows Chamberlain's social programme and old age pensions pledges covered over by the slogan "Vote Khaki".'

Grisette'.[38] The 'cad' has the same tastes in Battersea as in Hanover Square. 'The Gay Grisette' had once delighted the artistic sensibilities of the 'cads' of central London but has now moved to the suburbs.

Today, both parties are holding their meetings. Let us visit the Conservatives first. We find ourselves in a building that greatly resembles a church. It is indeed a chapel of the Methodists, those militant supporters of imperialism, who have let the Conservative candidate use it for his meeting.[39] Half of the church is filled with gentlemen in black frockcoats and yellow ties edged with red (the patriotic *khaki* colour), with portraits of Roberts on their breasts.[40] The other half of the audience is wearing jackets without any patriotic symbols. On the platform are several gentlemen in black frockcoats, three or four pastors and five or six showily dressed ladies. These are members of the 'Primrose League', who have arrived here to help Garton capture the Shevardino Redoubt of Radicalism.[41]

Applause rings out. A handsome, thickset, ruddy-cheeked gentleman with a rakishly curled military-style moustache comes out: the brewer Garton, the Conservatives' hope. The candidate begins to speak. Whether it's because Garton was too poor to get a decent education or because he considers his public uncouth in the last degree, he addresses them in a manner that is not customary for English public speakers.[42]

'Now then, my dear chaps, there are two sides to everything', he begins, slamming his fist into his palm.

'Except your beer, which has only one side: it's just foul!' someone cuts in sharply from the hall.

'Shut up there, you idiots!' Garton yells out, turning a deep shade of red.

'Boo-o!' dozens of voices begin to intone in the depths of the church. This is how the English always express their scorn.

'You can roar and howl all you like, lads', Garton definitively adopts the master's manner, 'but I am still going to fight for true patriotism in

---

[38]   The Shakespeare Theatre opened in 1896 next to Battersea Town Hall near Clapham Junction and presented musical comedies and plays, as well as films. *The Gay Grisette* was a popular musical comedy by George Dance, first staged in 1898, which played in theatres all over the country in these years.

[39]   'Garton held his first election meeting on Monday evening, September 24, at the Primitive Methodist Schoolroom, Plough-road. The building was packed to overflowing' (Schneer, 252).

[40]   Field-Marshal Roberts, the Boer War hero.

[41]   A reference to the 1812 Battle of Shevardino between the French and Russian armies. The French captured the redoubt.

[42]   Garton was educated at Owens College, Manchester and Marburg University, Germany as a chemist. See Fiona Wood, 'Garton, Sir Richard Charles (1857–1934)', *Oxford Dictionary of National Biography*, 23 September 2004, https://doi.org/10.1093/ref:odnb/47512.

this election. I am a supporter of the policies of the Honourable Lord Salisbury.'[43]

Applause and jeers break out.

'You should rather be ashamed to pay your workers fourpence-ha'penny an hour', someone remarks reproachfully.

'Wait, hold on you fellows!', the speaker gets worked up. 'I will prove to you later that those are all lies. When I'm elected to the House of Commons, what will I do?'

'You'll go to sleep, Harry Garton',[44] comes a mocking reply from the depths of the church.

'No, damn it! Not it! I am a patriot. I will give all my energies to see the British flag fly everywhere, in all the four corners of the earth. Together with the greatest statesman of our time, Joseph Chamberlain.'

'Kynoch!' a voice rings out at one end of the hall.

'Hoskins!' deep voices echo from the choir gallery.[45]

'Boo-o-o!'

The ladies from the 'Primrose League' fidget nervously, jump up and sit back down again.

'Three cheers for John Burns!' suggests some gentleman in a chequered tweed jacket. The suggestion is received with enthusiasm.[46] Garton, meanwhile, continues to speak of patriotism, the glorious war, the necessity of reforming the army, so that 'England could swiftly and decisively defend its interests everywhere.'

[43] Compare some of Garton's actual words as quoted in Schneer, 253: 'You may howl and boo [...] but I tell you this – you'll have to take me for Battersea whether you want it or not.' The meeting broke up at this point without Garton finishing his speech.
[44] Garton's first name was Richard not Harry.
[45] These are allusions to the charges of corruption and profiteering that plagued Joseph Chamberlain during the Boer War. See chapter 16, 'The Last of the Gentlemen's Wars?', in Denis Judd and Keith Surridge, *The Boer War: A History* (2002; London: I. B. Tauris, 2013): 'Chamberlain's brother Arthur was prominent in the armaments firm Kynoch Ltd, which supplied cordite to the army, and [the Radical Liberal] Lloyd George insinuated that Joseph had helped his brother's business.' See also Peter T. Marsh, *Joseph Chamberlain: Entrepreneur in Politics* (London: Yale University Press, 1994) and chapter 8, 'Back Home and Into Harness', in Walter Reid, *Neville Chamberlain: The Passionate Radical* (Edinburgh: Birlinn, 2021): the Chamberlain 'family network' were also majority shareholders in or owners of Elliott's Metal Company Limited and 'another metalworking firm, Hoskins & Son [...] which manufactured and fitted berths for ships all over the world'. The reference to Elliott's is below. None of the modern historians and biographers give anywhere near as much detail on the Chamberlain family's involvement in these companies as Shklovsky – drawing on contemporary pamphlets and newspaper articles – does in the pages omitted from the translation above.
[46] Cf. Schneer, 253: 'Instead the other side called for cheers for John Burns. These were given, upon which three cheers for Garton were also supplied, to much groaning.'

'And now let me tell you that the man who mentioned fourpence-ha'penny an hour has uttered the most vile, damnable and hateful lie', Garton concludes.

It was Joseph Chamberlain and not the nouveau-riche uneducated brewer Garton who first introduced coarse and vigorous language into electoral addresses.[47]

A poorly clad young man of about twenty-three comes quickly up to the platform and calls out to Garton: 'Listen, *you* paid me fifteen shillings a week when I worked for you. I received a "child's wage" though I worked the night shift in the oasthouse where you can't even wear a shirt on account of the dreadful heat.'

Shouts of 'Sweater! Sweater!' erupt everywhere.

'Come, you won't shout me down!' Garton's thunderous bass rises over the noise. 'Hey, John Philpot![48] I've recognised you! Come over here! Tell us, how much did you get when you worked for me?'

A workman – no longer young, timid, cowed and ill-clad – comes forward. He explains that he began on nine shillings a week and went on to earn twenty-three shillings.

'So, what do you say to that?' Garton exclaims triumphantly.

'And how many years had you worked, John Philpot', somebody asks, 'before you began to earn twenty-three shillings?'

'Twenty years.'

'And you're exulting, Mr Garton?'

'And why did you give Philpot the sack?' some tweed jacket demands to know. It seems that in Battersea everyone knows everyone else.

'Why, he's a drunk.'

'And it took you twenty years to find that out?' a man asks.

'Of course, as if one could get drunk on your stuff, made out of saccharine!',[49] another remarks ironically. John Philpot protests loudly.

'Sir! you've told a lie!' he addresses himself to Garton. 'You didn't dismiss me for drunkenness but because I'm old and weak.'

'Sweater! Sweater!' dozens of voices chant.

'Silence! Shut your traps!' Garton waves his arms. But the noise only grows.

The chairman of the meeting waves his hand, rings the bell, says something to the audience and then to the gentleman sitting next to him. One can only gather that somebody will soon be brought over, that some very important personage is about to make an appearance.

---

47 Garton was neither nouveau riche (his father owned a brewing firm, though Garton did achieve much greater success and was knighted in 1908) nor uneducated. It is entirely possible that Shklovsky knew nothing about Garton's background.
48 The original has 'Phlipot' throughout.
49 The company of Garton's father 'pioneered the production of saccharine [...] in 1855' (Wood). Garton owned a sugar refinery.

'Bring the Viy!',[50] comes to mind for some reason. The 'Viy' does indeed arrive, except he is not a dreadful gnome covered with soil, but a refined, perfumed, elegant young man with a monocle screwed into his eye: Wyndham, the Under-Secretary of State for War.[51] But the 'Viy' fails to instil any deference in the audience. Some applause is indeed heard, but protracted shouts of 'boo-o!' resound even louder. The ladies become agitated. The chairman performs an entire symphony with his bell. The elegant Wyndham rises and signals with his well-groomed hand that he is about to speak:

'John Burns!' he begins.

'Three cheers for our Jack!' someone suggests enthusiastically.

'We know all about Burns, but why don't you tell us about Kynoch?'

'Or Hoskins for that matter?'

'Or at least about Elliott's? We'll hear you out with pleasure!' The shouts once again merge in a single roar. Wyndham orders some fellow to be apprehended (not, of course, by policemen, who are prohibited by English law from entering a hall where a meeting is being held) and brought to him.

'Well, my good man', the elegant Under-Secretary asks in a condescendingly scornful tone. 'Why do you shout so? Do you wish, perhaps, to ask a question?'

'Yes, sir!' the young man replies with the utmost calm. 'I wanted to ask you, when you have finished, to tell us how Mr Chamberlain procures contracts for the Treasury.' Deafening laughter erupts.

'Fine!', Wyndham shrugs his shoulders contemptuously. 'It appears that we are unable to talk; but this will not prevent the honourable candidate from entering Parliament.' The speaker sits down.[52] Garton announces that he will now present his programme.

'I ask you, who shall be in charge in South Africa – the Boers or the British?' he begins with pathos.

'Sweater, it would be better if you paid your own workers decent wages! What do you want with South Africa?' someone rebukes him.

'Cut down the number of your pubs!' another advises.

---

[50] A quotation from Nikolay Gogol's 'The Viy' in *Mirgorod* (St Petersburg, 1835), which concludes with a witches' sabbath in a church, when a witch summons the Viy – the monstrous king of the gnomes. The implication is that a riotous Tory meeting (also in a 'church') is a monsters' gathering like the one in Gogol, although Shklovsky, unlike Gogol's protagonist, does not fall down dead.

[51] George Wyndham (1863–1913) was a Conservative imperialist politician, Under-Secretary of State for War under Lord Salisbury from 1898 to 1900.

[52] Cf. Schneer, 255: 'That Chamberlain's family had purchased shares in companies which then were awarded war contracts only confirmed a more general sense in their minds that the war was being fought for capitalists anyway. And when Wyndham protested his treatment by the crowd, they laughed at him.'

'Better go and sleep – why do you need politics!' The laughter, witticisms, shouts of 'boo-o!' (that's addressed to Joe) drown out the resolution. Indignant gentlemen in black frockcoats shout 'To hell with Burns!' and begin to sing '**God Save the Queen**', and then a patriotic song taken from the music hall, 'The Soldiers of the Queen'. From the platform, the chairman shouts into a speaking trumpet, 'Three cheers for Roberts!'.

Let us now go to the other meeting; fortunately, it begins much later. The doors of the town hall are still locked, but a huge crowd of Burns supporters is already waiting outside. Many have stuck the candidate's portrait into their hat bands. Suddenly, a large sheaf of agitational literature shoots up into the air out of the dense crowd: pamphlets, leaflets, political cartoons fall on all sides. Leaflet No. 1232 lands in my hands, a pamphlet issued by the 'Liberal Federation' and entitled 'A Rake's Progress' after a series of Hogarth caricatures.

[Shklovsky quotes a paragraph from the pamphlet about the Government squandering its budget surplus on 'wars, gifts to landlords, the clergy and denominational schools' and going into deficit as a result, instead of using it to introduce the promised old age pensions. The 'shameful Kynoch affair' (the War Office arms procurement scandal) is again invoked.]

But it looks like the public does not need to be won over by propaganda. Judging by the jokes and sporadic exclamations, it is sufficiently charged with animosity towards 'Birmingham politics' as it is.[53] Several 'khaki'-clad people are handing out pamphlets and leaflets with portraits of Burns to the crowd. I recall that the '**Pall Mall**' [*Gazette*] and the '**Daily Express**' had solemnly condemned Burns for outfitting his 'canvassers' (voting agents) in 'khaki', the patriotic colour. To which Burns replied that his canvassers were genuine army reservists who had returned from South Africa. They had come back with such a hatred of the war and the Government that they had offered their services (entirely disinterestedly) to Burns. In total, there are around seventy thousand army reservists.[54] They say that the vast majority of them are against the Government. And 'Joe' had brought forward the general election, among other reasons, to prevent those reservists who are still in South Africa from voting against the Government.

---

53   'Birmingham politics': Chamberlain's or Liberal Unionist politics. See Andrew Reekes, *The Birmingham Political Machine: Winning Elections for Joseph Chamberlain* (Alcester: West Midlands History Limited, 2018).

54   It is possible that Shklovsky is referring to the Royal Reserve Regiments established in 1900. For a contemporary imperialist account of the Reserves, see Filson Young, *The Relief of Mafeking* (London: Methuen, 1900), chapter 1, 'How the Reserves Came Up'.

There is an explosion of laughter in the crowd. Someone begins to sing verses newly composed in parody of the English nursery rhyme, 'Who Killed Cock Robin?'. 'Who started the war? I, Old Joe, for my own ends I started the war!', sings a gentleman in a flat cap and a resplendent red tie. 'Who lied to the public? I, Cecil Rhodes, empire builder, I lied to the public.' 'And who'll have to pay for the war? The public, the stupid public, will have to pay for the war.'

The song is such a success that improvisors appear on the spot to carry on the parody. 'And who'll line their pockets after the war? The stock-jobbers! They'll line their pockets.'

V.

The clock strikes eight. The doors open. The crowd surges into the hall like a great living stream and at once overflows into all the seats below and in the galleries. It looks like they know each other very well. On the platform, the guests are still arriving. For the most part, these are local notables, members of the parish council,[55] secretaries of Radical clubs, and so on. Now loud applause breaks out. They are welcoming a tall old man with a shaved moustache and a somewhat eccentric suit: the former professor of political economy and well-known figure in Parliament, Leonard Courtney.[56]

[Shklovsky proceeds to give a synopsis of Courtney's political career, his opposition to the South African War, the indignation of his jingoist Bodmin constituents and his resignation of his seat in Parliament together with the Conservative Edward Clarke. After a peroration on the persistence of that 'old England which commands such respect around the world', Shklovsky invokes Gogol's Cossack hero Taras Bulba to assert that if a leader like John Bright were to arise now to throw back the hordes of 'financial capital and Birmingham politicians', he would gain support from representatives of 'both parties'.]

Leonard Courtney was hounded by the patriotic press, such as the **Daily Mail** and the **Daily Express**. Thugs were bribed to smash the old man's windows and to pursue him in the streets, but like a true Englishman, Courtney remained tenacious and persistent. Leonard Courtney's views differ from Burns's on many points, but they respect each other and both strive for the same goal: the good of England. In

---

55 By 'parish council' Shklovsky means not a powerless rural body but the Vestry, which was the local authority before the Metropolitan Borough Councils were elected on 1 November 1900; the general election was the month before.

56 Leonard Courtney (1832–1918) was an anti-imperialist Radical Liberal MP and prominent politician who resigned over the Boer War. See Eleanor Tench, 'Joseph Chamberlain and Leonard Courtney: Freely Disagreeing Radicals?', in Cawood and Upton, 116–29.

view of this, Courtney has made an appearance at the meeting and taken his place on the platform... There is more thunderous applause. They are welcoming a lady who is leading by the hand a little, chubby three-year-old boy in a white cloak.[57] It is Burns's wife and son.

'Three cheers for young Jack Burns!' someone in the audience proposes. The mother wants the boy to bow, but the toddler stands motionless, his chubby little legs spread wide apart. The applause becomes deafening. John Burns appears on the platform, a broad-shouldered sturdy man with a grey beard and sparkling black eyes. I have heard him speak many times, in Parliament and at meetings,[58] but Burns must be heard in Battersea, where he seems to be on close friendly terms with his audience. Burns's powerful voice has grown much weaker lately, whether by reason of frequent open-air meetings or the electoral campaign. He gives a sign with his hand, and everyone falls silent. He must begin, he says, contrary to his wish, by talking about himself. His political adversaries are slandering him mercilessly and so he must, before all else, establish the truth. Burns recounts how he used to be a mechanic and how he defended the interests of the working class at meetings to the best of his ability, until the people of Battersea sent him first to the London County Council and then to Parliament. 'All my life thereafter is well-known to you.' There is loud applause. My neighbour tells me that 'Jack', like other MPs, has received numerous offers of various company directorships, but has refused categorically and continues to live on the three pounds a week allotted to him by his constituents.

'If you judge me as a man', Burns continues, 'you will re-elect me now.'

'Take heart, John! Your seat in Parliament is secure!', shouts a gentleman who is, judging by his clothes, a navvy.

Burns presents his programme.

[Shklovsky summarises Burns's speech, which sets out his position as 'a Collectivist in economics and a Democrat in politics'; his support for the 'abolition of the House of Lords, land nationalisation, old age pensions, the eight-hour working day and free education'; and his criticisms of the Tory government and the Boer War (in which he is supported by the people of Battersea), with particular blame allotted to Chamberlain, the 'patriotic' press and Cecil Rhodes's connections with the Daily Mail. *He concludes by wishing to see the day when the* Mail's *Harmsworth is 'sentenced to seven years' hard labour'.]*

---

57   The original text has 'burnous' – a white cloak with a pointed hood.
58   See *Hansard* for Burns's speeches in Parliament in 1900: 'Mr John Burns: Contributions, 1900', *Hansard*, https://api.parliament.uk/historic-hansard/people/mr-john-burns/1900.

To loud applause, the meeting passes a vote of confidence in John Burns. But he is not the hero of the evening. That honour goes to another speaker, Dr Clifford – a pale, withered, bent old man with large round spectacles and one of the most popular public speakers in England.[59] Burns speaks very well: he completely captivates his audience, knows it to perfection and can work in a witticism or a pun, which the English love so much, in a timely manner. But you always feel that the speaker has it all mapped out and calculated beforehand. He is a skilled mechanic who is firmly and calmly manipulating the movements of a complex machine. John Burns can always tell – in the moment of speaking – whether a joke is needed, and if so, what kind, to help his listeners understand his reasoning better. He is a Scotsman through and through,[60] never at a loss for words but also never touching the heights of poetry. Burns appeals to the public by his logic, the clarity and force of his arguments and, finally, by that dedication to the cause which even his political opponents value highly.

Dr Clifford, on the other hand, is a poet-orator. When he begins to speak, he transforms completely. He stands before his listeners, no longer a frail, stooping old man, but a vigorous tribune of the people. Both Burns and Clifford come from humble origins. But Burns has retained the broad shoulders of a mechanic, whereas Clifford, who was a weaver before the age of twenty and read for his bachelor's degree in fits and starts, is a sheer bundle of nerves.

Dr Clifford's speech is a passionate denunciation of the policies of the Government and Joe in particular.

[Shklovsky gives a transcript of the highlights of Dr Clifford's speech, inclusive of audience reactions, such as the boos and whistles that greet the mentions of Chamberlain and the applause lasting 'two minutes' that greets Clifford's enumeration of worthy 'ancestors' such as Milton ('freedom of speech'), Cromwell ('freedom of conscience'), Robert Owen, the Chartists, Cobden and Bright and 'last but not least', Gladstone. This is a Liberal genealogy that is explicitly juxtaposed with the Tory 'brewers, landlords and clergy'. Clifford concludes with a call to arms to fight for rights and the truth like 'our great grandfathers did!'.]

The feeble, frail old man draws himself up. He seems now a head taller than he was. He truly does now produce the impression of being a worthy heir of great ancestors. A little old lady in a white bonnet and spectacles who is seated on the platform wipes her eyes with a

---

59 John Clifford (1836–1923) was a Nonconformist minister with several degrees from the University of London and a prominent anti-Boer War campaigner.
60 Burns's father was Scottish, though he himself, as Shklovsky notes above, was a Battersea native. It is interesting to observe the Scottish national stereotypes at play here.

handkerchief and claps her wrinkled, withered hands. This is Dr Clifford's wife, his faithful companion, who has shared in many of his sorrows. Dr Clifford is a Dissenting minister. 'The *khaki*-coloured religion' has become the province of almost all the churches,[61] Anglican and Methodist, but there are exceptions, though not many...

The meeting is at an end. They are still applauding the speakers in the hall, but most of the audience are on their way out. In the street, there is a large, close-packed crowd – those of Burns's supporters who did not make it into the hall for lack of space. Now applause and shouts of *hurrah!* fill the air. Burns has arrived. The crowd details a deputation to request him to say a few words. A huge box is produced immediately out of nowhere, which Burns mounts as he would a rostrum.

Again, pamphlets, caricatures and proclamations circulate through the crowd.

[For the next several pages Shklovsky departs on a rhetorical flight praising the awakening of the freedom-loving English 'Demos' and a historical excursus into the various Reform Acts from 1832 onwards. He concludes by noting that the political demands which were considered impossibly absurd in the time of the Chartists are now considered 'completely natural even by extreme Conservatives'.]

Battersea is bathed in the bright rays of the autumn sun. The number of posters and caricatures has increased tremendously. The caricatures put up by the imperialists predominate. The pub windows are plastered all over especially thickly, and from their wide-open doors come patriotic exclamations and snatches of songs like 'The Soldiers of the Queen'. At the bar is an impenetrable crowd of beer-swollen men and blowsy women in broken hats. Speeches are delivered in support of Joe, the Queen and the destruction of traitors.

[In the following paragraph Shklovsky describes several patriotic, pro-war and anti-Radical posters.]

One cannot say that there are no caricatures put up by Burns's supporters. Their aim is to show how destructive the imperialist policies are for England.

---

[61] I have been unable to locate a specific source for the phrase; however, the association between religion, patriotic support for war and the khaki colour was firmly established at the turn of the century and continued into World War I. See Jane Potter, *Boys in Khaki, Girls in Print: Women's Literary Responses to the Great War 1914–1918* (Oxford: Oxford University Press, 2005), 27 referring to the *Girl's Own Paper* of 1900 where 'An open-air religious service, for instance, is called "a study in khaki", and the colour becomes emblematic of the War itself'; and Jonathan F. Vance, *Death So Noble: Memory, Meaning, and the First World War* (Vancouver: UBC Press, 1997) on patriotic support for the war preached from the Methodist pulpit in Canada in 1914, with khaki being declared 'a sacred colour' (35).

The streets are unusually busy. Crowds of voters are moving towards the 'booths', i.e. the polling stations where they cast their votes. Voters are being brought in carriages, traps, cabs, automobiles, covered wagons, and so on. Gentlemen in top hats and black frockcoats have pinned on huge patriotic rosettes with portraits of Garton. They seem to have high hopes for victory. The *Evening News*, the evening edition of the *Daily Mail*,[62] predicts that 'with one exertion the patriots of London will cover themselves in lasting glory. The conquest of Battersea will mean the final defeat of England's detractors.'

There are shouts of 'hurrah!' in the street. Burns quickly passes by on his bicycle, hastening to one of the 'booths'.[63]

'Traitor!', a bloated woman emerging from a pub shouts after him, her dirty, undone hair escaping from under her hat.

'Well, how's it going?' one passer-by in a corduroy jacket asks another with a carpet bag full of tools over his shoulder.

'Looks like it's going well. Johnny's safe.'

And here is a handmade poster in the window of an optimistic barber, forecasting victory. 'A shave: Radicals – 2d., Conservatives – 3d., on account of more work – they'll have long faces after Johnny is elected. Surely contractors from Hoskins, Kynoch, Elliott's and Co. won't rule England?'

The local paper analyses the odds in favour and against the candidates. Burns has the support of all trade unionists and the majority of people of liberal professions who live in the constituency. Garton has the support of the 'villa' dwellers, i.e. clerks, many shopkeepers and those who *buy from them on tick*, also the pubs and the pub down-and-outs.[64] The words 'those who buy on tick' are very significant. The laws on voter bribery are now very strict and anticipate many of the tricks that were widely practised as recently as the seventies.[65] Direct or indirect bribery

---

[62] The *Evening News* was a very popular London halfpenny evening newspaper from 1881, which was bought by the Harmsworths (owners of the *Daily Mail*) in 1894.

[63] See Schneer, 256–57 for a description of the polling day: Burns on his bicycle, the behaviour of the supporters of the two candidates, the 'linen screen, lit from behind by an electric light' that announces the winner, Burns hoisted on the crowd's shoulders, etc.

[64] Such people would not have had the vote until the 1918 Representation of the People Act anyway. For an in-depth analysis of the political attitudes and voting patterns of the London 'poor', including some mentions of the situation in Battersea in 1900, see Marc Brodie, *The Politics of the Poor: The East End of London 1885–1914* (Oxford: Oxford University Press, 2004).

[65] Shklovsky is probably referring to the 1883 Corrupt and Illegal Practices Act, which criminalised attempts to bribe voters during parliamentary elections. The sanguine views he expresses in this paragraph of English respect for the law are not borne out by the long history of legislative attempts to deal with electoral corruption in the Victorian period. On electoral culture, see Angus Hawkins, *Victorian Political Culture: 'Habits of Heart and Mind'* (Oxford:

Fig. 52. Awaiting Election Results.

can now not only lead to the election being declared void but result in severe punishment (penal servitude). But even though the legislators had foreseen all the existing direct and indirect routes to bribery and had closed them off, they could not foresee that new loopholes would be found... To tell the truth, the English, whichever party they belong to, have a profound respect for the law in general and for anything to do with Parliament in particular. But exceptions are always possible...

It is getting dark. The streets are growing busier. Belated voters returning from work are hurrying to the 'booths' before they've even had a wash. The clock strikes eight. The voting is finished. The ballot boxes are moved to the town hall for the count. Supporters of both candidates have gathered in a huge crowd before the town hall. The

Oxford University Press, 2015). See also 'Reforming Elections', *UK Parliament*, www.parliament.uk/about/living-heritage/transformingsociety/electionsvoting/ elections-and-voting-in-the-19th-century/reforming-election-methods/.

clock strikes nine, ten, eleven o'clock. The crowd waits patiently and in a dignified manner, like true Englishmen. It can maintain order on its own, without the police, which is entirely surplus to requirements here.[66] Midnight strikes. Presently, a huge board above the entrance is illuminated by electricity. The name of the elected candidate is about to appear. A movement of impatience is noticeable in the calm crowd. 'John Burns' – a coloured sign lights up.

'Three cheers for Burns!' the crowd shouts.

'Hoorah! our Johnny!'

'Honest Jack for Battersea! hoorah!'

The shouts grow louder. Burns appears on the threshold. The crowd catches him up and carries him home on its shoulders.

'For he's a jolly good fellow!' a thousand voices sing the English song of praise... Burns's victory means more than just the simple defeat of Garton. It signifies that there are still places in England not intoxicated with the brew of imperialism distilled by Chamberlain. It proves that when the self-consciousness of the masses has awakened, it cannot be clouded even in such moments as England has lived through during the war.[67]

---

[66] This depiction contrasts sharply with contemporary English accounts of election violence, although Schneer confirms, quoting the *Southwestern Star*, that on this occasion 'the crowd was [...] well behaved, "orderly [...] anxious not to cause any disturbance." Perhaps they were aware of the large contingent of police, horse and foot, waiting in a side street to deal with the expected riots if Burns had lost' (257).

[67] Burns received 51.1 per cent of the vote (5,860 votes to Garton's 5,606).

Isaak Shklovsky [Dioneo], from 'Koroleva Viktoriya' ['Queen Victoria']

Sketches of Contemporary England (St Petersburg, 1903): 224–53[1]

I.

The enormous English newspapers are full of endless articles framed in black. The Queen, who outlived several generations and during whose reign the country so radically changed its aspect, is dead. The period that England is living through at the moment – the period that has bred its cultured savages, its all-powerful gutter press and other phenomena – has left its mark on the obituaries too.[2] The Queen's name is accompanied by strong adjectives, in the superlative degree to boot: she is 'the greatest', 'the wisest', 'the most brilliant', etc. The authors of the obituaries attribute even the recent rains to 'heaven itself weeping for the greatest of monarchs'. They then proceed to speak of the grief-stricken Englishmen, of the 'gloom of despair hanging over London', of 'the country's great loss', etc. The court Pindar, the Poet Laureate Austin, speaks of the victories she achieved, of 'Semiramis of the northern seas'.[3]

I think our readers will find it interesting to pick through the piles of funerary literature and ascertain to what extent we foreigners, as people of a different parish, can accept these strong adjectives. First, let us go to the London Forum, to Hyde Park. It is Saturday, the second of February. Today, the Queen's remains will be carried through London and on to Windsor, where she will be buried alongside the Prince Consort.[4] The endless park and all the streets converging on it are flooded by a living sea. All the shops, factories, houses, offices and banks are shut (on the initiative of the owners themselves). Hundreds of thousands of working people have now taken to the streets. Moreover, since yesterday trains have been bringing in provincials who have spent the whole night in the street. There are several million people in the park and the adjoining avenues. On the roofs, on the balconies, in the windows, on the ledges, everywhere one can drag some seats, there are thousands of spectators

---

[1]   Originally published as a Letter 'From England' under the pseudonym Dioneo in the monthly journal *Russkoe Bogatstvo*, February 1901, 74–102. The periodical publication begins: 'For more than ten days now, the enormous English newspapers […]'. Queen Victoria died on 22 January 1901.

[2]   Passages like this make it clear where Chukovsky picked up his notion of English people as 'cultured savages' and his wonderment at the size of English broadsheets.

[3]   Alfred Austin was Poet Laureate from 1896 to 1913. Part of his job description, like that of his predecessor in the post, Alfred Lord Tennyson, was the production of poems in praise of the reigning monarch.

[4]   British Pathé footage of 'Queen Victoria's Funeral (1901)' is available on *YouTube*: www.youtube.com/watch?v=t9yiG3EUz_A&ab_channel=BritishPath%C3%A9.

Fig. 53. Postcard Published on the Death of Queen Victoria, January 1901.

who have shown up with binoculars, with baskets full of victuals and with bottles of whisky.

Patriotism is all well and good, but business is business. As soon as the first news of the Queen's illness broke, a syndicate rented all the windows and roofs along the entire route between Victoria and Paddington stations along which the monarch would be carried if she died. The rented spaces were subject to massive speculation: a window on Piccadilly was being let out for 1,500 roubles, while a poor spot on the roof next to the smokestacks was going for seventy roubles, etc.

A living sea, like any other sea, is subject to ebbs and flows. A wave, having arisen at one edge of the living sea, travels to the other, where it forms a veritable breaker. In this living surf, women faint from the stifling heat produced by the breath coming from millions of lungs, while ribs, arms and legs crack and break. Then the surf suddenly recedes; there is a lull until a new wave comes. However, on the whole, this crowd's self-discipline is extraordinary. The mood is not at all funereal. Gentlemen in tweed caps try to extricate their arms from the living press to offer some vodka to the factory girls in huge hats decorated with bunches of garish feathers.[5] The girls shriek with laughter, pour the vodka over the gallants who are trying to treat them, etc. Now a wave of laughter rolls over the sea of heads, growing stronger and stronger as it passes. In the distance, a lady in a black hat, a pleated coat of the same colour and baggy tweed bloomers – apparently

---

[5]   As usual, Shklovsky uses 'vodka' to refer to spirits (gin).

Fig. 54. The Procession Through London: A Bird's-Eye View of the Cortège
Passing Through the Apsley Gate.

a member of the women's 'rational' dress society – is running across a
green towards a tall and mighty oak tree. Slung over the lady's shoulder
is a photographic camera; in her hands is a kind of coiled lasso.[6] A pair
of fat 'bobbies' (policemen) are chasing after the lady, panting for breath
and gesticulating. The lady has reached an elm tree, uncoiled her lasso,
thrown it over a thick branch, quickly and deftly climbed up the knotty
rope, straddled the branch and brought up her lasso. The 'bobbies' catch
up and invite the lady to get down, but she calmly points her camera at
the spot where the procession is due to appear. The crowd applauds and
shouts 'hurrah'. The 'bobbies' give it up and leave the lady in peace.

In one place, the crowd is observing some gentlemen in top hats in
a house opposite the park attempting to prise open a window frame so
they can gain a better view. The frame is well-fixed and does not give
way; the crowd's interest grows. Ironic remarks about the gentleman's
[*sic*] feebleness are heard; he is advised to drink some 'bovril' (beef
extract), etc. But now the frame cracks and gives way, and the crowd,
forgetting its taunts, is captivated by this success. It gives three cheers
for the gentleman whom it had just been mocking.[7]

---

6   This is a typical 'New Woman' of the 1890s. Shklovsky is referring to the Rational
    Dress Society, founded in 1881 to advocate for practical women's clothing, and
    discussed at more length in some of his other Letters, such as 'The Crank'.
7   Editor's paragraph break.

The public, wishing to get a better view, choose some extremely risky lookout points. All the trees are dotted with spectators. From afar, they look like enormous magpie nests among the bare branches. Here is someone crawling up the very steep roof of a belfry. There is a small stair near the cross, and it is this that the intrepid observer is trying to reach. The crowd is in a cheerful mood and is watching the daredevil attentively. Now his foot has slipped. He loses his balance and starts to roll but manages to grab hold of some bolt with his hand. And the sight of a man convulsively seeking some prop for his foot provokes laughter down below. But now the gymnast makes a desperate effort, pulls himself up with a strain of the muscles, finds a ledge with his foot, crawls up and soon reaches the little stair on the steps of which he takes his seat with a triumphant air. The crowd applauds. He accepts the applause as his due and takes a bow.

Normally, in a vast crowd, the living wave that forms a breaker is produced by the mounted guards trampling over the people. In the crowd gathered on the second of February, one could observe altogether distinctive, typically English scenes. The chain holding back the crowd consists of mounted yeomen. Familiar relations are soon established between them and the townspeople, especially the townswomen. In one spot, one can see a boy of eleven, proud as a lord, in the saddle in front of a yeoman; behind, on the horse's rump, sits a lady. Further on, an even more bucolic scene. A yeoman lifts up to his saddle a parlour maid in a white apron and white cap with long ribbons. The parlour maid puts an arm around the soldier's neck. Some young, handsome foreigner with a small blonde beard and long blonde hair seemingly arrives at the conclusion that he could see better from a horse's back. He approaches a yeoman and tugs at the hem of his tunic, but the foreigner's stock of English words must be severely limited. The young man confines himself to pointing at the saddle and saying: 'two shillings'. The yeoman silently offers the stirrup. But a ragged, beer-swollen gentleman clutches at the young man's short overcoat. A '*Kroojer*' is not fit to sit on a British horse, he shouts, the German can jolly well stand.[8]

Boom! Boom! resound the cannon shots announcing that the funeral procession has set off. The damp wind brings from afar the solemn, mournful sounds of Mozart's Funeral March. Soldiers appear, in red, blue and black. Now the crowd applauds and gives three cheers. A small, shrivelled old man in a cocked hat with a plume of cockerel feathers rides by on a horse. This is Roberts. In his hand is a red field-marshal's

---

[8]   Kruger is a German surname, but there is a further layer of irony here because of the direct reference to the Boer president (see previous notes). Anti-German sentiment was rife at the start of the twentieth century, as a result of economic and imperial competition (see the references to Tariff Reform *passim*), the German–Boer connection (see the Kruger Telegram), and invasion fears peddled by the popular press.

baton decorated with golden bees.[9] And looking at this shrivelled old man, I am reminded of an article I had read that very day. The patriotic papers had once reported, in order to illustrate the commander-in-chief's magnanimity of soul, that an orderly, appearing on one occasion before Roberts, found him with an infant Boer on his lap – the General was teaching the boy his ABCs.

'Do not interrupt the lesson!' the General told the orderly, 'business can wait.'

Patriots were exceedingly touched by this telegram;[10] lady patriots shed rivers of tears as they retold its contents. A popular artist painted a picture of the subject, which was a great success at the last Academy Exhibition and sold hundreds of thousands of prints.[11] In it, Roberts was depicted with a dishevelled black-haired boy on his lap, at a Boer inn in the Orange Free State. The success of the painting prompted another famous artist, Arthur Drummond, to adopt the same subject.[12] In the new painting, Roberts was no longer teaching a dishevelled lad but a smoothly combed fair-haired girl, gazing in awe at the courageous General. A City Volunteer was standing in the doors.[13] This painting, too, had enormous success, which moved a third artist, **Cress Woollett**,[14] to try his hand at the same subject. Out of patriotic feeling, the painter rendered the pupil in the guise of an English girl and drew a portrait of the Queen on the wall. A fourth artist took up the same theme, but wishing to be realistic, approached Roberts for instructions. The latter replied that the entire account was made up and without any basis, that he had much more important business than teaching little Boers their letters. Thus, three artists illustrated a fantasy; moreover, two poets eulogised it and three military historians inscribed it in the pages of their lucubrations. This is a minor fact, but it illustrates the scale of voluntary servility.

---

9   The baton awarded to Field-Marshal Roberts in 1895, to be carried on ceremonial occasions, was covered in crimson velvet and decorated with gold lions (it may be seen in the National Army Museum). Shklovsky must have mistaken the lions for bees, possibly because French marshals' batons did feature golden bees.

10   On newspaper 'telegrams', see note 33 in Shklovsky's 'Richard Kelly'.

11   See the catalogue of *The Exhibition of the Royal Academy of Arts MDCCCC: The One Hundred and Thirty-Second* (London: William Clowes and Sons, Limited, 1900) available at *The Royal Academy*, www.royalacademy.org.uk/art-artists/exhibition-catalogue/ra-sec-vol132-1900.

12   Arthur Drummond (1871–1951) was a student of Lawrence Alma-Tadema and Benjamin Constant and exhibited at the Royal Academy until 1901. He specialised in history, genre and neoclassical subjects.

13   See footnote 5 on Lord Mayor Newton in Shklovsky's 'Imperialism' Letter above.

14   See MacKenzie, *Propaganda and Empire*, who mentions Cress Woollett's painting 'Lord Roberts and the Innkeeper's Child' when discussing 'patriotism and militarism' in schools: the painting was reproduced as 'a supplement to the *Christian Globe* of January 1901' and was 'framed and hung' in schools (183).

[Shklovsky digresses to reflect on an exemplar of servility in Dostoevsky's The Idiot *and compares the character with his English real-life counterparts.]*

Meanwhile, the cannon are still thundering. If you close your eyes, you might think that the great metropolis is in danger of an enemy assault. One detachment of soldiers follows another. Only the British army and navy are represented in the procession. Voltaire's Micromégas,[15] were he to descend here on this day, might think that England has no literature, no science, no courts, no Parliament, no citizens, nothing except soldiers in uniforms of all colours. Now appears the funeral hearse drawn by eight bay horses, but it, too, has an overwhelmingly military character. The coffin (extremely small, one would think it was a child's, were it not for its width) is placed on a gun carriage. The bronze muzzle of a cannon sticks out from underneath the platform on which the coffin stands.

'She approaches!', the courtly Pindar hymns the funeral. 'Along the silent streets overflowing with multitudes, they carry her remains who was the nation's pride and honour. From shore to shore resound the thunders of her fleet and the music of her valiant host which has never known defeat... Instead of an epitaph, we need only enumerate the victories achieved by Britons.'[16] Reality is optional for the bards, and of course we shall not criticise the proposition that Her Majesty's warriors have never known defeat. Because the funeral has a predominantly military character, exclusively warlike notes also sound in the hymns of the Pindars. They say that the Queen herself worked out the details of the ceremony long before her death. They also say that the aim of an overwhelmingly military demonstration at the funeral of a very elderly lady famous for her family virtues is to strike a note in tune with the mood that has been prevalent in England for several years now and has taken particularly dramatic form recently, during the war.[17] However it may be, the Queen has now descended to her grave surrounded by universal love.[18] Sixty-three years ago she was extremely unpopular. Now her name has become a cult of sorts, especially among a certain class. How can we explain it? How much is the country's great progress really tied to the Queen's personality? To what extent must we, as impartial and alien observers, accept the term 'Victorian age',

---

[15] An alien visitor to planet Earth in Voltaire's *Le Micromégas* (1752) who observes human foibles.

[16] I have not been able to locate the original source, so this is a back-translation.

[17] Shklovsky devoted a lot of space to analysis of the causes and expressions of British militarism at the time of the Boer War in articles written during those years and collected in the 1903 volume.

[18] For more on Victoria's death and funeral, see Stewart Richards, *Curtain Down at Her Majesty's: The Death of Queen Victoria in the Words of Those Who Were There* (Stroud: The History Press, 2019).

which is now so widely used in England? I shall attempt to answer these questions. First, let us get a clear picture of the Queen's character and determine when exactly the cult of Victoria took hold and why.

[The rest of the Letter retails Victoria's biography in the context of the history of the Victorian period, assessing the reasons for the growth of her popularity over the decades and the evolving characteristics of the 'Victorian Age' itself, and including extensive quotations from her published diaries. Shklovsky reflects on the Queen's cultural tastes and political opinions, her 'cult' and her political co-optation; and concludes by quoting from the Liberal historian James Bryce and from Hammond's Speaker *newspaper on the role of the monarchy after Victoria's death.]*

Isaak Shklovsky [Dioneo], from 'Delo Beka' ['The Beck Case'] On the Themes of Liberty: An Article Collection, vol. 1 (St Petersburg, 1908): 129–57[1]

[Shklovsky opens this Letter – dedicated to miscarriages of justice – by enumerating various examples from Russian, French, etc. history and folklore. Every lawyer, he laments, knows that the wrongfully accused are far from an exception in judicial practice, although the public only rarely finds out about such errors (as in the Dreyfus Case). He concludes with a warning that even in the most civilised states, the innocent can be convicted because of the existence of investigative institutions not subject to public oversight that would rather send them to jail than admit their mistakes.]

II.

It is April 1903.[2] A cramped, dark and dirty hall, which seems bespattered with spittle however much it is cleaned, is gloomy despite the fine day.

---

[1] Originally published as a Letter 'From England' under the pseudonym Dioneo in the monthly journal *Russkoe Bogatstvo*, October 1904, 22–45. In the excerpted section of the Letter, Shklovsky describes the trial of the serial killer George Chapman (1865–1903) for the murder of Maud Eliza Marsh that took place in the Central Criminal Court, Old Bailey, London, in March 1903; he was executed in April. George Chapman was one of the Jack the Ripper suspects. See Helena Wojtczak, *Jack the Ripper at Last? The Mysterious Murders of George Chapman* (Hastings: The Hastings Press, 2014) and chapter 22 on Chapman in Philip Sugden, *The Complete History of Jack the Ripper*, rev. ed. (London: Constable & Robinson, 2006). A useful collation of primary sources may be found in 'George Chapman (1865–1903)', *Casebook: Jack the Ripper*, www.casebook.org/suspects/gchapman.html; a part of the trial transcript is available in 'Trial of SEVERINO KLOSOWSKI (36) alias GEORGE CHAPMAN (t19030309-318)', March 1903, *Old Bailey Proceedings Online*, www.oldbaileyonline.org; see also Hargrave L. Adam, ed. *Trial of George Chapman* (Edinburgh: William Hodge, 1930) in the Notable British Trials series. The spelling 'Klosowski' will be used here to conform with the original usage in the trial transcript.

[2] There is an uncanny resemblance between Shklovsky's account in this section and George R. Sims's chapter 'A Trial at the Old Bailey', in Sims, *Living London* 1, 107–13, published the year before the Chapman trial. Sims describes the trial of an unnamed murderer, but though his account is entirely unsympathetic to the prisoner, unlike Shklovsky's, it gives a good insight into Shklovsky's method of composition. Sims opens, like Shklovsky, by introducing the small chamber of the Old Bailey, Newgate prison and the mobs who gathered there for public executions; he concludes, like Shklovsky, with the newsboys shouting the verdict; and along the way he references the same details, such as the 'Black Maria' waiting in the courtyard and the distinguished public figures among the spectators, including literary men, actors and a general. The proceedings on the day of the trial are described in the same order and sometimes in the exact same words: the entrance of the Lord Chief Justice preceded by the Lord Mayor and other City officials,

This is the **Old Bailey**, the famous chamber of the London criminal court that before 1905 had been located next to Newgate Prison, in which several hundred people were executed.[3] Once upon a time, on the night before an execution, a great mob of vagabonds, prostitutes, thieves and the blasé rich would assemble before the prison gates where a gallows was being erected. They would drink deep, sing, dance and brawl until dawn, while from the belfry opposite the prison the death knell tolled for the man who was still, at that moment, alive. When the wicket in the *debtor's gate* was opened and the condemned man appeared, tied hand and foot, the drunken mob would greet him with shouts, catcalls and obscene curses that mingled with the sounds of the death knell. Sometimes the condemned man would faint. The crowd would then not only whistle but pelt him with dirt. Sometimes, he proved to be a courageous man with nerves of steel. In that case, he would toss the mob a grim joke or an obscene curse as he ascended the scaffold. Then the mob would applaud and shout 'hooray'. Smollett (*Roderick Random*), Fielding (*Jonathan Wild*), and then in the nineteenth century Dickens (*Oliver Twist*) have all given us dreadful portraits of the mob awaiting an execution.[4] In the early sixties, a brilliant French political writer and historian wrote: 'An immense multitude, excited to an extraordinary degree, and, if I may say so, famished with curiosity, inundates, several hours before the time of the looked-for performance, all the approaches

---

the speech of the Counsel for the Defence, which raises the prisoner's hopes, the aspersions cast on the police who have prepared the evidence for the case, the King's Counsel (for the prosecution), who 'reweaves the evidence, twisting the separate strands into a hangman's rope' and 'drives nail after nail into the coffin of a living man', the two warders who support the apprehensive prisoner, the rumour that 'one Juryman is against capital punishment', the journalists who wonder 'Will there be time for dinner? Will it be safe to go to a restaurant?', the jury's quick return, the exchange between the judge and the foreman, the prisoner's response: 'Only that I am innocent, sir', the judge's black cap, the chaplain's 'Amen' and the crowd in the street. It is therefore almost certain that Shklovsky's version of the Chapman trial is not eyewitness testimony, but a fictionalisation closely based on Sims's *Living London* chapter (Shklovsky's 'errors' are, in fact, details borrowed from Sims). He may also have had in mind the many fictional courtroom scenes set in the Old Bailey chambers, such as the trial of Fagin in Dickens's *Oliver Twist* and the murder trial of Josh Perrott in Morrison's *A Child of the Jago*. See also the brief *Punch* interlude 'A Full Measure of Justice', 11 March 1893, with illustration, to get a sense of the choreography of Old Bailey court proceedings in the period. An image of a courtroom at the Old Bailey at the turn of the century may be seen in Mark D. Herber, *Criminal London: A Pictorial History from Medieval Times to 1939* (Chichester: Phillimore, 2002).

3   The original periodical publication continues 'until the beginning of this year'.
4   Shklovsky is referring to Tobias Smollett's *The Adventures of Roderick Random* (London: J. Osborn, 1748), Henry Fielding's *The History of the Life of Mr Jonathan Wild, The Great* (London, 1743) and Charles Dickens's *Oliver Twist; or, The Parish Boy's Progress* (London: Richard Bentley, 1838).

to the spot devoted to executions. It is quite natural. There is always a crowd waiting at the door of a theatre when a good piece is announced. But how pass the time until the hangman appears, which corresponds to what is called the *lever du rideau*? Sleep? Impossible, not because it would be necessary to sleep under the canopy of the stars, but because the expectation of a great pleasure drives away sleep. Accordingly, the time is passed in drinking, singing, swearing, chaffing... The business of hanging having for its object to terrify criminals by example, the spectacle is especially intended for all the thieves, all the pickpockets, all the rogues in the capital. They know it, and consequently are eager to honour the place with their presence, the more so that such a vast assemblage of individuals, and the confusion that must ensue therefrom, offer to these folks in process of conversion by example, an admirable opportunity of gathering in a harvest of purses, watches, and handkerchiefs.'[5]

Subsequently, executions were moved inside the prison, to a special *shed* where not even representatives of the press were admitted. Nevertheless, there would always be a crowd waiting outside the walls of Newgate Prison on the morning of an execution, to listen to the death knell tolling for a person who was still alive and to watch the black flag being raised over the roof when the doctor pronounced the condemned man dead. In 1905,[6] the ancient Newgate Prison that stood in the heart of the City was torn down. Executions were moved to another prison, but the court, the **Old Bailey**, just as dreadful and dismal as it was a hundred years ago, has remained.

We are in the courtroom. The session has not yet begun. In the press box hasty preparations are afoot. Three or four dozen old and very young reporters are sharpening their pencils hurriedly. The trial, which is supposed to finish today, has agitated Londoners and the evening editions of newspapers are selling like hotcakes. The courtroom is still empty. Occasionally, young men in black gowns and grey wigs with braids hurry past fussily. These are beginner barristers who are studying 'precedents'. In England, jurisprudence is studied not in universities but in solicitors' offices and law chambers. The art consists in learning as many 'precedents' as possible. The ethics of advocacy here are highly

---

5   Shklovsky's note: Louis Blanc, 'Lettres sur l'Angleterre'.
     Editor's note: Shklovsky is quoting Letter XXXV, 'The Gallows' of 20 October 1861. I have reproduced the text from Louis Blanc, *Letters on England*, trans. James Hutton, vol. 1 (London: Sampson Low, Son, and Marston, 1866), 174–75. Shklovsky omits the sentence describing female spectators. *Lever du rideau* means 'the raising of the curtain'.
6   The original periodical publication has 'this year'. It is not clear why Shklovsky put 1905 here when Newgate was, indeed, demolished in 1904. Hangings took place outside the prison until 1868, when they were moved inside. Shklovsky's favourite Dickens was one of the campaigners against public executions.

flexible and have not advanced far beyond those which were described by Swift. Beginner barristers sometimes search out their '**briefs**', i.e. their practical training, in courtrooms. They get a rich harvest from trials ensuing from breach of promise of marriage. Young barristers seek out such suits and undertake them on a 'half-and-half' basis.[7]

The courtroom has begun to fill with people. Prominent generals, men of letters, artists and public figures are pointed out. The trial is a cause célèbre and has given rise to endless rumours. The jury benches are already occupied. The faces there, clean-shaven or moustachioed, are for the most part expressionless. Or, more precisely, these faces are frozen in a single expression: 'I wish I could get this over with quickly and get back to work in the office or shop.' The majority of the jurors are clerks or shopkeepers. Presently, the courtroom grows silent. The court bailiff or *Usher* flings the doors wide open and jumps aside. The main judge or **lord chief justice** walks in, pacing slowly, in a grey wig and long robe trimmed with ermine.[8] The court is in the City, so the judge is preceded by the Lord Mayor and two Aldermen, also wearing medieval crimson robes trimmed with fur. These are not judicial advisors but only an honorary escort. In England, cases are heard by a single judge. The face of the Justice seems hewn of stone. No movement can be discerned in it. The eyes under the bushy eyebrows are also stone-like. For a man with such a face, there are no live human beings who are moved by joys or sorrows, there are only more or less complicated 'precedents'. English judges, as is well known, are selected from amongst the most talented and knowledgeable barristers. To make them entirely independent, judges are surrounded with such esteem as nowhere on the Continent. They are replaced only if they commit a crime. Their colossal remuneration should make bribery completely impossible. Theoretically, a judge is outside all parties, although in practice, unwittingly perhaps, he sometimes reflects the views of the class to which he belongs. On the whole, English judges command the most profound respect of foreign observers thanks to their impartiality. This is especially true of those who try criminal cases, although exceptions are, of course, possible.[9]

7   Shklovsky uses the old-fashioned Russian word for the metayage (halving) system, in which the cultivator of land pays half the produce as rent to the landowner.
8   In fact, the judge was Mr Justice William Grantham, also at some point a Tory MP, and not the Lord Chief Justice.
9   Cf. George Orwell's description in *The Lion and the Unicorn: Socialism and the English Genius* (1941), in Sonia Orwell and Ian Angus, eds. *The Collected Essays, Journalism and Letters*, vol. 2 (Boston, MA: Nonpareil Books, 2000): 'The hanging judge, that evil old man in scarlet robe and horse-hair wig, whom nothing short of dynamite will ever teach what century he is living in, but who will at any rate interpret the law according to the books and will in no circumstances take a money bribe, is one of the symbolic figures of England. He is a symbol of the strange mixture of reality and illusion, democracy and privilege, humbug and decency,

Fig. 55. A Trial at the Old Bailey Before the Lord Chief Justice.

The main judge lowers himself into his ancient black armchair. After a minute, the sign being given, the defendant is brought in. His character is an enigma to everyone.[10] He is a man of about thirty-eight years, with a strong, energetic and handsome face. His name is Chapman. He was the proprietor of an inn.[11] One of the barmaids who worked for him, with whom Chapman was close, died in circumstances which raised suspicions of poisoning. The autopsy revealed the presence of antimony. Chapman was very affectionate towards Maud Marsh (that was the dead girl's name), whom he intended to marry. When the young woman was ill, Chapman took care of her and spent whole nights sitting by her bedside, administering the medicines himself. Chapman was arrested, although he kept swearing that he knew nothing. It was then recalled that he had been married twice to barmaids who had served in his establishments. Both wives died after living no more than a year with their husband.[12] Their corpses were exhumed, and the autopsy showed the presence of antimony. Chapman was put on trial on the charge of

---

the subtle network of compromises, by which the nation keeps itself in its familiar shape' (63).

[10]   'Character': the Russian word Shklovsky uses also means 'identity', which is significant given the centrality of Chapman's true identity to the trial and Shklovsky's concerns later in the article.

[11]   Shklovsky is presumably referring to the Monument Tavern that Chapman leased, though he ran other pubs before that.

[12]   They were Mary Spink (d. 1897) and Bessie Taylor (d. 1901). Both were poisoned with the same compound as Marsh (d. 1902).

poisoning three women.[13] Preliminary investigations in England are carried out by **Scotland Yard**, i.e. police detectives who collect facts for the trial. The **Scotland Yard** officials found in Chapman's possession several medical books, including a pharmacopeia bookmarked at a page describing the effects of antimony. The bookmark turned out to be a chemist's receipt for dispensing antimony. At the preliminary hearing, which is held in open court in England in the presence of the jury, the defence counsel and the public, Chapman denied his guilt. He insisted that he had never purchased antimony and never bookmarked any pages in the pharmacopeia. All this was done by others, possibly the **Scotland Yard** policemen.

The mere circumstance of the three poisoned wives would have made the trial the talk of the town; but the **Scotland Yard** detectives had an even more sensational fact in reserve for the public. George Chapman, the detectives announced, was not the man he purported to be. He was not an American at all, but the Pole Severin Klosowski, who first worked as a doctor's assistant in Kalisz and then moved to London in the eighties.[14] The police produced two witnesses: a barber for whom Klosowski had worked when he arrived in London and a Polish woman to whom he had been married in Russia.[15] The witnesses identified Chapman as Klosowski (that being said, the wife made a mistake at first), although the defendant categorically denied this identification and stubbornly insisted that he was a natural-born American of Irish parentage. The following circumstance is curious. A foreigner can master any Continental language perfectly and speak it without the least accent. Neither is it difficult to learn to speak English more correctly and formally than many Englishmen; but it is very hard to get rid of all traces of an accent. The reason is the peculiar nature of English diphthongs, whose nuances are very hard to catch and even harder to get across. An Englishman who is used to his native diphthongs finds it very hard to shed them when learning a foreign language. An Englishman finds it just as difficult to get rid of his accent when speaking, say, French as a Russian does to acquire a perfect English pronunciation. Chapman, or Klosowski, spoke English without any foreign accent whatever, unless you count an American '**twang**' (a rapid nasal manner of speech).[16] The

---

13 Chapman was only tried for the murder of Marsh.
14 'Kalisz': it is not clear why Shklovsky mentions this Polish city. Chapman was apprenticed to a surgeon in Zwoleń and then worked as a doctor's assistant in Warsaw.
15 Chapman was from Congress Poland, which de facto belonged to the Russian Empire. The 'Polish woman', still his legal wife, later came to London, by which point Chapman was already living with someone else. The barber was probably Abraham Radin.
16 It would be interesting to know if Shklovsky invented this detail or was relying on the testimony of native speakers. Chapman did spend about a year living in the

magistrate committed Chapman-Klosowski for trial. For seven days now his case has been examined. For seven days, the defendant has borne up surprisingly well and has denied everything categorically. The day I was in court the closing arguments finally began.

The public prosecutor (the *King's Counsel* as he is called) began to adduce facts which told against the defendant with remarkable cogency.[17] Each fact represented a kind of nail which the King's Counsel drove into the coffin of a living man. The newspaper reporters, reproducing the speech later, wrote: 'the prosecutor once again wove together all the charges and wound the individual facts into a noose for Klosowski's neck'. Sometimes defendants break down during this process of 'noose-winding' and faint, which is why two burly warders stand behind them during the prosecutor's speech. They were standing behind Chapman-Klosowski as well, ready to support him in case of a swoon. But the defendant was, it seemed, a tough man. A few times his face grew pale. Once or twice his thick hairy hands shook nervously; but then his face would resume its calm, confident expression.

The prosecutor finished. In the courtroom in that moment many were reminded of a verse from Oscar Wilde's ballad:

'That fellow's got to swing.'[18]

But presently, the Counsel for the Defence began to speak. The average English juror will not yield to any sentimental inducements. He only wishes to know: did such and such a man commit a crime or not? If he has committed it, then he is guilty, because motives are of no concern for the ordinary English clerk. He will pronounce a man 'guilty' and send him to the gallows whatever motivations had driven him to murder. Defence solicitors know this, of course, and their only system of defence is denial. The Counsel's speech was masterful. He tried to tear every thread woven by the prosecutor. But in practice, in English courts, the defender's job ends when the witnesses have been examined. A skilful defence solicitor can throw a dangerous witness and compromise him in the eyes of the jury by a clever cross-examination, or worm out important testimony even from experienced police officials.

USA in 1891–1892, but one of the reasons he is frequently disqualified from being a Jack the Ripper suspect is because of the assumption that his English could not have been good enough. Shklovsky's observations about the difficulty a Pole would have had in losing his accent are borne out in the case of Chapman's contemporary Joseph Conrad, who reputedly never lost his heavy Polish accent despite learning to write English 'more correctly and formally than many Englishmen'.

17 All senior barristers were KCs; in this case the Solicitor-General, a law officer of the Crown who was also an MP, prosecuted.

18 Oscar Wilde's *The Ballad of Reading Gaol* (London: Leonard Smithers, 1898) about his incarceration in Reading Gaol from 1895 to 1897. The poem is dedicated to a man who was executed by hanging for murdering his wife, so is particularly appropriate in the circumstances.

But during closing arguments, as I saw for myself, rank-and-file jurors *never* listen to the Defence Counsel.

It was not hard to see that only one person was listening to the solicitor with rapt attention – Chapman himself. In all likelihood, the arguments put forward by the defence appeared to the accused to be incontrovertible. Blood once again flowed to his cheeks. It seemed the speech had awoken hope within him. But now the solicitor had finished. The King's Counsel rose again and in a few minutes not a trace was left of the entire line of defence. Chapman grew pale once more. The stony-faced judge proceeded to sum up the case for the jury in a cold, calm tone. Then the jurors were led away to the deliberation room. It grew dark. The gas was lit. The spectators, agitated by the trial, huddled together in groups, trying to guess the verdict. Many were anxious not about the outcome – they knew a guilty verdict was inevitable – but about when the jurors would return. Would there be time to run across the road to a pub to get some dinner? According to English law, the jury has to reach a unanimous verdict. If even one juror doggedly holds his ground, the others must bring him around, which can take a long time. If the jurors fail to persuade their comrade, then the case has to be tried again with a new composition of the court. One of the journalists predicted that the jurors would probably deliberate for a while because one of them was a principled opponent of the death penalty. But twenty minutes later, a bell sounded from the deliberation room. Two minutes more, and the judge, the defence solicitor, the King's Counsel and the defendant were in their places. Next to the judge now stood a new personage: the prison chaplain in a black cassock with hanging sleeves – a smooth, well-fed man in spectacles, with a carefully trimmed beard. Behind the defendant were the two burly warders, ready to support him at any moment.

'**Gentlemen of the jury**', the cold voice of the Chief Justice rang out amidst the leaden silence, 'have you reached a unanimous verdict?'.

'Yes', came the laconic response from the foreman, a clerk at some large bank.

'Do you find the prisoner at the bar guilty or not guilty?'

'**Guilty**', said the foreman with a light tremor in his voice. He knew that this word meant death. I could see that in the courtroom many had turned pale. Chapman swayed slightly and clutched the railing convulsively. The warders sprang to support him, but the defendant had already recovered and looked at the judge boldly when the latter asked:

'Do you know of any reason why the sentence of death should not be passed upon you?'

'Only one: I am not guilty!' Chapman almost shouted.

A sign was given and a clerk came up and placed a handkerchief-sized piece of black cloth on the judge's wig, the infamous *black cap* that signifies a sentence of death.

'Severin Klosowski', began the judge. 'The Lord endowed you with an exceptional intellect and great energy. You have studied and read widely. But you have used all your talents to commit a dastardly, treacherous, vile and cruel crime of which you now stand convicted. For this, I sentence you to be hanged by the neck till you be dead. **And may the Lord have mercy on your soul.**'

'Amen', intoned the black-clothed chaplain, folding his plump arms. Chapman, or Klosowski, barely managed to shout out 'I'm not guilty' before the warders seized him and dragged him towards the entrance where the prison carriage, or *Black Maria* as it is called, was already waiting.[19] The crowd in the street started to hoot and jeer. Even before Chapman reached the prison, he could already hear boys crying the 'extra-special editions' of the evening papers that carried reports of the death sentence.

The Chapman case made a horrifying impression upon me. I came out of the courtroom shattered and subdued. To this day I do not know what to make of this case. On the one hand, a series of categorical witness statements; on the other, categorical denial until the last moment. Chapman declared that he was innocent of the crime not only in court, when there was hope of acquittal, but also later, awaiting execution, when the condemned sits

> **... with silent men**
> **Who watch him night and day;**
> **Who watch him when he tries to weep,**
> **And when he tries to pray;**
> **Who watch him lest himself should rob**
> **The prison of its prey.**[20]

Chapman, or Klosowski, was a devout Catholic and spent a long time praying with his confessor before his death. Nevertheless, already standing on the scaffold, Klosowski for the last time made the same declaration he had made in court.

'Everything that is about to happen', he says in his last letter on the eve of the execution, 'I shall accept as a punishment for my sins but not for the crime which I did not commit... You have heard that a Russian woman discovered by the police swore in court that I was her husband, Klosowski. I swear to you that I have never seen her in my life.'

Chapman's execution involved an episode which led to a Parliamentary Question. When the convict was standing on the scaffold with a sack over his head and a noose around his neck and the executioner was preparing to lower the trapdoor, the confessor exclaimed:

---

[19]   Horse-harnessed Black Marias were still used by the police in the 1910s.
[20]   Shklovsky's note: [Russian translation of quotation given] **"The Ballad of Reading Gaol"**, *Oscar Wilde.*

'Severin Klosowski, here on the threshold of eternity, will you confess your guilt or not?'

'No!' a hoarse voice was heard.

A second later, the trapdoor under the convict's feet opened.[21]

Until recently, many of those who were unsettled by the description of this horrible scene had reassured themselves with the thought that the testimony of the witnesses established Klosowski's guilt. The testimonies were very precise. Each of them formed a separate link in a long chain. Now that the case of Adolf Beck has surfaced and perturbed the whole of England, the public's confidence in – not witness testimony, but the impartiality of those who pre-select facts for the prosecution, has wavered considerably. Before recounting the Beck case, let us see how a preliminary investigation is conducted in England. Court proceedings here are close to ideal. The defendant's identity is, it seems, guaranteed by the widest possible disclosure, as much at the preliminary hearing (with the magistrate) as in court. However, can it be said that those who gather facts for the prosecution are just as impartial as the English justices and magistrates?

[There follows a detailed account of the illegal activities of the Criminal Investigation Department of Scotland Yard in suborning witnesses and committing perjury in order to protect 'corporate honour' and ensure swift convictions, drawing on contemporary publications such as 'The Detective at Work', Daily Express, *2 September 1904 and James Timewell's pamphlet* Police Work! *(London, 1904). The rest of the Letter is devoted to the case of Adolf Beck – an infamous example of a* **'miscarriage of justice'**. *Beck was wrongfully convicted and imprisoned in 1896 and was tried again in 1904 before being pardoned and compensated following a public outcry after the real culprit was apprehended. The Beck case was compromised by inaccurate eye-witness testimony and riddled with judicial errors and refusals to admit mistakes; it led to the creation of the Court of Criminal Appeal. Shklovsky draws on the Central Criminal Court Session Papers for Beck's original trial transcripts, which he reproduces at length, as well as contemporary newspaper and pamphlet accounts both of the case and its aftermath. He concludes by asking rhetorically: 'if such incidents are possible in England, then what must go on on*

---

[21] Editor's paragraph break. *The Times*'s account of the 'Execution' from 8 April 1903 sums up: 'Severino Klosowski, otherwise George Chapman, 37, a Russian Pole, described as a licensed victualler, of the Borough, was executed yesterday morning within the walls of Wandsworth Prison for the wilful murder of Maud Eliza Marsh by poisoning her with antimony in October last. Billington was the executioner, and death was instantaneous. At the inquest which was afterwards held by Mr. Troutbeck, Major Knox, the prison governor, said that the convict made no confession. The jury found that Chapman had been duly executed according to law, and a notice to this effect was afterwards posted outside the gaol.'

the Continent, where organisations with infinitely broader powers than **Scotland Yard** *operate? What happens in those places where the activities of such organisations are shrouded in even greater secrecy than the operations of the inspectors from* **Scotland Yard?** *' The implicit comparison with Russia could hardly have escaped his readers.]*

BIBLIOGRAPHY

PRINT SOURCES IN ARCHIVES AND SPECIAL COLLECTIONS

'Books and Sermon Sheets Produced by the Agapemonite Church, Clapton and by the Agapemonite Church in Spaxton, Somerset'. 1896–1908. Hackney Archives. D/F/Wood.

'City Imperial Volunteers'. Catalogue. London Metropolitan Archives. CLA/051. https://search.lma.gov.uk/LMA_DOC/CLA_051.PDF.

Duckworth, George H. 'Notebook: Police District 28 [Kensington Town], District 29 [Fulham], District 30 [Hammersmith]'. 1899. LSE Library Charles Booth Archive. Booth/B/361. https://booth.lse.ac.uk/notebooks/b361.

'Fabian Tracts: 1884–1901'. *LSE Digital Library*. https://digital.library.lse.ac.uk/collections/fabiansociety/tracts1884-1901.

'Notebook: Nonconformist District 30 [Hammersmith]'. 1899. LSE Library Charles Booth Archive. Booth/B/268. https://booth.lse.ac.uk/notebooks/b268.

'Post Office London County Suburbs Directory, 1911 [Part I: Street & Commercial Directories]'. *University of Leicester Special Collections Online*. http://specialcollections.le.ac.uk/digital/collection/p16445coll4/id/25458.

VISUAL SOURCES

Benson, S. H. and W. H. Caffyn. 'Alas! My Poor Brother'. 1905. Victoria and Albert Museum, London. *Victoria and Albert Museum Collections*. https://collections.vam.ac.uk/item/O74315/bovril-alas-my-poor-brother-poster-benson-s-h/.

Crane, Walter. 'The Triumph of Labour'. 1891. The British Museum, London. *British Museum*. https://www.britishmuseum.org/collection/object/P_1955-0420-7.

Gould, Francis Carruthers. 'Caricatures of Politicians by Sir Francis Carruthers Gould, circa 1889–1912'. National Portrait Gallery, London. *National Portrait Gallery*. www.npg.org.uk/collections/search/set/90/Caricatures+of+politicians+by+Carruthers+Gould.

'Lambeth Baths and Washhouses, Kennington Road, Lambeth'. 1898. Lambeth Archives, London. *Lambeth Landmark*. https://boroughphotos.org/lambeth/lambeth-baths-and-washhouses-kennington-road-lambeth-2/.

'London County Council Election of 1907'. *LSE Digital Library*. https://digital.library.lse.ac.uk/collections/posters/londoncountycouncilelect ion1907#images.

'London Jewish Bakers' Union'. The Jewish Museum, London. *Jewish Museum*. https://jewishmuseum.org.uk/50-objects/1984-126_0001/.

'Ordnance Survey Maps: OS London, 1:1,056, 1893–1895'. The National Library of Scotland, Edinburgh. *National Library of Scotland: Map Images*. https://maps.nls.uk/.

'Political and Tariff Reform Posters'. *LSE Digital Library*. https://digital.library.lse.ac.uk/collections/posters/politicalandtariffreform.

'Queen Victoria's Funeral (1901)'. *YouTube*. British Pathé. www.youtube.com/watch?v=t9yiG3EUz_A&ab_channel=BritishPath%C3%A9.

'Steamer BLUCHER, built 1901'. Mystic Seaport Museum, Mystic. *Mystic Seaport Museum*. http://mobius.mysticseaport.org/detail.php?kv=109051&module=objects.

Van Dyck, Anthony. 'Drunken Silenus Supported by Satyrs'. 1620. The National Gallery, London. *National Gallery*. www.nationalgallery.org.uk/paintings/possibly-by-anthony-van-dyck-drunken-silenus-supported-by-satyrs.

NON-ENGLISH-LANGUAGE PRIMARY SOURCES

Barbier, Auguste. 'Londres' ['London']. *Iambes et Poèmes [Iambics and Poems]*. Paris: Paul Masgana, 1841.

Chekhov, Anton. *Medved': Shutka v Odnom Deystvii [The Bear: A Joke in One Act]*. Moscow, 1888.

—. *Predlozhenie: Shutka v Odnom Deystvii [A Marriage Proposal: A Joke in One Act]*. Novoe Vremya [New Times]. 3 May 1889.

Chukovsky, Korney. *Angliya Nakanune Pobedi [England on the Eve of Victory]*. Petrograd, 1916.

—. *Sobranie Sochineniy [Collected Works]*. 2nd ed. 15 vols, Moscow: Agentstvo FTM Ltd, 2012–2013.

Entsiklopedicheskiy Slovar' Brokgauza i Efrona [The Brockhaus and Efron Encyclopaedic Dictionary]. 86 vols, St Petersburg, 1890–1907.

Gogol, Nikolay. 'The Viy'. *Mirgorod*. St Petersburg, 1835.

Gorky, Maxim. 'London'. Kaznina and Nikolyukin, 323–26.

Harkavi, A. and L. Katzenelson, eds. *Evreyskaya Entsiklopediya Brokgauza i Efrona [The Brockhaus and Efron Jewish Encyclopaedia]*. 16 vols, St Petersburg, 1908–1913.

Huysmans, Joris-Karl. *A Rebours [Against Nature]*. Paris: Charpentier, 1884.

Kaznina, O. A. and A. N. Nikolyukin, eds. *'Ya Bereg Pokidal Tumanniy Al'biona...': Russkie Pisateli ob Anglii, 1646–1945 ['I Was Leaving Albion's Foggy Shore...': Russian Writers on England, 1646–1945]*. Moscow: ROSSPEN, 2001.

Marshak-Fainberg, Yu. Ya. 'Chastitsa Vremeni' ['A Piece of Time']. *'Ya Dumal, Chustvoval, Ya Zhil': Vospominaniya o Marshake ['I Thought, Felt and Lived': Reminiscences of S. Ya. Marshak]*. Eds. B. E. Galanov, I. S. Marshak and Z. S. Paperny. Moscow: Sovetskiy Pisatel', 1971, 13–42.

Marshak, Samuil. 'Na Detskoy Vistavke' ['At the Children's Exhibition']. *Birzhevie Vedomosti*. 10 January 1913, 3.

—. 'Pod Zheleznodorozhnim Mostom' ['Under the Railway Bridge']. *Nedelya 'Sovremennogo Slova'*. 1 April 1913, 2222–23.

—. *Sobranie Sochineniy [Collected Works]*. 8 vols, Moscow: Khudozhestvennaya Literatura, 1968–1972.

Milyukov, P. N. *Vospominaniya [Memoirs]*. 1955. Moscow: Izdatel'stvo Politicheskoy Literaturi, 1991.

Molière. *Les Femmes Savantes [The Learned Ladies]*. 1672. *Œuvres Complètes de Molière [The Complete Works of Molière]*. Vol. 3. Paris: Charpentier, 1910, 505–81.

Nabokov, V. D. *Iz Voyuyuschey Anglii: Putevie Ocherki [From England at War: Travel Sketches]*. Petrograd, 1916.

Nekrasov, Nikolay. 'Ritsar' na Chas' ['Knight for an Hour']. 1862. *Polnoe Sobranie Sochineniy i Pisem v 15 Tomakh [Complete Collection of Works and Letters in 15 Volumes]*. Vol. 2. Leningrad: Nauka, 1981.

Pasquet, D. *Londres et les Ouvriers de Londres [London and the Workers of London]*. Paris: Librairie Armand Colin, 1914.

Piron, Alexis. 'Dernière épitaphe' ['Last Epitaph']. *A Book of French Verse: From Marot to Mallarmé*. Ed. L. E. Kastner. Cambridge: Cambridge University Press, 1936, 132.

Rapoport, Semyon. *Delovaya Angliya [Business England]*. Moscow, 1903.

—. *Extracts from Periodicals Relating to English Life and Letters*. [1895–1917].

—. 'Moya Poezdka v Shotlandiyu' ['My Trip to Scotland']. *Vestnik Evropi*. July 1902, 79–139.

—. *Narod-Bogatir': Ocherki Politicheskoy i Obschestvennoy Zhizni Anglii [A Warrior People: Sketches of the Political and Public Life of England]*. St Petersburg, 1900.

—. 'Rapoport, Semyon Isaakovich: Avtobiograficheskaya Spravka' ['Rapoport, Semyon Isaakovich: Autobiographical Notice']. *Kritiko-Biograficheskiy Slovar' Russkikh Pisateley i Uchyonikh [A Critical-Biographical Dictionary of Russian Writers and Scholars]*. Ed. S. A. Vengerov. Vol. 6. St Petersburg, 1897–1904, 201–03.

—. *Statyi Ekonomicheskie i Politicheskie [Economic and Political Articles] Extracts from Periodicals.* [1900–1916].

—. *Stroiteli Angliyskoy Zhizni: Ocherki Reform i Sotsial'nikh Dvizheniy [The Builders of English Life: Sketches of Reforms and Social Movements] (Extracted from Mir Bozhiy).* [1905–1906].

—. *U Anglichan v Gorode i Derevne [With the English in City and Country].* Moscow, 1900.

Rogachevskii, Andrei and Rose France, eds. *Russian Writers on Britain: An Annotated Reader.* Tallinn: Avenarius, 2001.

Russkie Vedomosti, 1863–1913: Sbornik Statey [Russian News, 1863–1913: An Article Collection]. Moscow, 1913.

Schiller, Friedrich. 'An Minna' ['To Minna']. *Anthologie auf das Jahr 1782 [Anthology of the Year 1782].* Stuttgart: J. B. Metzler, 1782, 190–92.

Shklovsky, Isaak [Dioneo]. *Angliyskie Silueti [English Silhouettes].* St Petersburg, 1905.

—. 'Chelovek s Prichudoy (Pis'mo iz Anglii).' ['The Crank (A Letter from England)']. *Russkoe Bogatstvo.* February 1903, 108–14.

—. *Menyayuschayasya Angliya [Changing England].* 2 vols, Moscow, 1914–1915.

—. *Na Temi o Svobode: Sbornik Statey [On the Themes of Liberty: An Article Collection].* 2 vols, St Petersburg, 1908.

—. *Ocherki Sovremennoy Anglii [Sketches of Contemporary England].* St Petersburg, 1903.

—. *Refleksi Deystvitel'nosti: Literaturnie Kharakteristiki [Reflections of Reality: Literary Portraits].* Moscow, 1910.

—. 'Staraya Londonskaya Emigratsiya (Chaikovsky, Kravchinsky i Drugie) ['The Old London Emigration (Chaikovsky, Kravchinsky and Others)']. *Golos Minuvshego [Voice of the Past]* 4, 1926, 41–62.

Shklovsky, Viktor. *Zhili-Bili [Once Upon a Time There Lived].* Moscow: Sovetskiy Pisatel', 1966.

Struve, G. P. 'Pis'ma K. I. Chukovskogo k G. P. Struve' ['Letters of K. I. Chukovsky to G. P. Struve']. *Noviy Zhurnal [New Journal]* 101, 1970.

Swedenborg, Emanuel. *Arcana Coelestia [Heavenly Mysteries].* 8 vols, London: John Lewis, 1749–56.

Tolstoy, A. N. *V Anglii, Na Kavkaze, Po Volini i Galitsii [In England, In the Caucasus, Across Volhynia and Galicia].* Moscow, 1916.

Uspensky, Gleb. *Zhivie Tsifri [Living Numbers].* 1888. *Sobranie Sochineniy v Devyati Tomakh [Collected Works in Nine Volumes].* Vol. 7. Moscow, GIHL, 1957.

Voltaire. *Siècle de Louis XIV [The Century of Louis XIV].* *Œuvres Complètes de Voltaire [Complete Works of Voltaire].* Vol. 15. Paris: Garnier, 1878.

ENGLISH-LANGUAGE PRIMARY SOURCES

'A Bicycle Interview with John Burns, Battersea's Man to Beat'. *Guardian.* 2 October 1900. www.theguardian.com/theguardian/2012/oct/02/john-burns-battersea-cycling-archive-1900.

'A Full Measure of Justice'. *Punch.* 11 March 1893.

A Holiday Book for Christmas and the New Year. London: Ingram, Cooke & Co., 1852.

'A Straight Talk on the Alien Question'. *Yorkshire Evening Post.* 6 November 1903, 6.

Adam, Hargrave L., ed. *Trial of George Chapman.* Edinburgh: William Hodge, 1930.

'Antivaccination at the Children's Welfare Exhibition'. *The British Medical Journal*, 11 January 1913, 97.

Ballantyne, R. M. *The Coral Island.* London: T. Nelson & Sons, 1857.

Barker, J. Ellis. *British Socialism: An Examination of Its Doctrines, Policy, Aims and Practical Proposals.* London: Smith, Elder, & Co., 1908.

Blanc, Louis. *Letters on England.* Trans. James Hutton. Vol. 1. London: Sampson Low, Son, and Marston, 1866.

Blatchford, Robert. *Britain for the British.* London: Clarion Press, 1902.

—. *Merrie England.* London: Walter Scott, 1894.

Booth, Charles, ed. *Life and Labour of the People in London.* Vol. 3. London: Macmillan, 1892.

—, ed. *Life and Labour of the People in London.* Series 3. Vol. 3. London: Macmillan, 1902.

Bradshaw, Frederick and Charles Emanuel. *Alien Immigration: Should Restrictions be Imposed?* London: Isbister and Co., 1904.

Brewer, E. Cobham. 'Brandy Nan'. *Dictionary of Phrase and Fable.* Philadelphia, PA: Henry Altemus, 1898.

Brooke, Rupert. 'A Channel Passage'. *The Complete Poems.* London: Sidgwick & Jackson, 1950, 85.

Burns, Robert. *Selected Poems and Songs.* Ed. Robert P. Irvine. Oxford: Oxford University Press, 2013.

Carpenter, Edward. 'England, Arise!'. *Chants of Labour: A Song Book of the People.* London: Swan Sonnenschein & Co., 1888.

Chesterton, G. K. 'A Defence of Patriotism'. *The Speaker.* 4 May 1901.

—. *The Man Who Was Thursday.* London: J. W. Arrowsmith, 1908.

Clarendon Report. Vol. 1. 1864. *Education in England: The History of Our Schools.* www.educationengland.org.uk/documents/clarendon1864/clarendon1.html.

Clodd, Edward. *Pioneers of Evolution from Thales to Huxley.* London: Grant Richards, 1897.

Danes, Richard. *Cassell's Illustrated History of the Boer War.* London: Cassell, 1901.

Davies, J. Llewelyn, ed. *The Working Men's College 1854–1904: Records of Its History and Its Work for Fifty Years, By Members of the College.* London: Macmillan and Co., 1904.

Dickens, Charles. *Hard Times.* 1854. Oxford: Oxford University Press, 2006.

—. *Oliver Twist; or, The Parish Boy's Progress.* London: Richard Bentley, 1838.

—. *The Life and Adventures of Martin Chuzzlewit.* London: Chapman & Hall, 1844.

—. *The Life and Adventures of Nicholas Nickleby.* London: Chapman & Hall, 1839.

—. *The Personal History of David Copperfield.* London: Bradbury & Evans, 1850.

—. *The Posthumous Papers of the Pickwick Club.* 1837. London: Hazell, Watson & Viney, Ltd, 1933.

Dixon, William Hepworth. *Spiritual Wives.* 2 vols, London: Hurst and Blackett, 1868.

Doten, Lizzie. *Poems of Progress.* Boston, MA: William White and Company, Banner of Light Office, 1871.

Doyle, Arthur Conan. *The Lost World.* 1912. Oxford: Oxford University Press, 1998.

—. 'The Man with the Twisted Lip'. *Strand Magazine.* December 1891.

'Execution'. *The Times.* 8 April 1903.

Fielding, Henry. *The History of the Life of Mr Jonathan Wild, The Great.* London, 1743.

Forster, E. M. *Howard's End.* 1910. London: Penguin, 2000.

Gissing, George. *Demos: A Story of English Socialism.* Vol. 1. London: Smith, Elder & Co., 1886.

—. *New Grub Street.* London: Smith, Elder & Co., 1891.

Gogol, Nicholas. 'The Night of Christmas Eve: A Legend of Little Russia'. *Cossack Tales.* Trans. George Tolstoy. London: James Blackwood, 1860, 1–67.

'Good Old Joe!'. London: Francis, Day & Hunter, 1903.

Gordon, W. E. Evans. *The Alien Immigrant.* London: Heinemann, 1903.

Green, J. R. *A Short History of the English People.* London: Macmillan & Co., 1874.

Haeckel, Ernst. *The Riddle of the Universe at the Close of the Nineteenth Century.* Trans. Joseph McCabe. London: Watts & Co., 1901.

Hallam, Henry. *The Constitutional History of England.* Paris: A. & W. Galignani, 1827.

Hardy, Thomas. *Poems of Thomas Hardy.* Ed. Claire Tomalin. London: Penguin, 2006.

—. *Tess of the D'Urbervilles.* London: James R. Osgood, McIlvaine & Co., 1891.

Heine, Heinrich. *English Fragments.* Trans. Sarah Norris. Edinburgh: R. Grant & Son, 1880.

Hobson, J. A. *Imperialism: A Study.* London: James Nisbet & Co., 1902.
—. *The Evolution of Modern Capitalism.* London: Walter Scott, 1894.
—. *The Psychology of Jingoism.* London: Grant Richards, 1901.
'Home Again. Mr. Chamberlain Returned Quietly to London Yesterday'.
    The Daily Illustrated Mirror. 16 April 1904, 2.
Howarth, William. *The Banks in the Clearing House.* London: Effingham
    Wilson, 1905.
Hughes, Thomas. *Tom Brown's School Days.* London: Macmillan, 1857.
Jameson, William. *The Coming Fight with Famine.* Clarion Pamphlet
    13. London: Clarion Newspaper Company, 1896.
Jerome, Jerome K. *Three Men in a Boat.* London: J. W. Arrowsmith,
    1889.
'John Barleycorn is a Hero Bold'. *Folk Song and Music Hall.*
    23 October 2020. http://folksongandmusichall.com/index.php/
    hey-john-barleycorn/.
Joyce, James. *Ulysses.* Paris: Shakespeare and Company, 1922.
Kareev, N. I. 'How Far Russia Knows England'. *The Soul of Russia.*
    Ed. Winifred Stephens. London: Macmillan, 1916, 96–101.
Knox-Little, William John. Letter to the Editor. *The Times.* 22 December
    1899.
—. Letter to the Editor. *The Times.* 31 October 1901.
—. Letter to the Editor. *The Times.* 15 January 1902.
—. *Sketches and Studies in South Africa.* London: Isbister & Co., 1899.
Light. The International Association for the Preservation of Spiritualist
    and Occult Periodicals. *IAPSOP.* http://iapsop.com/archive/materials/
    light/.
Lion, Leon M. *The Surprise of My Life: The Lesser Half of an
    Autobiography.* London: Hutchinson & Co., 1948.
London, Jack. *The People of the Abyss.* New York: Macmillan, 1903.
Lytton, Edward Bulwer. *The Coming Race.* Edinburgh, 1871.
Mackay, John Henry. *The Anarchists: A Picture of Civilization at the
    Close of the Nineteenth Century.* Trans. George Schumm. Boston,
    MA: Benjamin R. Tucker, 1891.
Macqueen-Pope, Walter. *The Melodies Linger On: The Story of the
    Music Hall.* London: W. H. Allen, 1950.
Magna Carta. 1215. *The National Archives.* www.nation-
    alarchives.gov.uk/education/resources/magna-carta/
    british-library-magna-carta-1215-runnymede/.
Mann, Tom. *The Independent Labour Party Programme and the
    Unemployed.* Clarion Pamphlet 6. London: Clarion Newspaper
    Company, 1895.
Marshall, Alfred. *Principles of Economics.* 3rd ed. Vol. 1. London:
    Macmillan, 1895.
Marx, Karl. *Capital: A Critique of Political Economy.* Trans. Samuel
    Moore and Edward Aveling. Vol. 1. London: Swan Sonnenschein,

1887. *Marx/Engels Internet Archive.* www.marxists.org/archive/marx/works/1867-c1/.

Mill, John Stuart. *On Liberty.* London: John W. Parker & Son, 1859.

Milner, Dan and Paul Kaplan, *Songs of England, Ireland and Scotland: A Bonnie Bunch of Roses.* New York: Oak Publications, 1983.

'Miss Love at the "Lane"'. *Daily Express.* 30 January 1904, 5.

Morfill, William. *A History of Russia.* London: Methuen, 1902.

Morris, William. *A Dream of John Ball and A King's Lesson.* London: Reeves & Turner, 1888.

—. *Chants for Socialists.* London: Socialist League Office, 1885.

—. *News from Nowhere and Other Writings.* 1890. London: Penguin, 1998.

Morrison, Arthur. *A Child of the Jago.* 1896. Oxford: Oxford University Press, 2012.

'Mr John Burns: Contributions, 1900'. *Hansard.* https://api.parliament.uk/historic-hansard/people/mr-john-burns/1900.

'Mr Walter Goldsworthy'. *Hansard.* https://api.parliament.uk/historic-hansard/people/mr-walter-goldsworthy/index.html.

Napier, William Francis Patrick. *History of the War in the Peninsula and in the South of France from the Year 1807 to the Year 1814.* 6 vols, London, 1828–1840.

Nesbit, Edith. *Five of Us, and Madeline.* London: T. Fisher Unwin, 1925.

—. *The Magic City.* London: Macmillan & Co., 1910.

—. *The Story of the Treasure Seekers.* London: T. Fisher Unwin, 1899.

—. *The Wonderful Garden; or, The Three C's.* London: Macmillan & Co., 1911.

Nicholson, William. *London Types.* London: William Heinemann, 1898.

Orwell, George. *A Clergyman's Daughter.* 1935. Oxford: Oxford University Press, 2021.

—. *Down and Out in Paris and London.* 1933. Oxford: Oxford University Press, 2021.

—. *The Lion and the Unicorn: Socialism and the English Genius. The Collected Essays, Journalism and Letters.* Vol. 2. Eds. Sonia Orwell and Ian Angus. Boston: Nonpareil Books, 2000, 56–109.

—. *The Road to Wigan Pier.* 1937. Oxford: Oxford University Press, 2021.

Phillips, W. L. *Why Are the Many Poor?* Fabian Society Tract 1. London: Fabian Society, 1884.

Priestley, J. B. *Lost Empires.* London: Heinemann, 1965.

'Public Schools Commission'. Debated on Friday, 6 May 1864. *Hansard.* Vol. 175. https://hansard.parliament.uk/Commons/1864-05-06/debates/8bde32a8-df93-4980-9afd-bda8def8ecd4/PublicSchoolsCommission.

Reeves, Maud Pember. *Round About a Pound a Week.* London: G. Bell and Sons Ltd, 1913.

Rogers, James E. Thorold. *The Economic Interpretation of History.* London: T. Fisher Unwin, 1898.

Rose, Clarkson. *With a Twinkle in My Eye.* London: Museum Press, 1951.

Russell, Charles. *The Jew in London: A Study of Racial Character and Present-Day Conditions.* London: T. Fisher Unwin, 1900.

Sexby, John James. 'Victoria Park – Meath Gardens'. *The Municipal Parks, Gardens, and Open Spaces of London: Their History and Associations.* London: E. Stock, 1898, 552–74.

Shaw, G. B. *John Bull's Other Island and Major Barbara.* London: A. Constable & Co., 1907.

—. *Widowers' Houses: A Comedy.* London: Henry & Co., 1893.

Sherard, Robert. *The White Slaves of England.* London: James Bowden, 1897.

'Shklovski, Isaac Vladimirovich'. *The Jewish Encyclopedia.* Ed. Isidore Singer. Vol. II. New York: Funk & Wagnalls, 1906, 299.

Shklovsky, I. V. [Dioneo]. *In Far North-East Siberia.* Trans. L. Edwards and Z. Shklovsky. 1895. London: Macmillan, 1916.

—. *Russia Under the Bolsheviks.* London: Wilkinson Bros. Ltd, 1919.

Sims, George R., ed. *Living London: Its Work and Its Play, Its Humour and Its Pathos, Its Sights and Its Scenes.* 3 vols, London: Cassell, 1902–1903.

—. 'Off the Track in London: I. In Alien-Land'. *Strand Magazine.* April 1904, 416–23.

—. 'Off the Track in London: II. In the Royal Borough of Kensington'. *Strand Magazine.* May 1904, 545–51.

—. 'Off the Track in London: V. In the Shadow of St. Stephen's'. *Strand Magazine.* August 1904, 152–58.

—. *Off the Track in London.* London: Jarrold & Sons, 1911.

—. 'Trips About Town: IV. Round St. George in the East'. *Strand Magazine.* June 1905, 685–91.

Smollett, Tobias. *The Adventures of Roderick Random.* London: J. Osborn, 1748.

Somerville, W. J. *Impressions of Mission Work in the Far East.* London: T. Cornell, 1904.

Stanley, Henry Morton. *In Darkest Africa.* London: Sampson Low, 1890.

Stephen, Leslie. *An Agnostic's Apology and Other Essays.* London: Smith, Elder & Co., 1903.

Stewart, Iain. *Montesquieu in England: His 'Notes on England', with Commentary and Translation Commentary.* 2002. *Oxford University Comparative Law Forum* 6. https://ouclf.law.ox.ac.uk/montesquieu-in-england-his-notes-on-england-with-commentary-and-translation-commentary/.

Thackeray, W. M. *The History of Pendennis.* 1848. London: Smith, Elder, & Co., 1891.

'The Agapemonites: Further Demonstrations'. *The Sydney Morning Herald.* 16 September 1902, 5.

The Bible. King James Version.
'The Eastern Crisis: Hyde Park Demonstration'. *South Wales Daily News.* 12 October 1896, 6.
'The Emigrant's Farewell'. *Broadside Ballads Online.* http://ballads. bodleian.ox.ac.uk/.
The Exhibition of the Royal Academy of Arts MDCCCC: The One Hundred and Thirty-Second. London: William Clowes and Sons, Limited, 1900.
The Graphic History of the South African War, 1899–1900. London: The Graphic Office, 1900.
'The John Bull Store'. *Daily Express.* 15 October 1903.
'The Late Mr S. Rapoport'. *The Hornsey Journal.* 23 February 1934, 22.
The Life of Count Ivan D. Orloff: The Only Living Transparent and Ossified Man. Liverpool: Nicol, Kendrick, 1900.
'The Lord Mayor as Company Promoter'. *Daily News.* 29–30 November 1899.
Thompson, Alex M., trans. *Collectivism. A Speech Delivered by Jules Guesde to the French Chamber of Deputies.* Clarion Pamphlet 5. London: Clarion Newspaper Company, 1895.
Thomson, John and Adolphe Smith. *Street Life in London.* London: Sampson Low, 1877.
'Topics of the Day: The Rubbish Heap'. *Evening Star.* 29 December 1903, 4.
'Tramps' Terror'. *Daily Mail.* 22 May 1908, 3.
'Trial of SEVERINO KLOSOWSKI (36) alias GEORGE CHAPMAN (t19030309-318)'. March 1903. *Old Bailey Proceedings Online.* www. oldbaileyonline.org.
Twain, Mark. *The Adventures of Tom Sawyer.* Hartford, CT: American Publishing Co., 1876.
'Virtual Heritage Centre'. *The Salvation Army.* www.salvationarmy. org.uk/about-us/international-heritage-centre/virtual-heritage-centre.
Wallis, Edward Walter. *Let Not Your Heart Be Troubled and Human Life After Death: Two Addresses Through the Mediumship of E. W. Wallis, in Cavendish Rooms, London.* London, c. 1900.
Webb, Sidney. *An Eight Hours Bill.* Fabian Society Tract 9. London: Fabian Society, 1889.
—. *Facts for Socialists from the Political Economists and Statisticians.* 2nd ed. Fabian Society Tract 5. London: Fabian Society, 1891.
—. *Practicable Land Nationalisation.* Fabian Society Tract 12. London: Fabian Society, 1890.
Wells, H. G. *The Wheels of Chance.* London: J. M. Dent & Co., 1896.
Welsh, Charles. *Neddy: The Autobiography of a Donkey.* Boston, MA, 1905.
West, Julius, trans. *Plays by Anton Tchekoff: Second Series.* New York: Charles Scribner's Sons, 1916.
Whitaker, Joseph. *Whitaker's Almanack.* London: J. Whitaker, 1895.

White, Gilbert. *The Natural History and Antiquities of Selborne.* London, 1789.

Whitelaw, Alexander. *The Book of Scottish Song.* Glasgow: Blackie & Son, 1843.

Wilde, Oscar. *The Ballad of Reading Gaol.* London: Leonard Smithers, 1898.

—. *The Picture of Dorian Gray.* 1891. London: Penguin, 2003.

Wilson, H. W. *With the Flag to Pretoria: A History of the Boer War of 1899–1900.* London: Harmsworth Brothers, Ltd, 1900.

Wyss, Johann David. *The Swiss Family Robinson.* Ed. W. H. G. Kingston. 1812. London, 1879.

Young, Filson. *The Relief of Mafeking.* London: Methuen, 1900.

NON-ENGLISH-LANGUAGE SECONDARY SOURCES

Chikalova, Irina R. 'England and Englishmen in Semen Isaakovich Rapoport's "Letters from London"'. *Britanskiy Mir. Istoriya Britanii: Sovremennie Issledovaniya [The British World. The History of Britain: Contemporary Studies].* Eds M. P. Isenstadt and T. L. Labutina. Moscow: IVI RAN, 2015, 218–29.

—. *Velikobritaniya: Osmislenie Istoricheskogo Opita v Rossiyskoy Imperii (XIX – Nachalo XX V.) [Great Britain: Interpretation of the Historical Record in the Russian Empire (19th – Early 20th c.)].* Minsk: Belaruskaya Navuka, 2018.

Dissanayake, Natalia. *Russkie Sud'bi v Londone [Russian Destinies in London].* London: NED Publishing, 2016.

Galanov, B., I. Marshak and M. Petrovsky, eds. *Zhizn' i Tvorchestvo S. Marshaka [S. Marshak's Life and Work].* Moscow: Detskaya Literatura, 1975.

Ivanova, Evgeniya. *Chukovsky i Zhabotinsky: Istoriya Otnosheniy v Tekstakh i Kommentariyakh [Chukovsky and Zhabotinsky: The History of a Relationship in Texts and Commentaries].* Moscow-Jerusalem: Gesharim-Mosti Kul'turi, 2004.

Kanonistova, Z. S. 'Mezhkul'turniy Dialog v Istoricheskom Kontekste: Vospriyatie Obraza Anglii i Anglichan v Russkom Obschestve vo Vtoroy Polovine XIX – Nachale XX Vv' ['Intercultural Dialogue in Historical Context: The Reception of the Image of England and the English in Russian Society of the Nineteenth and Early Twentieth Centuries']. Thesis, Saratov State University, 2006.

Kaznina, O. A. 'I. V. Shklovsky (Dioneo) – Publitsist, Pisatel', Perevodchik' ['I. V. Shklovsky (Dioneo) – Journalist, Author, Translator']. Parkhomovsky and Rogachevskii, 260–72.

—. *Russkie v Anglii: Russkaya Emigratsiya v Kontekste Russko-Angliyskikh Literaturnikh Svyazey v Pervoy Polovine XX Veka*

[Russians in England: Russian Emigration in the Context of Russo-English Literary Connections in the First Half of the Twentieth Century]. Moscow: Nasledie, 1997.

Krivosheina, Maria. 'Ob Odnom Anglofil'skom Proekte: Iz Istorii Petrogradskogo Zhurnala "Argus"' ['About one Anglophile Project: From the History of the Petrograd Journal *Argus*']. *Tekstologiya i Istoriko-Literaturniy Protsess: Sbornik Statey [Textual Criticism and the Historical-Literary Process: An Article Collection].* Moscow: Buki Vedi, 2017, 134–45.

Makarova, N. V. and O. A. Morgunova, eds. *Russkoe Prisutstvie v Britanii [Russian Presence in Britain].* Moscow: Sovremennaya Ekonomika i Pravo, 2009.

Parkhomovsky, Mikhail and Andrei Rogachevskii, eds. *Russkie Evrei v Velikobritanii: Statyi, Publikatsii, Memuari i Esse [Russian Jews in Great Britain: Articles, Publications, Memoirs and Essays].* Jerusalem: Nauchno-Issledovatel'skiy Tsentr 'Russkoe Evreystvo v Zarubezhye', 2000.

Romanyuk, Sergey. *Russkiy London [Russian London].* Moscow: AST, 2009.

Rossiya-Velikobritaniya: Pyat' Vekov Kul'turnikh Svyazey [Russia-Great Britain: Five Centuries of Cultural Connections]. St Petersburg: Evropeyskiy Dom, 2015.

Shestakov, Vyacheslav. *Russkie v Britanskikh Universitetakh: Opit Intellektual'noy Istorii i Kul'turnogo Obmena [Russians in British Universities: A Record of Intellectual History and Cultural Exchange].* St Petersburg: Nestor-Istoriya, 2009.

Vorobyova, L. V. 'Londonskiy Tekst Russkoy Literaturi Pervoy Treti XX Veka' ['The London Text in Russian Literature of the First Third of the Twentieth Century']. Thesis, Tomsk University, 2009.

ENGLISH-LANGUAGE SECONDARY SOURCES

'191–193 Whitechapel Road'. *The Survey of London: Histories of Whitechapel.* https://surveyoflondon.org/map/feature/1468/detail/.

'A Walk Down Hill Street'. *London Borough of Richmond Upon Thames.* www.richmond.gov.uk/a_walk_down_hill_street.

'Ahmed Madrali'. *WrestlingData.com.* www.wrestlingdata.com/index.php?befehl=bios&wrestler=5933&bild=0&details=10.

Alderman, Geoffrey. *London Jewry and London Politics, 1889–1986.* London: Routledge, 1989.

Alston, Charlotte. *Tolstoy and His Disciples: The History of a Radical International Movement.* London: Bloomsbury, 2014.

'Amalgamated Society of Woodworkers'. *Trade Union Ancestors*. www.
unionancestors.co.uk/amalgamated-society-of-woodworkers/.

Andersson, Peter K. *Streetlife in Late Victorian London: The Constable
and the Crowd*. Basingstoke: Palgrave Macmillan, 2013.

Argent, Alan, ed. *The Angels' Voice*: *A Magazine for Young Men in
Brixton, London, 1910–1913*. London: London Record Society, 2016.

Attridge, Stephen. 'The Soldier in Late Victorian Society: Images and
Ambiguities'. PhD thesis, University of Warwick, 1993.

Bailey, Peter, ed. *Music Hall: The Business of Pleasure*. Milton Keynes:
Open University Press, 1986.

Baker, Bruce E. and Barbara Hahn. *The Cotton Kings: Capitalism and
Corruption in Turn-of-the-Century New York and New Orleans*.
Oxford: Oxford University Press, 2016.

Baker, Prue. 'House of a Thousand Destinies – The Jews' Temporary
Shelter'. *Jewish East End of London*. www.jewisheastend.com/
shelter.html.

Banerjee, Jacqueline. 'Henry James Prince and the Agapemonites'.
Victorian Web. https://victorianweb.org/religion/agape.html.

Barrow, Logie. *Independent Spirits: Spiritualism and English Plebeians,
1850–1910*. New York: Routledge & Kegan Paul, 1986.

Bartels, Sarah. *The Devil and the Victorians: Supernatural Evil in
Nineteenth-Century English Culture*. London: Routledge, 2021.

Bashford, Alison and Catie Gilchrist. 'The Colonial History of the 1905
Aliens Act'. *The Journal of Imperial and Commonwealth History*
40.3, September 2012, 409–37.

Bavidge, Jenny. 'Exhibiting Childhood: E. Nesbit and the Children's
Welfare Exhibitions'. *Childhood in Edwardian Fiction*. Eds A. E.
Gavin and A. F. Humphries. Basingstoke: Palgrave Macmillan, 2009,
125–42.

Beasley, Rebecca. *Russomania: Russian Culture and the Creation of
British Modernism, 1881–1922*. Oxford: Oxford University Press,
2020.

Beasley, Rebecca and Philip Ross Bullock, eds. *Russia in Britain,
1880–1940: From Melodrama to Modernism*. Oxford: Oxford
University Press, 2013.

Bermant, Chaim. *Point of Arrival: A Study of London's East End*.
London: Eyre Methuen, 1975.

Berry, Herbert. 'The Bell Savage Inn and Playhouse in London'.
Medieval and Renaissance Drama in England 19, 2006, 121–43.

Betts, Oliver. '"The People's Bread": A Social History of Joseph
Chamberlain and the Tariff Reform Campaign'. Cawood and Upton,
130–52.

Bright, Rachel. *Chinese Labour in South Africa, 1902-10: Race, Violence
and Global Spectacle*. Basingstoke: Palgrave Macmillan, 2013.

Brinkmann, Tobias, ed. *Points of Passage: Jewish Migrants from Eastern Europe in Scandinavia, Germany, and Britain 1880–1914.* Oxford: Berghahn, 2013.

Brodie, Marc. *The Politics of the Poor: The East End of London 1885–1914.* Oxford: Oxford University Press, 2004.

Brown, Simon. *Cecil Hepworth and the Rise of the British Film Industry 1899–1911.* Exeter: Exeter University Press, 2015.

Callow, Simon. 'Charles Dickens and the Victorian Christmas Feast'. *British Library.* 8 December 2017. www.bl.uk/romantics-and-victorians/articles/a-victorian-christmas-feast.

Cawood, Ian and Chris Upton, eds. *Joseph Chamberlain: International Statesman, National Leader, Local Icon.* Basingstoke: Palgrave Macmillan, 2016.

'Clarion Movement'. *Working Class Movement Library.* www.wcml.org.uk/our-collections/creativity-and-culture/leisure/clarion-movement/.

Cowdrey, Jacky. '1890–1913: The Truth Toy and Doll Show'. *Royal Albert Hall.* 12 December 2013. www.royalalberthall.com/about-the-hall/news/2013/december/the-truth-toy-and-doll-show/.

Curth, Louise Hill, ed. *From Physick to Pharmacology: Five Hundred Years of British Drug Retailing.* Aldershot: Ashgate, 2006.

Davis, John. 'Pro-Boers'. *Oxford Dictionary of National Biography.* 24 May 2008. https://doi.org/10.1093/ref:odnb/95545.

Diment, Galya. *A Russian Jew of Bloomsbury: The Life and Times of Samuel Koteliansky.* Montreal: McGill-Queen's University Press, 2011.

Estes, J. Worth. 'The Pharmacology of Nineteenth-Century Patent Medicines'. *Pharmacy in History* 30.1, 1988, 3–18.

Ewence, Hannah. *The Alien Jew in the British Imagination, 1881–1905: Space, Mobility and Territoriality.* Basingstoke: Palgrave Macmillan, 2019.

Featherstone, Simon. 'The Blackface Atlantic: Interpreting British Minstrelsy'. *Journal of Victorian Culture* 3.2, 1998, 234–51.

Fellom-McGibboney, Martie. 'The Skirt Dance: A Dance Fad of the 1890s'. PhD thesis, New York University, 1985.

Fishman, William. *East End Jewish Radicals: 1875–1914.* London: Duckworth, 1975.

'Foresters Music Hall, 93 Cambridge Heath Road, Bethnal Green, London'. *ArthurLloyd.co.uk: The Music Hall and Theatre History Site Dedicated to Arthur Lloyd, 1839–1904.* www.arthurlloyd.co.uk/Foresters.htm.

Forman, Ross G. *China and the Victorian Imagination: Empires Entwined.* Cambridge: Cambridge University Press, 2013.

'(Former) Agapemonite Church of the Ark of the Covenant, Upper Clapton, London (Exterior)'. *Victorian Web.* https://victorianweb.org/art/architecture/churches/77.html.

Foster, Laura. 'Christmas in the Workhouse: Staging Philanthropy in the Nineteenth-century Periodical'. *Journal of Victorian Culture* 22.4, December 2017, 553–78.

'Furniture and Timber Unions'. *Working Class Movement Library*. www. wcml.org.uk/our-collections/working-lives/furniture-and-timber/ furniture-and-timber-unions/.

Gainer, Bernard. *The Alien Invasion: The Origins of the Aliens Act of 1905*. London: Heinemann Educational Books, 1972.

Genzeleva, Rita. 'Marshak, Samuil Iakovlevich'. *The YIVO Encyclopedia of Jews in Eastern Europe*. https://yivoencyclopedia.org/article.aspx/ Marshak_Samuil_Iakovlevich.

'George Chapman (1865–1903)'. *Casebook: Jack the Ripper*. www. casebook.org/suspects/gchapman.html.

Girouard, Mark. *Victorian Pubs*. London: Studio Vista, 1975.

Glover, David. *Literature, Immigration and Diaspora in Fin-de-Siècle England: A Cultural History of the 1905 Aliens Act*. Cambridge: Cambridge University Press, 2012.

—. 'London, Liberalism, and the Chinese Labour Question'. *London: City of Paradox*. 3–5 April 2012. University of East London. Eds. Paolo Cardullo, Rahila Gupta and Jamie Hakim. London, 2012, 66–73. https://repository.uel.ac.uk/download/95e3f053437f9fbfb eb6a808a7fb446f4f9a438698102a91812945d6ede1e570/1256564/ LondonCityofParadox.pdf.

Green, Jeffrey. '*In Dahomey* in London in 1903'. *The Black Perspective in Music*. 11.1, Spring 1983, 22–24.

—. 'Minstrelsy'. *The Oxford Companion to Black British History*. Oxford: Oxford University Press, 2007. www.oxfordreference.com/view/ 10.1093/acref/9780192804396.001.0001/acref-9780192804396-e-271.

Gurney, Peter. *The Making of Consumer Culture in Modern Britain*. London: Bloomsbury, 2017.

Gwynne, Robin D. *Huguenot Heritage: The History and Contribution of the Huguenots in Britain*. London: Routledge & Kegan Paul, 1985.

Harrison, J. F. C. *A History of the Working Men's College 1854–1954*. London: Routledge and Kegan Paul, 1954.

—. *The Second Coming: Popular Millenarianism, 1780–1850*. London: Routledge and Kegan Paul, 1979.

Hawkins, Angus. *Victorian Political Culture: 'Habits of Heart and Mind'*. Oxford: Oxford University Press, 2015.

Heathorn, Stephen. *For Home, Country, and Race: Constructing Gender, Class and Englishness in the Elementary School, 1880–1914*. Toronto: Toronto University Press, 2000.

Heffernan, Hilary. *Hop Pickers of Kent and Sussex*. Stroud: History Press, 2008.

—. *Voices of Kent Hop Pickers*. Stroud: Tempus, 1999.

Henderson, Robert. 'Aleksei Teplov and the Free Russian Library in Whitechapel'. *Solanus* 22, 2011, 5–26.

—. "'For the Cause of Education": A History of the Free Russian Library in Whitechapel, 1898–1917'. Beasley and Bullock, 71–86.

—. 'Liberty Hall: Apollinariia Iakubova and the East London Lecturing Society'. *Revolutionary Russia* 28.2, 2015, 167–90.

—. *The Spark that Lit the Revolution: Lenin in London and the Politics that Changed the World.* London: I. B. Tauris, 2020.

Herber, Mark D. *Criminal London: A Pictorial History from Medieval Times to 1939.* Chichester: Phillimore, 2002.

Higginbotham, Peter. 'Salvation Army Establishments'. *The Workhouse: The Story of an Institution.* www.workhouses.org.uk/SA/.

—. 'Tooting Bec Asylum, Tooting Bec'. *The Workhouse: The Story of an Institution.* www.workhouses.org.uk/MAB-TootingBec/.

Hobbs, Andrew. 'Local Newspapers in the Victorian Era: Early "Rolling News" and Reading as Pub Activity'. *Press Gazette: The Future of Media.* 27 December 2018. www.pressgazette.co.uk/local-newspapers-in-victorian-times-early-rolling-news-and-reading-as-a-pub-activity/.

Hochberg, Severin Adam. 'The Repatriation of Eastern European Jews from Great Britain: 1881–1914'. *Jewish Social Studies* 50.1/2, Winter 1988–Spring 1992, 49–62.

Hofmeester, Karin. *Jewish Workers and the Labour Movement: A Comparative Study of Amsterdam, London and Paris, 1870–1914.* Trans. Lee Mitzman. Aldershot: Ashgate, 2004.

Holmes, Rachel. *Eleanor Marx: A Life.* London: Bloomsbury, 2014.

Hunter, J. Michael. 'Mormonism in Europe: A Bibliographic Essay'. *Faculty Publications.* 1389. *Brigham Young University ScholarsArchive.* 2014. http://hdl.lib.byu.edu/1877/3270.

'Imperial Units: City Imperial Volunteers'. *AngloBoerWar.com.* www.angloboerwar.com/unit-information/imperial-units/542-city-imperial-volunteers.

Jackson, Lee. *A Dictionary of Victorian London: An A–Z of the Great Metropolis.* London: Anthem Press, 2006.

JewishGen: The Global Home for Jewish Genealogy. Museum of Jewish Heritage. www.jewishgen.org/.

Johns, Adrian. *Piracy: The Intellectual Property Wars from Gutenberg to Gates.* Chicago, IL: Chicago University Press, 2009.

Johnson, Paul. *Saving and Spending: The Working-Class Economy in Britain 1870–1939.* Oxford: Clarendon Press, 1985.

Jones, Gareth Stedman. *Outcast London: A Study in the Relationship Between Classes in Victorian Society.* Oxford: Oxford University Press, 1971.

Jones, Richard. 'Immortalised by Charles Dickens?'. The Old Curiosity Shop: A Detailed History. *London Walking Tours.* www.london-walking-tours.co.uk/dickens-london/old-curiosity-shop.htm.

Judd, Denis, and Keith Surridge. *The Boer War: A History.* 2002. London: I. B. Tauris, 2013.

Keating, Peter, ed. *Into Unknown England, 1866–1913: Selections from the Social Explorers*. Manchester: Manchester University Press, 1976.
—. *The Working Classes in Victorian Fiction*. London: Routledge and Kegan Paul, 1971.
Kelly, Debra and Martyn Cornick, eds. *A History of the French in London: Liberty, Equality, Opportunity*. London: Institute of Historical Research, 2013.
Kingsway Conservation Area Statement. Conservation & Urban Design Team. *London Borough of Camden*. www.camden.gov.uk/documents/20142/7871262/Kingsway.pdf/.
Kolsky, Rachel and Roslyn Rawson. *Jewish London: A Comprehensive Guidebook for Visitors and Londoners*. London: New Holland, 2012.
Koven, Seth. *Slumming: Sexual and Social Politics in Victorian London*. Princeton: Princeton University Press, 2004.
Lansbury, Coral. *The Old Brown Dog: Women, Workers and Vivisection in Edwardian England*. Madison, WI: Wisconsin University Press, 1985.
Low, Rachael and Roger Manvell. *The History of British Film*. 7 vols, London: George Allen, 1948–1985.
Mackenzie, John M. *Propaganda and Empire: The Manipulation of British Public Opinion, 1880–1960*. Manchester: Manchester University Press, 1984.
Macleod, Jock. *Literature, Journalism, and the Vocabularies of Liberalism: Politics and Letters, 1886–1916*. Basingstoke: Palgrave 2013.
Mader, Jodie N. 'W. T. Stead and the Pro-Boer Response to the South African War: Dissent Through Visual Culture'. *Victorian Institute Journal Annex* 40, 2012. https://nines.org/exhibits/_W_T_Stead_and_the_Pro-Boer_Re.
Maltby, Josephine. '"To Bind the Humbler to the More Influential and Wealthy Classes": Reporting by Savings Banks in Nineteenth Century Britain'. *Accounting History Review* 22.3, November 2012, 199–225.
Marriott, John. *Beyond the Tower: A History of East London*. London: Yale University Press, 2011.
Marsh, Peter T. *Joseph Chamberlain: Entrepreneur in Politics*. London: Yale University Press, 1994.
Mazower, David. 'London-New York, or The Great British Yiddish Theatre Brain Drain'. *Digital Yiddish Theatre Project*. https://web.uwm.edu/yiddish-stage/london-new-york-or-the-great-british-yiddish-theatre-brain-drain.
McCrae, Niall and Peter Nolan. *The Story of Nursing in British Mental Hospitals: Echoes from the Corridors*. London: Routledge, 2016.
McDonald, Jan. 'Chekhov, Naturalism and the Drama of Dissent: Productions of Chekhov's Plays in Britain before 1914'. *Chekhov on the British Stage*. Ed. Patrick Miles. Cambridge: Cambridge University Press, 1993, 29–42.

McGrath, Melanie. *Hopping: The Hidden Lives of an East End Hop Picking Family*. London: Fourth Estate, 2009.

McKernan, Luke. 'Diverting Time: London's Cinemas and Their Audiences, 1906–1914'. *The London Journal* 32.2, July 2007, 125–44.

Mendelovitch, Bernard. *Memories of London Yiddish Theatre*. Oxford: Oxford Centre for Postgraduate Hebrew Studies, 1990. www.ochjs. ac.uk/wp-content/uploads/2011/09/7th-Stencl-Lecture-Memories-of-London-Yiddish-Theatre.pdf.

'Metropolitan Police Historical Timeline: Events Between 1829 and 1899'. *Friends of the Metropolitan Police Heritage Charity*. https:// fomphc.com/timeline-1829-to-1899/.

Middleton, J. 'The Overpressure Epidemic of 1884 and the Culture of Nineteenth-Century Schooling'. *History of Education* 33.4, July 2004, 419–35.

Nash, David. 'Secularist History: Past Perspectives and Future Prospects'. *Secularism and Nonreligion* 8, 2019, 1–9.

Newman, Aubrey. 'The Poor Jews' Temporary Shelter: An Episode in Migration Studies'. *Jewish Historical Studies* 40, 2005, 141–55.

Newton, Jennifer. 'Life Before the Great War: Incredible Black-and-White Images from a Grand Tour of Europe in 1904'. *MailOnline*. 21 September 2018. www.dailymail.co.uk/travel/travel_news/article-6189675/Incredible-black-white-images-grand-tour-Europe-1904. html.

O'Neill, Gilda. *Lost Voices: Memories of a Vanished Way of Life*. London: Arrow Books, 2006.

'Odessa'. *The YIVO Encyclopedia of Jews in Eastern Europe*. https:// yivoencyclopedia.org/article.aspx/Odessa.

Oppenheim, Janet. *The Other World: Spiritualism and Psychical Research in Victorian Britain, 1850–1914*. Cambridge: Cambridge University Press, 1985.

Orbell, John and Alison Turton. *British Banking: A Guide to Historical Records*. New York: Routledge, 2017.

Panayi, Panikos, ed. *Germans in Britain since 1500*. London: The Hambledon Press, 1996.

—. *Migrant City: A New History of London*. New Haven, CT: Yale University Press, 2020.

Percy, John. 'Political Cartoons of Sir Francis Carruthers Gould'. *Working Class Movement Library*. www.wcml.org.uk/blogs/Lynette-Cawthra/ Political-Cartoons-of-Sir-Francis-Carruthers-Gould/.

Perriton, Linda and Josephine Maltby. 'Working-Class Households and Savings in England, 1850–1880'. *Enterprise & Society* 16.2, 2015, 413–45.

Picard, Liza. 'Health and Hygiene in the 19th Century'. *British Library*. www.bl.uk/victorian-britain/articles/health-and-hygiene-in-the-19th-century.

Pickering, Michael. *Blackface Minstrelsy in Britain*. Aldershot: Ashgate, 2008.

Porter, Roy. *Quacks: Fakers and Charlatans in English Medicine*. Stroud: Tempus, 2000.

Potter, Jane. *Boys in Khaki, Girls in Print: Women's Literary Responses to the Great War 1914–1918*. Oxford: Oxford University Press, 2005.

Poulsen, Charles. *Victoria Park: A Study in the History of East London*. London: Stepney Books and the Journeyman Press, 1976.

Prawer, S. S. *Frankenstein's Island: England and the English in the Writings of Heinrich Heine*. Cambridge: Cambridge University Press, 1986.

Pritchard, Jane and Peter Yeandle. '"Executed with remarkable care and artistic feeling": Music Hall Ballet and Popular Imperialism'. Yeandle, Newey and Richards, 152–73.

Pye, Denis. *Fellowship is Life: The National Clarion Cycling Club, 1895–1995*. Bolton: Clarion Publishing, 1995.

Read, Jane. 'Bringing Froebel into London's Infant Schools: The Reforming Practice of Two Head Teachers, Elizabeth Shaw and Frances Roe, from the 1890s to the 1930s'. *History of Education* 42.6, 2013, 745–64.

—. 'The Froebel Movement in Britain, 1900–1939'. PhD thesis, University of Roehampton, 2012.

Reekes, Andrew. *The Birmingham Political Machine: Winning Elections for Joseph Chamberlain*. Alcester: West Midlands History Limited, 2018.

'Reforming Elections'. *UK Parliament*. www.parliament.uk/about/living-heritage/transformingsociety/electionsvoting/elections-and-voting-in-the-19th-century/reforming-election-methods/.

Rehin, George F. 'Blackface Street Minstrels in Victorian London and Its Resorts: Popular Culture and Its Racial Connotations as Revealed in Polite Opinion'. *The Journal of Popular Culture* 15.1, Summer 1981, 19–38.

Reid, Walter. *Neville Chamberlain: The Passionate Radical*. Edinburgh: Birlinn, 2021.

Reisenauer, Eric Michael. 'Anti-Jewish Philosemitism: British and Hebrew Affinity and Nineteenth Century British Antisemitism'. *British Scholar* 1.1, September 2008, 79–104.

Richards, Jeffrey. 'Drury Lane Imperialism'. Yeandle, Newey and Richards, 174–94.

Richards, Stewart. *Curtain Down at Her Majesty's: The Death of Queen Victoria in the Words of Those Who Were There*. Stroud: The History Press, 2019.

Rose, Jonathan. *The Intellectual Life of the British Working Classes*. London: Yale University Press, 2001.

Rosenberg, David. *Rebel Footprints: A Guide to Uncovering London's Radical History*. London: Pluto Press, 2015.

Routh, Guy. 'Civil Service Pay, 1875–1950'. *Economica* 21.83, August 1954, 201–23.

Rowe, Mortimer. *The Story of Essex Hall*. London: Lindsey Press, 1959.

Royle, Edward. *Radicals, Secularists, and Republicans: Popular Freethought in Britain, 1866–1915*. Manchester: Manchester University Press, 1980.

—. *Victorian Infidels: The Origins of the British Secularist Movement, 1791–1866*. Manchester: Manchester University Press, 1974.

Rule, Fiona. *London's Docklands: A History of the Lost Quarter*. Hersham: Ian Allan Publishing, 2009.

Schneer, Jonathan. *London 1900: The Imperial Metropolis*. London: Yale University Press, 1999.

Scott, Peter. 'Early Public Miniature Railways in Great Britain (1901–1918)'. *Minor Railways – Histories*. April 2021. www.minorrailways.co.uk/history1.php.

Senelick, Laurence. 'Politics as Entertainment: Victorian Music Hall Songs'. *Victorian Studies* 19, 1975, 85–98.

Shaw, Jane and Philip Lockley, eds. *The History of a Modern Millennial Movement: The Southcottians*. London: Bloomsbury, 2017.

Slatter, John. 'The Russian *Émigré* Press in Britain, 1853–1917'. *The Slavonic and East European Review* 73.4, October 1995, 716–47.

Smith, Victoria Ford. 'Exhibiting Children: The Young Artist as Construct and Creator'. *Journal of Juvenilia Studies* 1, 2018, 62–81.

Soloway, Richard Allen. 'Neo-Malthusians, Eugenists, and the Declining Birth-Rate in England, 1900–1918'. *Albion* 10.3, Autumn 1978, 264–86.

Stein, Peter. 'Vinogradoff, Sir Paul Gavrilovitch'. *Oxford Dictionary of National Biography*. 23 September 2004. https://doi.org/10.1093/ref:odnb/36664.

Strange, Julie-Marie. *Death, Grief and Poverty in Britain, 1870–1914*. Cambridge: Cambridge University Press, 2005.

Sugden, Philip. *The Complete History of Jack the Ripper*. Rev. ed. London: Constable & Robinson, 2006.

Summerfield, Penny. 'Patriotism and Empire: Music Hall Entertainment, 1870–1914'. *Imperialism and Popular Culture*. Ed. John M. Mackenzie. Manchester: Manchester University Press, 1986, 17–48.

Tananbaum, Susan L. 'Britain: Nineteenth and Twentieth Centuries'. *Shalvi/Hyman Encyclopedia of Jewish Women*. 31 December 1999. *Jewish Women's Archive*. https://jwa.org/encyclopedia/article/britain-nineteenth-and-twentieth-centuries.

Tench, Eleanor. 'Joseph Chamberlain and Leonard Courtney: Freely Disagreeing Radicals?'. Cawood and Upton, 116–29.

The London Project: The Birth of the Film Business in London. AHRB Centre for British Film and Television Studies. http://londonfilm.bbk.ac.uk/.

'The Pavilion Theatre and Wonderland, Whitechapel Road, Stepney'. *ArthurLloyd.co.uk: The Music Hall and Theatre History Site*

Dedicated to Arthur Lloyd, 1839–1904. www.arthurlloyd.co.uk/ PavilionTheatreAndWonderlandWhitechapelRoad.htm.

The Untold Stories. Yad Vashem: The World Holocaust Remembrance Center. www.yadvashem.org/untoldstories/database/homepage.asp.

Thomas, Jim. *Alien Immigration and the London School of Economics: Some Early Connections*. Technical Report. February 2016. *ResearchGate*. DOI: 10.13140/RG.2.2.19986.25286

Thompson, James. '"Pictorial Lies"? Posters and Politics in Britain c. 1880–1914'. *Past & Present* 197, November 2007, 177–210.

Toulmin, Vanessa. *Electric Edwardians: The Story of the Mitchell and Kenyon Collection*. London: British Film Institute, 2006.

Ueyama, Takahiro. *Health in the Marketplace: Professionalism, Therapeutic Desires, and Medical Commodification in Late-Victorian London*. Palo Alto, CA: Society for the Promotion of Science and Scholarship, 2010.

Vance, Jonathan F. *Death So Noble: Memory, Meaning, and the First World War*. Vancouver: UBC Press, 1997.

Vandrei, Martha. '"Britons, Strike Home": Politics, Patriotism and Popular Song in British Culture, c. 1695–1900'. *Historical Research* 87.238, November 2014, 679–702.

Vaninskaya, Anna. 'Between Fact and Fiction: The Fabrication of Migrant Knowledge in Professional and Personal Correspondence'. *Migrant Knowledge*. 16 December 2021. https://migrantknowledge. org/2021/12/16/between-fact-and-fiction/.

—. 'Korney Chukovsky in Britain'. *Translation and Literature* 20, 2011, 373–92.

—. *William Morris and the Idea of Community: Romance, History and Propaganda, 1880–1914*. Edinburgh: Edinburgh University Press, 2010.

Vervaecke, Philippe. 'The Primrose League and Women's Suffrage, 1883–1918'. *Suffrage Outside Suffragism: Women's Vote in Britain, 1880–1914*. Ed. Myriam Boussahba-Bravard. Basingstoke: Palgrave Macmillan, 2007, 180–201.

Vorachek, Laura. 'Whitewashing Blackface Minstrelsy in Nineteenth-Century England: Female Banjo Players in *Punch*'. *Victorians: A Journal of Culture and Literature* 123, Spring 2013, 31–51.

Weissman, Stephen. *Chaplin: A Life*. New York: Arcade Publishing, 2008.

White, Jerry. *Rothschild Buildings: Life in an East End Tenement Block, 1887–1920*. 1980. London: Pimlico, 2003.

'Whitechapel Gallery, former Whitechapel Library'. *The Survey of London: Histories of Whitechapel*. https://surveyoflondon.org/map/ feature/396/detail/.

Willburn, Sarah and Tatiana Kontou, eds. *The Ashgate Research Companion to Nineteenth-Century Spiritualism and the Occult*. Farnham: Ashgate Publishing, 2012.

Winter, James. *London's Teeming Streets, 1830–1914*. London: Routledge, 1993.

Wise, Sarah. *The Blackest Streets: The Life and Death of a Victorian Slum*. London: Vintage Books, 2009.

Wojtczak, Helena. *Jack the Ripper at Last? The Mysterious Murders of George Chapman*. Hastings: The Hastings Press, 2014.

Wood, Fiona. 'Garton, Sir Richard Charles (1857–1934)'. *Oxford Dictionary of National Biography*. 23 September 2004. https://doi.org/10.1093/ref:odnb/47512.

Yeandle, Peter, Katherine Newey and Jeffrey Richards, eds. *Politics, Performance and Popular Culture: Theatre and Society in Nineteenth-Century Britain*. Manchester: Manchester University Press, 2016.

Yeandle, Peter. *Citizenship, Nation, Empire: The Politics of History Teaching in England*. Manchester: Manchester University Press, 2015.

—. 'Exotic People and Exotic Places in Victorian Pantomime'. *Staging the Other in Nineteenth-Century British Drama*. Ed. Tiziana Morosetti. Oxford: Peter Lang, 2015, 125–51.

Zipperstein, Steven J. *Pogrom: Kishinev and the Tilt of History*. New York: Liveright Publishing Corporation, 2018.

INDEX

Page numbers in *italic* indicate figures; page numbers followed by 'n' refer to footnotes.

Ark of the Covenant Church fracas
261
and Chapman case 314
election violence 301n66
and homeless people 80–1
Limehouse and Wapping 120
London Metropolitan Police 120n11
police corruption 314, 318
Queen Victoria's funeral 304
St Martin-in-the-Fields Church fracas
268
surveillance activities 119n7, 137n9
unemployment demonstration clash
171–5
political cartoons 277, 281, 282, 286,
289n37, 294, 298
Poor Jews' Temporary Shelter 61n20,
62n22, 74n54
Port Arthur 18n32, 51, 252
Port of London 36, 60–1
postcards 1, 55, 100, 178, 193, 224, 272,
303
posters 84
anti-immigrant sentiments 44, 45,
65
Bovril poster 82–3
Chinese dance troupe 87
election campaigns 29, 281, 285–9,
287, 288, 298–9
patriotic posters 281
sandwich men 106
Tariff Reform League 170, 114n5
Yiddish posters and advertisements
70n40, 71
press *see* magazines; newspapers;
periodical press
Primrose League 282, 285, 290, 291
Prince, Henry James 259
prostitutes/prostitution 3, 17, 28, 39, 82,
181, 310
protectionism 48n4, 55n1, 67, 114, 170,
218, 219–21
see also Tariff Reform League
Protestants *see* Nonconformists
public meetings/debate 79n66, 239,
266n34
election campaigns 276, 290–8
'Forum' at Victoria Park 168–9n27
opposition to Boer War 283–4
Speakers' Corner, Hyde Park 166–7,
166, 169n27, 171, 249–58
see also religious sects
'Public Meetings in Hyde Park'
(Chukovsky) 249–53

public schools 194–8
bursaries 195
clubs 202–3
curriculum 195, 201
'fagging' system 195–6
fights 196, 200–1
'old boys' 203
school journal 203–4
sport 201–2
support for Boer War 200–1
pubs 6, 14, 26, 54, 119, 122, 126, 141,
144, 151, 211, 279, 313
Bell Savage, The 172
in Battersea 282, 283, 293
Elephant and Castle 160
'Goose Clubs' 206–7
and hop-pickers 279–80
in Lambeth 278, 281
and patriotism 272, 275, 276, 281,
298, 299
political meetings 276
Punch (periodical) 111, 148, 277n11,
310n2
Pushkin, Alexander 52

'Queen Victoria' (Shklovsky) 302–8
Queen's Hall 223

Radicals 66, 121n13, 197n28, 227, 254n3,
281, 283n27, 290, 291, 295, 298, 299
see also Liberals
'ragging' 226–7
Randle family (Dalling Road,
Hammersmith) 141–56
Rapoport, Semyon Isaakovich 2n3,
5n9, 7–8, 15–17, 18, 19n35, 22,
28, 30
background of 15–16
children of 17n31
Chukovsky's contempt for 20–1
'English Workmen at Leisure' 179
'My Trip to Scotland' 16, 30n53
obituary of 17n31
'Story of One Street' 17, 180–2
subjects covered by 16
Rational Dress Society 7, 183n2, 304
reading habits 118, 131, 142
autodidacts 20, 52n9, 109, 131n30,
142n18, 146n28, 151–3
children 193–4n22, 230n10
middle-class 187, 193, 202
'one book readers' 224
Reading Room *see* British Museum
Rech' (*Speech*) 5, 15, 32

LONDON RECORD SOCIETY

The London Record Society was founded in December 1964 to publish transcripts, abstracts and lists of the primary sources for the history of London, and generally to stimulate interest in archives relating to London. Membership is open to any individual or institution. Prospective members should apply to the Hon. Membership Secretary, Dr Penny Tucker, Hewton Farmhouse, Bere Alston, Yelverton, Devon PL20 7BW (email londonrecordsoc@btinternet.com).

The following volumes have already been published:

Previously published titles in the series are available from Boydell and Brewer; please contact them for further details, or see their website, www.boydellandbrewer.com